Poetry and the Making of
the English Literary Past

Poetry and the Making of the English Literary Past 1660–1781

RICHARD TERRY

OXFORD

UNIVERSITY PRESS

OXFORD
UNIVERSITY PRESS

Great Clarendon Street, Oxford OX2 6DP

Oxford University Press is a department of the University of Oxford.
It furthers the University's objective of excellence in research, scholarship,
and education by publishing worldwide in

Oxford New York

Athens Auckland Bangkok Bogotá Buenos Aires Cape Town
Chennai Dar es Salaam Delhi Florence Hong Kong Istanbul Karachi
Kolkata Kuala Lumpur Madrid Melbourne Mexico City Mumbai Nairobi
Paris São Paulo Shanghai Singapore Taipei Tokyo Toronto Warsaw

with associated companies in Berlin Ibadan

Oxford is a registered trade mark of Oxford University Press
in the UK and in certain other countries

Published in the United States
by Oxford University Press Inc., New York

British Library Cataloguing in Publication Data

Data available

Library of Congress Cataloging in Publication Data

Data available

ISBN 0-19-818623-1

1 3 5 7 9 10 8 6 4 2

Typeset in Sabon by Kolam Information Services Pvt. Ltd, Pondicherry, India
Printed in Great Britain
on acid-free paper by
Biddles Ltd,
Guildford and King's Lynn

TO CAROL

Acknowledgements

I BEGAN writing this book in 1993 and am deeply grateful for the help given to me since then by many friends and institutions. The book was started after I was awarded a Sir James Knott Fellowship at the University of Newcastle, and I would like to express gratitude for the hospitality extended to me there by the Department of English Literary and Linguistic Studies. What enabled me to bring it to completion was a research leave award from the Arts and Humanities Research Board. In addition, I am grateful for periods of research leave granted me by the University of Sunderland. The book was researched in various libraries, including the British Library, the Senate House Library of the University of London, the University Library in Cambridge, Palace Green Library of the University of Durham, and the Robinson Library of the University of Newcastle. I am grateful for the assistance given me by numerous library staff at these institutions and at my own university, but especially to the staff of the Literary and Philosophical Society of Newcastle upon Tyne, where the book in large part was written.

Many individuals have supported the project or lent assistance in various ways. Brean Hammond and Marcus Walsh supported me in the AHRB application that was indispensable to the work's completion, and David Fairer sent me a copy of the introduction to his edition of Thomas Warton's *History of English Poetry*. Numerous friends and colleagues were kind enough to read and comment on draft chapters: Stephanie Hodgson-Wright, Carol McKay, David Money, Valerie Sanders, John Strachan, and David Walker. Stephanie Hodgson-Wright also let me see unpublished material written by her and Alison Findlay; Paulina Kewes, as well as reading with minute attention several chapters, sent me a big pile of her research notes; and Pamela Clemit was happy to receive and criticize the most incipient versions of my ideas. In the final weeks of work on the book, Fiona Price acted as a research assistant, helping me to check references and edit out errors.

The book incorporates some material published in different form elsewhere. Chapter 1 contains material based on two earlier articles: 'The Eighteenth-Century Invention of English Literature: A Truism Revisited', *British Journal for Eighteenth-Century Studies*, 19 (1996), 47–62; and 'Literature, Aesthetics and Canonicity in the Eighteenth Century', *Eighteenth-Century Life*, 21 (February 1997), 80–101. Chapter 4 uses material from 'Thomson and the Druids', in R. Terry (ed.), *James Thomson: Essays for the Tercentenary* (Liverpool University Press, 2000), 141–63; and Chapter 5 draws on '"Metempsychosis": A Metaphor for Literary Tradition in Dryden and his Contemporaries', *Bunyan Studies*, 6 (1995/96), 56–69. I am grateful to editors and publishers for permission to redeploy this material.

Contents

Illustrations   x

Abbreviations   xi

Introduction   1

1. 'Literature': The Morphology of a Concept   11

2. The Progress of Poesy: Making an English Canon   35

3. Authorial Dictionaries and the Cult of Fame   63

4. Myths of Origin: The Canon of Pre-Chaucerian Poetry   93

5. Dryden and the Idea of a Literary Tradition   142

6. Teaching English Literature   169

7. Johnson's *Lives of the Poets*   216

8. Making the Female Canon   252

9. Classicists and Gothicists: The Division of the Estate   286

Appendices   324

Bibliography   328

Index   345

Illustrations

1. Frontispiece in William Winstanley, *The Lives of the most Famous English Poets, or the Honour of Parnassus* (1687). Courtesy Palace Green Library, University of Durham. 66

2. Frontispiece in Thomas Fuller, *Abel Redevivus: or the Dead yet Speaking. The Lives and Deaths of the Moderne Divines* (1651). Courtesy Palace Green Library, University of Durham. 67

Abbreviations

Cue titles are employed for the most commonly cited printed sources, as follows:

Anderson (ed.)	*The Works of the British Poets*, ed. Robert Anderson, 13 vols. (1795–5).
Butt (ed.)	*The Poems of Alexander Pope*, ed. J. Butt *et al.*, 11 vols. (London, 1939–69).
Davis (ed.)	*The Prose Writings of Jonathan Swift*, ed. H. Davis *et al.*, 14 vols. (Oxford, 1939–68).
Jonson	*Ben Jonson*, ed. C. Herford and Percy and Evelyn Simpson, 11 vols. (Oxford, 1925–52).
Kinsley (ed.)	*The Poems of John Dryden*, ed. James Kinsley, 4 vols. (Oxford, 1958).
Lives	Samuel Johnson, *Lives of the English Poets*, ed. George Birkbeck Hill, 3 vols. (Oxford, 1905).
Of Dramatic Poesy	John Dryden, *Of Dramatic Poesy and other Critical Essays*, ed. George Watson, 2 vols. (London, 1962).
Poems	*The Poems of John Milton*, ed. John Carey and Alastair Fowler (London, 1968).
Smith (ed.)	*Elizabethan Critical Essays*, ed. G. Gregory Smith, 2 vols. (Oxford, 1904).
Spectator	*The Spectator*, ed. D. F. Bond, 5 vols. (Oxford, 1965).
Spingarn (ed.)	*Critical Essays of the Seventeenth Century*, ed. J. E. Spingarn, 3 vols. (Oxford, 1908).
Yale	*The Yale Edition of the Works of Samuel Johnson* (New Haven, 1958–).
Zimansky (ed.)	*The Critical Works of Thomas Rymer*, ed. Curt A. Zimansky (New Haven, 1956).

Introduction

CONCENTRATING ON the period between 1660 and 1781, this book tells how the English literary past was made. It seemed appropriate to start at the Restoration since the late seventeenth century is an era of increasing sensitivity to the literary past, in part due to the posthumous staging of plays by the likes of Shakespeare, Johnson, and Fletcher; and the book's terminal point is fixed against the completion of two landmark literary historical works, Thomas Warton's *History of English Poetry* and Samuel Johnson's *Lives of the English Poets*. By 'making the past', I mean to indicate a range of scholarly or imaginative activities. One of these is the recital of narratives about the rise of native literature: when it is engendered, how it subsequently progresses, and where (within the time span of the book) it ends up. Another is constituted by the attempts made by some antiquarians to take complete stock of the contents of the tradition in the form of compendious dictionaries of authorial biography. Still another derives from those commentators who concentrated on assembling the illustrious writers of the past into canons of national or cross-cultural greatness, as Mark Akenside, for example, does in his exercise in arithmetical criticism, 'The Balance of the Poets'.

Just as various as the mental activities through which the literary past is appropriated are the venues at, and occasions on, which its contents come to be rehearsed. Included in my book, for example, is a short discussion of Poets' Corner in Westminster Abbey, the most important marmoreal shrine for the consecration of literary worthies, and also discussed here are a wide range of poetic genres that proved auspicious for recitals of the literary past: the funeral elegy, the progress-of-poesy poem and the session-of-the-poets poem. When it comes to prose writings, works which propound or foster versions of the literary past include tomes of antiquarian recovery, taste-forming anthologies, and the rhetorical, grammatical, and elocutionary primers, often incorporating literary gobbets, which were used in schools and academies.

The literary past investigated here was inevitably a disputed one: much of the book speaks of unbridgeable differences and the restless jockeying of scholarly factions. Some commentators believed that a literature in English could only come into being as a straight replication of the earlier literatures of Greece and Rome, but others maintained that the native tradition was at liberty to devise its own distinctive forms indifferently to the classics; most critics agreed a literature could only become great at a point contemporaneous with its language attaining an apex of refinement but then squabbled over when that point actually occurs; and while some critics demonized the barbarism of the medieval era, others discovered in the modish aesthetic of gothic the ingredients of the great Renaissance works of Spenser, Shakespeare, and even Milton. And, then, there is the whole vexed issue of the laws governing cultural progress. It was generally believed that a literature would flourish and decline in accordance with the general principles ruling the motions of cultures, except that no consensus existed as to exactly what these principles were. Was it that a culture would follow a virtuous curve of continuous improvement? Or might it be that cultures would inevitably decline the greater distance they put between themselves and the freshness of their first flourishing? Or might it be, as a further alternative, that the development of cultures consists of periods of illustrious achievement being punctuated by more barren ones. On such matters, no firm consensus was, or was ever likely to be, achieved.

The process through which the literary past gets made is a muddled one, much riven by disagreement and discontinuity, yet for all this my book does tell a story of sorts and moreover generates a body of (perhaps unlikely) heroes: men such as Thomas Birch, the father of modern literary biography; George Ballard, the first meticulous chronicler of the lives of literary women; and William Enfield, an early advocate of the classroom use of literature to inculcate taste. Although this book covers in detail only the period after 1660, the making of the English literary past begins rather earlier. It is to Elizabethan critics like George Puttenham, William Webbe, Francis Meres, and Sir Philip Sidney, as well as to the shadowy E. K., that we owe the pioneering leap of imagination of conceiving that England had come into possession of a literature of its own, a body of writings both counterpart to, and rivalling, those of classical Greece and Rome. Yet these critics had only a flimsy understanding of what the literary past consisted of: for them to raise an English standard was little more than to champion the merits of their illustrious contemporaries and a few recognizable earlier figures, such as Chaucer. A short time later, however, another Elizabethan, John Weever, begins his long traipse around the churchyards of England, recording 'antient funeral monuments'. Weever had in his early days cut a respectable figure as a poet, and his eye was especially keen for monuments to deceased poets. What drove him in his indefatigable peregrinations was the conviction that a culture should feel duty-bound to preserve and memorialize its dead, and this notion coalesced with a further key recognition: namely, that poets stand in a particularly intense relation to this preservatory ethic, the poet's calling being, more than any other, a sort of wager with futurity. In the later seventeenth century, antiquarians like Thomas Fuller and collectors of authorial lives like Edward Phillips and William Winstanley capitalize on Weever's recognition. The very point of excavating the literary past becomes an ethical one: it has to do with perpetuating the memory (or the 'fame') of the dead, and this imperative is met most satisfactorily by a recovery of past authors conducted as inclusively and non-judgementally as possible. Literary history, itself, becomes conceived elegiacally, as an aggregation of individual literary deaths.

The idea of fame, indispensable to the excavation of the literary past during the seventeenth century, becomes less persuasive in the eighteenth. It matters little to what later collectors of authorial lives such as Giles Jacob and Robert Shiels understood themselves to be doing, and it figures only in an incidental way in the authorial lives written by Samuel Johnson for *The Works of the English Poets* (1779–81). The brilliance and lordliness of Johnson's critical insights in the *Lives* (as his biographical prefaces subsequently became) has persuaded critics to see the work as ground-breaking; some, indeed, have claimed wildly that the *Lives* constitute nothing less than the inaugurative assertion of a native literary canon. However, Johnson's achievement was rather that of adopting a recognized scholarly form but improving its use, in part because he had the efforts of predecessors at his disposal. It is perhaps the reception of the *Lives*, rather than the *Lives* themselves, that constitutes the real landmark. No work of Johnson's was so much harried by critics, the author's discomfiture being all the greater for his being pincered between two nearly opposite sorts of attack. He was savaged for the hostility of his treatment of individual authors, while also being blamed for creating a canon (albeit that Johnson had selected only five of the fifty-six poets included) that seemed to others so perversely indiscriminate. Vicesimus Knox, for example, in an essay 'On the Prevailing Taste in Poetry' (1782) berated Johnson for restoring 'to temporary life many a sickly and dying poet, who was hastening to his proper place, the tomb of oblivion'. This complaint, shared by others, that Johnson's *Lives* sought to preserve the memories of authors who in reality deserved to be forgotten, sounds the final death-knell of the honourable old idea of fame. It represents the final extinction of the idea that the preservation of the literary past should be conducted in non-judgemental terms, as an essentially ethical and elegiac activity.

That Johnson's *Lives* include no author earlier than Milton was purely a matter of financial pragmatism, insisted on by the project's backers, and not representative of any limitation of literary historical awareness on Johnson's part. However, when Elizabethan critics, two hundred years earlier, cite Chaucer as the earliest English poet, this is because the then state of literary antiquities made it impossible for them to conceive of a literary tradition dating back any earlier. However, in 1605, a little book by the antiquarian William Camden entitled *Remains Concerning Britain*, a work dedicated to the author's enthusiasm for the 'English-Saxon tongue', vouchsafed for the first time a list of names of authors antecedent to Chaucer. These belong almost exclusively to Anglo-Latin writers domiciled in monasteries, but Camden also names the seventh-century Saxon poet Caedmon, celebrated in his home town of Whitby and also in Poets' Corner as the earliest of all English bards. Although Camden's *Remains* falls well short of what could be called a work of literary history, amounting to little more than a scrappy inventorizing of names and excerpts, it comprises the first raid into the previously uncharted territory of the pre-Chaucerian literary past. Over the next hundred and fifty years, however, the opening up of a primitive British literature, either through scholarship or imagination, is one of the great achievements of antiquarians and poets. Scholars like George Hickes enthuse over the treasures of Anglo-Saxon verse; critics argue, mostly wrongheadedly, about the influence on Chaucer of the troubadour poets of Provence; and academic and poetic myths are spawned about the descent of poets in the British Isles from the verse culture of the ancient Druids.

What characterized the collectors of authorial lives and antiquarians studying the primitive literary past was a determination to be as inclusive as possible, to take stock non-judgementally of all recuperable writings. In this sense, it would be wrong to see them as constructing a canon: that is, an assemblage solely of the best. This having been said, however, such works do hint at the possibility of a canon, intimated by the amount of coverage conceded to different writers and by the relative terms of approbation in which different literary careers are written up. William Winstanley's *Lives of the most Famous English Poets* (1687) also carries a frontispiece engraving in which a bust of Shakespeare sits between two pillars, these bearing the names of Chaucer and Cowley, this image clearly indicating a form of rationalization that could be applied to the canon. Much the same imagistic convention is used also in Giles Jacob's *Poetical Register*, a two-volume collection of lives published in 1719–20. In the first volume, a miniature portrait of Shakespeare is ringed by smaller ones of Jonson, Fletcher, Wycherley, Dryden, Otway, and Beaumont, as representing a canon of English drama; in the second, Milton, Cowley, Butler, and Waller surround an image of Chaucer, as constituting a canon of non-dramatic verse.

One of the main cases I argue here is that the invention of the canon, the idea that certain authors in the tradition stand out from others, rising above the contingency of their particular historical moment, occurs earlier than is apt to be supposed. I see the English canon, the exclusive grouping of the best, as instantiating itself, beginning to generate its own rhetorical momentum, before the end of the seventeenth century. An interesting illustration of this is provided by Joseph Addison's canonizing poem of 1694, his 'Account of the Greatest English Poets'.

Addison, perhaps as we all do, brings certain items of ideological baggage with him to the construction of the nation's canon: his is a Whig version, in which English literature purifies itself through time, reaching a pinnacle of perfect refinement in the neo-classical figure of Dryden, Addison's poetic mentor. What might be expected is that Addison would jettison from his canon authors incompatible with his governing principle of refinement, but curiously he stops short of doing this. Instead, in a curious and testy exercise, he pays lip-service to an established canonical ordering, while reprimanding the major writers before Dryden for their individual shortcomings: Spenser for his aesthetic uncouthness, and Milton for his odious politics. Even in 1694, Addison shows himself brow-beaten by the canon's own weight of precedent: he can besmirch Spenser and Milton but such is their canonical intransigence that he still fears to extirpate them from a poem billed as an 'Account of the Greatest English Poets'.

As I have said, this book argues for an earlier inauguration of the canon than has recently been fashionable; and I argue along similar lines in connection with the canonical credentials of female writers. Of course, the factors governing women's canonization are very different from those affecting men's; and even though, as early as 1675, Edward Phillips produces in his *Theatrum Poetarum* a list of 'Women among the Moderns Eminent for Poetry', taking note of Katherine Philips, Aphra Behn, Elizabeth Cary, Margaret Cavendish, and Lady Mary Worth, there is no sense of female authors coalescing into a publicly recognized canon until the mid-eighteenth century. At this point, a sudden access of interest in women writers seems to occur. The pertinacious George Ballard produces his *Memoirs of Several Ladies of Great Britain* documenting the lives of several literary figures; a year later the collection of authorial lives compiled by Robert Shiels is unprecedentedly hospitable to female authors; a further year on sees the appearance of John Duncombe's *The Feminiad*, championing the merits of a female literary pantheon; and 1755 sees the first significant anthology of female poets, gathered by George Colman, the younger, and Bonnell Thornton.

The mid-century surge of enthusiasm for the canonical credentials of women writers ought to dispel the notion that the eighteenth century, especially as vouched for by the absence of female writers from the great verse collections made by Robert Anderson and Alexander Chalmers around its turn, simply does not countenance the possibility of female membership of the canon. Yet, having said this, it remains the case that women writers tend to gain ground as constituting their own canon, rather than as making inroads into the established male one. Indeed, even women's advancement within the sorority of their own canon is impeded by considerations, imposed by men on female canonization, that scarcely ever entered into male canon formation. Chief among what men tended to value as canonizable traits in women writers were private morality and professional reticence, a combination of virtues that allowed Katherine Philips to assume the centre ground of the developing female canon in the place of the most obvious other contender, the licentious and mercenary Aphra Behn.

Canon-formation tends to be based on the notion that the merit of a literary work transcends any localized factors impinging on its creation. Yet, during the eighteenth century, we see the rise of an opposite contention to this: namely that judging a work correctly depends on scrutinizing the literary period from which it emerges in order to see how an author's task has been eased, or possibly made harder, by local circumstances. This idea is what we normally term 'historicism'. An effect of the rise of the historical outlook was to bolster in the canon writers who had come to be seen as deficient against Augustan standards of taste but whose achievements became more comprehensible when viewed more narrowly against the particularities of their own cultures: in particular, it precipitates a new wave of regard for works of the medieval or gothic era, or works of the early Renaissance which show gothic traces. Chief among the beneficiaries of the new outlook was Spenser. Though Spenser had always had an elevated status in the canon, this was something that Augustan commentators, like Addison, had to concede somewhat against their better judgements. Now those qualities that had always been invoked to Spenser's detriment, such as his barbaric style and exaggeratedly profuse imagination, become cited as his strengths, and as the proper and inevitable vestiges of the time at which he wrote. The powerful case made for gothic writers by the likes of Richard Hurd and the Warton brothers leads to a split in the tradition as the credentials of Spenser and Milton are asserted over and against the pallid neo-classicism of a writer such as Pope. Indeed, for the first time the literary tradition became seen as fractured, as an estate querulously divided between the classical and gothic.

This book is expressly concerned with the drafting and reciting of versions of the past, and makes no sustained effort to document how these versions ripple outwards through the various activities of publishers, theatre companies, educational institutions, and legal representatives battling over literary copyright. I am concerned with the intellectual convolutions through which versions of the past are invented, not with the commercial and institutional processes through which these are disseminated. Yet, having admitted so much, I do include one chapter that discusses the rise of 'English literature' as a material taught on educational syllabuses, those of schools, universities, and academies. It should be said at the outset that, throughout the eighteenth century, there is little evidence of literature being taught as a subject for its own sake, or as a way of impressing on initiates, in a patriotic way, the coherence and illustriousness of their own literary culture. Literary examples instead appear on syllabuses at various levels in the service of more pragmatic objectives: teaching pupils to spell, to pronounce words 'correctly', and to recognize and use rhetorical figures. However, in the later eighteenth century, we move a little closer to modern educational conceptions of the value of literary study as literary texts begin to assume a key role in the teaching of taste. 'Taste' remains a muddled notion in much eighteenth-century debate, combining sensory delicacy with mental judiciousness, its possession being achieved through exposure to such objects, chiefly works of 'literature', as were thought to provoke its exertion. Taste was also seen as an essentially *useful* acquisition, a quality that could be advantageously carried out into the world of affairs; and it should hardly surprise that the teaching of taste through literature was pioneered in England in dissenting academies, perhaps especially the one at Warrington, staffed by the likes of Joseph Priestley, William Enfield, and John Aikin. It is under the aegis of 'taste' that, within educational circles, literary works come together with a form of attention or a mode of consumption that might itself be spoken of as 'literary', characterized by qualities of sensory and mental refinement.

Finally, a word on what is not here and on what is owed to others. Though it is hoped that the reader will think that this book performs much, there is also much not undertaken here. There is no treatment of the canonical travails of individual writers, not even of Shakespeare; nor is there any of the process by which English authors become canonical, or are turned into 'classics', by becoming subject to the scholarly editorial treatment that had previously been the preserve solely of classical ones. I have also steered clear, as already intimated, of the issue of literary copyright, one which has been crucial to some recent historicizing of the concept of literature, for the reason that such an issue could not have been treated with justice within the word limit of the book. There is also here no discussion of the 'Englishness' of English literature, as of how identity in modern letters is constructed out of rivalry with the literature of other countries, especially with that of France. It is worth admitting here that dubieties of national identity, between saying 'English' or saying 'British', have been a plague on the whole book. To say 'English' when what is at issue is more largely 'British' constitutes a culpable form of exclusion; but, then again, to say 'British' in situations when what is meant is predominantly 'English' is to use a piece of modern-day rhetorical correctness to efface a partiality or injustice of the past that ought to be seen for what it was. The only other alternative, endlessly to have said 'British (but mainly English)', would have been to impose grievously on the reader's patience. My policy has been, as in the title itself, to use whichever formula seemed in the circumstances the least objectionable. Finally, it is well to admit to a particular partiality, in that my book is mainly concerned with poetry as opposed to prose, and mainly concerned too with non-dramatic poetry. When commentators in the eighteenth century look back on, or bring into being, their literary heritage, what they understand as constituting it is almost exclusively poetic; and poems themselves provide significant opportunities for the rehearsal of versions of the literary past. The process by which the upstart form of the novel begins to be recognized as itself forming an aspect of the literary historical past, in works like Clara

Reeve's *The Progress of Romance* (1785) and Sir Walter Scott's *Lives of the Novelists* (1821–4), occurs too late for treatment here.

Although my book dissents from several orthodoxies attaching to developments in eighteenth-century culture, it remains the case that I have absorbed much from strong work in the field. That even the word 'field' can be applied here owes much, for example, to René Wellek's pioneering study of *The Rise of English Literary History* (1941) which identified and assembled the source-materials within which debates about literary historiography continue to be conducted. Lawrence Lipking's *The Ordering of the Arts in Eighteenth-Century England* (1970) is indispensable for charting a historical sense as applied to literature against parallel developments in painting and music, and contains detailed expositions of Warton and Johnson. Some more recent studies were more troublesome to me, as being ones that my book had to tiptoe around before finding its own patch of territory. Howard Weinbrot's *Britannia's Issue: The Rise of British Literature from Dryden to Ossian* (1993) is a powerful study of national identity as it encroaches on literature and the construction of a native literary past; John Brewer's *The Pleasures of the Imagination* (1997) is the best book about how different eighteenth-century art forms commercialize themselves, making themselves available to tasteful consumption; and Trevor Ross's several articles on canon-formation and his book-length study of *The Making of the English Literary Canon* (1998) comprise a sophisticated examination of changing principles of literary reception and evaluation. I tussle with these critics at certain points but do not call into question the importance of their contribution.

I

'Literature': The Morphology of a Concept

I

THIS BOOK is about how cultured people in the seventeenth and eighteenth centuries understood their 'literary past'. Subsequent chapters will address how this past was unearthed, invented, or mythologized, as well as the occasions on which, and formulae through which, its contents were recited. My first chapter, however, is concerned with something different, with the provenance of literature as a concept: concerned, that is, not so much with the literary past as with the past of 'literature'. A book written about literary historiography between 1660 and 1781 nowadays stands in need of a special dispensation on which to proceed, a dispensation to speak of literature as if the concept has meaningful existence prior to the point to which several modern commentators have dated its inception. In recent times, a consensus has built up that not just does the 'invention' of literature occur no earlier than the mid- or late eighteenth century, but that the application of the term to periods or writings earlier than this constitutes an unwarrantable anachronism. This is a view with which this opening chapter is dedicated to taking issue, since unless the idea of literature can be invoked meaningfully in connection with many works discussed in this book, then neither also can the idea of the *literary* past—the subject to which my whole book is devoted.

It has become something of a commonplace that the modern-day concept of literature, not unlike the idea of 'Romanticism', came only retrospectively to be applied to many of the works that have come to be categorized under it. Take Roland Barthes: 'Depuis que la "Littérature" existe (c'est-à-dire, si l'on en juge d'après la date du mot, depuis fort peu de temps), on peut dire que c'est la fonction de l'ècrivain que de la combattre.'[1] Although Barthes asserts here only the general recentness of the concept, several commentators have gone further in pinpointing literature as not just a modern phenomenon but as one whose genesis should be located specifically in the eighteenth century. Alvin Kernan (1973) has suggested that 'The idea of literature seems to have begun taking shape during the latter half of the eighteenth century.'[2] Douglas Lane Patey (1988) has more recently underscored the commonplace in an article whose very title proclaims the conviction that 'The Eighteenth Century Invents the Canon': his argument being that until the eighteenth century 'there was no grouping together of all and only those forms which we would consider literary art—because no such conceptual category yet existed'.[3] Yet probably most influential has been the ringing endorsement of the claim in Terry Eagleton's *Literary Theory: An Introduction* (1983). Eagleton, drawing upon Raymond Williams's investigation of the idea of literature in works such as *Keywords*, argues that prior to the Romantic period the 'concept of literature' was not restricted to creative or imaginative writing but encompassed the whole body of writings valued in society. And he suggests, provocatively, that our current notion of literature would have been thought 'extremely strange by Chaucer or even Pope'.[4]

The claim that literature was invented in the eighteenth century is, to some extent, a variation on a generic one, to do with literature's being a cultural, rather than an essential, category. Accordingly, even the more exact arguments for the eighteenth-century emergence of literature have often, though perhaps covertly, been in the service of this more thoroughgoing hypothesis. Yet this is not to dispute that some historical grounds do exist for seeing literature's origination as an eighteenth-century phenomenon, certainly in as much as this century indubitably witnesses a change in the context in which the concept has to operate. The period experiences a rapid expansion in the market for print merchandise; the second half of the century sees litera-

---

[1] Roland Barthes, *Essais critiques* (Paris, 1964), 125.

[2] Alvin Kernan, 'The Idea of Literature', *New Literary History*, 5 (1973), 32.

[3] Douglas Lane Patey, 'The Eighteenth Century Invents the Canon', *Modern Language Studies*, 18 (1988), 17.

[4] Terry Eagleton, *Literary Theory: An Introduction* (Oxford, 1983), 18.

ture getting on to (without expressly being taught on) educational syllabuses; and from this era date the first full-blown English literary histories, as opposed to the mere biographical or bibliographical recording of authors and works.[5] The eighteenth century, moreover, also witnesses the earliest contributions to a seminal new discourse: that of *aesthetics*. The word 'aesthetics' was coined in 1735 by Alexander Baumgarten, but only came to be popularized with his two-volume *Aesthetica* of 1750–58.[6] Its cardinal precept, however, namely that human beings have a sensory aptitude for beauty, had already surfaced in England in Addison's influential *Spectator* essays on 'The Pleasures of the Imagination' (1712) and Francis Hutcheson's *Inquiry into the Original of our Ideas of Beauty and Virtue* (1725). The effect of the aesthetic discourse was to specify a particular form of attention to be brought to bear on literary works and, accordingly, to help define what literary works actually were: in effect, writings distinguished by a verbal beauty that could be disclosed through the exertion of taste.

Probably the single most influential rationale for the rise of literature, which also doubles up as an explanation for the emergence of the discourse of aesthetics, stems from Raymond Williams. His claim is that literature emerges as a response to sociological change, especially to the proliferation of trades and employments that was a feature of eighteenth-century industrialization. The space of literature was 'created' for its promise of commonality: a commonality that seemed the more valuable against the backdrop of a society visibly fragmenting into myriad opaquely specialized discourses of trade; and the withering aridity of the whole culture of competitive production created a desire for a discourse that could lay forceful claim to those human values and sensitivities that the new industrial realities seemed to be placing increasingly under siege. Thus arose the sociological requirement for literature. One of Williams's most

---

[5] Literary examples were studied, sometimes as part of elocutionary training, in dissenting academies like Kibworth and Warrington and in certain Scottish universities. Early biographical dictionaries such as Edward Phillips's *Theatrum Poetarum* (1675), William Winstanley's *Lives of the Most Famous English Poets* (1687), and Gerard Langbaine's *An Account of the English Dramatick Poets* (1691) are discussed in Ch. 3. Thomas Warton's *The History of English Poetry* (1774–81), sometimes hailed as the first significant treatise of literary history, is discussed in Ch. 9.

[6] See Patey, 'The Eighteenth Century Invents the Canon', 20.

succinct statements of literature's emergence as a response to just such sociopolitical factors comes in *Marxism and Literature* (1977):

The process of the specialization of 'literature' to 'creative' or 'imaginative' works is . . . complicated. It is in part a major affirmative response, in the name of an essentially general human 'creativity', to the socially repressive and intellectually mechanical forms of a new social order: that of capitalism and especially industrial capitalism. The practical specialization of work to the wage-labour production of commodities; of 'being' to 'work' in these terms; of language to the passing of 'rational' or 'informative' 'messages'; of social relations to functions within a systematic economic and political order: all these pressures and limits were challenged in the name of a full and liberating 'imagination' or 'creativity'.[7]

Changes in the cultural superstructure, including the invention of the modern concept of literature, are referred directly to changes in the nature of the economic base. One possible misgiving about the argument is its insistence that shifts in labour practice brought on by the Industrial Revolution make their earliest pronounced impact at the end of the eighteenth century: neither before nor after. Yet its main shortcoming concerns the precise nature of the cultural shift that Williams is purporting to rationalize. Is it the invention of a new conceptual space (that of literature), or the mere specialization of the word 'literature' into an application exclusive to 'creative' or 'imaginative' writings? Or might it be that to speak of one is to speak, as it were by logical entailment, of the other? While I will eventually present some lexical evidence pointing to the currency of the modern notion of literature throughout the eighteenth century, I want, in the first instance, to apply some logical pressure to the case for its eighteenth-century invention, especially as put forward by Williams and others.

II

The word 'literature' comes to us from the Latin 'litteratura', itself derived from the root 'littera' or letter, meaning knowledge

[7] Raymond Williams, *Marxism and Literature* (Oxford, 1977), 49–50.

of writing or reading.[8] The earliest usages of the word in English carry the same meaning, denoting knowledge of letters or, to use a closely cognate word, 'literacy'. This acceptation harks back to the Renaissance, but after this period, with the development of a more extensive print culture, the meaning of 'literature' modifies into knowledge, not of letters, but of books. Giles Jacob, for example, reports of Addison that in his early years he travelled into Italy 'and other polite Parts of the World, for the polishing of his Talents, and refining of his Literature'.[9] By the term 'Literature', Jacob here means book-learning, as does Johnson fifty years later, when he writes of Milton's father that 'He had probably more than common literature, as his son addresses him in one of his most elaborate Latin poems'.[10] This last example also suggests that the general association of literature with learning was prone to contract into its equation with knowledge specifically of the classical languages. *Tatler* 197 (1710), for example, equates 'literature' rather disdainfully with 'the Refuge of learned Languages', and Defoe's *The Compleat English Gentleman* (*c.*1729) expresses the regret that 'such is the vanity of the times, such the humour or usage of the day, that nothing but classic reading is call'd litterature'.[11] The general point, though, remains that in this period not only does 'literature' not refer to a roster of élite, imaginative texts (as we now understand it)— it does not refer to a body of writings at all. It refers, instead, to an activity and to a mental accomplishment, the word 'book-learning' embracing both ideas.

This acceptation of 'literature' can be seen to persist well into the eighteenth century as Johnson's *Dictionary* (1755) glosses

---

[8] My lexical history of 'literature' naturally makes use of the OED. Other useful sources are René Wellek, 'What is Literature?', in *What is Literature?*, ed. Paul Hernadi (Bloomington, Ind., 1978), 16–23; the same author's entry on 'Literature and its Cognates', in *Dictionary of the History of Ideas: Studies of Selected Pivotal Ideas*, ed. Philip P. Wiener, 4 vols. (New York, 1973), 3: 81–9; and Raymond Williams, *Keywords: A Vocabulary of Culture and Society*, revised edn. (London, 1983). What I offer here is intended as the fullest treatment of the term's eighteenth-century field of meaning.

[9] Giles Jacob, *The Poetical Register or the Lives and Characters of the English Dramatick Poets* (1719), 2.

[10] 'Life of Milton', in *Lives*, 1: 85.

[11] *Tatler* 197, 13 July 1710, in *The Tatler*, ed. D. F. Bond, 3 vols. (Oxford, 1987), 3: 61; Daniel Defoe, *The Compleat English Gentleman*, ed. Karl D. Bülbring (London, 1890), 222.

one sense of the term as 'skill in letters'. However, coeval with this sense was another one which progressively gained ground: this was the use of 'literature' to refer to a general culture of learning. In 1756, for example, Johnson set up under his own editorial aegis a periodical entitled the *Literary Magazine*. This was intended as a cultural and scholarly review, in which Johnson was to set in front of an English audience a sample of the productions of a Continental learned culture. 'Literary', in the title, denotes that which pertains to 'learned culture' or to 'knowledge', conceived as a social entity rather than an individual attribute; and this is probably the intended sense when, for example, Johnson states elsewhere that 'the sequel of Clarendon's history, at last happily published, is an accession to English literature equally agreeable to the admirers of elegance and the lovers of truth'.[12] Not just for Johnson, but also for Edward Gibbon, to speak of literature is to speak predominantly of a scholar's milieu. Gibbon's *Memoirs* begin with the explanation that 'In the fifty second year of my age...I now propose to employ some moments of my leisure in reviewing the simple transactions of a private and litterary [sic] life': 'litterary life' here refers to Gibbon's profession of miscellaneous scholarship.[13] The same association of literature with humane learning is especially salient in Gibbon's first published work, *An Essay on the Study of Literature*, which appeared originally in French (1761) before coming out in an English edition three years later. The title could easily mislead the unwary modern reader, for the book does not address itself to a body of texts ('creative' or otherwise) but sets out to defend certain principles and protocols of scholarly activity. 'Literature', once more, refers to the practices of a broadly conceived, scholarly enterprise.

The process by which 'literature' changes from being a noun of condition (referring to the *state* of being well read), or from specifying a learned culture, to its objective sense as a corpus of writings is one that also affects related terms, such as 'poesy' and 'fiction'. Both the latter originally denoted a mind-set or an internalized skill before shifting over to refer to the objective

---

[12] *Idler* 65, 14 July 1759, in *The Idler and Adventurer*, ed. W. J. Bate, John M. Bullitt, and L. F. Powell (1963), in *Yale*, 2: 201.
[13] Edward Gibbon, *Memoirs of My Life*, ed. George A. Bonnard (London, 1966), 1.

writings that the mind-set or skill enabled to be produced.[14] The date of this new semantic inflection, as regards 'literature', is hard to fix, not least because the OED's proposal of 1812 is obviously too late. The matter is complicated in any event because objective and subjective senses are often hard to differentiate. René Wellek has proposed, as the earliest instance of the objective sense, a critical remark of George Colman the elder (1761): 'Shakespeare and Milton seem to stand alone, like first-rate authors, amid the general wreck of old English literature.'[15] The acceptation appears to have caught on quickly, and in 1774 we find Johnson using 'literature' in this new sense as a corpus of writings when he talks about recalling to notice 'our stores of antiquated literature'.[16]

Neither the objective nor subjective senses of the word current at this point equate to our modern understanding of 'literature' as restricted exclusively to creative writings. Indeed, the sense of literature as meaning the whole gamut of learned or cultivated writings survives well into the following century; and this persistence of the older sense has certainly heartened critics such as Douglas Lane Patey, Terry Eagleton, and Alvin Kernan who have been vocal for a late inception of the very idea of literature. Yet late occurrences of the older sense are perhaps less immediately relevant than early ones of the modern sense. Here, however, there exists a problem. Rather extraordinarily, the OED does not recognize the more catholic and the more specialized versions of 'literature' as distinct senses, and so does not record when the second of these comes to supersede the first. The result has been that all those who have conducted arguments about the emergence of literature based on the semantic history of the word have been condemned to labour in the lexical dark.

Words often acquire new senses as a result of a tropological extension from an older sense. In the case of 'literature', the trope is synecdochic (part for whole): a sub-category of the word's original field of meaning becomes identified with the entire compass of its meaning. Where such a sense-change

---

[14] OED 'fiction' *1.a.*: 'The act of fashioning or imitating'; 'poesy' *1.c.*: 'Faculty or skill of poetical composition'.

[15] Cited from Wellek, 'What is Literature?', 19.

[16] Letter to George Horne, 30 Apr. 1774, in *The Letters of Samuel Johnson*, ed. Bruce Redford, 5 vols. (Oxford, 1992–4), 2: 139.

occurs, it will often begin with people using the word in an unofficial way, in a spirit of semantic latitude, before this new sense becomes hardened and publicly accepted. There is some evidence that this starts happening in connection with 'literature' as early as the mid-eighteenth century. In March 1752, for example, Henry Fielding published an essay in *The Covent-Garden Journal* on the conceit of the 'Commonwealth of Literature', the paper exploring, in allegorical form, the idea that the literary world possesses its own petty polity. Fielding traces this polity from its earliest beginnings, at which time the 'literary State' was an 'Ecclesiastical Democracy', all 'Literature' then being confined to the ranks of the clergy. At this moment, Fielding takes literature to mean 'learning' or, more specifically, cognizance of Latin. But as the allegory scrolls forward from the Renaissance right up until Fielding's own time, the 'literary' state is defined exclusively in terms of creative writers: Shakespeare, Jonson, Beaumont, Fletcher, Dryden, Pope, Swift, Young, and so on.[17] This state of affairs is puzzling: for either Fielding believed that for a century and a half, in the broad field of learned composition, there were no writers other than creative ones whose works were of consequence, or (which seems more probable) he is actually slewing the word 'literature' into a more restricted association with creative writing.

I am not so much suggesting that Fielding is using the word in its modern restricted sense as that he is using it in the old sense, but in a way that puts pressure on the old sense to turn into the new one. Of course, so much remains surmise: lexical 'facts', as facts in all other domains of research, are the product of interpretation, and should be treated as such. But if I am right that Fielding's usage in 1752 can be seen as prefiguring the emergence of a new sense, then this sense may have become officially acceptable by the final quarter of the same century. The earliest incidence known to me of 'literature' being used to equate unequivocally with our modern sense of 'creative writing' occurs in William Enfield's celebrated elocutionary primer *The Speaker*, published in 1774. Here the word is used to designate a group of writings described as 'works of taste', these being set apart from

---

[17] See Henry Fielding, *The Covent-Garden Journal and A Plan of the Universal Register-Office*, ed. Bertrand A. Goldgar (Oxford, 1988), 149–54.

a rival category termed 'works of knowledge'. Enfield, in other words, is invoking the term 'literature' in connection with a specialized group of writings that has clearly broken away from the miscellaneous category of learned or cultivated writings in general.[18] Some more evidence, though of a circumstantial kind, for dating this key lexical change to the late eighteenth century derives from Edward Gibbon's *An Essay on the Study of Literature* of 1761. As I have said, the use of 'literature' in the title belongs to its time, referring to the catholic notion of 'learning'. However, thirty or so years later, in his *Memoirs* of 1790, Gibbon took the trouble expressly to repudiate his earlier usage of the term: 'Instead of a precise and proper definition, the title itself, the sense of the word *Litterature* is loosely and variously applied.'[19] Clearly, by 1790, he had decided that the word 'literature' ought properly to command a more specialized meaning, and this conviction *may* reflect his awareness of a semantic drift towards the word's exclusive application to creative writing.

In suggesting that the semantic shift from the inclusive to the exclusive sense of 'literature' occurs in the second half of the eighteenth century, I am arguing for a date slightly earlier than is usually supposed; but my arguments are not in a material way at variance from the established consensus. It can still be said that the lexical shift that introduces our modern sense of 'literature' occurs at an historically specific moment, a moment moreover occurring not earlier than the middle of the eighteenth century. However, the question that immediately poses itself concerns what relevance such lexical information bears to the larger problem of when literature as an idea comes into being. Nearly all previous commentators on this subject have assumed that its relevance is very strict, such that the history of the word (as outlined above) can effectively pass muster as a history of the concept. Let me set down some examples of this attitude in practice, as drawn respectively from Alvin Kernan, Terry Eagleton, James Engell, and Gary Kelly:

---

[18] William Enfield, *The Speaker or Miscellaneous Pieces Selected from the Best English Writers* (1774), xxix.
[19] Gibbon, *Memoirs*, 103.

The idea of literature seems to have begun taking shape during the latter half of the eighteenth century. It was then that the word began to shed its earlier meanings and to replace the slightly older 'belles lettres' and the much older 'poetry' as a general term for the best imaginative fictional writing.   (Kernan 1973)

In eighteenth-century England, the concept of literature was not confined as it sometimes is today to 'creative' or 'imaginative' writing. It meant the whole body of valued writing in society: philosophy, history, essays and letters as well as poems.   (Eagleton 1983)

[The] narrowed conception of literature began, as Raymond Williams and countless others have pointed out, with an increased refinement and specialization of *belles lettres* in the eighteenth century.   (Engell 1989)

[In the Romantic era literature came to represent the interests and values of the middle classes through changing] from a humanist institution of 'polite learning' designed to serve court culture, *and* from an Enlightenment institution of demystification and social criticism... into a written verbal art.   (Kelly 1990)[20]

There are two points to be made about these excerpts: first, in every case, the argument being conducted for the eighteenth-century or Romantic inception of literature is based squarely on lexical evidence; and, second, in all but the case of Kernan, this fact that the evidential basis is *lexical* remains unstated. The passage cited from Kelly, for example, is part of a forthright opening argument about the bourgeois elevation of imaginative writing in the Romantic era, in which literature supposedly transmogrifies from 'polite learning' into 'written verbal art'. Yet the sole footnoted authority vouchsafed for this historical narrative is the relevant entry in Raymond Williams's *Keywords*, a book that never exactly purports to be a history of concepts but instead details the semantic histories of individual words. Kelly's whole argument, in other words, rests on the unstated assumption that no meaningful distinction obtains between the history of a word and the history of the concept that has come to

[20] Kernan, 'The Idea of Literature', 32; Eagleton, *Literary Theory: An Introduction*, 17; James Engell, *Forming the Critical Mind: Dryden to Coleridge* (Cambridge, Mass., 1989), 127; Gary Kelly, 'The Limits of Genre and the Institution of Literature: Romanticism between Fact and Fiction', in *Romantic Revolutions: Criticism and Theory*, ed. Kenneth R. Johnston, Gilbert Chaitin, Karen Hanson, and Herbert Marks (Bloomington, Ind., and Indianapolis, 1990), 158.

be associated with that word. Exactly the same slippage from word to concept is apparent also in the passage cited from Eagleton's *Literary Theory*. When, in the second sentence, Eagleton claims that 'It meant the whole body of valued writing', he is referring to the *word* 'literature' and its semantic history; yet Eagleton's first sentence makes a statement not about the word but about the concept, again as if what were true of the one held automatically for the other.

Two problems arise from the line of reasoning illustrated above. For one thing, the notion that in order to be in mental possession of a concept, one needs to be able to apply correctly some corresponding key term is inherently suspect. Yet even if one were to accept that proposition, this only begs the further question of exactly what term or terms one needs to be acquainted with in order to possess any given concept. This general quandary is revealingly in evidence in the excerpt from Alvin Kernan's essay 'The Idea of Literature'. Kernan argues that the concept of literature starts up 'during the latter half of the eighteenth century' and that coincidental with its genesis is a semantic shift under which the meaning of the word 'literature' narrows to mean the 'best imaginative fictional writing', thereby replacing two earlier terms, 'belles lettres' and 'poetry', which formerly occupied that semantic space. Yet, if these terms had already been laying claim to the same semantic territory of literature, how can Kernan be claiming that a mere semantic adjustment to the word 'literature' signals the invention of a whole new concept? The argument, in other words, is self-subverting, subtly realizing the opposite of what it purports to be claiming.

No rational ground exists for supposing that the history of any word will encapsulate the history of the concept that has come to be associated with it.[21] A semantic archaeology of the word 'missile' will not produce a history of the science of ballistics; nor does the word 'home' somehow internalize a history of human habitations. Interestingly, critics like Terry Eagleton and Douglas Lane Patey who use lexical evidence to argue for a late inauguration of literature also attach importance to the

---

[21] Some pertinent observations on the relation of concepts to their cultural keywords can be found in Quentin Skinner, 'The Idea of a Cultural Lexicon', *Essays in Criticism*, 29 (1979), 205–24.

eighteenth-century rise of aesthetics. Patey suggests that aesthetics is fundamental to (what he terms) the 'radical reconstitution of the literary', and Eagleton argues that the cult of the aesthetic was basic to the hegemony of the eighteenth-century middle class.[22] Yet from a lexical point of view, these arguments are wholly without warrant. As Raymond Williams reminds us, the word 'aesthetics' does not appear in English before the nineteenth century and remains uncommon until the middle of that century.[23] In other words, Patey and Eagleton construct arguments about aesthetics based on the premise of a dissociation of concept from word, yet at the same time their arguments about literature presuppose the very opposite, the inextricability of word and concept.

III

It should go without saying that one important reason why one cannot extrapolate from word to concept is that at an earlier time a concept may have been expressed by a word different from the one we nowadays associate with it. For much of the eighteenth century the main schema within which creative writing could be conceived was vouchsafed by the imported French term *'belles lettres'*: an expression for which the most frequent English renderings were 'polite letters' or 'polite literature'. *'Belles lettres'*, as a cultural buzz-word, seems to have been invented by the French critic René Rapin, figuring in the long title of both volumes of his 1684 collected works.[24] Rapin uses the term as a catch-all to embrace the four disciplines of poetry, history, philosophy, and rhetoric; and the equation of *belles lettres* with a repertoire of learned discourses something akin to what we now term 'the humanities' comprises, for the first half of the century, one important branch of its usage. William Wotton, in his *Reflections on Ancient and Modern Learning* (1694), for example, invokes 'Oratorie, Poesie, and all that which

---

[22] Patey, 'The Eighteenth Century Invents the Canon', 19. See Terry Eagleton, *The Ideology of the Aesthetic* (Oxford, 1990), 3.

[23] *Keywords*, 31.

[24] I am indebted hereabouts to W. S. Howell, *Eighteenth-Century British Logic and Rhetoric* (Princeton, 1971), 520 ff.

the *French* call *Belles Lettres*': exactly what the French consider *belles lettres* is not disclosed but the indication is that the category must be miscellaneous.[25] This catholic understanding of *belles lettres* is also to the fore in two important French texts. Dominique Bouhours's *La Manière de bien Penser dans les Ouvrages d'Esprit*, which came out in Paris in 1687, directed its readership to the formation of correct judgements about works of 'eloquence' and 'belles Lettres', by which expressions Bouhours explained that he meant works of genius in the fields of history, poetry, and oratory. A good deal later appeared Charles Rollin's influential pedagogic work *De la Manière d'Enseigner et d'Etudier les Belles Lettres*, which was made English in 1734 under the title *The Method of Teaching and Studying the Belles Lettres, or An Introduction to Languages, Poetry, Rhetoric, History, Moral Philosophy, Physicks &c*. The event of the work's appearance saw the term '*belles lettres*' for the first time making it into one of the regularly reprinted dictionaries. It is glossed in Nathan Bailey's *Dictionarium Britannicum* (1736) as 'Literature, and Knowledge of Languages and Sciences also'.[26]

Yet this construction of '*belles lettres*' was complemented by a different strand of usage, in which the term was taken as referring to the culture of imaginative writing: either to imaginative writings alone or to these and their subaltern discourse of literary criticism. The earliest English usage of '*belles lettres*' occurs in the writings of a devotee and translator of Rapin; a dedicatory epistle to Thomas Rymer's *A Short View of Tragedy* (1692) praises Cardinal Richelieu 'for his Encouragement to the *Belles Lettres*'.[27] Richelieu had founded the Académie française in 1634, a body that fostered literary discussion as well as undertaking projects such as the compilation of a national dictionary and the codification of rules for rhetoric and poetry. The fact that the Académie was essentially a literary society (rather than a society of learning) means that, notwithstanding Rymer's having almost certainly encountered the term first in its more catholic usage by Rapin, he may have been intentionally slanting it towards a more fixed association with literature. This association, in any event, is increasingly enforced. On 28 September

[25] William Wotton, *Reflections upon Ancient and Modern Learning* (1694), 19.
[26] See Howell, *British Logic and Rhetoric*, 532.
[27] Zimansky (ed.), 83.

1710, Swift contributed a polemical letter to the *Tatler* berating the 'great Depravity of our Tast, and the continuous Corruption of our Style'. Taking pains to clarify exactly whom he was attacking, he went on: 'I say nothing here of those who handle particular Sciences, Divinity, Law, Physick, and the like; I mean the Traders in History and Politicks, and the *Belles Lettres*.'[28] Although it is impossible to be certain what '*Belles Lettres*' designates here, the boundary-pressure applied by the run of other terms dictates that its meaning must be narrow. It applies, almost certainly, to imaginative works, to criticism of such works, or to both.

Occurrences in English of the actual phrase '*belles lettres*' remain thin on the ground in the first two decades of the century. When Basil Kennet and others undertook a translation of *The Whole Critical Works of Monsieur Rapin* (1706), they opted against merely borrowing the French expression, which Rapin uses a lot, and instead rendered the term through a repertoire of circumlocutions: 'fine Letters', 'Politeness', 'Polite Learning', 'Learning', and 'fine Learning'.[29] Accordingly, if one is charting the entry of the concept of *belles lettres* into English critical thought, one needs to consider its occurrence in these various periphrastic forms. As early as 1701 John Dennis can be found hymning the praises of 'Polite Learning': ' 'tis the Polite Learning of any Nation, that contributes most to the extending its Language, and Poetry is the Branch of Polite Learning, which is the most efficacious in it.'[30] Dennis suggests that the desire to acquire the polite learning of other countries is perhaps the overriding incentive behind the learning of foreign languages, for polite learning is 'more easy, and has more of Imagination in it' than 'Literature which is barely Solid'.[31] The remark is interesting, for polite learning, rather than figuring as coextensive with 'literature', or even as one of its subcategories, is actually set against it as a countervailing category. Polite learning admits of 'imagination' in that it creates images of things not immediately present to the eye, and one of its most illustrious branches

---

[28] No. 230, 28 Sept. 1710, in *The Tatler*, 3: 191.

[29] See Howell, *British Logic and Rhetoric*, 525.

[30] John Dennis, *Critical Works*, ed. E. N. Hooker, 2 vols. (Baltimore, 1939–43), 1: 204.

[31] Ibid. 1: 205.

is poetry. It seems plausible that Dennis's 'polite learning', then, maps on to the modern concept of creative writing, and this surmise gains muted support if one consults related usages in Addison. Addison regularly employs common circumlocutions for *'belles lettres'*, these being the terms 'fine' or 'polite' ascribed to 'writing', 'learning', 'literature' and so on. Such expressions themselves are often collocated with the further term 'taste'. *Spectator* 409, for instance, refers to 'that fine Taste of Writing, which is so much talked of among the Polite World'.[32] Taste was a mental aptitude to be nurtured through familiarity with 'Polite Authors', for someone with 'any Relish for fine Writing' either discovers 'new Beauties, or receives stronger Impressions from the Masterly Stroaks of a great Author every time he peruses him'.[33] 'Fine Writing', of course, is a rendering of *'belles lettres'*, taken in Addison's usage as referring to creative works or to those non-creative ones which were susceptible to appreciation in aesthetic terms. At this juncture, 'taste' refers to a sophistication of response that can be elicited by both creative and non-creative writings. But, as the century goes on, it joins the term 'criticism' in having relevance almost exclusively to works of imagination.

Some evidence exists suggesting that the category of *belles lettres* undergoes a subtle shift from the century's mid-point onwards. Early usages, especially by Dennis and Swift, indicate that *belles lettres* was considered as a category of writings contra-distinguished from other such categories: Swift, for instance, runs through 'Divinity, Law, Physick . . . History and Politicks' as scholarly discourses from which *belles lettres*, considered as a discursive field, was differentiated. Yet later invocations seem to bespeak a widening of the term's application, without, though, returning it to a meaning so broad as 'the humanities' in general. Adam Smith's influential lectures on 'Rhetoric and Belles Lettres', for example, delivered in Edinburgh in 1748–9, discuss poetry and polite prose only in accompaniment with treatment of the discourses of history and oratory.[34] *Belles lettres*, here,

---

[32] No. 409, 19 June 1712, in *Spectator*, 3: 527.
[33] Ibid. 3: 529.
[34] See *Lectures on Rhetoric and Belles Lettres Delivered in the University of Glasgow by Adam Smith Reported by a Student in 1762–63*, ed. John M. Lothian (London, 1963). Also see Howell, *British Logic and Rhetoric*, 536–76.

tends to flatten down into an application to all writings that are rhetorically crafted, yet it is not that the distinction between literary texts and historical or oratorical ones is simply lost, for these discourses are accorded separate lectures, but that the distinction ceases to be marked by the term 'belles lettres' itself. A similar development occurs in a series of essays on belles lettres written for the British Magazine by Tobias Smollett and published between July 1761 and January 1763. Smollett begins by identifying the broad category of 'liberal arts', grouped within which are poetry, painting, sculpture, music, eloquence, and architecture. From this grouping he withdraws those disciplines that depend upon 'manual operation', to leave those, namely poetry and eloquence, which are the product of the mental faculty: these are what constitute belles lettres.[35] Once more, belles lettres does not equate with a single genre or discursive type but, instead, under the guise of a generalized 'eloquence', ranges freely across a range of compositional forms.

As a term sometimes used to mark out the conceptual space of literature, 'belles lettres' had some singularities. One was that it straddled a division, one wont to run deep in the eighteenth century, between the cultures of pedagogy and criticism. Belles lettres became a feature of several prescribed educational syllabuses as well as a buzz-word amongst literary critics.[36] Another trademark, as I have suggested, was its tendency to conflate creative and critical discourses, to assimilate writings of both kinds to the one category. This fact, however, should not be taken as implying that the category distinction between the creative and the critical remained unavailable, for had that been the case no example of literary criticism could ever have been produced. One further trait of 'belles lettres' is that although it sometimes maps out the space of imaginative writing, the phrase tends not to define this space in specific terms of the imagination. Instead two alternative criteria mainly obtain: levity and politeness. Although the invention of the now stock

---

[35] These essays were long misattributed to Goldsmith. I have consulted them as they appear in Oliver Goldsmith, Works, with a memoir by William Spalding (London, 1858), 337–58; see 342.

[36] Lecture courses on belles lettres become an established part of humanities curricula in Scottish universities. The teaching of belles lettres seems to have been pioneered in England at Warrington Academy 1757–83, where Joseph Priestley amongst others lectured on the subject.

sense of *belles lettres* as denoting the more light or trifling sort of literary effusion belongs to the nineteenth century, the principle of levity matters even from the expression's outset. *Belles lettres* is 'more easy', states John Dennis, and Joseph Priestley's popular textbook *The Rudiments of English Grammar* (1761) breaks off from its thread of discussion to declaim against the whimsical irrelevances of literary critics, demanding 'What is more remarkable than the conceit, the spleen, and the petulance of critics in language and the *Belles Lettres*'.[37] The context makes clear that it is not so much the asperities of belletristic critics, as these combined with their trifling inconsequence, that prove so obnoxious. Stoking Priestley's annoyance is a staunch fidelity to utilitarian ideals in education and scholarship, ideals that conflict with one other particular dimension of *belles lettres*. *Belles lettres*, through its association with 'polite' culture, had very definite sociological bearings. Politeness was not merely a cultural accoutrement but a general accessory of leisured society. One effect of *belles lettres*, accordingly, was to bring the realm of literature into convergence with a particular echelon of social living: it was 'easy' rather than professionally intense, a consummation of a more general urbanity and social finesse, and a means of occupying leisure.

IV

If we are to explore the extent to which the modern concept of literature is reified in eighteenth-century culture, we need to look at a gamut of associated terms rather than stop at the word 'literature' itself. Yet if the term *'belles lettres'* with its various periphrases comprised a nomenclature through which the concept of literature could be realized, a more household term, and a much older one, that served to announce the idea of literature was the plain word 'poetry' (or 'poesy'). The idea that 'poetry' designates only that which is committed to verse is surprisingly recent: the Greek 'poesis', from which our own term derives etymologically, meant 'making' or 'fabrication' and did not

---

[37] Joseph Priestley, *The Rudiments of English Grammar Adapted to the Use of Schools. With Observations of Style* (1761), 63.

imply versification. This generalized understanding of the term is also indigenous to the English Renaissance, and is evident, for example, in Sidney's *Apology for Poetry* (1595) which posits that verse is 'but an ornament and no cause to Poetry'.[38] In other words, according to Sidney, verse is *inessential* to poetry, such that a poem in principle can be composed in prose; and the same distinction between the categories of poetry and verse is evident in Puttenham's *Arte of English Poesie* (1589), where Puttenham declares that a derivative writer (one translating, or working from, a 'foreine copie or example') 'may well be sayd a versifier, but not a Poet'.[39] In addition, then, to Sidney's notion that the category of 'poetry' may include non-versified composition, Puttenham suggests that not all writings committed to verse ought properly to count as poetry, for what remains intrinsic to the latter is the fact of artistic fabrication not the particular medium through which that fabrication is expressed.

Such an application of the term 'poetry' to works of imagination, versified or not, is common in the Augustan era and throughout the eighteenth century. This usage, naturally enough, is Dryden's, so that when, in one of his prefaces, he speaks of the ill-considered length of his play *Don Sebastian* (1690), he actually remarks that 'the poem was insupportably too long': 'poem', here, means a literary work of any kind.[40] Failure to appreciate this equation of 'poetry' with imaginative writing of any description can lead us to misconstrue even a remark so famous as Fielding's designation of *Joseph Andrews* as a 'comic Epic-Poem in Prose': 'comic' and 'epic', here, represent polarities, but 'poem' and 'prose', received nowadays as being wittily paradoxical, were not, to an eighteenth-century reader, irreconcilable terms.[41] Some verbal juddering, no doubt, was always intended, but the paradox might not have seemed quite so pert as it does now. Fielding's 'Preface', in any event, was to alert subsequent critics to the possibility of assimilating the comic novel to the example of Homer's lost comic epic, the *Margites*; and, of course, by seeing the comic novel as epic, it naturally

[38] Sir Philip Sidney, *An Apology for Poetry or The Defence of Poesy*, ed. Geoffrey Shepherd (Manchester, 1973), 103.
[39] Cited from Smith (ed.), 2: 3.
[40] *Of Dramatic Poesy*, 2: 44.
[41] Henry Fielding, *Joseph Andrews*, ed. Martin C. Battestin (Oxford, 1967), 4.

followed that it should be seen as a type of poem. Accordingly, Lord Monboddo can refer to *Tom Jones* as 'a species of narrative poem', and James Beattie nominates *Tom Jones* and *The Merry Wives of Windsor* as 'the two finest Comic poems, the one Epic, the other Dramatical, now in the world'.[42]

The process of reasoning is that the Fieldingesque novel is epic and *on that account* poetical, but there is also the sense that it would be unjust to withhold from it the label of poetry on the mere scruple of its lack of versification. All good literary works, so it is implied, accede naturally to the status of poetry. This honorific acceptation of 'poetry' is also to the fore in an essay written by Tobias Smollett for the *British Magazine* (1762) and entitled 'Poetry distinguished from other writing', in which he defines 'poetry' in general and magnanimous terms.[43] Poetry is constituted by a free-wheeling rhetorical panache, by a principle of aesthetic tact ensuring 'propriety to the subject' and by its production of salutary effects on the heart, imagination, and reason. 'Poetry', in effect, becomes the accolade to which all writings, in their highest flights of aesthetic realization, can aspire.

This applausive construction of the term gets some endorsement from Dr Johnson: although the *Dictionary* records 'poetry' only as a metrical composition, Johnson found himself drawn into one literary debate that centred on the much broader application of the word. This took off from Joseph Warton's severe judgement, contained in his *Essay on the Genius and Writings of Pope* (1756, 1782), that Pope's imaginative powers were so feeble as properly to disqualify his writing from being thought of as 'poetry'. Johnson was famously dismissive of the calumny ('If Pope be not a poet, where is poetry to be found?'), but still expressed opposition to Warton in terms making clear his acceptance, to some extent, of the honorific understanding of 'poetry' on which Warton's accusation was founded.[44] His conviction of the impertinence of Warton's argument was summed up in

---

[42] James Burnett, Lord Monboddo, *The Origin and Progress of Language* (1776), cited from *Novel and Romance 1700–1800: A Documentary Record*, ed. Loan Williams (London, 1970), 291; *An Essay on Poetry and Music as They Affect the Mind*, cited from James Beattie, *Essays* (Edinburgh, 1776), 563.

[43] *Works of Oliver Goldsmith*, 346–9.

[44] 'Life of Pope', in *Lives*, 3: 251.

typically gnomic and lordly fashion: 'To circumscribe poetry by a definition will only shew the narrowness of the definer.'[45] 'Poetry', here, has escaped altogether its narrow association with versified composition: 'poetry' resists definition just as human creativity in general resists it, or just as the satisfactions of the aesthetic also inevitably prove obdurate to rational enumeration. Although this honorific sense of 'poetry' survives into the Romantic era, it increasingly vies with an insistence on a more absolute disjunction between prose and poetry. Wordsworth's 'Preface' to the *Lyrical Ballads* (1800), for example, gives us a glimpse of the older usage in its last throes: 'I have used the word "Poetry" (though against my own judgement) as opposed to the word Prose, as synonomous with metrical composition.'[46]

V

It is indubitable that at some point between 1660 and 1830, the dominant sense of the word 'literature' shrinks down from applying to the entirety of all cultured writings to relating only to those that are imaginative. One school of thought has seen this semantic modification as symptomatic of much larger changes at the level of cultural and economic organization. Yet surprisingly little has been made of the fact that in process of coming to denote 'imaginative writing', 'literature' is expanding itself into semantic territory that had previously been occupied by adjacent terms like 'poetry' and 'belles lettres' (at least in one of the latter's acceptations). By the mid-eighteenth century, rather than a new concept suddenly being born from a narrowing down of the sense of 'literature', there exists a veritable glut of terms relating to creative or made-up compositions, or to the mental activities from which they arise. Johnson's *Dictionary*, for example, gives 'fiction' (1) as 'The act of feigning or inventing': the term, it should be noted was general, implying no slant (as nowadays) towards prose works. The term 'invention' is defined circularly as 'fiction'; and also defined in terms of each

---

[45] Ibid.
[46] Wordsworth and Coleridge, *Lyrical Ballads*, ed. R. L. Brett and A. R. Jones, rev. edn. (London, 1984), 254.

other are 'imagination' and 'fancy', these meaning 'the power by which the mind forms to itself images and representations of things'. A third term also mapping on to the same semantic space is 'wit' (2) meaning 'Imagination; quickness of fancy'. If we are to search out the modern idea of literature, then, as existing before the mid-eighteenth century, we need to find it not in the word 'literature' but in a jostle of other, collocating terms. Yet in suggesting that the idea of literature predates the mid-eighteenth century, my book is not claiming that literature has always been looked at in the same way or defined through the same set of descriptors. In the Renaissance, for example, the notion is understood predominantly in terms of the idea of 'feigning' or 'fabrication', and defined against the countervailing category of 'history'—a discourse specific to the non-fabricated. From about 1660, however, a new paradigmatic construction of literature comes into being, in which it gets defined in dialectical relation to a new concept: that of 'criticism'.[47]

The *OED* identifies two main senses of the word 'criticism', the first a quotidian sense, and the second more specialized. Sense 1 is 'The action of criticizing, or passing judgement upon the qualities or merits of anything; *esp*. the passing of unfavourable judgement; fault-finding, censure'; sense 2 refers to 'The art of estimating the qualities and character of literary or artistic work; the function or work of a critic'. Amongst these, the more generalized sense is also the more long-standing, the earliest recorded usage dating to 1607; only in the post-Restoration era did the word acquire a more restricted application to judgements expressed about works of art or literature. The earliest recorded exponent of this acceptation is Dryden (1677), who associates the activity of criticism with the precedent of Aristotle. In the 'Preface' to *The State of Innocence*, he observes that by 'Criticism, as it was first instituted by Aristotle, was meant a standard of judging well.'[48] The same year finds him acclaiming Thomas Rymer's *Tragedies of the Last Age* as 'the best piece of criticism in the English tongue', and two years on, he brings the

[47] A recent discussion of the rise of criticism, though not one compatible with my discussion here, is Douglas Lane Patey, 'The Institution of Criticism in the Eighteenth Century', in *The Cambridge History of Literary Criticism, vol. 4. The Eighteenth Century*, ed. H. B. Nisbet and Claude Rawson (Cambridge, 1997), 3–31.

[48] *Of Dramatic Poesy*, 1: 196–7.

same acceptation of the word into more marked prominence by affixing to his play *Troilus and Cressida* a preface entitled 'The Grounds of Criticism in Tragedy'.[49] By the early eighteenth century, this sense of criticism has become commonplace, as witnessed by works such as John Dennis's *The Grounds of Criticism in Poetry* (1704), Samuel Cobb's *A Discourse on Criticism and the Liberty of Writing* (1707), and Pope's *Essay on Criticism* (1711).

The rise of criticism, as a discourse parasitic on, and defined in relation to, literature owed much to an earlier lexical dichotomy, that between 'wit' (or 'fancy') and judgement. Before 1700, fancy and judgement often figure as the contrary elements within an overall pathology of creativity, Thomas Hobbes's 'Answer' to Sir William Davenant's 'Preface to *Gondibert*' (1650) being the first text to dovetail the twin faculties of judgement and fancy into a composite theory of literary creation: 'Judgment begets the strength and structure, and Fancy begets the ornaments of a poem'.[50] This formula is endorsed when Dryden, for instance, describes the gestation of composition as 'when the fancy was yet in its first work, moving the sleeping images of things towards the light, there to be distinguished, and then either chosen or rejected by the judgement'; and it also underlies Swift's famous admonition in *A Tale of a Tub* about a 'Man's Fancy get[ting] *astride* on his Reason'.[51] In these instances, 'fancy' and 'judgement' (or 'reason') describe opposed mental aptitudes, one doing the creating and the other disciplining the results of that creation. After 1700, however, these terms cease to refer to a creative psychomachia and instead come to equate with distinct categories of written texts. Pope's *Essay on Criticism*, for example, relentlessly contrasts the different sort of books produced by creative writers and critics and the different mental skills underpinning them, beginning with the conundrum raised in the opening lines about whether 'greater Want of Skill | Appear in *Writing* or in *Judging* ill'. Later in the poem, he stipulates that 'A perfect Judge will *read* each Work of Wit | With the same Spirit that its Author *writ*' where 'work of wit'

---

[49] Letter to Charles, Earl of Dorset, in ibid. 1: 209.
[50] Cited from Spingarn (ed.), 2: 59.
[51] 'To Roger, Earl of Orrery', prefixed to *The Rival Ladies* (1664), in *Of Dramatic Poesy*, 1: 1; *A Tale of a Tub* (1704), in Davis (ed.), 1: 108.

expressly means an imaginative or literary work, such as might become an object for the attention of critics.[52]

Unlike literature, criticism came into being at the same time as the lexical acceptation that now conveys its idea (the restricted sense of 'criticism') was also conceived. If Dryden is the first to use 'criticism' in its specialized sense, then the likes of Dryden and Rymer are also those to whom we look as the earliest exponents of a recognizable literary criticism. From its inception, criticism, as a secondary discourse, attached itself to the primary discourse of literature. Pope, for example, refers to criticism as 'the Muse's Handmaid'; and Johnson remarks in *Rambler* 3 that 'Criticism came down to survey the performances of those who professed themselves the votaries of the Muses'.[53] Indeed, Johnson's several essays on criticism are particularly useful in detailing the nature of the writings he thinks it criticism's particular remit to address. In *Idler* 61, for instance, his spoof-critic, Dick Minim, plans an 'academy of criticism' in which every 'work of imagination' will be read out before being printed; and, similarly, *Rambler* 23 discusses how easy it is for captious critics to triumph over creative writers by suggesting bogus improvements, since 'in every work of imagination, the disposition of parts, the insertion of incidents, and use of decorations, may be varied a thousand ways with equal propriety'.[54]

This first chapter, as I have indicated, is foundational to the rest of my book. For unless a case can be made for speaking of 'literature', as a concept meaningful throughout the eighteenth century, then no case or justification can exist for speaking of the 'literary past'. English studies is now a beleaguered discipline, its state of beleaguerment being evident from nothing so much as the feeling entertained by its practitioners that unless an intellectual case can be made in the most sensationalistic terms, it can hardly be worth making at all. Thus it is that whereas an older generation of critics made much of changing attitudes towards literature in the eighteenth century, it has fallen to ours to assert

[52] 'An Essay on Criticism', lines 1–2, 233–4, in Butt (ed.), 1, ed. E. Audra and Aubrey Williams (1961), 239, 266.
[53] 'An Essay on Criticism', line 102, ibid. 251; *Rambler* 3, 27 Mar. 1750, in *The Rambler*, ed. W. J. Bate and Albrecht B. Strauss (1969), in *Yale*, 3: 17.
[54] *Rambler* 23, 5 June 1750, ibid. 3: 127.

in more strident terms that literature actually gets 'invented' in
this period. Of course, as the eighteenth century goes on, literature does come to be influenced by a syndrome of ideas to do
with originality, artistic inspiration, imagination and so on; and,
moreover, even if one can not quite say that these ideas *constitute* literature, they become so entangled with it, that the concept looks different once they have emerged. Yet a change in
how a concept is used or applied, or in the descriptors invoked in
connection with it, does not amount to the same concept's being
invented or reinvented. You can use a horse to pull a plough or
to leap a fence, but reverting from one activity to the other does
not invent or regenerate the idea of a horse. Similarly, you can
describe a horse in terms of its anatomy or in terms of its DNA
sequence, but understanding a horse in a new way is not the
same as inventing a new animal. So it is also with new attitudes
towards, and new descriptions of, literature.

The Progress of Poesy: Making an English Canon

The constitution of a literary heritage brings into play two axes: those of selection and combination. It depends on the veneration of select authors and works (that is, their adoption into a canon) and on the combination of these into an intelligible 'tradition' or creative genealogy. In this book, I intend the word 'canon' in its blandest sense as simply a list of books maintained by personal or public opinion to be illustrious, rather than in the more ideologically hard-edged application of it as a corpus of texts accredited and promulgated by some force of authority (as school, university, publishing house). But, bland though the definition is, it still allows for a distinction between canon-making, as involving a principle of selection, and the *exhaustive* recovery of the cultural past undertaken by some antiquarians whose work I discuss in later chapters.

The words 'canon' and 'classic' (the 'canon' being an assemblage of 'classic' books), as used of vernacular works, are of long vintage—though curiously even now the *OED* does not record a sense of 'canon' as relating to the roster of a culture's or nation's élite literary works. Like many others, the two words acquired their current meanings through metaphoric extension from older ones, 'canon' being a word drawn from the religious realm, and 'classic' being drafted into wider service from its earlier, more specialized application to works belonging to classical culture. The secular use of both terms precedes by some stretch the Augustan era. As early as 1592, for example, in his *Greene's Vision*, Robert Greene enquires 'who hath bin more *canonized* for his works than Sir Geoffrey Chaucer'.[1] Similarly, the earliest application of the word 'classic' to secular works may date as far back as the 1630s: Richard West in an elegy on Ben Jonson claimed that '*Thou* shalt be read as *Classick Authors*; and | As *Greeke* and *Latine* taught in every Land'.[2] By the early eighteenth century, the expression seems to have become a staple one for works of high canonical value: in 1710–11, for example, Elijah Fenton praises Thomas Southerne's plays on the grounds that their 'immortal' scenes 'shall stand | Among the chosen classics of our land'.[3]

When the English literary canon comes into being remains a vexatious question. In recent times, it has become the norm for a relatively late date, usually falling in the eighteenth century or Romantic period, to be accorded to its inception. Douglas Lane Patey, for example, suggests that literary canons 'both in name and in fact, are an Augustan invention'; Harold Bloom in his controversial study of *The Western Canon* has claimed William Collins's *Odes*, published in 1746, to be 'among the earliest poems in English written to propound a secular tradition of canonicity'; and Lawrence Lipking has stated that prior to Johnson's *Lives of the Poets* (1779–81) 'there was ... no canon of what was best'.[4] Yet, notwithstanding these asseverations, an interest in literary canonization can be traced back much earlier, in particular to the final quarter of the sixteenth century. This era sees an extraordinary efflorescence of canon-forming texts, including ones by William Webbe (1586), George Puttenham (1589), Sir Philip Sidney (1595), and Francis Meres (1598).[5] Up until this point, native writing had been seen as little more than a codicil tagged on to the classics, and these works make the pioneering leap of drawing attention to

---

[1] Robert Greene, *Greenes Vision* (1592), sig. C3^r; cited from Trevor Ross, 'Just When *Did* "British bards begin t'Immortalize"?', *Studies in Eighteenth-Century Culture*, 19 (1989), 391.

[2] *Jonson*, 11: 470.

[3] Elijah Fenton, 'An Epistle to Mr. Southerne', in Anderson (ed.), 7: 660.

[4] Patey, 'The Eighteenth Century Invents the Canon', 17; Harold Bloom, *The Western Canon: The Books and Schools of the Ages* (London, 1994), 20; Lawrence Lipking, *The Ordering of the Arts in Eighteenth-Century England* (Princeton, 1970), 3.

[5] Webbe, *A Discourse of English Poetrie*; Puttenham, *The Arte of English Poesie*; Sidney, *An Apologie for Poetrie*; Meres, *Palladis Tamia*. All can be consulted in Smith (ed.), *Elizabethan Critical Essays*. These works are discussed further in Ch. 4.

English literature as a phenomenon distinct in itself. Thus even while William Webbe, in his *Discourse of English Poetrie*, can admit that addressing English poetry as a self-standing entity, separated off from the classical poetic tradition, might seem 'like vnto the drawing of ones pycture without a heade', this reservation does not restrain him from doing that very thing.[6]

Although the canon available to the Elizabethans was mainly a late medieval one, consisting of Chaucer, Gower, Skelton, and Lydgate, the literary past was all the same not a frozen heritage so much as an unfolding tradition, to which even contemporary writers could be annexed. Webbe, for example, cites Spenser as 'the rightest English Poet that euer I read', and Puttenham recommends both Spenser and Sidney for 'Eglogue and pastorall Poesie'.[7] In much the same spirit, Ben Jonson's masque *The Golden Age Restor'd* (1615), sees the eminent bards Chaucer, Gower, Lydgate, and, significantly, Spenser (born only two decades before Jonson himself) being summoned by the goddess Astraea 'To waite vpon the age that shall your names new nourish'.[8] A year later, the death of Shakespeare provides occasion for Jonson to propose a further addition to the canonical roll. His 'To the Memory of My Beloved, the Author Mr William Shakespeare' (1618) draws Shakespeare into association not just with his direct contemporaries but with a cabal of writers seen as the luminaries of an unfolding and unified tradition (Chaucer, Spenser, Beaumont, Kyd, and Marlowe), before according him canonical ascendancy over all of them. Similarly, in commemoration of Abraham Cowley's death and stately interment in Westminster Abbey, Sir John Denham composes his 'On Mr. Abraham Cowley His Death and Burial Amongst the Ancient Poets' (1667), attaching Cowley to a line of canonical descent from Chaucer, Spenser, Shakespeare, Jonson, and Fletcher.

By the early seventeenth century, then, a literary canon had not only been drawn up but had become subject to its own tradition of recital, yet its most visible symbol remained less textual than monumental, provided by the conversion of the south transept of Westminster Abbey into what eventually

---

[6] Smith (ed.), 1: 247.   [7] Ibid. 1: 245; 2: 65.   [8] *Jonson*, 7: 425.

became known as Poets' Corner.[9] Although Chaucer had originally been buried in the transept on his death in 1400, this honour owed to his being Clerk of the King's Works and to his living in the precincts of the Abbey at the time of his death. The first step towards a more specialized elevation of the burial site was in fact taken only in 1556 when a monument was belatedly erected to the poet in specific commemoration of his career as a writer. The next such step probably occurs in 1599 when on the death of Edmund Spenser in indigent circumstances friends raised funds for him to be interred in close proximity to Chaucer's resting place, out of recognition of his lifelong desire to emulate Chaucer's literary precedent. Of course, Spenser's relation to Chaucer constituted a very precise sort of literary filiation, and thus early the cathedral seems not to have fixed its credentials as a general site for the consecration of literary worthies. Such a development belongs instead to the seventeenth century. Francis Beaumont was buried in the cathedral in 1616, and even though Shakespeare's death in the same year led to his being interred in his home town of Stratford-upon-Avon, there are signs that this event was seen as anomalous. In 1631, Michael Drayton was buried in the Abbey; Ben Jonson's tomb was installed there in 1637; and in 1667, after a funeral of considerable public pomp, Abraham Cowley was committed to the same burial site. By this time, the cathedral's status as providing a monumental ratification of the native literary canon was well established. When the turncoat poet Tom May was interred in the Abbey in November 1650, for example, Marvell responded with a satire on 'Tom May's Death' in which he depicts the dust of Chaucer and Spenser rising in élitist indignation to resist the burial. It was, however, only in the following century that a further commemorative tradition was set in motion, the retrospective recognition of writers who had died earlier and been interred elsewhere. In 1737, a bust of Milton was set up, and in 1740 a cenotaph was erected to the honour of Shakespeare.

---

[9] See Ross, 'Just When *Did* "British bards begin t'Immortalize"?', 386. The most useful short essay on Poets' Corner, which I have drawn on here, is 'Poets' Corners: The Development of a Canon of English Literature', standing as introduction to Andrew Sanders's *The Short Oxford History of English Literature* (Oxford, 1994), 1–15.

Some of the earlier writers buried in the Abbey, as Spenser, Drayton, and Jonson, possessed credentials as national poets; and the fact that Pope never got to be interred in the same place may reflect that his Catholicism stripped him of that credential. Yet the honour of being recognized in Poets' Corner was originally a matter of aristocratic rather than of state or religious patronage; as Andrew Sanders has noted, 'distinguished citizens, and not the state, decreed that, with the Dean of Westminster's permission, men of letters might rest or be sculpturally remembered in the ancient Roman manner'.[10] The degree of accident or casualty that entered into such acts of commemoration was significant, not to say notorious in connection with one illustrious figure, Dryden. After Dryden was laid to rest in St Anne's, Soho on 2 May 1700, the Earl of Dorset, scandalized by the ignominy of this first interment, paid for the body to be exhumed and embalmed, and reinterred in Westminster Abbey on 13 May.[11] Dryden's mortuary canonization, in other words, owed everything to the sense of propriety, and munificence, of a single benefactor. Yet whatever the somewhat random processes by which poets came to have their remains committed to the Abbey, the iconography of such interments was publicly understood well before 1700: to be so commemorated was to be accepted into the fold of the native literary canon.

Far from literary canonization being an invention of the eighteenth century, by this time the canonical roll was already beginning to sound wearily familiar, even becoming susceptible to mild ridicule on this account. The earliest instance known to me of the canon's being sent up in this way occurs in Sarah Fielding's novel *The Adventures of David Simple* (1744), where David, visiting a tavern, is introduced to 'a modern Critick', who regales him with a set-piece peroration on the merits of the canonical poets, including English, French, and classical. The expression of these merits is irksomely clichéd (Shakespeare is the great poet of imagination, Jonson that of learning; Waller's verse is pleasingly smooth; Cowley is a great wit but a poor versifier; and so on), the real point of the satire being how the memorization of a repertoire of pat canonical judgements has

[10] Sanders, *Short Oxford History of English Literature*, 2.
[11] See James Anderson Winn, *John Dryden and His World* (New Haven, 1987), 512.

come to be seen as 'the only Qualification necessary to make a modern Critick'.[12] This episode in *David Simple* may have been the seed of Samuel Johnson's very similar attack on the follies of modern criticism, as epitomized by the feckless Dick Minim, in his *Idler* papers 60 and 61 (9 and 16 June 1759). As one aspect of Minim's critical self-fashioning, he learns to intone the names and characters of the 'great authors'. These latter are made up of four Renaissance figures (Shakespeare, Jonson, Spenser, and Sidney), the three acclaimed reformers of English versification (Denham, Waller, and Dryden), a clutch of post-Restoration dramatists, and the associated authors, Pope and Swift. Minim, though, goes beyond merely detailing a file of names, for he also expresses the terms of each author's canonical strength or weakness. So Shakespeare, through 'committing himself wholly to the impulse of nature' lacked correctness, whereas Jonson was guilty of trusting over much to learning and hence disregarding nature; similarly, had Denham and Waller been able to combine the 'strength' of the former with the 'sweetness' of the latter, 'there had been nothing wanting to complete a poet'.[13] This incantation of the national literary canon is, of course, a joke, though one aimed not against the occupants of Minim's list but against the hackneyed rhetoric of canon formation in which Minim shows himself so appallingly word perfect. Both his canon of greats, and the critical adjudications on which this is based, have been souped up from earlier sources, and were, like those of Fielding's 'modern Critick', already the stuff of cliché. What Fielding and Johnson demonstrate, indeed, is that by the mid-eighteenth century not just have certain illustrious authors been canonized but so has the canon itself. It has acquired the venerability of having, like its constituent authors, survived the ravages of time.

II

Recitations of an English canon are spurred by different sorts of occasion and appear in a variety of guises and locales. One such

---

[12] Sarah Fielding, *The Adventures of David Simple*, ed. Malcolm Kelsall (Oxford, 1994), 88–91.
[13] See *Yale*, 2: 184–93, 186.

is the prose treatise of literary history, but the incidence of these, at least prior to the appearance of Thomas Warton's *History of English Poetry* (1774–81) is surprisingly thin: a case of aspirations frustrated or relinquished. We know, for example, that Dryden's *Of Dramatic Poesy* (1668), written a full century before Warton's great study, was projected only as the first of a bipartite work, the second part being wherein 'the virtues and faults of the English poets who have written either in... the epic, or the lyric way, will be more fully treated of'.[14] This sounds like an abstract, however hazy, for a prospective literary history, though unfortunately no such volume ever appeared, possibly because Dryden felt his pitch had been queered by the appearance of Thomas Rymer's *Tragedies of the Last Age* (1678). Dryden, moreover, was not alone amongst Augustan critics who, while never producing a fully-fledged literary historical work, evidently felt some enticement towards doing so. In 1703, John Dennis released proposals for a grandiose undertaking, a treatment of the 'works of the most Celebrated English Poets Deceas'd'. As well as supplying biographical entries on chosen poets, the project pledged itself to elucidate the 'laws' and genres of poetry and to illustrate the proper interconnectedness between literature and religion. Yet, in spite of the broad compass of the proposed work, fewer than eighty subscribers bothered to come forward. As a result, Dennis aborted his plan, though the fragment he had already composed eventually appeared as *Grounds of Criticism in Poetry* (1704).[15]

It may have been that Dennis decided that a diachronic approach to literature was simply less marketable than writings about literature of a more critically judgemental or moralistic bent, but, in any event, in the first half of the eighteenth century, the most significant literary historical documents, those most immediately prefatory to Warton's *History*, all remain unpublished. Probably no text exerted more influence relative to length on the course of English literary history than Alexander Pope's 'scribbled paper' on the 'birth and genealogy of English

---

[14] See 'To the Reader', appended to *An Essay of Dramatic Poesy*, in *Of Dramatic Poesy*, 1: 17.
[15] Hooker (ed.), 2, 'Introduction', li.

poetry'.[16] No satisfactory date has been offered for the document; nor does any evidence exist of Pope's interest in composing a literary history other than the bare survival of the
document itself. Yet, unearthed by his literary executor William
Warburton, it passed through the hands of Richard Hurd, William Mason, and Thomas Gray (in whose *Common-Place Book*
it is transcribed in full), before being communicated to Warton.

What is interesting about Pope's document is not his enumeration of a pantheon of authors so much as the complex classifi-
catory system into which they are put. His schema is exclusive to
poets (though one or two dramatic works are included), and
splits into two 'eras' sustaining six 'schools' (see Appendix 1).
The break between the two eras falls roughly around the beginning of Elizabeth's reign, though it is defined in main part by the
segregation of writers into schools. Pope identifies four schools
belonging to the first era, these being the schools of 'Provence',
'Chaucer', 'Petrarch', and 'Dante'; the second era meanwhile
consists of the schools of 'Spenser' and 'Donne', as well as a
separate category for translators from Italian and a rather undi-
gested group of writers seen as providing models for the later
seventeenth-century poets Waller and Butler. The general project
is compact in scope: it begins in the late medieval era (though the
twelfth-century Welsh poet Walter Map is mistakenly cited as a
disciple of Chaucer's) and breaks off at the Restoration, with the
effect that Milton's later poetry and all of Dryden's is excluded.

Although the method of organization remains chronological,
writers are accommodated by school rather than by period;
moreover, Pope's application of the concept of school is especially singular. For Pope, a school does not comprise a group of
writers enclustering a central, influential writer, as we think of
the 'School of Ben' as consisting of those young writers who
actually danced attendance on Ben Jonson. Rather, in Pope's
schema writers post-date the era of the great author to whose
school they belong: so Lydgate and Skelton, for example, are

---

[16] The first expression is Gray's, the second Warburton's; see *The Correspondence
of Thomas Gray*, ed. Paget Toynbee and Leonard Whibley, 3 vols. (Oxford, 1935),
3: 1124. Pope's draft plan was first published by Owen Ruffhead in his *Life of
Alexander Pope* (1769), 424–5. It is also printed in *The Works of Thomas Gray*, ed.
T. J. Mathias, 2 vols. (1814), 2: vi–vii, from a manuscript in Gray's *Common-Place
Book*.

given as members of the 'School of Chaucer', but Chaucer himself belongs to the earlier 'School of Provence'. The idea of the school is harnessed, in other words, to express literary influence rather than the sociology of literary association. Pope's sensitivity to how authors could be associated on the basis of influence or imitation is also discernible in several of his stray remarks on English poets, collected in Joseph Spence's *Observations, Anecdotes, and Characters of Books and Men*. In one place, he observes that 'Michael Drayton was one of the imitators of Spenser, and Fairfax another', and elsewhere that William Davenant was a 'scholar of Donne's, and took his sententiousness and metaphysics from him'.[17]

In spite of remaining unpublished during Pope's lifetime, his literary historical scheme quickly got abroad after his death. Thomas Gray was one who became apprised of it, using it as the basis of his own draft-plan for a history of English poetry. Gray began pursuing his own researches into early British literature during the 1750s, and his *Common-Place Book* contains various materials compiled towards this end. These include an essay on the fifteenth-century poet Lydgate, a discussion of early Welsh poetry and an attempt to document every metrical scheme indigenous to British poetry. By 1770, however, it is evident that Gray had given up these researches, for on April 15 of this year he sent Thomas Warton a copy of his draft-plan (see Appendix 2), with assurances of his confidence in Warton to do better justice to the project than he himself felt able to.[18] Like Pope's earlier plan, Gray's excludes drama, but other than in this regard the differences are more pronounced than the similarities.

Gray's schema reflects the antiquarian nature of his interests as well as his reading proficiency in Middle English, Old English, and early Welsh. Thus he boldly proposes to begin with 'the poetry of the *Galic* (or Celtic) nations, as far as it can be traced'. The earliest stirrings of British poetry are to be dealt with in an introduction, after which the ensuing course of poetry is broken down into four parts. The first of these embraces English and Continental poetry prior to the late fourteenth century; the second details a host of late medieval poets such as Chaucer,

---

[17] Joseph Spence, *Observations, Anecdotes, and Characters of Books and Men*, ed. J. M. Osborn, two vols. (Oxford, 1966), no. 433, 440.
[18] See Gray to Warton, 15 Apr. 1770, in *Correspondence*, 3: 1122–5.

Gower, Hoccleve, Lydgate, and so on; the third encompasses English and European poets of the Renaissance, spanning from Wyatt through to the Restoration and ending with Cowley and Sprat; the fourth period aims to treat poetry virtually up until Gray's own present, including such figures as Waller, Denham, Dryden, Addison, Prior, and Pope. Added to this temporal partitioning of the tradition, Gray inherits from Pope the idea of the literary 'school'. His use of it, however, differs from Pope's, in as much as none of the schools are named after some eponymous single author. Gray's schools instead embrace writers drawn together by common practices as inherited from an earlier, foreign literary school. Thus he identifies a '*third Italian School*', peopled by exponents of the metaphysical conceit and bringing together Donne, Crashaw, Cleveland, Cowley, and Sprat, while the '*School of France*' is the one in which Gray proposes to accommodate poets of the post-Restoration era. What Pope and Gray do share, however, is the belief that practically every major English writer can best be understood in regard of a pan-European—rather than narrowly native—tradition.

Neither Pope's nor Gray's project for a native literary history was ever realized, though both became known to Warton, albeit Gray's too late to have exerted much influence on the larger project. A work falling into a rather different category, but sufficiently important to have been plausibly described as 'the earliest History of English Poetry', belongs to a friend of Pope's, Joseph Spence, sometime Professor of Poetry at Oxford. The work in question, written in French and entitled by Spence 'Quelques Remarques Hist: sur les Poets Anglois', was belatedly discovered by James Osborn, and printed by him in 1949. Nineteen years later, Osborn reported another exciting find in connection with Spence and literary historiography. This was a group of papers, donated to the Harvard College Library, and entitled by an auctioneer's cataloguer 'Collections Relating to the Lives of the Poets'.[19] The latter as mentioned of the two manuscripts was begun the earlier (probably 1720s) and seems to have been augmented throughout Spence's life. It consists of a

---

[19] James M. Osborn, 'The First History of English Poetry', in *Pope and his Contemporaries: Essays Presented to George Sherburn*, ed. James L. Clifford and Louis A. Landa (Oxford, 1949), 230–50; and id., 'Joseph Spence's "Collections Relating to The Lives of the Poets"', *Harvard Library Bulletin*, 16 (1968), 129–38.

dictionary of poets, with a ranking scheme running from the highest category ('a great Genius, & fine writer') to one beneath classification ('one never to be read'), plus a bibliography of source-books and an earlier English draft of 'Quelques Remarques'. Osborn is somewhat embarrassedly at pains not to make strong claims on behalf of the 'Collections', finding the biographical drafts scrappily anecdotal and derivative. Of most interest he takes to be the occasional traces of Spence's intimacy with Pope, some of his biographical entries quoting remarks of Pope's that were also to be assimilated into the *Observations*.[20]

It was probably in 1732–3, while travelling in France and Italy, that Spence brought to completion and rendered into French his earlier draft of a history of English poetry. It is clear that he was conscious of being a pioneer, for in 1736 he wrote in his 'Preface' to *Gorboduc* that 'Literary History has not to this day got much ground in our Island.'[21] One way of approaching Spence's 'Quelques Remarques' is through briefly consulting another project whose relation to it remains problematic. The 'Remarques' have come down to us in the form of a bound manuscript, the first leaf of which is headed 'Lessons, in learning French; and Italian'. The same title-leaf also contains some jottings in connection with an envisaged 'Preface' to Spence's poetical dictionary, in the form of a 'His^y of Poetry for above 2000 yrs'. Spence's schema for this history is as follows:

1. Druidical Poetry.
   Roman Poetry? Contr[acte]d from Pol[ymeti]s

2. How far in this Island
   Revival of Poetry: in Provence
   Italian shoot from it.

3. Chaucer, Piers Plowman, Mir[roi]r &c.
   Revival of Classical Learning in Italy
   Improvement of the Italian Poetry.

4. Our Fourth Age of Poetry
   Improvement of Fr[ench] Poetry

---

[20] See Osborn, 'Joseph Spence's "Collections"', 131–3.
[21] 'Preface' to *Gorboduc* (1736), iv; cited from Osborn, 'The First History of English Poetry', 238.

5. Our Fifth Age
6. Our Last Age.[22]

The 'Hist[y] of Poetry', so Osborn concludes, was always designed
as something distinct from 'Quelques Remarques', but the over-
lap in span and progression between the two projects would
have been marked. Like the 'Hist[y]' would have done, Spence's
'Remarques' locates the origin of British poetry in the verses of
the Druids, and he attempts to recite its subsequent history all
the way through to the 'Last' ('latest') age. If one studies Spence's nomenclature, one can note that the two words indicative of
literary historical development are 'revival' and 'improvement':
the first occurs where literary history changes in accord with
some external influence as with the recovery of a past literary
culture, the second where an indigenous tradition develops and
matures. The big difference, however, between Spence's plan and
'Remarques' is that in the latter, authors are grouped by century,
an immediate effect of such a strategy being to throw into sharp
relief the yawning gaps still existing in the historical record. So
while Spence can assign at least a solitary poet to each century
from the sixth to the ninth, he comes up with no name whatso-
ever for the tenth, eleventh, and twelfth centuries, a period of
literary drought caused by the minatory influence of the Vikings,
'grands ennemis de la litterature'.

   The 'Remarques' offer scant evidence of Spence's being a
highly original thinker about literature, and his judgements on
particular authors are for the most part perfunctory and conventional. The tone adopted throughout the work stops short of
hagiography, and even for a work of such slightness (no more
than five thousand words), Spence leans more towards compre-
hensivity of notice than towards the erection of a pantheon of
greats. Chaucer is dutifully acknowledged as the 'father' of
English poetry; Shakespeare wins the longest and most partisan
entry; and Dryden is praised as having elevated both English
poetry and the language in general. Probably most interest
attaches to Spence's treatment of poets near in time to himself,
since his remarks are here less compliant with a settled body
of critical opinion. In spite of rejecting the Popean notion of
schools as his organizing paradigm and instead proceeding in

[22] Ibid. 238–9.

dogged century-by-century fashion, he equates the beginning of his own modern era not with the century's own beginning but with the Restoration. Gray was later to label the post-Restoration period as the 'School of France', but Spence instead opts for the 'Augustan Age', a verbal usage that is prescient without being original. Even here, though, Spence eschews any high degree of selectivity, managing for example to crowd Prior, Garth, Gay, Parnell, King, Swift, John Philips, and Thomson into a single paragraph. Perhaps predictably, a climax to Spence's literary history is provided by a glowing reference to Spence's friend, Pope, described as 'Le Premier Poëte de ce siècle, ou en Angleterre, ou ailleurs'.

III

It remains something of an historical anomaly that figures such as Dryden, Dennis, Pope, and Spence, for all the preliminary motions they go through, never bring a literary historical work to fruition in printed form. Before Thomas Warton's *History*, indeed, the main vehicles for intimating or reciting an English canon are poetic ones. One obvious such vehicle is the sort of funereal elegy which lauds a deceased writer by promoting him into a larger canonical firmament: good examples of this form are Jonson's famous elegy on Shakespeare, Denham's on Cowley, and Alexander Oldys's dream poem, *An Ode ... on the Universally Lamented Death of the Incomparable Mr. Dryden* (1700). Another form, though, that is sometimes directed to canonical ends is the 'session of the poets' poem, in which poets are judged before a tribunal normally headed by Apollo though occasionally by some canonical luminary such as Ben Jonson. The inaugurative work of this kind seems to have been Sir John Suckling's 'A Session of the Poets' (wr. 1637) from which descend other attempts along similar lines including Marvell's 'Tom May's Death' (a rather underdeveloped illustration of the form), a poem uncertainly attributed to Rochester and sometimes entitled 'A Session of the Poets' (1680) and Anne Finch's 'The Circuit of Apollo'. As often as not these poems provide occasion for debunking satire against contemporaries. Suckling's 'Session' for example ends with the laurel being conferred not on any of the supplicating bards but on a rich alderman, on the grounds that 'the best Sign | Of good Store of Wit's to have good Store of Coyn'.[23] Similarly, in the later, possibly Rochesterian 'Session', a host of contemporary poets and dramatists assert their credentials for possessing 'the Bays' only for them to be awarded instead to the actor Thomas Betterton for having had the modesty to keep his plays un-published.[24] Perhaps the most interesting among such works in raising issues to do with canon formation is the anonymous prose work, *A Journal from Parnassus*, probably written in 1688. Here again much of the energy of the piece is given over to topical mockery of a contemporary poet, Dryden. At the beginning of the work, several authors process into an assembly in the sequence of an understood literary tradition: Gower and Chaucer come first followed by Shakespeare and Jonson, 'Whose unparallel'd work never mett with any Rivals'. At a later point, some of the more illustrious figures are nominated to inspect and license 'the several Species of Poetry', and here again the appointments are made in a way that seems to deline-ate an English canon, one which includes Spenser, Cowley, Waller, Oldham (whose appointment to supervise 'Satyrs' may be a calculated snub to Dryden), Shakespeare (to oversee tragedy), Jonson, and Beaumont and Fletcher.[25]

The 'session of the poets' poem, as I have said, was a form mainly put in service of satire of contemporaries, but from the late sixteenth century onwards, poets begin to write poems reflecting more neutrally, or more genially, on the contemporary literary scene. Thomas Churchyard's 'A Praise of Poetrie' (1595) has magnanimous things to say about several fellow poets such as Surrey, Spenser, Drayton, and Sidney; and John Weever's *Epigrammes* (1599) is also full of laudatory references to a host of contemporary writers. One beneficiary of Weever's friendliness (complimented on his 'hony words') is Michael Drayton, and a signally important example of early seven-

---

[23] *The Works of Sir John Suckling* (1709), 4–7, 7.

[24] The poem is omitted from David Vieth's edition of Rochester's poems. It is included, however, as an appendix in *The Poems of John Wilmot Earl of Rochester*, ed. Keith Walker (Oxford, 1984). See 133–5 and the editor's note on the attribution issue (312). 'Session of the poets' poems are discussed in Trevor Ross, *The Making of the English Literary Canon* (Montreal and Kingston, 1998), 175–82.

[25] *A Journal from Parnassus*, ed. Hugh MacDonald (London, 1937), 5–6, 38.

teenth-century canon-making is the latter's verse epistle 'To Henry Reynolds, of Poets and Poesy', included in Drayton's *Elegies upon Sundry Occasions* (1627).[26] The poem begins with Drayton reminiscing on evenings of literary conversation spent with his friend Reynolds, in which not just contemporary writers but also the older writers of the tradition are discussed, this because Reynolds was always pleased 'Of those who liued long agoe to heare'.[27] From this point, the poem details Drayton's adolescent aspiration to be a poet, before, from line 47, shifting into a recital of the major poets of the English tradition.

Drayton claims to have dispensed from his account the work of non-publishing authors whose works merely 'by transcription daintyly must goe'; and he also suggests he has refrained from interesting himself in successful dramatists, in those that 'applause haue wonne, | Vpon our Stages', though this statement is not borne out by the poem. The poets, excluding translators, who are acknowledged in a more than perfunctory way are Chaucer, Gower, Surrey, Wyatt, Gascoigne, Churchyard, Spenser, Sidney, William Warner, Marlowe, Nashe, Shakespeare, Daniel, Jonson, Sir William Alexander, Drummond of Hawthornden, Francis Beaumont, Sir John Beaumont, and William Browne: it might be noted that Warner, Alexander, Drummond, John Beaumont, and Browne were all friends of Drayton.[28] The introduction of each significant author is accompanied by a pithy character note: Spenser is 'Graue' and 'morrall', Marlowe in possession of a 'fine madnes', and Jonson, given the longest and most enthusiastic notice, is praised for his depth of learning. The list (excepting Drayton's particular friends) might seem a surprisingly prescient rendition of a medieval and Renaissance poetic canon easily familiar to us nowadays, yet it still evinces some quirks and anomalies. Of particular note are that Drayton seems unconversant with the fifteenth-century poets Lydgate and Skelton, who had already been enshrined in earlier versions of the pre-Renaissance tradition; also that Jonson is here accorded the pre-eminent place on the

---

[26] John Weever, *Epigrammes in the Oldest Cut and Newest Fashion (1599)*, ed. R. B. McKerrow (Stratford, 1922), 11.
[27] The poem is cited here from Spingarn (ed.), 1: 134–40, 134.
[28] See Bernard H. Newdigate, *Michael Drayton and his Circle* (Oxford, 1941).

Jacobean stage, being termed 'Lord...of the Theater', with Shakespeare being allowed only a more modest status as an essentially comic writer; that no mention is made of John Fletcher; and finally that the raffish Thomas Nashe is admitted to the tradition, albeit in spite of the fact, as Drayton embarrassedly admits, that 'he a Proser were'.

Drayton's poem is slanted by his friendly partiality for several of the poets mentioned, and so much can be said of Joseph Addison's similar catalogue of poets, 'An Account of the Greatest English Poets' (1694). The poem, a piece of prentice-work composed when Addison was just twenty-one, puffs itself as 'A short account of all the muse-possest...down from Chaucer's days to Dryden's times'.[29] Unlike Drayton's epistle, Addison does not simply list the major publishing poets known to him; rather the 'Account' traces a trajectory of refinement in English poetry from its uncouth beginnings with Chaucer through to an apex of correctness and limpidity represented by Dryden, a poet to whom Addison, in his first significant writerly act, had already composed a poem of glowing sycophancy. Such a procedure contributes to an odd sharpness of tone, for even while progressing through his pantheon of greats, Addison constantly chivies his entrants over their poetic deficiencies. Chaucer's style, for example, is 'unpolish'd' and his language obscured by time; Spenser's supernaturalism and overt moralizing make him suitable only for an age 'uncultivate and rude'; Cowley is overlavish of wit; and Milton 'profan'd his pen, | To varnish o'er the guilt of faithless men'. This emphasis on what each canonical figure lacks is a necessary preliminary to the enshrinement of Dryden as the most perfect embodiment of the poet, Dryden's Muse affording 'The sweetest numbers, and the fittest words'.

Leaving aside poets mentioned at the end, who belong to his own generation, Addison's poetic canon runs as follows: Chaucer, Spenser, Cowley, Milton, Waller, Roscommon, Denham, and Dryden. Amongst these, only the Earl of Roscommon, author of the well-regarded *Essay on Translated Verse* (1684), might have been considered an exceptional figure. In any event, Addison's roster of greats formed the basis of another

---

[29] *The Works of the Right Honourable Joseph Addison*, ed. Richard Hurd, 6 vols. (1811), 1: 29–33, 29.

poem of literary canon-formation published only six years later (1700) by another stripling poet, Samuel Cobb, entitled 'Of Poetry: Its Progress'.[30] Its worthies, drawn from both poetry and drama, were by now household names in such a context: Chaucer, Spenser, Jonson, Fletcher, Beaumont, Shakespeare, Cowley, Milton, Waller, Denham, Roscommon, Oldham, Lee, and Otway. Cobb has added the dramatists Nathaniel Lee (d. 1692) and Thomas Otway (d. 1685) as well as the satiric poet John Oldham (d. 1683), but the other names are either identical with those of Addison's 'Account' or are already generic to canon-forming histories of the English stage. What needs to be stressed is that by the beginning of the eighteenth century, a canon of English literature had not just been formulated but been stabilized and consecrated.

Cobb's 'Of Poetry' was the first of a clutch of progress-of-poesy poems which, during the first half of the eighteenth century, formed perhaps the principal generic vehicle for literary canon-making, the others being Elijah Fenton's 'An Epistle to Mr. Southerne' (wr. 1711), Judith Madan's 'The Progress of Poesy' (1721), William Collins's 'An Epistle addressed to Thomas Hanmer' (1743) and Thomas Gray's 'Progress of Poesy' (1757). Progress poems were a staple literary form, narrating the aetiology, generally expressed in mythological terms, of some object or invention. However, poems like Cobb's and Gray's were also probably invoking the same sense of the term 'progress' as is to the fore in the title of John Bunyan's *The Pilgrim's Progress* (1678), a sense represented by *OED* 1: 'The action of stepping or marching forward or onward... a journey, an expedition.' The idea of journeying was applicable to progress-of-poesy poems, since the rise of poetry in England was seen as having been achieved through its geographical translation from those cultures in which it had originally flourished, Greece and Rome.

Cobb's 'Of Poetry' sets out to expound the 'Antiquity', 'Progress', and 'Improvement' of poetry from its early origins and across its several continents. What is sketched out is a

---

[30] I have consulted the poem in Samuel Cobb, *Poems on Several Occasions*, 3rd edn. (1710), 176–226. Prefixed to it is W. Worts's 'To his Friend on the Following Poem', 172–4, in itself an interesting statement about the relation of English literature to an antecedent classical tradition.

mythology or pseudo-history of poetry's progress, beginning from its rise, in the person of Moses, among the biblical peoples, and its subsequent migration to the heathen cultures of Greece and Rome. From here, in course of time, poetry decamps to England, taking root in the breast of Chaucer (the 'English Ennius'). In spite of stressing poetry's longevity as a phenomenon, Cobb lays a pronounced emphasis on 'improvement': poetry should ideally contain a primary creative force supplemented by art, the latter seen as being the product of discipline and labour. The gamut of issues that Cobb addresses become generic to progress-of-poesy poems. Where and when does poetry actually begin? If poetry is common to both ancient and modern cultures, what can we say it consists of? And what indeed are the respective merits of the 'primitive' poetry of previous cultures and the refined poetry of the modern era?

If these questions are not entirely answered, they are certainly raised by Elijah Fenton's 'Epistle to Mr. Southerne', written in 1710–11.[31] By this time, Thomas Southerne's career, which had peaked with his tragedies *The Fatal Marriage* (1694) and *Oroonoko* (1695), had gone into a somewhat pitiable decline; Fenton, on the other hand, only 27, was launching a literary career chiefly recalled nowadays for his involvement as co-translator on Pope's *Odyssey*. The 'Epistle' falls into two sections. It begins with a panegyric on Southerne and Thomas Otway and on the achievements of post-Restoration tragedy, before reciting an earlier dramatic tradition comprising Shakespeare, Jonson, Beaumont, and Fletcher. Reawakening a metaphor more famously used by Dryden, Fenton states that 'in those days were giants in the land'. Next he proceeds to lambast the era of the Civil war and Interregnum, 'Discolour'd with the pious monarch's blood', and then praises the post-Restoration revival of comedy at the same time as lamenting the poverty of tragedy, a poverty offset only by the efforts of Southerne.

At this point in the poem, Fenton shifts tack to a mythology of poetry's rise and progress. In his account, poetry rises in Greece, where she first attaches herself to the epic form and then to the pastoral one. At length, however, the nymph loses her bloom and transports herself to Rome, where she initially finds herself

---

[31] See Anderson (ed.), 7: 660–2.

enchained by 'wars abroad, and civil discord'. Only when the sword of Octavius brings peace is she at liberty to install herself in a succession of Roman poets, such as Virgil, Horace, and Sappho. It is the overrunning of the Roman state by the Goths that leads to the Muse decamping to England where she takes up residence amongst the Druids, infusing herself into their hymns of natural religion. After this mythological account of the arrival of poesy in England, Fenton's 'Epistle' reverts back to reciting the major canonical poets. A line of poetic worthies is sketched out from the fourteenth century through to Fenton's own day, consisting of Chaucer, Surrey, Waller, and Granville.

The excessive culminatory praise of Granville should discourage us from taking Fenton's poetic pantheon too seriously. Rather more interesting than his literary historical schema, in fact, is his detailing of a fanciful aetiology for poetry in England. Yet in so far as historical factuality matters, Fenton's aetiology is confused. The Roman empire being overrun by Gothic swarms, the Muse supposedly repairs to the English Druids; but the era of the Druids actually predates the fall of Rome, since their existence was documented by Caesar during his Gallic expedition of the first century BC. All progress-of-poesy poems are, in one sense, allegories of influence: to say that the Muse passes from Greece to Rome and thence to England is to surmise along the lines that literature in Rome is born out of a cognizance of Greek literature, and literature in England from a cognizance of the Roman literary tradition. Yet this fails to hold for Fenton's scheme, since the Druids did not acquire poetry from the Romans, nor did the subsequent English tradition, headed by Chaucer, acquire it from the Druids. Other progress-of-poesy poems avoid the anomalies of the Druids by holding up Chaucer as the Muse's first recipient in England. This is true of Cobb, but also of Judith Madan's 'The Progress of Poesy' (1719). In her account, having begun in Greece and then migrated to Rome, the Muse flies to Britain and lodges herself in Chaucer, then infusing herself in a poetic lineage comprising Spenser, Cowley, Waller, Milton, Dryden, Denham, Addison, Garth, Pope, Prior, Granville, and Rowe.

A modification of this scheme is proposed by William Collins in his 'Epistle to Thomas Hanmer' (1743), this being that the Muse, having vacated Greece and Rome, stops off in Provence, home of the thirteenth-century troubadours (though Collins mistakenly supposes a fifteenth-century date). Moreover, on arrival in England, she incarnates herself not in Chaucer but in Shakespeare, this fact being an eloquent testimony to Shakespeare's growing status as the champion of native letters. A further complication of the picture is evident if we turn to Thomas Gray's 'The Progress of Poesy' (1757). Here poetry is seen as enjoying a primitive origin amongst the ancient cultures of the Laplanders and South American Indians:

> In climes beyond the solar road,
> Where shaggy forms o'er ice-built mountains roam,
> The Muse has broke the twilight-gloom
> To cheer the shivering native's dull abode.
> And oft, beneath the odorous shade
> Of Chile's boundless forests laid,
> She deigns to hear the savage youth repeat
> In loose numbers wildly sweet
> Their feather-cinctured chiefs and dusky loves.[32]

That Gray should suppose the Muse's first abode to have been amongst primitive peoples reflects a new appreciation both that poetry had been native to early cultures and that primitive poetry possessed merits comparable with the more refined verse of modern ages. Having admitted primitive poetry, however, Gray returns to convention, documenting the Muse's progress to Greece, followed by, 'in Greece's evil hour', her migration to the 'Latin plains'. Next, seeking out the 'sea-encircled coast' of Albion, she occupies a line of august poetic worthies: Shakespeare, Milton, Dryden, and (with a self-congratulating egoism untypical of the poet) Gray himself.

One or two further aspects of the myth of poetry's progress should be drawn out. A patriotic undertow throughout all the progress-of-poesy poems is that the Muse (that is, poetry itself) can only thrive amidst conditions of individual liberty. Her flight from Greece and Rome is normally seen as necessitated by tyranny, and her happy settlement in Albion is accountable to the ancient liberty supposedly enjoyed by Englishmen, such liberty itself being a myth cherished especially by Tories and

---

[32] 'The Progress of Poesy', lines 54–62, in *The Poems of Thomas Gray, William Collins, Oliver Goldsmith*, ed. Roger Lonsdale (London, 1969), 169–70.

Whig patriots. Judith Madan, for example, sees Britain as ultimately transcending Rome as a sanctuary for poetry on the strength of her reputation for freedom:

> 'Twas sacred Liberty's celestial smile
> First lur'd the Muses to thy generous isle;
> Twas Liberty bestow'd the power to sing;
> And bid the verse-rewarding laurels spring.[33]

In similar vein, Gray suggests that wherever the Muse travels, there will be found 'Freedom's holy flame'; and the same point is made in Michael Wodhull's *Ode to the Muses* (1760) which records how when the Muse took flight from Rome, 'Expell'd by Gothick arms', she set course to England 'In quest of liberty'.[34] At the heart of this myth lies an assertion of continuity between classical culture and that of Britain (or more narrowly England), but it also proposes the political and literary supremacy of the English over national rivals like the French.

Progress-of-poesy poems, especially where they lashed together narratives of political and cultural progress, *translatio imperii* and *translatio studii*, inevitably took their own liberties with the historical record. Nobody, for example, could languish unaware that the greatest flowering of Roman literature had occurred coevally with the despotic rule of Augustus. One work particularly revealing about the intractability of the historical material in the face of this myth-making zeal is James Thomson's *Liberty* (1735–6). As regards English politics, Thomson is concerned to show that the full flowering of 'political liberty', a state equated throughout the poem with power-sharing government, arises no earlier than the 1689 political settlement. But to argue this also entails that he propose that the high-point of national letters must occur at the same time (political liberty and cultural maturity being intertwined), with the further entailment that the efforts of the great Renaissance poets, such as Shakespeare and Spenser, have to be played down and skirted over.[35]

---

[33] Line 65, ibid. 170; *The Progress of Poetry. By Mrs. Madan* (1783), 15.
[34] *Ode to the Muses. By Mr. Wodhull* (1760), 8.
[35] See Robin Dix, 'James Thomson and the Progress of the Progress Poem: From *Liberty* to *The Castle of Indolence*', in *James Thomson: Essays for the Tercentenary*, ed. Richard Terry (Liverpool, 2000), 117–39.

The invoking of liberty as a key concept within progress-of-poesy poems has one other consequence: the depredations supposedly inflicted on it by the Goths could be used to explain the embarrassing hiatus in the literary historical record, evident in all the works I have discussed here, stretching from the fall of Rome to the reawakening of poetry in the modern figure of Chaucer. Admittedly, Fenton cites the Druids (though wholly implausibly) as an intermediate stage, and Collins turns to the medieval troubadours of Provence, but these gentle whimsies do little to solder up the historical gap. This sense of a literary vacuum prior to Chaucer was not, however, the preserve solely of progress-of-poesy poets, for it mapped on to a general schematization of secular history into three eras: eras of classical and modern enlightenment separated by one of cultural darkness.

The expressions that we use nowadays to designate the period dividing the ancient from the modern world, the 'Middle Ages' or 'medieval' epoch, were uncommon before the nineteenth century.[36] The original *OED* could find no example of the first of these before 1722 (though earlier ones have been incorporated in the revised dictionary); and even now the *OED* can offer nothing before 1827 for the word 'medieval'. This situation does not bespeak the fact that the eighteenth century lacked a clear sense of the medieval period as a temporal entity, but rather that such terms as 'Middle Ages' and 'medieval' reflect a historical neutrality towards the period that few actually entertained. More common designations were the 'dark ages' (current from the late seventeenth century) and, most notably, the 'gothic age'. In the first half of the eighteenth century, hostility to the gothic age was grimly uniform and based on an ensconced historical orthodoxy. Its details were that the Roman empire had eventually crumbled and been overrun by the Goths whose influence thenceforth sank the European continent into an age of ignorance and barbarism. This situation was only relieved with the Turkish sack of Constantinople in 1453 which led to a diaspora westwards of classical scholars, with the effect that a new age of learning broke across Europe.

---

[36] See Pat Rogers, 'Thomas Warton and the Waxing of the Middle Ages', in *Medieval Literature and Antiquities: Studies in Honour of Basil Cottle*, ed. Myra Stokes and T. L. Burton (Cambridge, 1987), 175–86, esp. 175.

The terms of the Augustan dehumanization of the Middle Ages can seem alarmingly histrionic. Dryden, in his verses 'To Godfrey Kneller' (1694) condemns how the '*Goths* and *Vandals*, a rude *Northern* Race, | Did all the matchless Monuments deface'; and Book II of Mark Akenside's *The Pleasures of Imagination* (1744) opens with an especially lurid vision of how the 'iron-swarms' 'swept the works | Of liberty and wisdom down the gulph | Of all-devouring night'.[37] These ritualistic denunciations are pretty much *de rigueur* in progress-of-poesy poems, so that Fenton stigmatizes the dark ages as a time when 'from the rugged North unnumber'd swarms | Invade the Latian coasts', while Collins condemns them as when 'resistless dulness rose'.[38] It is telling that the only poet of those dealt with here to eschew indignant satirizing of the gothic age is Gray, the sole one who had actually undertaken a serious body of literary historical research. Instinct within the progress-of-poesy format was the smug conviction that English literature enjoyed an immediate descent from the literatures of the classical world, this conviction inevitably reducing the period intervening—the Middle Ages—to a cultural void that could safely be subject to any amount of uninformed derogation. Yet as the eighteenth century unfolds, a more enlightened view of the Middle Ages slowly makes itself heard, indeed became one of the triumphs of antiquarianism as well as an important moment in the onset of Romanticism. The new sensibility is epitomized by no work so much as Richard Hurd's *Letters on Chivalry and Romance* (1762), beginning as it does with the pertly iconoclastic statement: 'The ages, we call barbarous, present us with many a subject of curious speculation.'[39] This discovery that these centuries, just as much as the classical epochs, contained the seeds of a subsequent vernacular tradition was to be a major achievement of eighteenth-century literary history. But the narration of this achievement must wait until my final chapter.

---

[37] Kinsley (ed.), 859; cited from *The Poetical Works of Mark Akenside*, ed. Robin Dix (London, 1996), 111.

[38] Anderson (ed.), 7: 661; line 35, in Lonsdale (ed.), 392.

[39] *Hurd's Letters on Chivalry and Romance with the Third Elizabethan Dialogue*, ed. Edith J. Morley (London, 1911), 79.

IV

As already said, progress-of-poesy poems were concerned with the translation of culture between regions and periods and not with 'progress' as consistent improvement. Yet literary quality was widely, though not invariably, spoken of as a factor of two other phenomena which *did* prove amenable to notions of progress: first, the state of the English language; and, second, the quality of English versification.[40] From the sixteenth century onwards, literature was customarily seen as contributing to a grand project of English 'eloquence', to an upwardly mobile maturation of the English language: when Drayton, in his epistle 'To Reynolds' notes that poets have 'inricht our language with their rimes', he is not merely saying that poets have created valuable linguistic works but also that they have made the language itself more valuable.[41] In the seventeenth and eighteenth centuries, the poets Waller, Denham, and Dryden all become hallowed for their role in perfecting the national tongue; and it is telling that Dryden speaks of his own creative vocation as an attempt to 'improve the Language, & Especially the Poetry'.[42] Perhaps only in the post-Restoration era, especially with the advent of descriptive criticism, do commentators begin to fashion judgements about literary works that are clearly divorced from being adjudications on the language in which they are written.

If writers acceded to greatness partly on the strength of their improvement of the tongue then it followed that a whole canon could be mapped out along these lines. This indeed is what happens in a set of verses appearing on the frontispece engraving of Christopher Smart's periodical *The Universal Visitor* (1756):

> To CHAUCER! who the English Tongue design'd:
> To SPENCER! who improv'd it, and refin'd:
> To Muse—fir'd SHAKESPEAR! who increas'd its Praise,

[40] The best general discussion of linguistic change remains Richard Foster Jones, *The Triumph of the English Language: A Survey of Opinions Concerning the Vernacular from the Introduction of Printing to the Restoration* (Oxford, 1953). See also the relevant sections of Albert C. Baugh and Thomas Cable, *A History of the English Language*, 3rd edn. (London, 1978).

[41] Line 14, in Spingarn (ed.), 1: 134.

[42] Letter to Mrs Steward of 7 Nov. 1699, in *The Letters of John Dryden*, ed. Charles E. Ward (Durham, NC, 1942), 123.

Rich in bold Compounds, & strong-painted Phrase,
To WALLER! Sweet'ner of its manly Sound:
To DRYDEN! who its full Perfection found.[43]

What is enumerated here is a canon of English literature relative to the single criterion of linguistic improvement. Taken on these terms, the canon is for the most part predictable: Chaucer 'designs' the English tongue, Waller's is an important contribution towards its purification, and Dryden brings it to full perfection. Yet thrown in amongst these three writers, whose names were bywords for linguistic purification, are two more enigmatic figures: Spenser and Shakespeare. While the case for Shakespeare's literary greatness was usually so incontestable as not to require arguments drawn narrowly from language, Spenser's impact on the tongue was most often seen as the rather retrograde one of having resuscitated the poetic phraseology of earlier English writers, especially Chaucer. The impression given by Smart's canon is that of stuttering between two distinct criteria: the one purely linguistic, and the other a covertly aesthetic one, though itself framed in linguistic terms.

One other blurring of criteria can be detected in Smart's lines. Although he begins by alluding to Chaucer, 'who the English Tongue design'd', it subsequently remains unclear whether his lines concern the advancement of the language in general or merely of poetic language or 'versification'. 'Versification' embraced a variety of issues: rhythm, diction, the manipulation of syllables, the handling of rhetorical figures and the relation between sense-units and the units of line and stanza. Although the Elizabethans had looked back to Wyatt and Surrey as having reformed 'our English meetre and stile', poets of the eighteenth century attributed this activity to their nearer predecessors, Waller, Denham, and Dryden.[44] Dryden himself praises Waller as 'the first whose Art | Just Weight and Measure did to Verse impart'; Sir Thomas Pope Blount notes that 'Mr. *Waller* remov'd all . . . [the] . . . Faults' of English poetic style; and Sir Richard Blackmore states that 'Before the two great Reformers *Denham*

---

[43] Cited from Ross, 'Just When *Did* "British bards begin t'Immortalize"?', 383. See also Ross, *The Making of the English Literary Canon*, 3–4. Ross is interested in the image accompanying the lines rather than the lines themselves, an image which casts Smart as a 'reproducer' of the canon of English poetry.
[44] Puttenham, *Arte of English Poesie*, in Smith (ed.), 2: 63.

and *Waller* flourish'd, poetical Pieces show'd that the Authors had little Taste of the Beauties of Diction, and Purity, Propriety and Splendor of Words; of the Harmony of Numbers, the Dignity of figurative Expression; and the Art of Versification'.[45] Although the role played by Denham and Waller was thought to have been crucial, it was equally truistical that the absolute purification of English numbers had been attained only by Dryden: Johnson's 'Life of Dryden', for example, venerates Dryden as the poet to whom 'we owe the improvement, perhaps the completion of our metre, the refinement of our language, and much of the correctness of our sentiments'.[46]

This supposed improvement of English versification, as well as of the language in general, enabled literature to be assimilated to a principle of progress. This fact is evident in a passage in Dryden's 'Preface' to *Fables Ancient and Modern* (1700) in which he absolves Chaucer from the disgrace of metrical irregularity:

We can only say that he lived in the infancy of our poetry, and that nothing is brought to perfection at the first. We must be children before we grow men. There was an Ennius, and in process of time a Lucilius, and a Lucretius, before Virgil and Horace; even after Chaucer, there was a Spenser, a Harington, a Fairfax, before Waller and Denham were in being; and our numbers were in their nonage till these last appeared.[47]

In its developmental arc from infancy to maturity, the literary tradition tracks the progress of English versification in general. That this was felt to be so bespeaks a sensitivity to poetic language that is now no longer extant: we do not nowadays cultivate a canon of writers who, regardless of their own intrinsic achievement, are fêted on account of having advanced the state of versification. Yet it is distinctive of the Augustans to keep in play the two alternative criteria of canon-construction: the literary and the linguistic. Addison's 'Account of the Greatest English Poets', for example, is clearly predicated on the linguis-

[45] Translation of Boileau's 'The Art of Poetry', lines 131–2, in Kinsley, (ed.), 335; Thomas Pope Blount, *De Re Poetica: or, Remarks upon Poetry. With Characters and Censures of the most Considerable Poets whether Ancient or Modern* (1694), 245; Sir Richard Blackmore, *Essays* (1717), cited from Earl R. Wasserman, *Elizabethan Poetry in the Eighteenth Century* (Urbana, Ill., 1947), 21.

[46] *Lives*, 1: 469.

[47] *Of Dramatic Poesy*, 2: 281.

tic model, with Waller being accorded a prominent status and Dryden being introduced as the apogee of the English tradition. It is Dryden alone whose adjectives are superlatives: his numbers are the 'sweetest' and his words the 'fittest'. So much does he bring the tradition to its apex that Addison suggests that his verse represents a pinnacle from which the only possiblity is decline: we should 'fear our English Poetry, | That long has flourish'd, shou'd decay with thee'.[48]

Yet accounts of the rise of the English language or of English versification never fully ensconced themselves as accounts of English literature as such. For one thing, they were inconsistent with the literary priority that critics, on the strength of other criteria, wanted to grant to Shakespeare. Perhaps, more acutely, linguistic schemas could also make nothing of Milton, a writer who underwent a pronounced vogue in the first decade of the eighteenth century. Addison went so far as to say that 'Our Language sunk under him', and nobody could plausibly claim that Milton, however great his 'literary' achievement, had done much towards the refinement of the tongue.[49] The two distinct criteria for literary canonicity for the most part subsist in a state of unruffled contradiction. Some commentators were ebullient about current-day achievements, while being sympathetic to earlier writers like Shakespeare for having had at their disposal a language still recalcitrant to high literary achievement; others were already acclaiming Shakespeare as the pinnacle of the native canon. In all this, the key confrontation is that between Dryden and Shakespeare, a competition the more momentous as not being for supremacy in a single unified canon, but for supremacy between competing canonical logics. Ultimately, it might be said, the literary canon that the Augustan era has bequeathed to the modern day is one in which Shakespeare's, and not Dryden's, comprises the apical achievement.

Canons and traditions inevitably change over time: as history scrolls forward, those authors available to be included in them constantly increase in number. Moreover, the selections and omissions of one era are always liable to be overturned by a later one. For the eighteenth century, Waller and Denham occupied positions of high cultural eminence that can easily seem

---

[48] Hurd (ed.), 1: 33.   [49] No. 297, 9 Feb. 1712, in *Spectator*, 3: 62.

baffling nowadays; on the other hand, Marlowe seems largely to have been suppressed from the Augustan canon, shouldered out by the powerful axis of Shakespeare, Jonson, and Fletcher; while Donne's poetry, though well enough known, was mostly derogated by critics and readers. Equally, the difficulty of Chaucer's language, and the rebarbative nature of Milton's politics, brought their own volatilities to eighteenth-century acts of canon-formation.

It could hardly have been otherwise. Yet, at the same time, amidst this flux, there remains a significant degree of continuity; moreover, there arises a pattern in which the canon itself *overrides* the different sorts of logic, or forms of narrative, that are applied to it. Those who promote a canon of linguistic progress find Shakespeare an insurmountable obstacle. But even when this particular canonical logic lapses into obsolescence, the author who had been most advantaged by it, Dryden, continues to hold a place in the higher echelons of a canon conceived on different grounds.[50] By the middle of the eighteenth century, the canon has acquired its own momentum, a lust to perpetuate itself, an awareness, in short, of its own canonicity. I concluded section I with Dr Johnson's spoof of canon recital in *Idler* 60, a spoof that depends entirely on a recognition that even by then the literary canon had ossified into truism. So much is evident even earlier. In 1736, for example, Pope can state with bluff certitude that: "Tis easy to mark out the general course of our [non-dramatic] poetry. Chaucer, Spenser, Milton, and Dryden are the great landmarks for it.'[51] This is not so much an adjudication on particular authors as a level enumeration of the contents of an understood tradition. The canon has already turned into a mantra.

[50] See Thomas Gray's 'The Progress of Poesy' in which Dryden figures in a canon drawn up on the basis, not of linguistic purity, but of sublimity.
[51] Spence, *Observations*, no. 410.

3

Authorial Dictionaries and the Cult
of Fame

I

In 1616, there occurs a notable event in the history of English publishing, the appearance of the monumental folio edition of *The Workes of Beniamin Jonson*.[1] Unlike E. K.'s dedication to Spenser's *Shepherd's Calendar*, its purpose was not to announce the arrival of a new poet, but instead to proclaim the accession of an older poet to the status of a vernacular classic. This claim of canonicity was conveyed in part by the lavish typographic appearance of the *Works* as well as by the magniloquence of its very title. The semantics of Jonson's 'works' are complex. The oldest acceptation of 'work' (*OED* 1) understands the term as an 'act' or 'deed', clearly implying the existence of an agent; but more precisely applicable is *OED* 13: 'A literary or musical composition (viewed in relation to its author or composer).' The parenthesis here is important, for it implies that for a writer to speak of his own 'works' was for him to issue a public statement of proprietorship over the corpus of his productions, an intimation that would not be conveyed by use of a neutral term such as 'plays'. The self-assurance of Jonson's use of the word 'works', in any event, drew comment: Sir John Suckling's *A Session of the Poets* (1637?), for example, written in the year of Jonson's death, has him blurting out that 'he deserv'd the Bays, | For his were call'd Works, where others were but Plays'.[2]

[1] See Richard C. Newton, 'Jonson and the (Re-)Invention of the Book', in *Classic and Cavalier: Essays on Jonson and the Sons of Ben*, ed. Claude J. Summers and Ted-Larry Pebworth (Pittsburgh, 1982), 31–55; David Riggs, *Ben Jonson: A Life* (Cambridge, Mass., 1989), 215–39; and Richard Helgerson, *Self-Crowned Laureates: Spenser, Jonson, Milton and the Literary System* (Berkeley and Los Angeles, 1983), 101–84.
[2] *Works* (1709), 4.

Over and above the semiotics of their very appearance, Jonson engaged in less obtrusive strategies of self-canonization. For one thing, he excluded from the folio a number (of unknown size) of plays, most notably *Bartholomew Fair*, and silently revised others so as to give the impression of a self-continuous and integrated corpus of work; the setting of *Every Man in his Humour*, for example, was switched from Florence to London, in keeping with the later plays set in the capital. Jonson, moreover, partly through omitting *Bartholomew Fair* and partly through departure from the strict chronological sequence of the plays included, sought to impose both a shapeliness and an upward trajectory on his canon. By printing as last in the folio a tragedy, *Catiline*, he tried to style his artistic development as a migration from the lower genre of comedy to the higher one of tragedy.[3] The overall effect of the folio was to exalt Jonson into the major literary celebrity of his age; its appearance, indeed, may have stimulated James I to confer on him a pension, as an unofficial poet laureate.

There are two aspects of Jonson's project that should be stressed. First, it shows him to have been very self-conscious, if not avidly calculating, about the public office of a poet. His *Works* represent a vigorous assertion of authorial ownership over a corpus of writing, as well as a studied exercise in the management of an audience. At the same time, however, as Jonson elevates his own 'canon', this canon represents only a winnowed selection from the complete body of his writings. Jonson, moreover, is keenly aware of an ideal of canonical graduation: a writer's canon should be animated by a principle of burgeoning maturity from the lower to the higher literary genres. This observance, indeed, of an ideal *gradus ad Parnassum* was to prove influential on later poets like Milton, Dryden, and Pope. The second aspect of Jonson's *Works*, however, has a more precise relevance to the rest of this chapter. Jonson's plays, it goes without saying, had previously been delivered to their audience (as well as in earlier quarto publication) through the evanescent nature of their theatrical performance; his lavish *Works*, therefore, represent an attempt to confer on the same plays a different sort of existence, both stable and permanent. In the *Works*, moreover,

---

[3] Riggs, *Ben Jonson*, 224–5.

the play-texts were printed in a way that made them conspicuously unsuitable for any theatrical usage—for use as something other than a book to be read. This was achieved by Jonson's adopting methods of scene division and lineation employed in the earliest editions of Plautus, Terence, and Aristophanes. Entrances and exits are unmarked, and dialogue is printed in unbroken verse lines, even where two or more speakers share the same line. Moreover, Jonson supplied larger textual paraphernalia, consisting of commentary and textual notes, at that time associated only with editions of classical authors.[4]

What is at issue here is partly Jonson's desire to lend to his work the same solemnities of presentation normally visited on classical writers—and therefore to register a claim for his own 'classic' status. In this, in fact, he seems to have been adroitly successful, since Richard West, in an elegy written 'On Mr. BEN. IOHNSON', can tell the deceased poet that *'Thou* shalt be read as *Classick Authors*; and | As *Greeke* and *Latine* taught in every Land'.[5] But also he had taken to heart that part of the office of a writer was to achieve a settlement with posterity. Both in the very fact of the self-canonizing enterprise, and in the mechanics of its textual production, Jonson was bidding to enshrine his literary deeds (his 'Works') in immutable form. Although a form of celebritization may have been an immediate upshot of the *Works*, the end Jonson had in view was a post-mortal and lasting fame. Jonson's *Works* represent a key realization of the idea that all literary creation is, almost inevitably, a project for fame. And from this idea is generated a complementary one with which the current chapter is expressly concerned: namely that the very purpose of a discourse of literary tradition is to minister to, to salve and to satisfy, the innate authorial desire for 'fame'.

II

In 1687 there appeared a biographical dictionary of English poets and dramatists compiled by William Winstanley and entitled *The Lives of the most Famous English Poets, or the*

---

[4] Ibid. 221–2.   [5] Cited from *Jonson*, 11: 470.

1. Frontispiece in William Winstanley, *The Lives of the most Famous English Poets, or the Honour of Parnassus* (1687). Courtesy Palace Green Library, University of Durham.

2. Frontispiece in Thomas Fuller, *Abel Redevivus: or the Dead yet Speaking. The Lives and Deaths of the Moderne Divines* (1651). Courtesy Palace Green Library, University of Durham.

Honour of Parnassus. Though not the first of its kind, it was nonetheless one of a relatively new breed: some of its precursors I will discuss later. The work came furnished with an elaborate frontispiece engraving allegorizing the bestowal of 'fame' on some venerable dead writers and clearly meant to represent Winstanley's own intention of restoring to fame numerous lost or little known English poets (Fig. 1). In the engraving's centre-ground, flanked on either side by twin pyramidical pillars, is a plinth on which sits a bust of Shakespeare. He sports a laurel crown, and bays of laurel also garland each pillar. Carved in relief on each pillar is a skeleton, laureated and lying supine, beneath which are engraved the names of three ancient writers. Further down, the name of a deceased English writer is etched in more prominent lettering. Hovering above the scene, a winged cherub poises a laurel crown above the apex of each pillar, and inside the circle of each crown, penned as if in air, is the word 'Imortality'. Finally, an extended trumpet or clarion, set to the cherub's pursed lips, is proclaiming the fame already signified by the abundant laurel.

Both emblems, the bays worn as a stigma of renown and the trumpet used to broadcast such renown, were commonplace in the pictorial and verbal imagination of fame. They appear together, for example, in an engraving entitled 'The Fame of the Royal Society' (1667) preserved in the British Library.[6] The conceit of fame's being broadcast through the blaring of a trumpet occurs much earlier in Chaucer's *House of Fame*, where Eolus, the God of wind, spreads renown and notoriety on two separate instruments: the one termed 'Clere Laude', the other 'Sklaundre'.[7] Further back, some salient figurative meanings of trumpet blowing derive from the bible. The sounding of trumpets, for example, could signify the gift of divine favour, and their being blown in a liturgical context became a strong external enactment of the inner will to praise God.[8] An especially

[6] See the illustrations between 338 and 339 in Leo Braudy, *The Frenzy of Renown: Fame & its History* (New York, 1986). Braudy's book provides the most wide-ranging treatment of the concept of fame.

[7] *The House of Fame*, 1567–82, in *The Riverside Chaucer*, ed. Larry D. Benson et al. (Oxford, 1988), 366–7.

[8] The biblical role of trumpets is detailed in the entry on 'Music and Musical Instruments', in *The Anchor Bible Dictionary*, ed. David Noel Freedman, 6 vols. (New York, 1992), 4: 936.

vivid depiction of trumpets being used in this latter way is the title-page engraving to the first edition of John Foxe's *Actes and Monuments* (1563). In *Revelations*, the final of seven trumpet peals signals the rewakening and judgement of the dead and the beginning of second time, this image of triumph over death having a very direct application to the concept of fame, described by Pope as 'that second Life in others' Breath'.[9] The investiture of deserving poets with laurel bays is of more dim-lit descent. The title 'poet laureate' long predates the crown's pensioning of a selected poet with a view to his composing verses praising King and country. Laurel crowns were bestowed on poets as far back as classical Rome, and probably the most famous of all laureations, that of Dante, took place in Rome in 1341. In the late medieval era, the title of laureate was conferred on deserving candidates by universities and carried a stamp of accreditation not unlike that of an honorary degree. John Skelton, for example, whose *Garland of Laurel* describes in allegorical fashion just such a ceremony, was thrice laureated, by the universities of Oxford, Louvain, and Cambridge.[10]

In the literary realm, the cult of fame was endorsed by the belief that writing was an inherently preservatory medium, fastening in perpetuity the memory of experiences, events, people, and, perhaps most importantly, of authors themselves. This permanent remembrance was often expressed figuratively by the image of a person's name being etched on a monument dedicated to fame. Such a monument would be constructed from durable material (most often marble) and would be pyramidical in shape, its pointing skywards signifying heavenly favour and hence immortality; exactly such a monument indeed embellishes the frontispiece engraving of Winstanley's *Lives*. However, this imagistic rendering of fame actually falsifies the real conceit underlying it, which is the old poetic boast, traceable to Horace's *Odes*, that 'Exegi monumentum aere perennius | regalique situ pyramidum altius' ('I have finished a monument more lasting than bronze and loftier than the Pyramids' royal

---

[9] *The Temple of Fame* (1715), line 505, in Butt (ed.), 2, ed. Geoffrey Tillotson, 271.
[10] See David A. Loewenstein, 'Skelton's Triumph: The *Garland of Laurel* and Literary Fame', *Neophilologus*, 68 (1984), 611–22.

pile').[11] In other words, an author's writings were conventionally seen as furnishing a memorial to fame altogether less per-
ishable than traditional mortuary monuments. Both Jonson and
Milton, in poems memorializing Shakespeare, make the express
point that he needs no 'star-ypointing pyramid' but will remain
alive while his 'Booke doth liue, | And we haue wits to read, and
praise to giue'.[12] This general point that verbal memorials can
outlast those of other materials is set down in Abraham
Cowley's poem 'On the Praise of Poetry':

> 'Tis not a *Pyramide* of Marble stone,
>   Though high as our ambition;
> 'Tis not a Tomb cut out in Brass, which can
>   Give life to th'ashes of a man,
> But Verses only; they shall fresh appear,
>   Whilst there are men to read, or hear.
> When Times shall make the Lasting Brass decay,
>   And eat the *Pyramide* away,
> Turning that Monument wherein men trust
>   Their names, to what it keeps, poor dust:
> Then shall the *Epitaph* remain, and be
>   New graven in Eternity.[13]

This image of a poem as 'living stone', more durable than brass
or marble, appears also in Robert Herrick's 'His Poetrie his
Pillar'; and the same author's 'Poetry perpetuates the Poet'
expresses the perhaps naive belief that 'eternall Poetrie' can
ward off death's total annihilation for the thirty thousand
years until the reawakening of the dead on judgement day.[14]

The claim that by his own writings an author could perpetuate
his memory is an existential conceit, and although it was sometimes brought into relation to facts about the actual physical
endurance of different forms of written material (as manuscript
v. print), it was never wholly dependent on them. Of course,
these certitudes of eternal endurance now seem naively unappre-
ciative of how few written works actually manage to evade an

---

[11] Horace, *Odes and Epodes*, ed. and trans. C. E. Bennett, rev. edn. (Cambridge,
Mass., 1966), 278–9.
[12] 'On Shakespeare' (1630), line 4, in *Poems*, 123; 'To the memory of my
beloued...Mr. WILLIAM SHAKESPEARE' (1623), 23–4, in *Jonson*, 8: 391.
[13] *Abraham Cowley: Poetry & Prose*, ed. L. C. Martin (Oxford, 1949), 2.
[14] *The Poetical Works of Robert Herrick*, ed. L. C. Martin (Oxford, 1956), 85,
265.

early obsolescence. Cowley can talk blithely of verbal memorials lasting 'Whilst there are men to read, or hear', but in that very specification lies a cramping contingency. Even by the time of Cowley's poem, the example of Chaucer, no edition of whose works was published in England between 1602 and 1687, existed as a standing rebuke to poets' casual expectation that their writing would long survive them. Chaucer provided a striking instance of how linguistic change could sentence a poet to languishing unread or misread. His plight indeed became occasion for an outpouring of poetic sympathy. Edmund Waller's 'Of English Verse', for example, a poem with a sharply sceptical attitude towards fame, cites the plight of Chaucer ('Years have defaced his matchless strain') as exemplifying the vanity of believing that our writings can indefinitely survive us; and Addison's 'Account of the Greatest English Poets' (1694) observes that 'age has rusted what the poet [Chaucer] writ, | Worn out his language, and obscur'd his wit.'[15] This decaying of Chaucer's wit and language presented a sober lesson to Augustan writers that even their own writings would in the course of time become dated and obscure, this anxiety being voiced most famously in *An Essay on Criticism*, 480–3:

> Now length of *Fame* (or *second* Life) is lost,
> And bare Threescore is all ev'n That can boast:
> Our sons their Fathers' *failing Language* see,
> And such as *Chaucer* is, shall *Dryden* be.[16]

Whatever the practical problems of achieving fame, it was assumed that writing was an activity almost uniquely driven by the desire for its attainment. William Davenant, for example, in 'The Author's Preface' to *Gondibert* (1651), observes that 'Men are cheefly provok'd to the toyle of compiling Bookes, by love of Fame'.[17] The same commonplace is given a more specific application much later in *Spectator* 253 (1711): 'there are none more ambitious of Fame, than those who are conversant in Poetry'; and it is noteworthy also that Pope's *Dunciad* reserves exclusively for poets the charge of being besotted by their 'vision

---

[15] *Poetical Works of Edmund Waller*, ed. Robert Bell (London, 1854), 192; Hurd (ed.), 1: 29.
[16] Butt (ed.), 1: 293.
[17] *Sir William Davenant's 'Gondibert'*, ed. David F. Gladish (Oxford, 1971), 25.

of eternal Fame'.[18] By the early eighteenth century, this feeling that writers stood in a different relation to fame from that of ordinary people was being attributed to the medium of print. The fact that printed works could be reproduced indefinitely gave them an in-built advantage over every other form of material legacy. This viewpoint is expressed eloquently in *Spectator* 166 where Addison remarks that 'Books are the Legacies that a great Genius leaves to Mankind', for these are the sole means by which our mental experience, the 'Thoughts which arise and disappear in the Mind of Man', can be conveyed forward from one generation to the next. The great happiness of authors is that 'they can multiply their Originals' without limitation and this 'gives a great Author something like a Prospect of Eternity'.[19] No other art has equal potential to afford our ideas such indefinite furtherance into the future. Statues and buildings ultimately crumble and perish; paintings fade and dull over.[20]

Fame remained a concept central to the office of poetry from the Renaissance through to the late eighteenth century, the reason for its invocation in such urgent terms being that it conferred a kind of secular after-life. Edmund Waller, for example, believed that the durability of 'lasting verse' could 'so preserve the hero's name, | They make him live again in fame'; and Pope more than once refers to fame as a 'second life'.[21] A second life gained through bodily death, just like that of the Christian after-life, presents itself as a paradox and, accordingly, the idea of fame was often formulated in paradoxical terms. Common amongst conceits about fame was that it was a sort of inheritance, only an inheritance whose condition of release was the writer's own death rather than that of somebody else. Milton invokes Shakespeare as 'great heir of Fame' and Cowley's

---

[18] No. 253, 20 Dec. 1711, in *Spectator*, 2: 481; *The Dunciad* (1742), III. 12, in Butt (ed.), 5, ed. James Sutherland, 320.

[19] No. 166, 10 Sept. 1711, in *Spectator*, 2: 154.

[20] Interest in the posterities of authors was mirrored by a satiri-comic interest in the posterities of books. So the works of hack authors are often imagined as suffering an after-life as pie-wrappings, arse-wipes, window patchings, lantern lighters, and the like. See e.g. Dryden's 'Mac Flecknoe', 98–101, in Kinsley (ed.), 267; and Swift's 'Epistle Dedicatory to His Royal Highness Prince Posterity', prefixed to *A Tale of a Tub* (1704), in Davis (ed.), 1: 21–2.

[21] 'Of an Elegy Made by Mrs. Wharton on the Earl of Rochester', in *Poetical Works*, 208; *Essay on Criticism*, line 480, and *The Temple of Fame*, line 505, in Butt (ed.), 1: 293; 2: 271.

'Upon the shortness of Mans Life' applauds the equanimity of he 'Who never thinks his end too near, | But says to *Fame*, thou art mine *Heir*'.[22] Cowley actually puts the conceit the other way around (Fame's being his heir rather than his being Fame's), but the paradox, as it was generally appreciated, entailed something akin to being named as a beneficiary of one's own will. The conceit was subsequently to achieve a new level of technicality with the likening of fame to the legal notion of 'reversion': the term meant a right of succession to an office or emolument after the death of an incumbent. John Dennis, in *The Impartial Critick* (1693) describes poetic fame as 'a sort of Airy Revenue', which only the poet himself can enjoy but which can be 'detained' from him by malignant critics, whose actions condemn him to only a 'vain Reversion'.[23] Similarly, Giles Jacob's *Poetical Register* refers to the 'Reversionary Fame' that great writers envisage from their works, and Edward Young declares that 'Fame's a reversion in which men take place | (O late reversion!) at their own decease'.[24]

The pursuit of fame was an inherently worldly drive and consequently difficult to square with orthodox Christian beliefs and principles of conduct. In the eighteenth century, indeed, a moral-minded disavowal of fame becomes something of a poetic topos: Pope, for example, whom Johnson describes as an author with an almost unique 'voracity for fame' is also uncommonly prolific in renouncing or deriding it.[25] One particular respect in which fame stood awkwardly to orthodox religious beliefs was in regard of its promised second life, a notion which could be seen as vying with the conventional Christian after-life. One way

[22] 'On Shakespear', line 5; *Poetry & Prose*, 3.
[23] Hooker (ed.), 1: 14.
[24] Giles Jacob, *The Poetical Register*, 'The Dedication', ii; Edward Young, 'Love of Fame, the Universal Passion', in *The Poetical Works of Edward Young*, 2 vols. (London, 1896), 2: 93.
[25] Samuel Johnson, *Lives*, 3: 136. Pope's poems and letters contain numerous statements of cynicism about fame's value. For example, in a letter of 20 May 1709 to William Wycherley, he remarks that as 'for gaining any [fame], I am as indifferent in the Matter as *Falstaffe* was, and may say of *Fame* as he did of *Honour, If it comes, it comes unlook'd for'*. Cited from *The Correspondence of Alexander Pope*, ed. George Sherburn, 5 vols. (Oxford, 1956), 1: 60. See also 1: 280. An overview is provided by Donald Fraser, 'Pope and the Idea of Fame', in *Writers and their Background: Alexander Pope*, ed. P. Dixon (London, 1972), 286–310. See also David Wheeler, '"So Easy to be Lost": Poet and Self in Pope's *The Temple of Fame*', *Papers on Language and Literature*, 29 (1993), 3–27.

of reconciling the two concepts was to see the hereafter vouch-safed by fame as a pre-image or foretaste of the Christian one. Accordingly, Davenant describes fame as 'the first, though but a little taste of Eternity'; and much later Edward Young praises Addison for having trod 'a splendid path, thro' fame immortal, into eternal peace'.[26]

As I have suggested, fame was always likely to find itself in dispute with traditional religious thinking, but probably the most common ground for scepticism about fame was a perceived illogicality internal to the concept itself. If fame makes available a second life, what exactly is the ontological status of such a life? In what sense can it be true to claim that if people re-collect us after our deaths, we are somehow kept alive by that recollection? For surely it is an elementary fact that once we are dead we are rendered insensible to whatever fame posterity sees fit to accord us. And if one is insensible to one's fame, what can be the point then of possessing it? This dilemma, one that was a constant trouble to adherents to fame, can be illustrated from two poems written fifty years or so apart, the first by Thomas Shadwell, the second by Edward Young:

> Fame's but a shadow of great action,
> And but the *Eccho* of't when we are gone,
> Than whose Trumpet no Musick is more sweet
> Nor none's alive more pleas'd with hearing it,
> But I do'nt know what pleasure I should have,
> When I am dead with Musick in my Grave.
>
> 'On the Dutchess of New-Castle her Grace'

> But, ah! not inspiration can obtain
> That fame, which poets languish for in vain.
> How mad their aim, who thirst for glory, strive
> To grasp, what no man can possess alive!
>
> 'Love of Fame, the Universal Passion'[27]

It may be that Shadwell and Young do fame a disservice in supposing that its devotees want not only to be spoken of after

---

[26] *Gondibert*, 26; Edward Young, *Conjectures on Original Composition* (1759) (London: Scolar Press Facsimile, 1966), 104.

[27] Shadwell's poem can be dated from the burial of the Duchess, 7 Jan. 1673–4; cited from *The Complete Works of Thomas Shadwell*, 5 vols. (London, 1927), 5: 234; 'Love of Fame', in *Poetical Works*, 2: 293.

death but actually to be privy to themselves being spoken of. But it is still hard to see how we can derive much satisfaction from post-mortal plaudits to which we inevitably remain oblivious. One way around this problem was to suppose that death might not totally incapacitate us from keeping in touch with our worldly reputations. Edward Phillips, for example, speculates on the disappointment all writers must feel if linguistic change cheats them out of a perpetual fame, but then admits that for this point to apply souls must have 'intelligence, after their departure hence, what is done on Earth'.[28] A good deal later, Dr Johnson writes a *Rambler* paper that posits that an exalted soul may still retain a cognizance of the upkeep and currency of its worldly reputation.[29] Of course, this circumvents one problem only then to raise another. Granted that we can keep tabs on our earthly posterity, will we want to? What sort of relish will a soul draw from the fame of its mortal exertions? These questions might seem knotty and arcane but they were inextricable from the project of the authorial dictionaries which I now want to address.

III

Some early seeds of a native genre of English literary history are probably to be found in the long popularity enjoyed by chronicles of kings and by lives of saints and martyrs. In the Restoration period, these were assimilated into more catholic histories of worthies, the most influential amongst such being Thomas Fuller's compendious *The History of the Worthies of England* (1662) which formed the groundwork for William Winstanley's less ambitious *England's Worthies: Select Lives of the most Eminent Persons of the English Nation* (1684).[30] For Fuller, 'worthies' were illustrious persons drawn from those occupations and echelons of society that were consistent with a general

---

[28] Edward Phillips, 'Preface' to *Theatrum Poetarum, or a Compleat Collection of the Poets* (1675); cited here from its most easily available location in Spingarn (ed.), 2: 264.

[29] No. 49, 4 Sept. 1750, in *Yale*, 3: 263–8.

[30] For treatment of the relation between collections of authorial biography and an emerging literary history, see René Wellek, *The Rise of English Literary History* (Chapel Hill, NC, 1941).

'notability'. His work is arranged on geographical principles, county-by-county. It documents such things as the predominant vegetation of each county, prolific manufactured commodities and unusual natural phenomena, as well as the lives of all notable people having lived inside the county boundary. Amidst the file of princes, saints, martyrs, cardinals, judges and eminent lawyers, soldiers and seamen, an inauspicious place is also found for noteworthy writers. Because of its geographical arrange-ment, Fuller's work reads as a sort of Baedeker and has parallels with a work like Defoe's *Tour through the Whole Island of Great Britain* (1724–6). It stands as a monument of dogged compilation, but this could hardly be said of Winstanley's follow-up attempt. *England's Worthies* jettisons the welter of largely geographical detail accumulated by Fuller and reverts to a plain catalogue of lives, ordered chronologically. Native writers included are Chaucer, Crashaw, Cleveland, Drayton, Daniel, Gower, Jonson, Shakespeare, Spenser, and Sir Philip Sidney. Moreover, as well as the table of contents, Winstanley provides a list specifically of 'The Names of the Authors cited in this Book', suggesting that lives of authors were beginning to enjoy a special status even in works of miscellaneous biography.

These were not the only works in which biographies of authors figured within a more general format. Anthony à Wood's *Athenae Oxonienses* (1691–2), a history of the writers produced by the University of Oxford, provided useful source material for later literary historians. Sir Thomas Blount's *Censura Celebriorum Authorum* (1690), written throughout in Latin, was a compendium of lives of humanists and scholars, but whereas it includes continental literary figures such as Dante, Petrarch, and Rabelais, only Chaucer and Bacon amongst its entrants could be said in any sense to belong to English litera-ture. More directly related to the growth of literary history, however, was the same author's *De Re Poetica* (1694) which fell into two sections: the first consisting of a treatise on poetry, mainly concerned with the definition of genres; and the second of critical biographies of classical and modern authors. The latter are largely cobbled together from earlier literary historical sources and embrace, as well as perennial figures, some more contemporary ones such as Katherine Philips and the Earl of Rochester.

It is customary to view as an important step in the mapping of the English literary heritage the appearance of a cluster of works dating from 1675 to 1691: Edward Phillips's *Theatrum Poetarum* (1675), William Winstanley's *Lives of the most Famous English Poets* (1687), and Gerard Langbaine's *Account of the English Dramatick Poets* (1691). All three are biographical dictionaries, though the latter two also provide bibliographical lists, their pioneering feature being that they were the first to corral together information concerning (if not quite exclusively) creative writers composing in the vernacular. In some respects, Phillips's *Theatrum Poetarum* makes for an inauspicious start. Even for a forerunning attempt, his entries are disarmingly flimsy: Shakespeare, for instance, is conceded less than a single side of what is only an octavo volume. And his work is the more vitiated by its perverse organization as a biographical dictionary based on forename (i.e. Shakespeare is listed under 'W'). Yet this quirk of adopting forenames perhaps matters less than the fact that any system of alphabetical listing inevitably frustrates our experience of the literary past as a chronology.

It is only with Winstanley's listing of writers in order of date that an experience of the chronology of English literature is expressly provided for. Indeed, as a result of Phillips's vagaries, René Wellek selects Winstanley's *Lives* as the inaugurative literary historical work and as instituting a line of development running through to Johnson's *Lives of the Poets*.[31] Each of Winstanley's entries consists of biographical details followed by a sometimes slapdash list of publications: each entry, moreover, is filled out with copious quotation, especially with character notes (sometimes epitaphic) on the author by his contemporaries. The explicit purpose of the book is to document English (or more largely British) writers from the Norman conquest to the reign of James II, and Winstanley accordingly starts out with Robert of Gloucester, Richard the Hermit,

---

[31] See Wellek, *The Rise of English Literary History*, 18. A detailed defence of Winstanley against the charge of plagiarism from Phillips is William R. Parker, 'Winstanley's *Lives*: An Appraisal', *Modern Language Quarterly*, 6 (1945), 313–18. For a comparison of the two works, see 317–18: 'Phillips is more the bibliographer and cataloguer, collecting names and titles; Winstanley is the amateur literary historian, seeking out the verse itself, arranging it in chronological order, and trying to pass judgement upon it.' Parker seems oblivious to Winstanley's indebtedness to Fuller's *History of the Worthies of England*.

Joseph of Exeter, and so on. Of the hundred or so authors included, the one most favourably treated in terms of space is Chaucer (who gets ten pages); surprisingly, given the frontispiece engraving in which he takes centre-stage, Shakespeare is granted only four pages, the same as Francis Quarles and Sir Thomas Overbury. It might be added that no female authors are represented. What might not have been appreciated by Winstanley's readers is the extent to which his book had been silently pieced together from Fuller's *History of Worthies* and Phillips's *Theatrum Poetarum*: for example, probably only a third of his Shakespeare entry is independent of its two main sources.

In contrast with Winstanley's project, Langbaine's *Account of the English Dramatick Poets* exudes an air of earnest professionalism. His work, in any event, was intended mainly to have a bibliographical utility, and was prepared as a successor to his earlier *New Catalogue of English Plays* (1687). The later work, though, sought to supersede the former on four expressly stated accounts: it offered a succinct relation of each author's life-history plus some appraisal of his writings; it provided 'a large Account of the Title-page of each Play'; where a plot was based on actual events, it filled in the real-life details so that representation and reality could be compared; and Langbaine troubled himself to sleuth out thefts and borrowings between authors.[32] Langbaine's fastidiousness about plagiarisms in fact came rather maliciously into its own in his long and controversially hostile entry on Dryden, whom he had already flyted at in the earlier *Catalogue*. Notwithstanding the notoriety of the Dryden entry, Langbaine's work generates sufficient briskness and clarity of purpose to represent an advance on the earlier projects of Phillips and Winstanley. For one thing, his entries, while admittedly being filled out with bibliographical matter, are markedly longer: Jonson's with twenty-six pages and Shakespeare's with sixteen being the most voluminous after Dryden's one of forty-seven. Langbaine also admits five women, these being 'Astraea' Behn, Lady Elizabeth Carew (Cary), the Duchess of Newcastle, the Countess of Pembroke,

[32] Gerard Langbaine, *An Account of the English Dramatick Poets, or some Observations and Remarks on the Lives and Writings of all those that have Publish'd . . . in the English Tongue* (1691), 'Preface'.

and Katherine Philips. As regards the biographical component of each entry, however, no great claims can be made for Langbaine's originality. He is still raiding from an established store-chest of anecdotes and truistical facts, though he is more scrupulous than Winstanley in recording his indebtedness to works like Fuller's *History of the Worthies* and Wood's *Athenae Oxonienses*. Only in fact with Giles Jacob's *Poetical Register* (1719) does one sense that a new supply of biographical data has come on stream.

The dictionary entries conform to what, in the eighteenth century, would have been called an 'epitome' or 'character': in other words, a condensed sketch of the salient traits of a person or thing. Most of the entries tend towards caricature in the foregrounding of a small number of select traits. What lies behind this is the reliance of seventeenth-century biography on the 'ruling passion' theory of character. Under such a theory, individuals were seen as distinguished by one predominant aptitude or disposition; each good aptitude, moreover, would be seen as coexisting in close relation to an opposite one (as dissipation being the opposite of thrift) and to one representing its deleterious extreme (as miserliness being an extreme form of thrift).[33] It goes without saying that this model fosters a somewhat abstract approach to character, but it nonetheless had a major impact on the emerging genre of critical biography. The same methods of delineating authorial characteristics are interestingly evident in Dryden's *Of Dramatic Poesy* (1668) which outlines the respective merits of Shakespeare, Jonson, and Beaumont and Fletcher. Dryden sees Shakespeare as a poet instinct with a high level of intuitive empathy that rendered unnecessary any particular conversancy with books: 'he needed not the spectacles of books to read nature.' Jonson, on the other hand, manifests an opposite trait, that of a somewhat sterile learning and correctness. Beaumont and Fletcher meanwhile are characterized as a synthesis of the two extremes already associated with Shakespeare and Jonson, in that they possess 'great natural gifts improved by study'.[34] In spite of its

[33] For some comments on the ruling passion, see my own ' "Ill Effects from good": The Rhetoric of Augustan Mockery (with illustrations from Pope and Fielding)', *British Journal for Eighteenth-Century Studies*, 17 (1994), 125–37.
[34] *Of Dramatic Poesy*, 1: 67–8.

being obvious here that Dryden is merely rotating the permutations spawned by a single binary opposition (wit or 'nature'
v. learning), his judgements were to prove enormously influential. Yet that they are generated as much by a desire for
dialectical shape as for a neutral rendering of fact is perhaps
suggested by Ben Jonson's poem 'To the memory of my beloued
...MR. WILLIAM SHAKESPEARE' (1623), supplied for the
first folio, which expressly repudiates any one-dimensional
view of Shakespeare's genius: 'Yet must I not giue Nature
all.'³⁵

The entries on Shakespeare and Jonson contained in the authorial dictionaries exhibit this same tendency to caricature and
to a diagrammatic wielding of character comparisons. Phillips,
for example, declares of Shakespeare that 'never any represented
nature more purely to the life', whereas Jonson, in spite of his
low origins as a bricklayer, is praised as an author 'learned,
judicious and correct'. Phillips has probably picked up this
distinction from its illustrious formulation by Dryden but perhaps also from Thomas Fuller's *History of the Worthies*.
Winstanley, in his turn, seems almost exclusively reliant on
Fuller. One conceit lifted from this source is the comparison of
Shakespeare to a species of Cornish diamond extracted from the
earth already in smooth and polished form. Another is the
rendering of the difference between Jonson and Shakespeare as
that between a 'Spanish great Gallion' and an '*English Man of
War*': the former distinguished by its bulkiness, the other by
agility, these qualities mapping on to the supposed ponderous-
ness of Jonsonian learning and the mercurial nature of Shake-
spearean wit. The same distinction has its rudiments preserved
in Langbaine, though Langbaine candidly identifies Dryden as
his source.

When we turn to entries on Jonson as well as remarking on his
learning, the dictionary-markers fix repeatedly on his early employment as a bricklayer and on his having educated himself and
risen against the odds. Winstanley thus repeats from Fuller how
'some Gentlemen' pitied that Jonson's natural endowments
'should be buried under the rubbish of so mean a Calling'; and
Langbaine likens Jonson to a whole file of classical poets, in-

³⁵ *Jonson*, 8: 392.

THE CULT OF FAME 81

cluding Homer, Euripides, Plautus, and Virgil, who were of inauspiciously mean birth. When Langbaine parades these antecedents, it is obvious how much his biographical treatment is in hock to a felt need to make Jonson conform to a recognizable 'type'. It holds true, in fact, to the entries in all the dictionaries that they render their subjects not through heaping up detail but through condensing a small body of anecdotal detail into a recognizable character type.

It might be useful to finish this section with some summary remarks on the posterity of these biographical dictionaries and on their relation to an unfolding articulation of an English literary heritage. Amongst the works of Phillips, Winstanley, and Langbaine, only the latter was to achieve an honourable survival beyond their own century. Phillips's and Winstanley's unseemly dependence on earlier sources may account for why in the eighteenth century both were cast in shadow by Langbaine's more illustrious light. Jacob's *Poetical Register*, for example, admits Langbaine's work to have been its formative precursor; and when Charles Gildon brings out *The Lives and Characters of the English Dramatick Poets* (1699), an enlarged revamp of Langbaine's *English Dramatick Poets*, he speaks slightingly of the two earlier works: 'I shall take no notice of Mr. *Winstanley*'s or Mr. *Phillips*'s [treatises], for one I never saw, and the other I could not read, and Mr. *Langbain* has discovered their Defects sufficient to justify his undertaking a more perfect Work.'[36] A similar attitude reveals itself in Johnson's 'Life of Milton' where Johnson records scathingly that the only 'product' of Milton's self-instituted educational academy was 'a small *History of Poetry* written in Latin by his nephew Phillips, of which perhaps none of my readers has ever heard'.[37] Referred to here is Phillips's *Tractatulus de Carmine Dramatico Poetarum Veterum* (1669), a forerunner of the *Theatrum Poetarum*, and Johnson's remark could be taken as implying his unfamiliarity with Phillips's later project. This contrasts with our knowledge that he was familiar with and sometimes used Langbaine's book, as in his 'Life of Dryden'.

---

[36] *Poetical Register*, 'Preface'; *The Lives and Characters of the English Dramatick Poets . . . First begun by Mr. Langbain, improv'd and continued down to this Time by a Careful Hand* (1699), 'The Preface'.
[37] *Lives*, 1: 101.

Langbaine indeed is the real bridge between the early spate of biographical dictionaries and Johnson's culminatory work in the same genre, his *Lives of the Poets*, treatment of which I want to reserve until Chapter 7.

It should be remembered that the works I have been discussing are heavily indebted to conventions of authorial biography now no longer extant: they are rooted in the 'worthies' tradition, in which the exposition of the life of a meritorious individual was supposed to have a morally exemplificatory role. Because writers, perhaps more than any other category of persons, tend to be valued for their creations rather than their deeds, the employment of worthies-style conventions might seem somewhat inapt and mistaken. Indeed, it is the use of such conventions that accounts for the sometimes grating attempts to moralize authors' lives, as in the insistence on Ben Jonson's triumph in clambering upwards from poverty and inauspicious beginnings. It is usual now to see literary *works*, not *authors*, as being the material of tradition, but the authorial dictionaries feature literary works only as adjuncts to each individual life. The biographical tradition also differs from most other discourses of literary heritage dealt with in this book in that it aimed at exhaustiveness. In this respect, such works were not intended to be canon-forming (though this is not to say that they do not intimate a canon); the guiding paradigm of fame mandated rather a recovery of past authors on a scale as generously comprehensive as possible. Indeed, exactly how ideas of fame influenced the convention of collecting authorial biographies is something that I now want to address.

IV

Thomas Fuller, later the author of the *History of Worthies*, was the compiler of an earlier collection of lives of distinguished men of religion, *Abel Redevivus: or the Dead yet Speaking. The Lives and Deaths of the Moderne Divines* (1651). The book was furnished with a frontispiece engraving of a mausoleum, reproduced here as Figure 2. In the lower half, a skeleton lies supine over a tomb, the words 'Mors ultima linea rerum est' ('Death is the final end of things') issuing from the mouth.[38] Piled above him is a pyramid of books, the one at the apex spread open to the onlooker's eye. The image's symbolism is intended to convey the idea that although physical death is absolute, our books can as it were ventriloquize us back into life, so that we can be 'dead yet speaking'. Yet *Abel Redevivus*, itself, makes only for a muted exposition of this general idea. Admittedly, Fuller states that saints and prophets have often won over hearts less by their manner of living than by their deaths, the Roman centurion converted at the foot of the Holy Cross being offered as a case in point, and the book accordingly pays particular attention to the manner of death of particular religious notables. Yet it is only with his subsequent *History of Worthies* that the idea that individuals can enjoy a second life in the posterity of their writings comes into its own.

Fuller's *History of Worthies* is perhaps the most important compilation of literary historical source-materials since the six-teenth-century catalogues of Leland and Bale, and without its prior existence Phillips's and Winstanley's collections of author-ial lives would simply not have been feasible. Yet more than just providing materials, Fuller establishes a conceptual framework in which the collecting of biographies (authorial or otherwise) can be rationalized and imbued with value. The concept crucial to this framework is fame. Moreover, even though Fuller's work contains innumerable entrants other than authors, he still gives a special prominence to the pet conceit of authors that written works provide the best hope of a person's achieving posterity:

It hath been the lawful desire of men in all ages to perpetuate their Memories, thereby in some sort revenging themselves of Mortality, though few have found out effectual means to perform it. For Monu-ments made of Wood are subject to be burnt; of Glass, to be broken; of soft stone, to moulder; of Marble and Metal, (if escaping the teeth of Time) to be demolished by the hand of Covetousness; so that, in my apprehension, the safest way to secure a memory from oblivion is (next his own Vertues) by committing the same in Writing to Posterity.[39]

The unique imperishability of the written word was, of course, a time-honoured brag of poets, but this is not the only writerly

---

[38] The line is a quotation from Horace, *Epistles*, 1. 16. 79 (my translation).
[39] Thomas Fuller, *The History of the Worthies of England* (1662), 1–2.

hyperbole that Fuller's project was taken as having endorsed. Fuller, himself, goes no further than saying that one of his objectives is 'To preserve the Memories of the Dead', but a commendatory verse first published in the Biographia Britannica (1747–63) annexes his work to the idea that for the dead to be recollected, as through the offices of Fuller's History, is tantamount to their being somehow resuscitated back into life:

> Who noblest do, most nobly must deserve;
> Great, who perform, but greater who preserve:
> If virtue most directs, which most dilates,
> The draught excels, that most communicates;
> Such copy spread, thus durably to all,
> Begets more virtue, than th'original:
> 'Tis an original; its own outvy'd;
> Where life less copied is, than multiply'd;
> And they are deathless made, who long since dy'd.[40]

The claims made here are disarmingly large. Fuller's virtue is stated to be that of preserving and disseminating ('dilating') the memories of the dead, but as a self-appointed custodian of the noble feats performed by others, he himself performs a deed of even greater nobility. For a start, his book is not merely a passive record of the active deeds of others, for by exemplifying virtue, it can 'Beget[] more virtue than th'original'. Yet the most grandiose claim is that the book does not merely register the expired lives of numerous worthies, it actually conjures them back to life so that 'they are deathless made, who long since dy'd'.

Even though Fuller's encyclopaedia of notables only admits writers as a small minority group, it is writers to whom his work is indebted for its attitude towards death and the preservation of memory. Subsequent collections of authorial biographies were also to recognize that by sending out their works as personal emissaries, writers made a claim on posterity's recollection that was uniquely vocal and insistent. Winstanley, for example, points out that of all the means by which men can 'give unto their Fames eternity... Books, and Writings, have ever had the

---

[40] 'To the Reader and Writer of Lives: Written in Fuller's Worthies', first published in, and cited from, Biographia Britannica: or the Lives of the most Eminent Persons who have Flourished in Great Britain and Ireland, from the Earliest Ages, down to the Present Times (1747–66), 3: 2067.

Preheminence'.[41] The vast number of petty dignitaries who make it into Fuller's collection may well have bothered little about their post-mortal reputations, but when we come to collections of authorial biography, we encounter a category of entrants almost by definition taken as having been solicitous for fame. This fact, moreover, has the effect of bringing some inequalities into sharper relief. Clearly some writers, such as Shakespeare, already enjoyed a fame sufficiently incontestable not to require the services of a Phillips or Winstanley, whereas for others just those services must have been their best hope against future oblivion.

The difference between writers securely in possession of fame and those needing to be helped to it easily passes into a distinction between authors most and least deserving of it. Phillips's lengthy 'Preface' to *Theatrum Poetarum* goes beyond Fuller specifically through bringing the concept into close proximity with questions of desert and finishes with his stating the fate he hopes to achieve for 'all deserving Writers' to be 'a lasting Fame, equal to ... [their] ... merit'.[42] He begins by spelling out those attributes that make up a person's overall prowess, which consist of natural endowments supplemented by education. To possess innate gifts without education (or vice-versa) is to be a person of tolerable parts, but those who have been visited with both are held up (in Phillips's nomenclature) as '*more* than *Men*'. And these are the illustrious specimens who he believes should rightfully be heirs to fame. Phillips, however, is reconciled to the fact that merely deserving fame can never be a guarantee of winning it, for

in the State of Learning, among the Writers of all Ages, some deserve Fame & have it, others neither have nor deserve it, some have it, not deserving, others though deserving yet totally miss it, or have it not equall to their deserts.[43]

This passage, with its vivid description of the plight of writers caught between the impersonal permutations of desert and reward, is lifted *verbatim* by Winstanley in the 'Preface' to his

---

[41] William Winstanley, *The Lives of the most Famous English Poets, or the Honour of Parnassus* (1687), 'The Preface to the Reader'.
[42] Spingarn (ed.), 2: 272.
[43] Ibid. 2: 258–9.

Lives. Amongst those mentioned, it is the last group, those whose fame has never caught up with the magnitude of their desert, whose cause Phillips is especially intent on championing. Phillips believes there to be 'an exact resemblance between the fate of writers & the common fate of Mankind', for many 'of the writing party' even though they have produced works 'more lasting sometimes than Brass or Marble...have fallen short of their deserved immortality of Name'. Taken as poignant instances of this syndrome are the numerous classical authors who in their own time supposedly achieved fame comparable with that of Homer and Euripides but whose works, and perhaps even whose names, have now perished, so that they 'sleep inglorious in the croud of the forgotten vulgar'.[44]

It is unsurprising that Winstanley's *Lives* should also rationalize its project in terms of fame since the work was to a large extent cobbled together from the earlier works of Fuller and Phillips. Winstanley thickens out his 'Preface' with a series of remarks by classical authors on the hope that their writings will enable them to survive into posterity; and he sees the human compulsion towards fame writ large in the feats of Alexander the Great and in the seven wonders of the world. The paradigm of fame, however, emerges not just from prefatory remarks but in the way that the biographers typically put together their entries. Fame's centrality is evident for example from how both Winstanley, and Phillips before him, include in their collections both those famous *as* poets and those who, while perhaps having written poetry, actually achieved their fame in some other area: in other words, the claim of fame takes precedence over that of poetic distinction. This policy accounts for Winstanley's admission of the likes of Thomas Sprat and Edward Phillips (the literary biographer) who, in spite of both writing poems, could not be said to have become famous, or to have deserved fame, by virtue of their poetry alone. The thematics of fame, as well as a residual influence from biographies of saints and martyrs, also entailed that a pronounced emphasis be placed if not on the deaths of poets, then on the details of their interment and memorialization. Winstanley, for example, records that Shakespeare was 'buried at *Stratford* upon *Avon*, the Town of

---

[44] Ibid. 2: 259.

his Nativity'; but because such a parochial burial might redound prejudicially to Shakespeare's fame, he adds wistfully that it had been 'more proper had he been buried in *Westminster Abbey*'. Fame moreover is a factor both of what authors have performed and of how their performances are viewed by others. Accordingly, Winstanley and Langbaine pad out their entries with statements by contemporaries, especially in the form of epitaphic verses or monument inscriptions that could be seen as standing witness to an author's fame. So Winstanley, for example, cites William Basse's mawkish elegy on Shakespeare: 'Sleep rare Tragedian *Shakespear*!'; and both Winstanley and Langbaine faithfully record the flatly uninspired inscription on Jonson's memorial slab: 'O *Rare* Ben Johnson'.

v

In the seventeenth century, the idea that poets could inherit fame through their writings was sufficiently pervasive as to be unpronounced. What was notable, however, was a modulation of that idea: namely, that it was incumbent upon an ethically mature society to exercise charge over, to tend and nurture, the fames of its reputable dead. One might even say that it is this particular discourse of cultural stewardship that turns into what we know today as 'literary history'. In the works looked at in this chapter, fame provides the principal aegis under which the preservation of the literary past takes place; yet as regards the inauguration of this idea, these works yield precedence to another one as yet unmentioned.

John Weever (1575?–1632) has become a teasing figure because of the way he steals across the landscape of that elusive period of Shakespeare's life known as his 'lost years': his sonnet 'Ad Gulielmum Shakespeare', printed in *Epigrammes* (1599), comprises some of the earliest praise of Shakespeare and indicates a close association between the two men.[45] But much as Weever is a busy literary figure of the late 1590s, his vocation as a poet comes to a sudden halt in 1601, after which, for reasons

---

[45] *Epigrammes*, 75. For Weever's life, see E. A. J. Honigman, *John Weever* (Manchester, 1987); also id., *Shakespeare: the 'lost years'* (Manchester, 1985).

that have proved irrecoverable, he ceases to publish verse under
his own name. Instead, he embarks on a career as an itinerant
antiquarian. The last half of his life was spent traipsing through
innumerable cathedrals and graveyards, hunting down and
recording memorials to the revered dead: the fruit of this dili-
gence, published in 1631, a year before his death, was a bulky
folio entitled *Antient Funeral Monuments of Great-Britain, Ireland, and the Islands adjacent.* Weever's groaning tome is a
Baedeker of tombs and mausolea but, more than this, across
its near nine hundred pages, it gathers momentum as a plangent
meditation on death and the preservation of fame. In his preface
'The Author to the Reader', he sets down his resolve, in the face
of the lamentable disrepair of so many monuments, to 'continue
the remembrance of the defunct to future posterity' and 'to
revive the memories of eminent worldly persons entombed or
interred'.[46]

By way of paradox, for all Weever's poring over lapidary
inscriptions, a persistent refrain of his book is that an assurance
of perpetuating one's posterity is something given alone to poets.
So, in a passage appropriated later by Winstanley, he maintains
that as regards conferring immortal fame 'books, or writings,
have ever had preeminence'. And later he asserts that 'only the
muses' works...give unto man immortality': indeed, how could
it be otherwise when 'in all things else there is vicissitude'.[47]
That Weever should subscribe so avidly to this sentiment owes
much to his having had a life-long interest in poetry, first as
a practitioner but later as a literary historical scholar. R. B.
McKerrow, for example, has pointed out that the sheer width
of reference to contemporary literary figures in Weever's *Epigrammes* renders it a literary historical treasure trove on much
the same scale as Francis Meres's *Palladis Tamia* of a year
earlier.[48] Moreover, probably the most remarkable aspect of
Ancient Monuments is its use of illustrative extracts drawn
from poets. These include pieces from very modern poets like
Sir John Beaumont and Thomas May, as well as from those of
the slightly dimmer past as John Skelton, Gavin Douglas, and

[46] *Antient Funeral Monuments, of Great-Britain, Ireland, and the Islands adjacent* (1767 edn.), 'The Author to the Reader'.
[47] Ibid., 'A Discourse on Funeral Monuments'.
[48] *Epigrammes*, 'Introductory Note'.

Thomas Churchyard; but perhaps most notable is that, albeit in haphazard fashion across a text of considerable length, Weever puts together the most extensive anthology of medieval verse, as by Chaucer, Gower, Lydgate, and Hoccleve, that had so far appeared. A taste of his localized technique can be had through glancing quickly at a single entry: that of Chaucer. Weever cites inscriptions adorning Chaucer's tomb and tomb-ledge, but also more or less in the same breath adduces a host of other non-mortuary testimonials by the likes of Hoccleve, Lydgate, Gavin Douglas, Spenser, and so on. All the testimonials, mortuary or non-mortuary, represent accolades to Chaucer's achievement and endorsements of his literary fame.

Weever's contribution to the construction of the literary past lies in his bringing together two ideas, which are then taken up by the later authorial biographers, only collocated in reverse order. What is striking in Weever is his use of poetic testimonials as accreditations of fame; what is pronounced in the authorial biographers is the role they accord to fame and mortuary inscriptions in the construction of a rudimentary literary past. Compilers like Fuller, Phillips, and Winstanley derive from Weever the perception of the literary past's being not an abstract tradition so much as an aggregation of individual literary deaths; they are concerned not to *unearth* the past so much as to *retain* it, just as Weever felt that in his own indefatigable recordings he was racing against time as the stones and inscriptions crumbled around him; and they share an understanding that all commentaries on previously-lived authors are, by their very nature, epitaphic.

In the eighteenth century, the compiling of the literary past gradually surrenders its link with the old discourse of fame, but it would be wrong to say that this discourse is entirely extinguished. One notable biographical work, for example, that finds a place for it is Elizabeth Cooper's *The Muses Library or a Series of English Poetry* (1737), which consists of an anthology of poetry together with a biographical sketch of each author included. It takes in poets 'from the Saxons to the Reign of Charles II' and is billed as the first volume of a larger project, though no further volumes subsequently appeared. Although the work first and foremost offers itself as an anthology, Cooper still takes her lead from the earlier authorial biographers, the three to whom she alludes as pre-eminent in the genre being Phillips, Winstanley, and Giles Jacob, whose *Poetical Register* appeared in 1719. That Cooper harks back to Phillips and Winstanley may explain why the idea of fame is flagged as the express pretext for her project. In a dedicatory address to the Society for the Encouragement of Learning, Cooper asks assistance in her effort 'to preserve the Memories of the *Dead*'.[49] In her 'Preface', she alludes to the many poets who 'have sacrific'd the *Substance* of present Life to the *Shadow* of future Fame' and yet, either through public neglect or the volatility of the language, have been disappointed in their aspiration. Cooper's volume, in her own words a sort of '*Poetical Chronicle*', accordingly fashions itself as an attempt 'to cure this Evil; and secure the Poet in his Idol-Reputation'.[50]

Yet the discourse of fame running through Cooper's 'Preface' is already sounding a note of anachronism. It is instructive that she cites Phillips and Winstanley as her most relevant seventeenth-century precursors and gives no regard to Langbaine, whose work she must have known. Langbaine, in spite of his entries being modelled in format on those of Winstanley and so deriving ultimately from premises about fame, was the one amongst the collectors of lives not to incorporate fame as a rhetoric and guiding paradigm. Subsequent authorial dictionaries moreover take their cue from him: Giles Jacob refers only fleetingly to fame; neither Charles Gildon's revamp of Langbaine nor the collection of lives published in 1753 under the name of Theophilus Cibber openly endorses the concept; and while Johnson's *Lives* contain scattered truisms on the subject, there exists no sense that fame is an underlying premise of the genre being expounded.

At an earlier time, however, fame provided a pretext and rationale for the collecting of authorial lives, as well as accounting for the sorts of detail that authorial biographies typically contained. In fact, one can go further and say that during the seventeenth century, with particular regard to collected lives, fame is fundamental to the recovery of an English literary past. Such a recovery was not 'academic' in nature. The projects of Phillips, Winstanley, and Langbaine are essentially ethical: they

[49] Elizabeth Cooper, *The Muses Library, or a Series of English Poetry from the Saxons to the Reign of Charles II* (1737), sig. A2ᵛ.
[50] Cooper, *The Muses Library*, vii–viii, ix.

encapsulate a conviction that it behoved a mature culture to preserve in memory the achievements of its noteworthy dead. Heritage equates to remembrance, and to fail to remember is to capitulate to oblivion. Such ideas are the more pronounced because by the mid-eighteenth century, even though the concept continues to be invoked by poets, fame has lost its way as a paradigm motivating the construction of a literary heritage. By this time, as I discuss later, the drive to recover the literary past has become intertwined with a broad antiquarian movement and a vogue interest in forms of cultural primitivism. The likes of Thomas Gray and Thomas Warton are not committed to paying a debt of human remembrance: theirs is a scholarly, not an ethical, attitude towards the past.

If in the late seventeenth century, fame is integral to the very possibility of conceiving of literature in historical terms, why should it cease to be so fifty years on? The answer is not, I think, that the idea of fame simply disappears from the agenda of cultural discussion. Throughout this chapter, in documenting the idea of fame, I have used illustrations drawn from writers sometimes separated in time by as much as a hundred years, and this policy was intended to demonstrate that some of the core issues surrounding fame remain consistent over a long period. What does happen, though, is that 'fame', itself, undergoes semantic change. The main change is that the word, rather than denoting an accolade conferred by posterity, comes increasingly to mean this-worldly reputation. It converges with the modern ideas of 'public profile' and 'celebrity status'. The medieval idea of fame's being an implacably capricious goddess to whom writers (as others) were subjugated is replaced by a growing confidence amongst writers that they can cultivate—even stage-manage—their own fames. In the eighteenth century and Romantic era, authors such as Pope, Sterne, and Byron exploit the print circulation of their works so as to create public personae or authorial alter-egos, a tendency witnessed for example in Pope's subterfuge of clandestinely arranging for publication of his correspondence.[51] The fact that books are

[51] See David B. Morris, *Alexander Pope: The Genius of Sense* (Cambridge, Mass., 1984), 29. For poetic self-fashioning, see Lawrence Lipking, *The Life of the Poet: Beginning and Ending Poetic Careers* (Chicago, 1981); and Helgerson, *Self-Crowned Laureates*.

produced and consumed within the perceived conditions of a print market leads to fame itself being reified in market-oriented terms. If it is understood that all writing is directed towards an increase in the stock of an author's fame, a natural corollary is that this stock can be depreciated—namely by the activities of critics. Critics in fact become perceived as violators of the fames of authors; and suffering the detraction of critics looms as a more baleful spectre than having one's writings merely forgotten.[52] The jostling of writers involves fame in a fierce economy. One of its effects is that the writer's here-and-now predominates over his posterity; and this in turn detracts from the moral imperative, felt especially by the early authorial biographers, to restore and sustain the posterities of dead writers. As a result, the old role of fame as a moral and conceptual pretext for recovering the literary past shrinks in importance.

[52] See e.g. Leonard Welsted's virulent attack on Pope as a mutilator of the fames of others ('No Fame not scarr'd, no Genius not decry'd'), in *Of False Fame. An Epistle to the Right Honourable Earl of Pembroke* (1732), 20.

4

Myths of Origin: The Canon of Pre-Chaucerian Poetry

I

Since long before the English Augustan era, it had been a commonplace that English literature began in the age of Chaucer, either through his offices or, more rarely, through those of his contemporary, Gower. Indeed, it was not unusual for Chaucer to be seen as the sole literary figure of consequence before the sixteenth century. Thomas Sprat, for example, states in his *History of the Royal Society* (1667) that 'Till the time of *King Henry* the *Eighth*, there was scarce any man regarded [the English language]...but *Chaucer*, and nothing was written in it which one would be willing to read twice but some of his *Poetry*.'[1] This exact point is reiterated by John Dennis in *The Usefulness of the Stage* (1698) where he observes that before Henry's reign, and excepting Chaucer, 'we had not had a first rate Writer'.[2] The most common conceit expressing Chaucer's priority in the literary tradition was that of his being the 'father' of English poetry, and I will say more about this figure later on. Another prevalent metaphor for Chaucer's initiation of the vernacular tradition, however, was that of his being a rising sun or new-breaking morn. The conceit appears in the opening couplet of Denham's 'On Mr Abraham Cowley' (1668): 'Old *Chaucer*, like the Morning Star, | To us discovers day from far'; it is taken up in Henry Keepe's (1681) description of Chaucer's 'being the Sun just rising' and surfaces again in Samuel Cobb's remark that Chaucer 'pointed out the day'.[3]

[1] Spingarn (ed.), 2: 113.
[2] Hooker (ed.), 1: 160.
[3] *Poetical Works*, 149; Henry Keepe, *Monumenta Westmonasteriensia* (1682), in *Five Hundred Years of Chaucer Criticism and Allusion (1357–1900)*, ed. Caroline F. E. Spurgeon, three vols. (Cambridge, 1925), 1: 255; Cobb, 'Of Poetry', in *Poems on Several Occasions* (1710), 188.

Chaucer's position was not altogether unchallenged. After all, to most readers his language remained more or less unintelligible, and only in the later eighteenth century, through the offices of such as Thomas Gray and Thomas Tyrwhitt, were the complexities of his versification first unravelled. Perhaps, however, a greater threat to Chaucer's canonical primacy than that provided by his obscurity came from the mid-eighteenth-century rise of bardolatry and the fashioning of a more rarefied concept of poetic creativity or 'poesy'. In both William Collins's 'Epistle to Thomas Hanmer' (1743) and Thomas Gray's 'Progress of Poesy' (1757), for example, when the godlike 'Muse', the animate spirit of creative genius, arrives in 'Albion', she first invests herself, not in Chaucer, but in Shakespeare, presumably because Chaucer's intractable rudeness was seen as incompatible with the solemnity of true artistic inspiration.

All heritage movements set great store by origins. The origin tends to act as guarantor of the integrity and sanctity of the tradition as a whole; but also origins are often unearthed (or 'selected') so as to reinforce values that have come to seem desirable in the subsequent tradition. In this chapter, I want to consider the hunt for a pre-Chaucerian origin to English literature, an origin that would satisfy the question of at what point, and in connection with which writers, English literature actually began. Such a question, as it was proposed during the eighteenth century, was never likely to bring a single, unequivocal response. One constituency of opinion continued to discover the earliest origins of native literature in classical culture; yet increasingly during the eighteenth century commentators found the confidence to assert more homespun origins for British or English literature. These themselves, however, take different forms: the scholarly recovery of Anglo-Saxon pointed not just to a Saxon literary inheritance but also to the rootedness of the whole subsequent tradition in the Saxon tongue; while at the same time there developed a vogue for mythic idealizations of the embryonic tradition, in the figures of the Celtic or Druidical bards.

II

Before 1600, those wanting to proclaim the existence of a native poetic tradition had no option but to define it against an earlier classical culture. So even while William Webbe, in his *Discourse of English Poetrie* (1586) can sing the praises of an emerging native poetry, he still remains self-conscious that to speak of English poetry as a thing unto itself, separated off from the classical poetic tradition, might seem 'like vnto the drawing of ones pycture without a head'.[4] Exactly the same edginess and lingering self-doubt appear in George Puttenham's compendious *Arte of English Poesie* (1589). The opening chapter consists of genteel flattery of Queen Elizabeth, whom Puttenham salutes, on the strength of some circuitous rhetoric, as the 'most excellent Poet' of 'any that I know in our time'. The next chapter, the one, however, that actually initiates the argument of the book, carries the banner-title 'That there may be an art of our English Poesie, aswell as there is of the Latine and Greeke'.[5] This conviction forms the nub of Puttenham's entire Olympian project: it is the postulate on which his whole book is implicitly based but also one that he feels obliged to set down and defend publicly at its very outset.

In chapter XXXI of 'The First Booke', Puttenham enumerates 'the most commended writers in our English Poesie', but perhaps of greater significance is an earlier chapter in which he identifies the 'sundry formes' of poetry and nominates the leading exponents in both Greek and Latin. So in the '*Heroick*' vein, for example, he declares that '*Homer* was chief and most auncient among the Greeks, *Virgill* among the Latines'.[6] Although this procedure hardly seems pronounced, impregnate within it are ideas that were to exercise considerable sway in future consideration of the English poetic canon. Puttenham accepts that the staple genres of poetry are few and unchanging; and that each culture will produce its own champions in each of these kinds. A mature poetic culture will throw up a great epic poet, a great lyricist, a great satirist, and so on. A little later on, these stipulations about genre are joined by the further ones, also procured from examining the classics, that a successful culture will have an originary figure who 'fathers' the subsequent tradition, plus a poet characterized by a god-like extremity of creative energy, and also perhaps one distinguished by an unswerving 'correctness', whose efforts will serve to refine the language as a whole.

---

[4] Smith (ed.), 1: 247.   [5] Ibid. 2: 4.   [6] Ibid. 2: 26.

What unites all these forms of stereotyping is a principle of cultural atavism, the belief that Roman culture does not just emulate, but also *re-enacts* Greek culture, and that a vernacular English culture will reproduce the structures and traits of classical culture in general.

We can see this idea in relation to English literature as early as Richard Carew's celebrated essay *The Excellency of the English Tongue* (1595–6), an early piece of linguistic propaganda, in which Carew discovers the origin of the English language in the 'old Saxon'. His concern is to demonstrate that 'what soeuer grace any other Languadge carryeth, in Verse or Prose...they maye all be liuely and exactly represented in ours'. The evidence for this statement is sought in a series of parallels between classical and vernacular figures:

Will you haue *Platos* vayne? reede Sir *Thomas Smith*: The *Ionick*? Sir *Tho. Moor: Ciceros? Aschame: Varro? Chaucer; Demosthenes?* Sir *Iohn Cheeke*... Will yowe reade Virgill? take the *Earll of Surrey: Catullus? Shakespeare,* and *Marlowes fragment: Ouid? Daniell: Lucane? Spenser: Martiall? Sir Iohn Dauis and others. Will yow haue all in all for prose and verse? take the miracle of our age Sir Philip Sidney.*[7]

The brio and confidence with which Carew strikes these patriotic notes is very different from Puttenham, but just as salient is the rhetorical framework in which he expresses his views. English poetry can claim to have come into its own because for every classical figure who has inaugurated a distinct 'vayne' of writing, there now exists a vernacular shadow. The way that English literature grounds its rivalry with classical culture is to re-enact it. It is in the spirit of this conception that Francis Meres's *Palladis Tamia, Wits Treasury* (1598) includes a chapter entitled 'A Comparatiue Discourse of our English Poets with the Greeke, Latine, and Italian Poets', which furnishes a plethora of whimsical and sometimes esoteric correspondences between writers drawn from the different cultures, the opening paragraph being indicative of the rest:

As Greece had three poets of great antiquity, Orpheus, Linus, and Musaeus, and Italy other three auncient poets, Liuius Andronicus,

---

[7] Ibid. 2: 293.

Ennius, and Plautus: so hath England three auncient poets, Chaucer, Gower, and Lydgate.[8]

The ideas set in motion by the Elizabethan critics retain their currency even after the Restoration. Speaking well of the native literary tradition still means, first and foremost, comparing it favourably with the achievements of classical culture. Moreover, to rival classical culture is not to do something different with equal distinction, but rather to do the same thing to the same standard, to confront the classical authors on their own ground. When John Denham, for example, composes his adulatory elegy on Abraham Cowley, the precise statement of commendation is that he has equalled those classical authors who stand as his immediate forebears: '*Horace*'s wit, and *Virgils* state, | He did not steal, but emulate'; and 'Old *Pindar*'s flights by him are reach'd, | When on that gale his wings are stretch'd'.[9] Similarly, in the 'Preface' to *Fables Ancient and Modern* (1685), Dryden champions the cause of Chaucer by drawing a systematic parallel between him and the Roman poet, Ovid, this being the first example of an extended comparison between a classical and a vernacular author in English criticism. Two years after Dryden's *Fables* appeared William Winstanley's *Lives of the most Famous English Poets* (1687), which was furnished with a frontispiece engraving (discussed earlier) illustrating the idea of 'fame': a bust of Shakespeare is flanked by two pyramidical pillars inscribed on which are the names of six classical authors (Homer, Ovid, Ennius, Pindar, Horace, and Virgil) as well as, in more prominent lettering, the two moderns, Chaucer and Cowley. A clear message of the image is that the attainment of poetic fame is synonymous with joining in fellowship the poets of the classical firmament. But the image goes beyond this truism, and with Shakespeare's image dominating the centre-ground, intimates the possibility of a native genius that might eclipse the pantheon of the ancients.

The last years of the seventeenth century saw the outbreak of the intellectual fracas that we now know as the 'battle of the books'. Its origin in England can be traced to the appearance in 1690 of a genteel essay by Sir William Temple on the respective merits of classical and modern culture. Temple had happened on

---

[8] Ibid. 2: 314.   [9] Anderson (ed.), 5: 679.

a short essay of Fontenelle's entitled a *Digression sur les An-cients et les Moderns* and took objection to it on the grounds that it 'falls so grosly into the censure of the Old Poetry and preference of the New'.[10] The controversy ensuing from Temple's innocuous essay ultimately fans out to embrace an issue as large-scale and arresting as through what means we should seek to encounter the past. Yet the initial question that Temple put in play was rather more diminutive. What were the claims that modern literature could justifiably make for itself in the context of the past achievements of Greece and Rome? Temple's essay immediately ignited a flurry of controversialist activity on the same issue, the first rejoinder of lasting account being by William Wotton in 1694. Moreover, in between the two works, there appeared Thomas Rymer's *A Short View of Tragedy* (1692), which while not explicitly dedicated to the controversy already rumbling, lambasted the Renaissance tragic dramatists, including Shakespeare, for their failure to comply with classical rules. This in its turn led to counter-attacks from the modern side, as Charles Gildon's 'For the Modern Poets Against the Ancients' (1694). Only three years later, the time was ripe for Swift to draft a defence of his patron, Temple, which, though published only so late as 1705, was to give its name to the entire controversy.[11]

It has been suggested that the 'battle of the books' is an epochal event in the formation of the English canon, witnessing over a period of time 'the gradual replacement of Latin by polite English, and the final establishment of a national canon on the model of the ancients'.[12] But there are reasons to think that the reality is more complex, and perhaps more confusing, than this picture allows for. For one thing, the controversy was character-ized throughout by modulation and blurring of the sides of the argument. This applies even to William Wotton's *Reflections upon Ancient and Modern Learning*, the work with which he won his spurs as a leading spokesman for the modern side against the *ancienneté* of Temple and his supporters. To those

[10] Spingarn (ed.), 3: 33.
[11] The best recent treatment of the controversy is Joseph Levine, *The Battle of the Books: History and Literature in the Augustan Age* (Ithaca, NY, 1991); an older one is R. F. Jones, *Ancients and Moderns*, 2nd edn. (St Louis, 1961).
[12] Jonathan Brody Kramnick, 'The Aesthetics of Revisionism, a Response', in *Eighteenth Century Life*, 21 (1997), 84.

visiting the controversy nowadays, what most stands out is the understated nature of Wotton's argument and the broad area of agreement between him and his main opponent. He is happy to concede that the works of the ancients 'give us a very solid Pleasure when we read them' and he accepts that across the broad area of cultivated writing including poetry 'the Ancients may have out-done the Moderns'. On the other hand, it would be to give the moderns less than their due not to concede that recent times 'have seen extraordinary Productions, which the Ancients themselves, had they been alive, would not have been ashamed of', but for Wotton to identify excellence amongst the moderns is for him to believe that this could come about only through painstaking imitation of classical originals.[13] And if Wotton, one of the great champions of the modern case, can approve of some of Temple's most elementary premises, then so can supporters of the ancients sometimes find themselves endorsing essentially modern assumptions. In 1709, for example, Henry Felton published his *Dissertation on Reading the Classics and Forming a Just Style* in which he set out a classical curriculum designed, in the first instance, to be of service to the young Marquis of Granby but which he envisaged would stand in good stead any young man of position. Felton was firmly aligned with Temple's party, his committed *ancienneté* being evident from his mockery of the pedantries of modern philology, but, contrary to what one might expect, he expresses a high regard for works of modern literature. For though Felton denies that modern works can ever do more than be 'almost equal to the Ancients', he is so won over by Spenser and Shakespeare as to think them 'as great Genius's as ever were produced in *Rome* or *Athens*'; and, even more provocatively, he discovers that '*Milton* ... in Epic Writing hath transcended the *Greek* and *Latin* Poet'.[14]

The 'battle of the books', especially as it addressed the status of the vernacular literary canon in comparison with the classical one, was one of those disputes whose very existence depended on a sound platform of unanimity between the opposing parties. English literature, it could be agreed, possessed its own distinct tradition and had produced many remarkable writers; and

[13] Spingarn (ed.), 3: 203.
[14] Henry Felton, *A Dissertation on Reading the Classics and Forming a Just Style* (1713), 222.

where these writers acceded to excellence they did so because, either loosely or more exactingly, they followed the precedent of the ancients. Both these factors made it possible to attempt to adjudicate between the comparative merits of classical and modern cultures, but which culture was deemed victorious was probably of lesser note than that the mere drawing of the comparison was seen to be appropriate. It is important that this point be recognized, because there *were* voices at the time clamouring for a more thoroughgoing review of the role of the classics in English education and culture, but their opinions never came to be assimilated into the 'battle of the books' controversy as such. Daniel Defoe, for example, a product of Newington Green academy, and therefore a beneficiary of the sort of realist education that flourished in such institutions, can be found lamenting that 'such is the vanity of the times, such the humour or usage of the day, that nothing but classic reading is call'd litterature [or 'learning']'.[15] What is at issue for Defoe, here, is more far-reaching than the technicality of relative cultural value: it is the monopoly exercised by classical writing through the entire process of gentlemanly education. And Defoe was far from alone in his resentment of this. Richard Steele had some years earlier included an essay in the *Spectator*, the house journal of a social 'politeness', one aspect of which was an easy conversancy with classical culture, attacking the forcible inculcation of Latin in grammar schools.[16] Such radical thinking does in time, as I explore later, impact on the rise of English literature, but it falls outside the strict ambit of the feud we now know as the 'battle of the books'.

Although it is convenient to think of Temple's unassuming essay as a catalyst for the ensuing controversy, even this work was itself a retaliation against an earlier one by Fontenelle. Indeed, it is impossible, without severe qualification, to assert when the fracas actually begins or ends. Moreover, as regards its outcome, Joseph Levine, the foremost modern historian of the controversy, can do no better than assert rather limply that it terminates 'in something of a draw'.[17] No reconciliation is effected between the warring parties; nor is there any decisive

[15] Bülbring (ed.), *Compleat English Gentleman*, 222.
[16] No. 157, 30 Aug. 1711, in *Spectator*, 2: 114–17.
[17] Levine, *Battle of the Books*, 84.

resolution of the matters at issue between them. As I have shown, attempts to assert, and construct the identity of, an incipient English literature date back to the Elizabethan critics; and even at the outset this involved scrutinizing the relation between indigenous poets and their Greek and Latin forebears. This process continues, throughout and after the period of the 'battle', with gathering conviction. On some occasions, this activity seems to take place under the aegis of the 'battle' itself, but on others, it seems to occur independently of it, its impetus and format largely unchanged from the time of Carew and Meres.

In 1710, for example, appears Samuel Cobb's 'Of Poetry', prefixed to which is William Worts's commendatory verse 'To his Friend on the Following Poem'. Here Worts commends the native tradition as a worthy successor to those of Greece and Rome, the best of the ancients being now 'transplanted to the *British* Coast'; and he amuses himself by nominating a leading English author as an equivalent to each of the great authors of Greece and Rome: so Homer is shadowed by Milton, Virgil by Dryden, Catullus by Waller, and so on.[18] The idea of an actual pitched battle between ancient and modern poets, a ploy capitalized on first by Swift, is also used in Colley Cibber's *A Rhapsody upon the Marvellous* (1751), the victory this time going to the moderns. This squaring up between the rival factions is necessary as

> Then shall we see 'twixt *Homer's* Gods,
> And *Milton's* Paradise, what Odds!
> What Pleasures *Virgil's* Plaines instill,
> Beyond the Views from *Cooper's* Hill?
> Or how far *Pindar* sweeps the Bays
> From *Dryden's* bright *Cecilian* Lays?[19]

In similar vein, Thomas Cooke's *Pythagoras An Ode* (1752) describes how each modern writer is infused with the transmigrated soul of the classical author most resembling him. So Shakespeare, for example, houses the soul of Aeschylus, while 'Old *Homer* shall revive again | In *Milton's* bold and sacred

---

[18] W. Worts, 'To his Friend on the Following Poem', in Cobb, *Poems on Several Occasions*, 172–4.

[19] Colley Cibber, *A Rhapsody upon the Marvellous...Being a Scrutiny into Ancient Poetick Fame, Demanded by Modern Common Sense* (1751), 7.

Strain'.[20] Michael Wodhull's 'Ode to the Muses' (1760) resists the conceit of transmigration but fashions a similar sequence of correspondences between classical and modern figures, with Pope matching Juvenal, Thomson Theocritus, and so on; and Edward Burnaby Greene's 'The Classic' (1768) shows a broad gamut of supposedly eminent moderns (including the likes of Colman, Akenside, and Hammond) equalling or eclipsing their classical counterparts.[21]

How, then, does the battle of the books stand towards the maturation of an English literary tradition? While it is hard to be categoric, its impact seems to have been chiefly retrograde. When Elizabethan authors such as Carew and Meres specify a series of analogies between classical and modern figures, their doing so actually submits English literature to a sort of initiation rite. They know that there is an English literary culture worth speaking about because this body of writing matches the template of the classics; and even though their reasoning rules out the possibility of a native literature in any way at variance from the classical models, this is of no concern to them. Yet, by the early eighteenth century, in ways that this chapter will go on to document, it had become possible to think that English or British literature might be successful in terms other than those laid down by the classics. The effect of the battle of the books was rather to distract from these new possibilities: even those ostensibly supporting the moderns were imprisoned within a rhetoric of debate which ruled out many claims that might otherwise have been made for the longevity and strength of the native literary tradition. Whereas Carew and Meres make use of classical parallels as an act of rudimentary affirmation of their own culture and its status, the same techniques trundled out in the mid-eighteenth century have dwindled to a hackneyed parlour game. It is a discourse no longer at the cutting edge of attempts to recover, invent, or promote a native literary culture. Already it is in process of being supplanted by newer explanations and narratives.

---

[20] Thomas Cooke, *Pythagoras An Ode. To which are Prefix'd Observations on Taste and on Education* (1752), 8.

[21] See Howard Weinbrot, *Britannia's Issue: The Rise of British Literature from Dryden to Ossian* (Cambridge, 1993), 129.

III

When Alexander Pope drew up his scheme for an English literary tradition, breaking the tradition into distinct 'schools', the second of these, containing Lydgate, Hoccleve, Walter Map, and Skelton, was designated the 'School of Chaucer'. The first, however, comprising 'Chaucer's Visions, Romant of the Rose, Pierce Plowman, Tales from Boccace', was dubbed the 'School of Provence'. By making in this way the 'School of Provence' the point of departure of his literary history, Pope was endorsing a literary historical theory that had rapidly—however misguidedly—acquired the status of an orthodoxy. The origin of the theory in England can be attributed to one single work, Thomas Rymer's *A Short View of Tragedy* (1692), a work that Pope explicitly acknowledges as his authority. Rymer's *Short View of Tragedy* is a rag-bag of intemperate critical opinionation, chiefly notorious for its high-handed criticism of Shakespeare's *Othello*, its overall argument being that English tragic drama compared unfavourably with that of ancient Greece and with modern tragic writing flourishing on the Continent. But Rymer is also at pains to insist that this situation does not reflect some more general poverty afflicting the entirety of English literary culture; and, to this end, he includes a general chapter on the 'Development of poetry and drama in England'. This chapter shows conversancy—if only on limited terms—with a number of ancient British authors, including the Celtic poets Taliessin and Merlin. What is singular, though, is that as Rymer moves forward chronologically, he allocates a prominent place in the development of modern European literature (including English) to the literary culture of Provence: '*Provencal* was the first, of the modern languages, that yielded and chim'd in with the musick and sweetness of ryme.'[22] Amongst those owing a major debt to Provençal troubadour poetry, Rymer names Petrarch; but he also describes Chaucer's particular furtherance of the English tongue as his assimilation into the native Saxon tongue, not just of Latin and French, but also of 'Provencial' words. All in all, the influence of the Provençal troubadours is so

---

[22] Zimansky (ed.), 126.

great that Rymer can generalize that 'all our *modern* Poetry comes from them'.[23]

The attractiveness of Rymer's theory is fairly obvious, for it circumvented a literary historical problem that has remained vexing even to this day. While the Augustans were conversant with a number of Latin and Saxon writers before Chaucer, and while they were ready enough to claim these for 'English litera-ture', the relation such early writers bore to Chaucer remained radically uncertain. Indeed, the question of how well Chaucer was versed in native writing prior to his own time has never been adequately resolved. Yet the theory of a Provençal influence on the rise of English literature did not just promise an answer to the conundrum of from exactly where Chaucer's unique achieve-ment had sprung. For the predication of such an influence seemed to clinch the case for English literature's being essentially 'polite'. One can, for example, detect a hint of nationalistic pride in an observation such as this by Dryden:

Chaucer (as you have formerly been told by our learned Mr. Rymer) first adorned and amplified our barren Tongue from the Provençal which was then the most polished of all the modern languages.[24]

The infusion of Provençal words and idioms, it was believed, assisted the language towards its 'refinement', a refinement for which it was otherwise difficult to account. It seemed to confirm that English literature belonged as part of a pan-European polite culture.

The merits of this general theory are something I want to address in a moment, but it is worth stressing just how widely influential Rymer's theory was. One of those who swallowed it without demur was Pope. In an introductory note to his *Temple of Fame* (1715), a poem based on a Chaucerian original, Pope suggests that both Chaucerian and Petrarchan dream-vision poems originally derive from Provençal poetry, for 'Almost all the Poems in the old *Provençal* had this Turn'.[25] In similar vein, Joseph Spence, Pope's friend, addressed himself to the Provençal literary heritage in a footnote to 'Quelques Remarques'. The

[23] Ibid. 120. See Curt A. Zimansky, 'Chaucer and the School of Provence: A Problem in Eighteenth Century Literary History', *Philological Quarterly*, 25 (1946), 321–42.
[24] 'Preface' to *Fables Ancient and Modern* (1700) in *Of Dramatic Poesy*, 2: 272.
[25] Butt (ed.), 2: 243.

footnote relates to a paragraph on fourteenth-century literature, exclusively devoted to Chaucer and Gower, in which Spence identifies Chaucer as the first polite English poet ('Enfin il ne lui manquoit rien pour devinir poli'); and the whole paragraph is glossed with the observation that 'Our first Poetry was chiefly either of the Lyric or ye Satirical kind: both of wch Fashions were probably deriv'd from ye Italians, as they receiv'd them fro [sic] the Provencals'. Spence then claims that an important ingredient of Provençal poetry was satire against princes, including those of the papacy (then settled at Avignon), and intimates vaguely: 'Hence many things in Chaucer; Piers Plowman; ye Mirrour for Magistrates, &c.'[26] Much the same cavalier enthusiasm for Provençal influence comes in William Collins's 'Epistle Addressed to Sir Thomas Hanmer' (1743). Here Collins incorrectly places the troubadours after the revival of learning in Italy and associates their output exclusively with love poetry:

> Then deeply skilled in love's engaging theme,
> The soft Provencial passion to Arno's stream:
> With graceful ease and wanton lyre he strung,
> Sweet flowed the lays—but love was all he sung.[27]

Collins's picture is blatantly tendentious. By connecting the troubadours with the revival of learning, he rescues them from the suffocating cultural miasma of the dark ages, assimilating them all the more vigorously to learned and polite culture. This then makes them seem aptly antecedent to what Collins identifies as the next great moment of European literary culture, the coming of Shakespeare.

The orthodoxy of a Provençal origin of English literature straddles the whole of the eighteenth century, and even those, unlike Pope, Spence, and Collins, who knew how to undertake original literary scholarship were persuaded by it. Thomas Gray, for example, notes in his *Common-Place Book* that Dante, Petrarch, and Chaucer all 'caught their fire from ... [Provençal] ... writers, & imitated their manner, style, & versification'.[28] Not surprisingly, the 'School of Provence' also figures

---

[26] Osborn, 'The First History of English Poetry', 244.
[27] Lines 39–42, in Lonsdale (ed.), 393.
[28] *Thomas Gray's Common-Place Book*, 3 vols., Pembroke College Library (unclassified), 2: 772.

centrally in the same author's literary historical scheme in which
Chaucer, the earliest poet documented in the plan, is claimed to
be the first to have 'introduced the manner of the Provençaux
inproved by the Italians into our country'.[29] And yet more
authority accrued to the theory from Thomas Warton's earnest
testimony that:

Chaucer manifestly first taught his countrymen to write English; and
formed a style by naturalising words from the Provencial, at that time
the most polished dialect of any in Europe, and the best adapted to the
purposes of poetical expression.[30]

The misconceptions at work here are understandable given the
inherent elusiveness of Provençal language and culture. The
main ambiguity was that 'Provençal' named both a group of
dialects indigenous to southern France and also an artificially
standard language employed by the troubadours and influential
well beyond the confines of that territory. The language of old
Provence was more Latinate than that of the northern regions of
France, and so in this finite sense more polite, but the ability of
critics such as Rymer to distinguish between different French
dialects was in fact minimal. As a result, they ended up conflat-
ing all medieval French dialects with that of Provençal. Such
confusion ramified all the more broadly because Rymer's account of the matter remained the one notionally 'first-hand'
source on which the subsequent observations of Dryden, Pope,
and others were based; yet Rymer's narrative was itself founded
on just one source-work, a work moreover so flawed as to have
been labelled by a modern critic as 'one of the baldest fabrica-
tions ever to confuse literary history'.[31]

Two general propositions about the impact of Provençal culture on English literature distilled out of Augustan debate on
the matter: first, that Chaucer refined the language partly by
importing into it Provençal words; and, second, that the same
author as well as other English writers inherited some of their
literary forms from the troubadours. Neither of these two ideas is
given much credence nowadays by Chaucerian scholars. Norman

---

[29] *Correspondence*, 3: 1123.
[30] Thomas Warton, *The History of English Poetry*, 3 vols. (1774–81), 1: 344.
[31] The work is *Les Vies des Plus Célèbres et Anciens Poètes Provencaux* by Jean
de Nostredame (1575); Zimansky, 'Chaucer and the School of Provence', 327.

Davis, for example, contributing to the great Riverside Chaucer edition of 1987, argues that while Chaucer did introduce to the language 'a substantial number of words and phrases', of which many were of French (though not Provençal) origin, his overall influence 'on the English language seems to have been more a matter of style than of substance'.[32] In other words, Chaucer did not so much change the language as fashion out of it new possibilities for poetic style. Davis concludes, in fact, that Chaucer wrote 'in the English familiar to him from business as well as from court circles in London and Westminster'.[33] Just as the picture of Chaucer refining the language by introducing words drawn from the inherently polite language of 'Provence' is chimerical, so the idea that Chaucer's literary forms are Provençal in derivation has also been discountenanced by modern literary historians. The myth of the Provençal origin of English literature is initially propagated by those, such as Rymer and Pope, who had much invested in the intrinsic 'politeness' of English letters. Yet its success can be measured by the extent to which poet-scholars like Gray and Warton, who had much less invested in that particular narrative, who indeed were constructing rather different narratives of the literary past, end up accrediting it.

IV

William Webbe's *A Discourse of English Poetrie* (1586), especially in regard of the candour it shows about its own ignorance, probably provides the most complete picture of the understanding of native literature prevalent at the end of the sixteenth century. Webbe, for example, is perfectly frank about being unfamiliar with any English poet between Lydgate and Skelton, a gap in his knowledge covering some hundred years; and in similar vein, while he is aware of the reputation for learning of Henry I (nicknamed 'Beaucleark'), he still remains at a loss to name any actual poet writing earlier than the fourteenth century: 'The first of our English poets that I haue heard of was *Iohn Gower*, about the time of king *Rychard* the seconde.'[34]

[32] *Riverside Edition*, 'Introduction', xxvi.
[33] Ibid.
[34] Smith (ed.), 1: 240–1.

Leaving aside some small-scale wrangling over whether Chaucer
or Gower should count as the earliest English poet, the tradition
as constructed and bequeathed by Elizabethan literary scholars
began no earlier than the late fourteenth century. Indeed, in light
of the prevailing state of literary antiquities, things could hardly
have been otherwise. However, inside two decades there appeared
a work that was to exert a profound influence in pushing back the
frontiers of knowledge about an early native literature: William
Camden's *Remains Concerning Britain* (1605).

It now appears that the *Remains*, rather than being pieced
together from the leftovers of Camden's majestic *Britannia*
(1586), had a separate provenance. Written in Latin, the *Britannia* had been aimed exclusively at a scholarly, and perhaps
largely Continental, audience; and, as the title suggests, it had
tried to take a snapshot of the British world at the time of the
Roman occupation. The *Remains*, however, was planned along
different lines: not just did Camden publish the book in English
but all along he had compiled his notes in the same language, as
distinct from his method of working on the bigger project.[35]
Moreover, as well as making the book more accessible to his
English countrymen, Camden projected it as a celebration of the
roots of Englishness. One of its objectives was to bring to public
notice the civility and piety of Anglo-Saxon culture, and to trace
the origins and sing the praises of the 'English-Saxon' tongue.

Unlike *Britannia*, the *Remains* was not a county or topographical study but rather a study of selected facets of early history
organized under an assortment of heads, including languages,
common Christian names and surnames, money, apparel, military engines, and so on. As regards early native literature, most
crucial were three chapters entitled 'Poems', 'Epigrams', and
'Rhythmes' in which Camden vouchsafed to subsequent historians a file of names of English writers antecedent to Chaucer.
Those referred to are such as Caedmon, Joseph of Exeter, Geoffrey of Monmouth, John of Hauville, Godfrey of Winchester,
Alexander Neckam, Michael of Cornwall, Walter Map, and
Gerald of Wales. In addition, in the work's first chapter, entitled
'Britaine', Camden quotes the start of Robert of Gloucester's
thirteenth-century verse chronicle, beginning 'England is a well

[35] See William Camden, *Remains Concerning Britain*, ed. R. D. Dunn (Toronto,
1984), xvi–xvii.

good land'. Camden was not the first to cite early verse of this kind, Leland, for example, had included examples in his *Itinerary*, but Camden is the first to anthologize such authors in a systematic way. It is as well to be clear, though, that the *Remains* in no sense represents even a trial-run at literary history: its relevant chapters consist of no more than a scrappy inventorizing of names and excerpts. But these names were soon to harden into an adoptive canon of early English writing.

Camden's canon of early English authors was to be incorporated into Edward Phillips's *Theatrum Poetarum* (1675), and half or so of the eleven poets cited by William Winstanley as writing prior to the later fourteenth century duplicate those named in Camden and Phillips. Yet what sort of canon does this amount to? For one thing, the pre-fourteenth-century writers whom Phillips and Winstanley assimilate into their collections spring from an age of which they had practically no understanding. Nor did the two of them probably have first-hand acquaintance with any of the authors whom they mention. Phillips, for example, in a supplement to *Theatrum Poetarum*, refers somewhat misleadingly to 'Gaulfrid' (Geoffrey of Monmouth), the author of an influential pseudo-history of Britain as 'one of the oldest of our Modern Poets'. Geoffrey *did* write poetry, but the work for which he is almost solely remembered is in Latin prose; and one suspects that Phillips's inclusion is more likely to be expressive of ignorance than erudition. Equally, while Phillips's and Winstanley's entrants from the fourteenth century onwards are exclusively literary authors, before that point their canons slacken into synonymity with writers of any sort whose works or reputations have survived. So historians (like Geoffrey or Gerald of Wales) are included, and Alexander Neckam, described by Winstanley as 'an exact Philosopher, and excellent Divine', also gets classed as a poet.

Yet the two most prominent features of this primitive early canon are that, for all Camden's vaunting of the Anglo-Saxon tongue, its authors were nearly all domiciled in monasteries and nearly all wrote in Latin.[36] At this juncture, the pre-fourteenth-century canon remains essentially an Anglo-Latin one. This obviously reflects the fact that reading competence in Latin was

---

[36] Information on Anglo-Latin authors is contained in A. G. Rigg, *A History of Anglo-Latin Literature 1066–1422* (Cambridge, 1992).

vastly more dispersed than in Anglo-Saxon or Celtic. But it also betrays a continuing desire that native literary culture prior to Chaucer should be Latinate (and therefore polite) rather than being confined to the barbarous vernacular tongue. So much might be surmised from an odd oversight committed by Phillips. Although his flimsy canon of early poets has been plucked almost straight from Camden, there remains another early poet, described in glowing terms by Camden, who makes it into neither Phillips nor Winstanley. This is the seventh-century Saxon poet Caedmon, of whom Camden says: 'by divine inspiration, about the yeare 680 [he] became so divine a Poët in our English tongue that, with his sweete verses full of compunction, he withdrew many from vice to vertue, and a religious fear of God.'[37] Such a description might have allowed Phillips, had he so wished, to have assimilated Caedmon as the earliest native poet known on reputable authority (that of Bede) to have existed. Moreover, the story of Caedmon's conversion to poetry, vividly related by Bede, would have provided exactly the sort of enigmatic anecdote so treasured by the collectors of biography.[38] In other words, Caedmon's pointed omission suggests that Phillips and Winstanley were determinedly extending favouritism to the Latin tradition at the expense of the vernacular one. That the prehistory of English literature should be seen as Latinate guaranteed that the entire literary tradition be threaded through by a principle of politeness, and so plain ignorance of early Saxon culture may have vied with an active determination to edit it from the cultural tradition. Yet Phillips's disregard of the Saxon vernacular belonged very much to its time: forty years later was to occur an extraordinary efflorescence of Anglo-Saxon scholarship, after which Saxon poetry, and moreover the Anglo-Saxon origins of the very language of native culture, would become more difficult to ignore.

V

Through successive editions of the *Britannia*, to which Camden continued adding material until 1607, and in the *Remains* of

[37] Camden, *Remains*, 287.
[38] Bede, *Ecclesiastical History of the English Nation*, IV. xxiv.

1605, we can see Anglo-Saxon culture and language acquiring more and more importance in the construction of the past. Yet Camden, in spite of acquiring an enthusiasm for the Anglo-Saxons, was not really an authentic Saxonist. Curiously, however, in the same year as the *Remains*, there appeared a work, by an author of whom Camden seems to have been unaware, that would prepare the ground for the great advancements in Anglo-Saxon studies to be made over the next hundred years. This was Richard Verstegan's *A Restitution of Decayed Intelligence* (1605), a collection of meanings and etymologies of Old English words and the first book in the language to be devoted exclusively to the Anglo-Saxon tongue. Verstegan, born in London into a family of Dutch immigrants, was a Catholic, who was forced to leave Oxford without a degree due to his inability to take the oath of loyalty. Nonetheless, his book, dedicated somewhat daringly to James I, is an exercise in patriotic scholarship. It celebrates the Saxons as the true ancestors of the English people, and the Anglo-Saxon tongue as the origin of the English language (if not of all languages).[39]

Verstegan's work was possible at this juncture because he had the achievements of an earlier phase of Anglo-Saxon scholarship on which to call, and which consisted of the locating and gathering of early manuscripts. Some progress in this direction had been made by the cataloguers Leland and Bale but most instrumental was Matthew Parker, sometime Vice-Chancellor of Cambridge University and, from 1559 to 1574, Archbishop of Canterbury. Parker and his secretary John Joscelyn sent out letters around the bishops requesting they report on books or manuscripts held in their cathedral churches and dioceses, and enjoining that particular note be taken of any Anglo-Saxon material. This early corralling of sources was to lay the groundwork for the great Anglo-Saxon manuscript collections now held in the British Museum, as the Cottonian, Harleian, and Royal.[40]

[39] See the chapter on Verstegan in Graham Parry, *The Trophies of Time: English Antiquarians of the Seventeenth Century* (Oxford, 1995). See also Hugh A. MacDougall, *Racial Myth in English History: Trojans, Teutons, and Anglo-Saxons* (Montreal, 1982).
[40] Hereabouts, I am heavily indebted to Eleanor N. Adams, *Old English Scholarship in England from 1566–1800* (New Haven, 1917).

The next step in the dissemination of Anglo-Saxon writing was naturally that of ushering such manuscript material into print, but here lay a problem. Because Anglo-Saxon used non-Roman characters, no set of printing types existed through which it could be reproduced. The surmounting of this impediment is another debt that Anglo-Saxon scholars came to owe to Parker, for it was he who furnished a font of Anglo-Saxon types for the printer John Day, enabling him to be the first to print Old English excerpts as part of a work entitled *A Testimonie of Antiquitie* (1566–7). Day's *Testimonie* contained an Anglo-Saxon sermon, epistles by Bishops Alfrike and Wulfsine, and the Lord's Prayer, the Creed, and the Ten Commandments, all in the Anglo-Saxon tongue. Because of the problem of types, the repertoire of Anglo-Saxon material in print was slow to increase, and tended to consist of more of the same. The seventeenth century, for example, saw the appearance of further religious material in Anglo-Saxon versions of the Psalms and the Heptateuch. This was supplemented by the printing also of legal and historical materials including the Anglo-Saxon Chronicle. Yet the mere printing of Anglo-Saxon materials, limited though this was, did not ensure their being understood. For this it was necessary that scholars have at their disposal a reliable Saxon lexicon and grammar, and the provision of such texts stands as one of the great achievements of seventeenth-century antiquarianism. The creation of an Anglo-Saxon lexicon was expedited by the existence of a Latin-Saxon grammar compiled by Ælfric, which ensured that antiquarians had at least something from which to work. But much still needed to be done. It was in an attempt to fill this void that Verstegan produced his *Restitution*, but it was only in 1659 with the appearance of William Somner's *Dictionarium Saxonico-Latino-Anglicum* that the absence of a sound, comprehensive dictionary was fully rectified.

So far Anglo-Saxon scholarship had been pushed forward by the offices of a small number of isolated enthusiasts, but in the final quarter of the seventeenth century a group of Saxon scholars, sufficiently integrated to be thought of as a 'school', assembled itself in Oxford. This group included the likes of Edmund Gibson, Edward Thwaites, Humphrey Wanley, and, at its centre, George Hickes; its principal legacy to posterity was to be the collaborative and elephantine *Thesaurus*, published under Hickes's name in 1705.[41] In so far as the *Thesaurus* draws together the work of an entire school acknowledging Hickes's leadership, its contents are hard to anatomize. It combines both history and comparative philology, and pushes back the frontiers of scholarship in several areas. Its contents number, among other things, the first Anglo-Saxon grammar to have been produced (though one vitiated somewhat by the erroneous supposition that the structure of Anglo-Saxon mirrored that of Latin), Hickes's treatise *Dissertatio Epistolaris* which lays down foundations for the study of Old English antiquities, and Humphrey Wanley's seminal 'Catalogue' of Anglo-Saxon manuscripts.

Sadly, however, Hickes's *Thesaurus* represents the high noon of Anglo-Saxon scholarship in the English Augustan era. The Oxford school breaks up with the deaths of Thwaites in 1711 and Hickes himself in 1715, and the foothold gained at this time by Saxon Studies on the Oxford curriculum is also lost. Moreover, in the cantankerous dispute between the ancients and moderns, the study of Saxon antiquities was easily seized on by detractors as the acme of modern pedantry and futility. It has to be admitted that the discipline hardly made things easy for itself. The forbidding learning and steep price of the *Thesaurus* resulted in many unsold copies and financial despair for Hickes. Even when William Wotton produced a more friendly synopsis, this still appeared in Latin as his *Conspectus brevis* (1708). It might have been thought that Hickes and Wotton would have seen their recovery of the primitive vernacular as consistent with a more general project for the elevation of the vernacular tongue. Yet, far from this being the case, their treatment of the early Northern languages remained uncompromising towards those unversed in the scholarly medium of Latin.

Anglo-Saxon scholarship, even from its advent, was pursued for reasons other than those of pure learning. Matthew Parker, for example, who first initiated the gathering of manuscripts, did so in the hope that he might demonstrate the existence of an established Anglo-Saxon church standing as a prototype for the

---

[41] See David Fairer, 'Anglo-Saxon Studies', in *The History of the University of Oxford*, general editor T. H. Aston, vol 5. *The Eighteenth Century*, ed. L. S. Sutherland and L. G. Mitchell (Oxford, 1986), 807–29. See also David C. Douglas, *English Scholars 1660–1730* (London, 1939).

reformed church in England over which he presided. This vein of acknowledged anti-Catholicism runs through Saxon studies even in the eighteenth century. George Hickes, a strong-willed Anglican, was happy to subordinate his capacious and highly original learning to the service of his church, to which nothing could be more useful than that he 'show the faith and other chief doctrines of the English-Saxon Church to be the same with ours'.[42] Similarly, in 1697, Edmund Gibson writes to his fellow Oxford Saxonist Edward Thwaites in connection with some Anglo-Saxon homilies: 'I hope you'll have an eye to all the passages against Popery...a collection of that kind...would be undeniable evidence to all posterity, that the belief of our Papists at this day is a very different thing from that of our Saxon ancestors.'[43] Given that Saxon studies were so much in hock to these prejudices, it is not surprising that the antiquarians should have been chiefly interested in religious writings and that, before the mid-eighteenth century, interest in the literary significance of written antiquities should remain minimal.

It was not that Anglo-Saxon poetry had not been recovered; only that nobody quite knew what to do with it. Sir Robert Cotton's great library, compiled in the Elizabethan period, for example, contained the unique manuscript of *Beowulf* as well as one of the only two manuscripts of *The Owl and the Nightingale*. However, the polemical agenda of seventeenth-century antiquarian studies, as well as the obscurity of Anglo-Saxon versification, led to their being disregarded. The first notable printing of Anglo-Saxon poetry in fact took place as late as 1655 in Amsterdam: this was Francis Junius's flawed edition (based on a serious manuscript misattribution) of the seventh-century poet, Caedmon. In England, developments were even more tardy, so that only in 1698, when Edward Thwaites included the poem 'Judith' in his *Heptateuchus*, did Anglo-Saxon poetry first issue from an English press.

The great leap forward in the dissemination of Anglo-Saxon poetry, as with so much else, comes with Hickes's *Thesaurus* of

---

[42] Hickes to Bishop of Bristol, 22 May 1714; cited from Douglas, *English Scholars*, 19.

[43] Gibson–Thwaites, 20 May 1697, quoted in Nichols's *Literary Anecdotes of the Eighteenth Century*, 9 vols. (1812–15), 4: 143; cited here from Fairer, 'Anglo-Saxon Studies', 808.

1705. In hindsight, we might think that of most lasting significance is Humphrey Wanley's inclusion of the manuscript of
Beowulf in his 'Catalogue' and, moreover, his provision of
the first printed extracts from the poem. Yet at the time more
arresting was the section of the volume written by Hickes and
entitled 'De Poetica Anglo-Saxonum'. This was not only the first
corralling together of Anglo-Saxon poetic fragments, but also
the first attempt at critical commentary on actual works. It
has to be remembered that some of the jewels of Anglo-Saxon
poetry, such as 'The Dream of the Rood', 'The Seafarer', and
'The Wanderer' had still not been discovered; accordingly, the
range of poetry noticed by Hickes now seems rather thin, consisting of little more than the poems 'Genesis', 'Judith', a translation of the Lord's Prayer, and the Caedmonic fragment cited
by Bede. What stood out was less the poetry itself than Hickes's
professed enthusiasm for its merits. Hickes was a man of
staunch and indeflectible Anglican credentials: a recent historian
has described him as 'profoundly conservative in sentiment,
even reactionary'.[44] Yet merely in enquiring into the Anglo-
Saxon tongue, Hickes was marking himself out as an inveterate
modern: for the supporters of the ancients, there was no discipline that reeked so much of modern pedantry as philology,
this being the discipline, after all, of the reviled Bentley. But
in actually *praising* Anglo-Saxon verse, Hickes had passed
beyond mere dronishness, and was effecting what many saw as
a wholesale perversion of cultural values. Even some of Hickes's
close allies, amongst whom his high opinion of Anglo-Saxon
verse must have been well known, looked slightly askance. In
a letter to Arthur Charlett, for example, Edmund Gibson
remarked sceptically on Hickes's views: 'Dr H——s has given
us a glorious character of their [Anglo-Saxon] poetry, and
will hardly allow the Ancients to take place of them in that
particular. I have read some of it formerly, but could never
meet with any thing that relish'd half soe well as Homer or
Virgil.'[45]

Interest in Anglo-Saxon poetry, however, in spite of Hickes's
exhortations, did not flourish in the eighteenth century. *Beowulf*
still languished as a largely neglected manuscript, and Hickes's

[44] Levine, *Battle of the Books*, 354.
[45] Cited from ibid. 355.

pregnant critical commentary remained inaccessible to all but the learned and wealthy. Moreover, Saxon poets appeared notably less amenable to the sort of mythical idealization that was being applied to the 'bards' of the earlier British or Celtic tradition. There was, however, one Saxon poet who enigmatically did conform (to some extent at least) to this bardic stereotype: the seventh-century poet Caedmon. Caedmon enjoyed a somewhat artificial status in the eighteenth century due to the erroneous manuscript attribution made in Junius's edition of 1655. However, it was less the actual details of what he had written than the biographical sketch of his life left by Bede that contained the seeds of his charisma. Bede recounts how until late in life Caedmon lived after a secular manner and possessed no aptitude for poetry. One night a presence entered his dream and bestowed on him the gift of verse, after which he took orders and devoted himself to composing verses in praise of the Lord. Thus arose an image of Caedmon as an unlettered poet made vocal through divine inspiration. As an inspired poet, Caedmon presented obvious parallels with the Greek Pindar, this comparison being invoked by Hickes and also by his colleague, Edward Thwaites, who claimed that Caedmon was possessed of 'a sort of Poetick madness'.[46]

As distinct from early British poetry, the virtues of Anglo-Saxon poetry were not thought to be at variance from qualities admired in conventional neoclassical verse. Hickes, for instance, stresses the Saxons' observation of strict metres and the general intricacy of their poetic style; and, in the same vein, Elizabeth Elstob, in her *English-Saxon Grammar* (1715) notes that 'The pure *Saxon* Verses are known by that Exactness of Grammatical Construction, which is to be observed in them'.[47] Similarly, in John Campbell's *Polite Correspondence* (1741), a collection of letters between fictitious characters, Leander, depicted incidentally with Elstob's grammar next to him on the table, convinces his friend 'that neither our *Saxon* Ancestors, nor any of their Neighbours, were so rude and illiterate as we are taught to

---

[46] Letter from Thwaites to Hickes preserved in the British Library; cited from Samuel Kliger, 'The Neo-classical View of Old English Poetry', *Journal of English and Germanic Philology*, 49 (1950), 520.

[47] Elizabeth Elstob, *The Rudiments of English Grammar for the English-Saxon Tongue... With an Apology for the Study of Northern Antiquities. Being very useful towards the understanding our ancient English Poets, and other Writers* (1715), 66.

believe them'.[48] Even Caedmon, whose powers were supposedly visited on him through an act of divine inspiration, is still held up as an accomplished technician:

They ascrib'd the Furor Poeticus, the Divine Rage of Verse, to a gift from Heaven; but they attributed the Structure and Elegance of Poetry to the Art and Application of Man as is evident from the Account they give us of Caedmon, the Saxon Homer.[49]

This belief that the Anglo-Saxons possessed a poetry of polish and sophistication justifies Campbell's conviction that even poets of his own time can profit from cognizance of the 'Saxon Manner of Writing'; indeed, he argues that Augustan topographical poems like 'Cooper's Hill' and 'Windsor Forest' are—albeit not knowingly—constructed along similar lines to earlier Anglo-Saxon poems.[50] Claims made in the earlier eighteenth century for the aesthetic stature of Anglo-Saxon poetry, like those being made around the same time on behalf of early British literature, can be extremely ebullient. J. Henly, for example, in his *Introduction to an English Grammar* (1726) refers his readers to Hickes's verdict on Caedmon's sublimity as 'equal to that of the Greatest Masters, whether Greek or Latin'.[51] Similarly, Campbell maintains that for all the virtues and felicities to be found in 'the Greek and Latin Poets, the same are to be found in our Saxons'.[52] These judgements are heady indeed. Moreover, familiarity with Caedmon, if not with a larger body of vernacular Saxon writing, diffuses outward from the straitened world of the philologists. Joseph Spence's 'Quelques Remarques' devotes a paragraph to Caedmon as the sole author recoverable from the seventh century, stressing his lack of education, the suddenness of his inspiration and his celebrated status. The rise of Caedmon is a milestone in the formation of the national literary past: regardless of the limited body of those qualified to make it, and the smallish number who might have felt inclined to approve it, a claim of stunning magnitude was now being mounted—that

---

[48] *The Polite Correspondence: or Rational Amusement; being a Series of Letters, Philosophical, Poetical, Historical, Critical, Amorous, Moral and Satyrical* (1741), 235.

[49] Ibid. 263.

[50] Ibid. 273.

[51] Cited from Kliger, 'The Neo-classical View', 520.

[52] *Polite Correspondence*, 270.

more than half a millennium before Chaucer these islands had
bred a poet of comparable stature with any of classical civilization.

VI

The vogue for Anglo-Saxon culture does not just issue in, but
also achieves one sort of apex with, grandiloquent claims of the
nature of those recorded above. But there is another dimension
to the issue. In 1614, William Camden made what now seems
the perplexing decision of assimilating into a late edition of his
otherwise single-authored *Remains Concerning Britain*, an essay
written by Richard Carew which had originally been published
nearly twenty years earlier as his *Epistle on the Excellency of the
English Tongue*. Camden must have thought the essay's ebullience about the state of English language and letters in tune with
the tone of his own book, and may have been heartened in
particular by Carew's conviction about the Saxon basis of
the vernacular tongue: the 'grounde of our owne [language]
apperteyneth to the old Saxon'.[53] Camden's work helped to
popularize, what Richard Verstegan's *Restitution of Decayed
Intelligence* had made demonstrable to more scholarly eyes, that
whatever people might think (or imagine) about the Anglo-
Saxons, it was essentially their language that modern society
had at its disposal.

Over the next hundred years, the ideas propounded by the
likes of Camden and Carew harden into truism. It becomes
received opinion that the Saxons' conquering of the indigenous
British tribes had been virtually total. Swift, in his *Proposal for
Correcting, Improving and Ascertaining the English Tongue*
concedes that the Saxons 'drove the *Britons* into the most
remote and mountainous Parts; and the Rest of the Country in
Customs, Religion, and Language, became wholly *Saxon*'; and
in 'The History of the English Language' prefixed to his *Dictionary*, Johnson asserts flatly that 'The whole fabrick and scheme of
the *English* language is *Gothick* or *Teutonick*.'[54] These convic-

---

[53] Smith (ed.), 2: 289.
[54] Davis (ed.), 4: 7; Samuel Johnson, *Dictionary of the English Language*, 2 vols.
(London, 1840), 'History of the English Language' (separately paginated), 1: 1.

tions about the morphology of the English tongue inevitably had a bearing on how the national literature was conceived. For it was a commonplace in the eighteenth century, though an idea to which we are now alien, that a literature represents the flowering of the language in which it is written. A great literary work can be seen as in itself an advancement of the tongue; and no achievement in letters is possible unless the language has arrived at a maturity which can support such achievement.

Unsurprisingly, there was no consensus in the eighteenth century as to how the language had actually evolved. It was generally assumed that at some point, there had been an infusion of French words into the more purely Saxon tongue, though there was disagreement concerning at which point this had occurred. One common view, endorsed by Dryden amongst many others, associated the process almost exclusively with Chaucer, and on this basis ascribed to him a seminal role in the refinement of the national tongue; but others, including both Swift and Johnson, took a slightly different tack, and proposed a more gradual refinement in the century or so after the Norman conquest, caused either by the importing of French words or by more inward mechanisms of linguistic change. But even these two positions allowed for further nuances of opinion. So, for example, the author of an essay in the *Muses Mercury* in 1707 argues that, while there had indeed been a decanting of French words into the English language after the Conquest, this did not so much refine the tongue as turn it into a mongrel ('a confus'd mixture of *Saxon* and the *Norman* jargon'), and that Chaucer's peculiar office was to homogenize and garnish this unappetizing mish-mash.[55]

Yet a far more vexing issue was what had been going on linguistically in more recent times. And here the division into rival camps was rather sharper. Probably the most prevalent belief was that the English language had gone through a continuous process of refinement up until the English Augustan age itself, with poets like Waller, Denham, and Dryden raising it to a pitch of lucidity and harmony that, while it could perhaps be maintained, could not be improved on. This line of reasoning is implicit in Joseph Addison's 'Account of the Greatest English

---

[55] *The Muses Mercury or Monthly Miscellany* i. 6 (June 1707), 128.

Poets' with its arc of poetical improvement stretching from
Chaucer to Dryden, but appears in more brash and summary
form in Leonard Welsted's *A Dissertation concerning the Perfection of the English Language* (1724): 'it seems to me plain, that
the *English* Language is not capable of a much greater Perfection, than it has already attain'd.'[56] There were though dissenters from this happy picture. When Swift takes stock of the
language in his *Proposal*, for example, he finds much to arouse
his concern. The state of the language around him confirms him
in the doleful opinion that the English tongue is inherently
impolite. The problems he diagnoses have to do with corrup-
tions and affectations that have entered the language and contaminated it at two key points: first, during the Cromwellian
'usurpation', and, second, during the licentious days of the
Restoration court. For the time of greatest linguistic maturity,
we have to revert back to a time before these unhappy eruptions:
'The Period wherein the *English* Tongue received most Improvement, I take to commence with the Beginning of Queen
Elizabeth's Reign, and to conclude with the great Rebellion in
Forty-two.' Just such a position is also taken up by Johnson. In
the 'Preface' to the *Dictionary*, he commits himself to collecting
'examples and authorities' preponderantly from writers before
the Restoration, on the basis that these works will represent '*the
wells of English undefiled*'.[57]

These different narratives of linguistic maturation are, to
some extent, political. Whigs like Addison and Welsted were
aware of the political capital to be gained from discovering that
the language had just happened to flower coevally with the
accession of William of Orange; similarly, for Tories such as
Swift and Johnson, linguistic nostalgia doubled up as a covert
form of political nostalgia.[58] Yet such narratives are not accountable *purely* to politics, for instrumental in them are a
gamut of issues and quandaries to do with the nature of linguistic change. Are languages governed by a virtuous curve of continuous improvement? Will they at some point reach an apex of

---

[56] Cited from *Critical Essays of the Eighteenth Century 1700–1725*, ed. W. H.
Durham (Oxford, 1915), 358.
[57] Davis (ed.), 4: 9; *Dictionary*, 'Preface' (separately paginated), 1: 8.
[58] See *Augustan Critical Writing*, ed. David Womersley (London, 1997), 'Introduction', esp. xv–xix.

non-improvable perfection, and can their state at this point be arrested and frozen? Or do languages develop in cyclical fashion, with periods of maturation being punctured by ones of corruption and decay? Of course, such issues themselves do not stand aloof from politics, but nor are they easily reducible to simple party political affiliations.

But another issue is what actually changes in the language to bring about the rival processes of refinement or corruption. For Welsted, the matter was straightforward. Over the centuries leading up to his own time, new words had been grafted on to the tongue, drawn from the ancients but also plucked from the more recent 'Gardens of *France* and *Italy*', and through this benign process 'the most beautiful Polish is at length given to our Tongue, and its *Teutonic* Rust quite worn away'.[59] In other words, improvement in the language is proportionate to its discarding of its Saxon origins: the flourishing of both language and culture depends on a purging of the Saxon inheritance. Curiously, this view of things is shared by Swift's *Proposal*, a text in other respects at loggerheads with Welsted's. The main innovation that has led to 'the spoiling of the *English* tongue' is, in Swift's opinion, the 'barbarous Custom of abbreviating Words', which 'is nothing else but a Tendency to lapse into the Barbarity of those *Northern* nations from whom we are descended'.[60] This habit of clipping words creates a roughness in their articulation, but also increases the incidence of monosyllables, these been seen as themselves detracting from the liquidity of the tongue. When we turn to Johnson, we might expect him to concur with Swift, especially since he agrees with him about the recent deterioration of the language and about the period of its greatest refinement having been in the Elizabethan era, but in fact he is entirely of another mind. According to Johnson, what has been going wrong with the language since the Elizabethan era is that it has 'been gradually departing from its original *Teutonick* character, and deviating towards a *Gallick* structure and phraseology', a malaise from which it can only be rescued by 'making our ancient volumes the groundwork of style'.[61]

---

[59] Durham (ed.), 358.   [60] Davis (ed.), 4: 11–12.
[61] *Dictionary*, 'Preface', 1: 8.

It should be stressed how much these linguistic matters bear upon the constitution of literature and the literary canon. All participants would have acknowledged the force of two central propositions. First, that literary achievement in general is bounded by the maturity of the language in which authors find themselves having to work; and, second, that linguistic maturity is mainly (though perhaps not entirely) a matter of a 'refinement' or 'purity' that is brought about by discharging from the language elements that are perceived to be foreign to it. Once, however, there is confusion over which linguistic elements are indigenous to a language and which foreign, this inevitably frustrates any consensus over the point at which the language achieves its greatest purity, and this in its turn complicates the process of assimilating writers into a canon of literary greatness.

A work that can help us explore some of these complexities is Elizabeth Elstob's *English-Saxon Grammar* which appeared in 1715, three years after Swift's *Proposal*, and which retaliated against some of its views. In particular, she scoffs at the idea that it should not be demanded of those individuals charged with 'correcting, enlarging and ascertaining' the language that they have a secure knowledge of Anglo-Saxon; and she argues, in flat contradiction of Swift's theory, that the sort of words necessary to be inserted into the language to assist its refinement should be ones 'confessing a *Saxon* Original for their native Stock'.[62] From here she turns to the vexed issue of monosyllables. Although Swift does not explicitly complain about the high incidence of monosyllables descending from the Saxon, he does talk about harsh syllabic abbreviations, associating them with the Saxon tongue. Swift, in any event, would have been aware that from early times the Saxon language had been characterized, fairly or otherwise, as being unusually profuse with monosyllables. Richard Carew, for example, suggests that Anglo-Saxon is distinguished by many of its ideas being 'suitablye expressed by woordes of one syllable', a point also made by Puttenham: 'our naturall & primitiue language of the *Saxon English* beares not any wordes (at least very few) of moe sillables then one'.[63]

By the early eighteenth century, Elstob was aware that this perception of its monosyllabic nature was bringing the Saxon

---

[62] *Rudiments of English Grammar*, x.
[63] Smith (ed.), 2: 287; 2: 71.

language into disrepute. She accordingly sets out to defend it in two distinct ways: first by claiming that the Northern languages do neither in fact 'wholly nor mostly consist of *Monosyllables*', and second by challenging the supposition that a copiousness of monosyllables should automatically be charged as a fault. To the latter end, she puts together a curious anthology of monosyllabic lines by English poets, beginning with instances from the two great 'refining' poets Denham and Dryden, and then embarking on a chronological progress through Chaucer, Gower, Lydgate, Drayton, Spenser, Jonson, and Cowley before eventually coming up to poets of her own time such as Anne Finch and Matthew Prior.[64] In effect, what Elstob has done is spell out an Anglo-Saxon tradition of English literature. Yet in the range of her selections, and leaving aside her unusual hospitality to female authors, the canon mapped out is uncontroversial. Chaucer and Gower prove the obvious place to start, and the rest of the canon then unfolds along conventional lines. One of the authors whose use of monosyllables is documented happens to be Addison; and, interestingly, the poem to which Elstob refers is his 'Account of the Greatest English Poets', a work that itself, and in more explicit terms, recites a canon. The canon Addison enumerates, however, is one of linguistic refinement, in particular a refinement seen in terms of movement away from Anglo-Saxon roots rather than back towards them.

Far from proposing a new canon, then, Elstob reads the existing canon, or at least one version of it, against itself. For Addison, the greatest poets are those against whose achievements we can chart a continuous line of refinement in English versification as it approaches a zenith of full politeness, a politeness associated implicitly with the polysyllables of the Romance languages. Elstob demonstrates that the very same texts can support a totally different narrative: that of the unconquerable persistence of the native Saxon tongue in the specific form of the quintessentially English monosyllable. Nor can we merely record Elstob's argument as an interesting counter-position: in a real sense, she is right. The ideal of linguistic politeness was one that even the canonical poets struggled to live up to. Dryden, for example, in keeping with his usually being seen as

---

[64] See *Rudiments of English Grammar*, xi–xxix.

the poet who brings the language to a pitch of politeness, associates the 'Barbarity, or the narrowness of modern Tongues' with
the unfortunate linguistic throw-back of monosyllables. And yet
Dryden, as Eric Griffiths has brilliantly shown, is perhaps our
finest exponent of a verse-line that acquired 'strength' through
being rough-hewn straight from the Saxon. He, after all, it is
who chooses to render the first line of Virgil's *Aeneid* in monosyllables: 'Arms and the man I sing, who forc'd by Fate . . .'; and
for whom the Saxon monosyllable becomes a ubiquitous token
of linguistic and nationalistic strength: 'Strong were our Syres;
and as they Fought they Writ'.[65]

VII

Even at the same time as Hickes is promoting the Anglo-Saxon
literary heritage, a potential exists for extending the literary
historical narrative further back even than this. In less than a
hundred years from the date of Webbe's uninformed flounder-
ings, a remarkable ebullience has crept into the raiding of the
nation's literary past. Thomas Rymer's *A Short View of Tragedy*,
for instance, contains a chapter entitled 'Development of poetry
and drama in England' in which he claims that a tradition of
native poetry can be dated back as far as 'the decay of the
Roman Empire'.[66] He seizes in particular on the fact that an
early British coin, recorded in the numismatics section of
Camden's *Britannia*, bears a harp on its reverse. In Rymer's
view, this image suggests that a poetic culture must have existed
even at the time of the coin's minting. In similar vein, Joseph
Spence had it in mind to write a 'Hist[y] of Poetry for above 2000
yrs' whose point of origin would be 'Druidical Poetry': a claim
for the longevity of the literary tradition that fifty years earlier
would have seemed quite unaccountable. Increasingly, literary
historians take for granted that the mysteries of the distant past
are as much their rightful province as the nearer achievements of
the post-Chaucerian inheritance. Thus Thomas Gray proposes

[65] The line is from Dryden's 'To my Dear Friend Mr. Congreve . . .', in Kinsley
(ed.), 852. See Eric Griffiths, 'Dryden's Past', in *Proceedings of the British Academy*
84: 1993, *Lectures and Memoirs*, 115–20.
[66] Zimansky (ed.), 119.

beginning his literary history with the poetry of 'the *Galic* (or Celtic) nations, as far back as it can be traced'. And while Thomas Warton's *History of English Poetry* eventually quarries no further back than the eleventh century, at an earlier point Warton considered beginning with the Saxons—but beginning here only because 'The Poetry subsisting among the Druids [is] lost.'[67]

Notwithstanding their poetry no longer being extant, for Warton to credit the Druids with having been poets is necessarily for him to identify them as being the *earliest* British poets—in effect the founding fathers of the vernacular tradition. The supposition, fanciful as it might seem to us, was one that secured wide endorsement in the eighteenth century, so much so that it might be useful to say something about the Druids themselves and about conceptions of them prevalent in the Augustan era. Because early Celtic culture was non-literate, knowledge of the Druids has descended to us through two main sources: from classical texts that document their existence and relation to the larger Celtic community; and from archaeological evidence that has enabled the spread of Celtic culture to be charted. The Celtic world was to a remarkable degree homogeneous in terms of culture and language. It occupied much of Europe, as far east as Asia minor, and flourished from the third century BC until, and in places beyond, the incorporation of the same land mass into the Roman empire. The unit of organization of Celtic culture was the tribe, whose leader was more of the nature of a local chieftain than a monarch. The highest echelon of society seems to have been divided between combative and non-combative élites: warriors, on the one hand, and on the other a priesthood or clerisy.[68]

As regards the structure of Celtic society, and the role within it of Druids, we are heavily reliant on the classical texts of Strabo, Diodorus Siculus, Athenaeus, and Julius Caesar, writings that as well as being elliptical in nature are also in large part derivative from an even earlier, lost source: the *Histories* of Posidonius.

---

[67] Thomas Warton, 'Plan of the History of English Poetry'; cited from David Fairer, 'The Origins of Warton's *History of English Poetry*', in *Review of English Studies*, NS 32 (1981), 42.

[68] For general information on the Druids, I am indebted to Stuart Piggott, *The Druids* (London, 1968). See also T. Kendrick, *The Druids: A Study in Keltic Prehistory* (London, 1927); and A. L. Owen, *The Famous Druids* (Oxford, 1962).

For most lettered people in the eighteenth century, however, it was probably enough to be acquainted with just two sources, Caesar's *The Battle for Gaul* and the solitary reference to British Druids in Tacitus's *Annals*. Caesar's account accords to the Druids a prominent role as educators and shows them disseminating their 'doctrine' in the form of large numbers of verses that initiates had to commit to memory. Yet, on a condemnatory note, he also stresses their officiation at judicial and religious ceremonies, the latter including human sacrifices in which victims were sometimes immolated inside huge wickerwork figures; and a similar sense of the barbarism of the Druids is conveyed by Tacitus's description of them execrating the Roman soldiers passing through the Menai Straits. Indeed, the cultural reverence accorded to Druids in the eighteenth century comes about only through a process of rehabilitation, in which a blind or tolerant eye was turned to the unsavoury aspects of Druidical practices dwelt on in the classical sources. For Caesar, the privileged status enjoyed by the Druids was symptomatic of nothing so much as the inveterate savagery of early British society.[69]

It remains unclear from the classical accounts whether the Druids should be seen as a caste (in other words, set apart by birthright) or merely a set of functionaries but, in any event, their three main functions seem to have been to do with the preservation and passing down of communal lore, the administering of justice, and officiation at religious ceremonies. But a further function or propensity that became associated with them was verse-making. Some grounds for the association arise, as I have indicated, from Caesar's *Battle for Gaul*, which records how the Druids inculcated their lore through the medium of verses. This was done, however, for practical, mnemonic reasons, and Caesar offers no suggestion that the Druids wrote verses as an end in itself.[70] The equivocality of the Druids' status as poets is also evident from both Strabo and Diodorus, in whose writings they are seen as only one of three denominations of holy or learned men, these being, in loose terms, 'bards', who wrote poems of eulogy and satire; 'Druids', who were

---

[69] For Tacitus, see *Annals*, XIV. 30. For Caesar, see *Battle for Gaul*, VI. 13–16. The relevant classical sources are available in Kendrick.

[70] *Battle for Gaul*, VI. 14.

philosophers and curators of knowledge; and augurers, who interpreted sacrifices. Under this nomenclature, Druids and bards, though part of a single clerisy, form distinct categories within it.[71]

Yet from the earliest writings in English in which Druids appear, a marked feature of their representation is the tendency for the two categories of Druid and bard to be conflated. In Michael Drayton's influential *Poly-Olbion* (1622), for example, references to bards and Druids are collocated in such a way as to make ambiguous the nature of their relation. In a passage in 'The First Song', for example, Drayton petitions the ancient British bards to inspire his verse so that it might achieve a fame beyond his own death:

> Ye sacred Bards, that to your harps' melodious strings
> Sung th'ancient Heroes' deeds (the monuments of Kings)
> And in your dreadful verse ingrav'd the prophecies,
> The Agéd world's descents, and genealogies;
> If, as those *Druids* taught, which kept the British rites,
> And dwelt in darksome groves, there counselling with sprites,
>
> · · · · · · · · · · · · ·
>
> When these our souls by death our bodies do forsake,
> They instantly again do other bodies take;
> I could have wish'd your spirits redoubled in my breast,
> To give my verse applause, to time's eternal rest.[72]

Although Drayton distinguishes between the two categories, it is also the case that they rise in his mind simultaneously, as if yoked together by mental association; moreover, what the bards supposedly versify (prophecies and genealogies) is material that would have formed part of the communal lore over which the Druids supposedly exercised a curatorial role. A much more emphatic conflation of the roles of Druid and bard, however, is evident in John Milton's elegiac poem 'Lycidas' (1637). The poem's subject, Edward King, had drowned off the Irish coast, close enough to Anglesea (Mona), the legendary home of the Druids, for Milton to build an allusion to them into his lament:

---

[71] See Kendrick, *The Druids*, 82–3.
[72] Cited from *The Complete Works of Michael Drayton*, ed. Revd. Richard Hooper, 3 vols. (London, 1876), 1: 2–3.

> Where were ye nymphs when the remorseless deep
> Closed o'er the head of your loved Lycidas?
> For neither were ye playing on the steep,
> Where your old bards, the famous Druids, lie,
> Nor on the shaggy top of Mona high,
> Nor yet where Deva spreads here wizard stream...[73]

The following year, in his Latin poem to Manso, Milton trumpeted England's credentials to be considered a poetical nation by again drawing attention to the Druids, as 'an ancient race' who 'were well practised in the rituals of the gods and used to sing the praises of heroes and their exemplary exploits'.[74] Such a conflation of bard and Druid was never, it might be said, strictly warranted by the classical sources on which poets such as Milton depended for their familiarity with early British history. Yet even by the early seventeenth century that the Druids were hybridically both priests and poets was becoming a stock assumption, leading, in somewhat trite fashion, to their appearance in a choric role in works such as John Fletcher's *Bonduca* (1618) and Thomas Carew's *Coelum Britannicum* (1634), in both of which Druids parade across the stage while incanting patriotic verses. It might be noted, however, that at this time the equation of Druids with bards did not contain the logic, as it came to do in the Romantic era, that verse-making was an intrinsically priestly and prophetic activity.[75]

This conflation of Druids and bards persists in the eighteenth century. In 1741, for example, a literary historical sketch contained in John Campbell's *The Polite Correspondence* is furnished with sections devoted to the early Saxon and British traditions. In a chapter 'On the antiquity of poesy', Campbell suggests that although 'the *Druids* had the Direction of Sacred

---

[73] Cited from *The Poems of John Milton*, ed. John Carey and Alastair Fowler (London, 1968), 243–44. For a comment on Milton's introduction of Druids here, see Joseph Warton, *An Essay on the Genius and Writings of Pope* (1756, 1782); here 1806 edn., 2 vols. 1: 7: 'The mention of places remarkably romantic, the supposed habitation of Druids, bards, and wizards, is far more pleasing to the imagination, than the obvious introduction of Cam and Isis, as seats of the Muses.'

[74] Ibid. 266.

[75] See William Cowper's 'Table Talk' (1782) for how in former times 'the graceful name | Of prophet and poet was the same' and how 'ev'ry hallow'd druid was a bard', in *The Poems of William Cowper*, ed. John D. Baird and Charles Ryskamp, 3 vols. (Oxford, 1980–95), 1: 254.

and Civil Affairs', in reality they 'were no other than Poets'.[76]
One of the most influential peddlers of such arcane imaginings
was the deist John Toland. In 1726, a posthumous collection of
his unpublished pieces appeared, incorporating *A Specimen of
the Critical History of the Celtic Religion and Learning, Containing an Account of the Druids*, a work that was reissued in a
separate volume in 1740. Toland, it might be noted, hailed from
near Londonderry in northern Ireland and was a voluble apolo-
gist for Celtic culture. Discussion of the Druids is largely confined to an appendix, entitled 'Mr. Tate's Questions about the
Druids and other Brittish Antiquities, with Mr. Jones's Answer
to Them'. The fourth answer distinguishes between three sorts
of Druidical bard: the *priveirdd, posweirdd*, and *arwyddveird*.
The former were inventors and teachers of philosophy; the
posweirdd were employed to disseminate the teaching of the
priveirdd; and the *arwyddveird* had a ceremonial function as
heralds and public genealogists.[77] In a similar vein, when Joseph
Spence touches on the Druids in his 'Quelques Remarques',
he also deliberates over the exact nature of their poetic function.
One of his principal sources hereabouts is Paul de Rapin Thoyras's *Histoire d'Angleterre* (1724); Spence footnotes Thoyras's
belief that the Druidical bards were wont to compose verses
celebrating the deeds of warrior heroes. Spence, himself, however, sticks close to the Caesarean account in which the use of
poetry figures as part of the Druids' larger pedagogic role, poetry
being the medium of instruction because of being easier than
prose to commit to memory.

These recondite wranglings over the exact role played by
poets in Druidical culture, however, matter less than that once
the Druids were construed as bards another proposition inevitably followed: that they must be the earliest poets to have
inhabited the British Isles—that they must, in effect, be the
originary figures of both the British and English poetic traditions. The Druidical origin of native poetry, in fact, becomes a
frequent assumption made by early literary historical writers. In
1711, for example, in Elijah Fenton's verse-epistle to the dramatist Thomas Southerne, poetry is shown migrating from the

[76] *Polite Correspondence*, 247.
[77] John Toland, *A Collection of Several Pieces*, 2 vols. (1726), 1: 184–203.

Greek to the Roman and thence to the British, her first residence here being among the Druids:

> Long in the melancholy grove she staid,
> And taught the pensive Druids in the shade;
> In solemn and instructive notes they sung
> From whence the beauteous frame of nature sprung,
> Who polish'd all the radiant orbs above,
> And in bright order made the planets move;
> Whence thunders roar, and frightful meteors fly,
> And comets roll unbounded through the sky;
> Who wing'd the winds, and gave the streams to flow,
> And rais'd the rocks, and spread the lawns below;
> Whence the gay spring exults in flowery pride,
> And autumn with the bleeding grape is dy'd;
> Whence summer suns imbrown the labouring swains,
> And shivering winter pines in icy chains:
> And prais'd the Power Supreme, nor dar'd advance
> So vain a theory as that of chance.[78]

Although progress-of-poesy poems are relatively common in the eighteenth century, this is the sole one with which I am familiar where the Druids are proposed as the earliest bearers of the British poetic flame: most often the first recipient is Chaucer or Shakespeare. Yet the Druids were particularly apt for Fenton's purposes since his poem is concerned to argue a close link between the flourishing of poetry and the waxing of political freedom, the successive migrations of poetry always enacting a flight from tyranny to liberty. Thus in their mythic role as opponents of Roman oppression, the Druids were well-suited to be considered as the first custodians of English verse. As regards the *sort* of poetry practised amongst them, Fenton falls in with the Caesarean account in the *Battle for Gaul*. The Druids' poetic notes are 'solemn and instructive', which suggests that their verse-making was confined to the dissemination of lore.

The enshrinement of the Druids as the founders of the native literary tradition is completed by the middle of the eighteenth century. In John Brown's *History of the Rise and Progress of Poetry* (1764), for example, the earliest native authors are given as the ancient '*British Bards*' who, while not technically Druids as such, are described as composing a lower order in a larger

---

[78] Anderson (ed.), 7: 661.

clerisy of which the Druids formed a part.[79] Similarly, as was noted earlier, Thomas Gray, in his jotted draft-plan for a history of English poetry, proposes beginning with 'the poetry of the *Galic* (or Celtic) nations, as far back as it can be traced'.[80] Such a project would also inevitably have involved discussion of the Druids, notes on whom (mainly deriving from Caesar and Strabo) can be found in his *Common-Place Book*.[81]

Although the draft-plan of Gray's envisaged history remains undatable, his research into early British literature had certainly been long set aside when, in a letter to Thomas Warton on 15 April 1770, he enclosed his plan in the hope that it might be of use for Warton's own research on the same subject. In fact, the document was too fragmentary, and was communicated to Warton too late, for it to have had any influence on the latter's *History of English Poetry*, which eventually came out in three volumes between 1774 and 1781. Surviving notebooks of Warton's confirm that early in his envisagement of the project, he had intended, like Gray, to incorporate treatment of the Druids. In one of these he penned a thumb-nail 'Plan of the History of English Poetry', in which the first of a sequence of numbered paragraphs, presumably corresponding to intended chapters, runs as follows:

1. The Poetry subsisting among the Druids lost: The Saxon's introduc'd it, of whom Hickes produces many Hymns: The old British Bards not yet lost: Robert of Glocester's Cronicle the Remain of them.[82]

A separate notebook contains successive drafts of 'part of a formal letter on the subject of English language and literature before the Norman Conquest', which again contains the near statutory reference to the Druids:

It was the office of the Bards, among the ancient Britons, to sing to the Harp the Atchievements of great Men in Metre. This Institution of Men was undoubtedly dissolv'd at the Roman Invasion, as was that likewise of the Druids, Prophets, & Priests who together with the Bards were highly esteem'd, when our Island was in Possession of its original Inhabitants.[83]

[79] John Brown, *The History of the Rise and Progress of Poetry* (1764), 200–1.
[80] Gray to Thomas Warton, April 15 1770, in *Correspondence*, 3: 1123.
[81] *Common-Place Book*, 1: 310.
[82] Cited from Fairer, 'The Origins of Warton's *History of English Poetry*', 42.
[83] Ibid. 52.

What Warton might have said about the Druids, had he not retrenched the project, remains, of course, irrecuperable, but it is hard to imagine how there would have been much scope for expansion beyond the ephemeral remarks of the notebooks. The two passages quoted even show a degree of wavering over whether the Druids, strictly so called, *were* indeed poets. The latter passage, for example, keeps separate the categories of bard and Druid, and even to say, as in the first passage, that poetry 'subsists' among the Druids is to stop short of saying that the Druids were actually poets.

The commonplace that the Druids (or the British bards) were the originators of the English poetic tradition vied perhaps only with the equal one that none of their compositions remained extant.[84] So that when Warton writes 'The Poetry subsisting among the Druids lost', this could be read equally as an indication of what he was intending his book would include or what it would necessarily have had to exclude, given the lack of available sources. Perhaps of even greater consequence was that, in spite of the hallowed status of Druidical poetry, no scholar could point with assurance to a single exponent, let alone come to a conclusion as to the worth of the poetry that the Druids had produced. It is true that John Toland's 'Account of the Druids' (1726) enlists Merlin Silvester, Merlin Ambrosius, and Taliessin as Druidical bards, but claims of this sort are in reality little more than a concoction of myth and anachronism.[85] What alone could be done with probity was to surmise that 'Druidical compositions' might have been known to poets of a later era, so that, as Thomas Gray suggests, the poems of the Druids could have 'served for a Model to Taliessin, Lhywarch, & others of the most ancient & best of ye British Poets'.[86]

Of course, the reason for the anonymity of the Druidical tradition owed less to the scattering or perishing of written sources than that such sources had probably never existed; Celtic culture was pre-literate, and its verse culture described

---

[84] See Jonathan Swift's fragment, 'An Abstract of the History of England': 'Their [the early Britons'] priests were called Druids: These lived in hollow trees, and committed not their mysteries to writing, but delivered them down by tradition, whereby they were in time wholly lost.' Davis (ed.), 5: 3.

[85] Toland, *A Collection of Several Pieces*, 1: 191.

[86] *Common-Place Book*, 2: 799.

by Caesar is an entirely oral one.[87] The literary historical research of the likes of Gray and Warton, in other words, was an attempt to place on historical record the cultural achievements of a prehistoric society. The very idea of Druidical poetry was (to introduce a modern parlance) an absence that, at the same time, constituted a presence: the lack of any evidence for a Druidical poetic culture doubled up as perhaps the single circumstance most authenticating of its having existed. Indeed, the Druids in the eighteenth century, most notoriously in the case of the antiquarian William Stukeley, come to be a *tabula rasa* on to which Druidicists could map any or all of the whimsies (and perhaps tomfooleries) of their own imaginations.[88]

VIII

The attempt to construct a native literary history extending back to the Druids would seem more like a work of myth than of history were it not that these two categories were not in the eighteenth century and earlier so firmly differentiated as is the case nowadays. This was mainly because the distinction, standard to the present-day practice of history, between original and derivative sources, the former being eyewitness statements contemporary with historical events, the latter the narratives or interpretations of events put together by people not actually witness to them, was applied only irregularly.[89] Most historical writing founded itself on earlier historical narratives, remaining aloof from original sources; and even the *relevance* of historical remains to the construction of the past was far from universally understood.[90] Yet even if this distinction between history and myth is an unsure one, it can still be said that the mapping of a

---

[87] *Battle for Gaul*, VI. 14.

[88] Stuart Piggott, *William Stukeley: An Eighteenth-Century Antiquary* (London, 1950; rev. and enlarged 1985).

[89] This distinction is stated concisely by the Italian historian Arnaldo Momigliano in a passage cited in John Kenyon, *The History Men: The Historical Profession in England since the Renaissance* (London, 1983), 7.

[90] See Joseph M. Levine, *Humanism and History: Origins of Modern English Historiography* (Ithaca, NY, 1987), esp. ch. 3, 'The Antiquarian Enterprise, 1500–1800'.

primitive literary heritage in which the Druids were the earliest begetters had no foundation in historical fact.

If the paucity of sources surrounding the Druids necessarily entailed that discussion of them compose a heady brew of supposition and myth, then the same applies to Augustan acquaintance with non-Druidical early British poetry. As I have said, the Druids were unable to provide the tradition with actual named poets, the two earliest such figures to be assimilated to a 'long' version of literary tradition being the sixth century Welsh poets, Taliessin and Merlin. Taliessin was almost certainly a real person despite the fact that the *Book of Taliessin* has descended to us in a manuscript dating only so far back as the tenth century. The figure of Merlin, on the other hand, is more appropriately assigned to legend. In one manifestation he was a wizard bard on whom various poetical works were subsequently (and spuriously) fathered; in another, largely through the whimsical offices of Geoffrey of Monmouth, he became a character in Arthurian romance.

From the end of the seventeenth century, Taliessin and Merlin become stock figures in antiquarian versions of the literary past. In 1692, for instance, Thomas Rymer draws attention to them, adding the equivocal comment that 'had they not written in Welch, [they] might yet deserve an esteem among us'. Rymer's information may have come from Pierre Daniel Huet's *Traité de l'Origine des Romans* (1671), rendered into English the following year.[91] This in any event is the source used by Joseph Spence in the ritual acknowledgement of the two poets in his 'Quelques Remarques'. It was because Taliessin's writings remained extant, albeit in fragmentary form, that they proved susceptible to being dragged into debates, beginning to animate scholars, to do with the merits of primitive and modern literary culture. During the mid-eighteenth century, moreover, these debates began to occupy a central place in the formation of the literary heritage.

---

[91] Zimansky (ed.), 119. See *A Treatise of Romances and their Originals. By Monsieur Huet. Translated out of French* (1672), 75: '*Taliessin* who is said to have lived about the middle of the sixth Age, under that King *Arthur* so famous in Romances; and *Melkin* [Merlin] who was somewhat younger, writ the History of *England*, their *Countrey*, of King *Arthur*, and of the round Table'.

The eighteenth century witnesses a vogue for (what we might call) poetic anthropology, for speculation about how the phenomenon of poetry might have come about as part of the rituals and practices of primitive societies. Sir William Temple's essay 'Of Poetry' (1690) provides an early example of this sort of musing. He invokes as a truism that poetry has been 'the first sort of Writing that has been used in the World', and then describes its earliest flourishing among several cultures. He wrangles over whether Job or Moses should count as the earliest Hebrew poet, names Orpheus, Linus, and Musaeus as the originary figures of the Greek poetic tradition, and identifies the Runic poetry of the Goths as the origin of a poetic tradition in England.[92] In its reflection on early poetry, Temple's essay is pioneering, and presages a more thoroughgoing interest in poetic primitivism burgeoning in the mid-eighteenth century. Typical of this is Tobias Smollett's essay on the 'Origin of Poetry', appearing in the *British Magazine* (1763). With all the aplomb and certainty of the lettered gentleman ensconced in his study, Smollett uncovers the origins of poetry in the emotions felt by the 'unlettered mind' at the great 'phaenomena' of nature. The passions of 'surprise or gratitude, terror or exultation' stirred up by the rising sun, the night firmament and so on 'must', so Smollett avers, 'have produced expressions of wonder and adoration', these being formulated along the lines of a Shaftesburian rhapsody: 'O glorious luminary! great eye of the world! source of that light which guides my steps!' And, in time, these spontaneous eruptions of religious sentiment will become assimilated into formal patterns of worship.[93]

While Smollett assumes poetry's origin to be in religious experience, John Brown, in his *History of the Rise and Progress of Poetry*, sees it as arising from the mere compulsion to vent 'agreeable' or disagreeable passions: those of love, pity, hope, joy, and exultation, on the one hand, and hate, revenge, fear, sorrow, and despair on the other. The lowest scale of savages can render these emotions only as howls and gabblings, but those of slightly higher ascent, possessed of the principle of order and proportion, become capable of turning their speech into metrical

[92] Spingarn (ed.), 3: 85–6.   [93] *Works of Oliver Goldsmith*, 342.

poetry.[94] Such a belief in the primitive origins of poetry was closely linked to an acceptance, on the part of some, of the non-rational basis of 'taste' or aesthetic appreciation. It was possible for primitive people to compose verses, and therefore to internalize the principle of harmony, because aesthetic qualities like harmony (so it was maintained) made themselves available to the senses rather than to the reason, the state of primitivism being defined above all else by its non-rationality.[95]

This recognition (or 'invention') of primitive poetry inevitably led to comparisons being made between the literary works produced by such societies and those belonging to more developed cultures. The issue is really a specialized version of a more general one that exercised the Augustans and that can be posed thus: at what chronological point in history did the human state most tend to excellence? And might it be that certain excellences are conferred on cultures simply by dint of their flourishing at particular points on the curve of human temporal existence?[96] This is, of course, ground over which the Battle of the Ancients and the Moderns was fought, an important element in the dispute being not just whether classical works were in a discernible way better than those of the moderns, but whether they *had to be* better since temporal priority necessarily conduced to a larger cultural superiority. When this matter was applied more narrowly to poetry, it tended to be filtered through some heavy stereotyping. Primitive poetry was thought of as passionate and 'naive', and as emanating with a high degree of immediacy from contact with the natural world: it arises from 'the effusion of a glowing fancy and an impassioned heart', as William Duff puts it; modern poetry, on the other hand, was seen as informed by craft and technique, by the need to imitate and emulate illustrious models, and, some people increasingly came to think, by the distortive

---

[94] See Brown's discussion 'Of Melody, Dance, and Poem, in the savage State', in *History of the Rise and Progress of Poetry*, 11–12.

[95] See Lois Whitney, 'English Primitivistic Theories of Epic Origins', in *Modern Philology*, 21 (1924): esp. 355–8; and id., *Primitivism and the Idea of Progress in English Popular Literature of the Eighteenth Century* (Baltimore, 1934), esp. 92–3.

[96] Of relevance here is the section on 'Chronological Primitivism', in Arthur O. Lovejoy and George Boas, *Primitivism and Related Ideas in Antiquity* (Baltimore, 1935), 1–7.

necessity of anticipating the reactions of critics.[97] The upshot is that primitive poetry triumphs in naturalness but loses in polish: as Johnson's Imlac says in *Rasselas*, the 'early writers are in possession of nature, and their followers of art . . . the first excel in strength and invention, and the latter in elegance and refinement'.[98]

Which of the two states and two aesthetics might be seen as superior was a matter on which no consensus was ever, nor was ever likely to be, achieved. One school of thought insisted that improvement in the arts was progressive, with whatever came late enjoying a distinct advantage over what had gone earlier. That this doctrine could foster smugness and self-satisfaction was realized by Swift in his *A Tale of a Tub*:

> But I here think fit to lay hold on that great and honourable Privilege of being the *Last Writer*; I claim an absolute Authority in Right, as the *freshest Modern*, which gives me a Despotick Power over all Authors before me.[99]

But this was not the only opinion on offer. Even where it was accepted that the primitive state could be improved on, many still felt that such improvement was likely to prove finite, at some point giving way to a decline into corruption or decadence. As Alexander Gerard, for example, says in his *Essay on Taste*: 'When poetry and eloquence are brought to perfection, the next generation, desiring to excel their predecessors, and unable to reach their end by keeping in the road of truth and nature, are tempted to turn aside into unbeaten tracks of nicety and affectation.'[100] This view that a period of gradual cultural improvement would eventually give way to degeneration was quite widespread, endorsed for example by Johnson in *Idler* 63; but a more radical variant was one in which the apogee of cultural perfection, the point after which decline would set in, belonged to the primitive state itself: poetry actually began at its peak.

---

[97] William Duff, *An Essay on Original Genius* (1767), ed. John Valdimir Price (Routledge/Thoemmes Press, 1994), 270.
[98] Samuel Johnson, *The History of Rasselas, Prince of Abyssinia*, in *Yale*, 16, ed. Gwin J. Kolb (1990), 40.
[99] Davis (ed.), 1: 81.
[100] Alexander Gerard, *An Essay on Taste* (1759), 130. See John D. Scheffer, 'The Idea of Decline in Literature and the Fine Arts in Eighteenth-Century England', in *Modern Philology*, 34 (1936), 155–78.

When, for example, William Collins notes in his 'Epistle to Thomas Hanmer' that the Muse 'graced with noblest pomp her earliest stage' (i.e. Greece), he is putting forward this conventional viewpoint: poetry, so Collins surmises, is not a progressive discipline but rather one that comes into the world already in a state of perfect formation.[101]

An early pioneer of the vogue for literary primitivism is the little known figure John Husbands. Husbands's only feat of note is in 1731 to have collected together a miscellany volume and to have prefaced it with an essay on 'primitive' or natural poetry. For Husbands, the 'primitive' is defined by two criteria: temporal priority and aesthetic naivety; its products belong to an unpolished or 'natural' condition. Husbands's importance here is that he is probably the first critic to apply emerging ideas about primitive cultures to early Britain, and moreover to invoke the 'first equals best' principle so as to confer on primitive British poetry the same ascendancy over modern writing as that more often yielded to classical works. Under his scheme, the classical and the primitive make common cause in alike asserting their temporal priority over the modern. Essentially, Husbands's 'Preface' is an exercise in poetic anthropology based on the premise that verse-making has been indigenous to all eras and climes: 'We may truly say it is the universal language of men.'[102] Having detailed the penetration of poetry within classical cultures, Husbands turns to its centrality in a variety of primitive ones:

But poetry was not confined only to the politer nations. We may find some remains of it among the most uncultivated people and trace its footsteps even beneath the pole. The frozen Laplander is susceptible of this fire, as well as the sunburnt American. Witness those beautiful odes preserved by Scheffer, and those noble strains of poetry which the learned Olaus Wormius has given us in his runic antiquities. The respect and distinction which their runes or scaldri met with was very extraordinary. And is it really surprising to find among those nations that are accounted barbarous poems that may vie with any of the

---

[101] The most complete recent treatment of these general ideas is David Spadafora, *The Idea of Progress in Eighteenth-Century Britain* (New Haven, 1990).

[102] John Husbands, 'Preface' to *Miscellany of Poems* (1731), in *Eighteenth-Century Critical Essays*, ed. Scott Elledge, 2 vols. (Ithaca, NY, 1961), 1: 419. See Ronald S. Crane, 'An Early Eighteenth-Century Enthusiast for Primitive Poetry: John Husbands', *Modern Language Notes*, 37 (1922), 27–36.

performances of Greece or Rome? Scallagrim's ode is very much in the spirit of Pindar, and comes up to almost anything we find in him. And I have been told by a gentleman of a very good taste, who understands that tongue, that the Welsh odes of Taliesin are equal to anything in antiquity. It is indeed very certain that the ancient Britains gave great encouragement to the Muses.[103]

That poetry occupied an important place in the cultures of the Laplanders and the South American Indians was appreciated more widely; Thomas Gray's slightly later 'Progress of Poesy', for example, describes the earliest abodes of poetry as 'Where shaggy forms o'er ice-built mountains roam' and 'beneath the odorous shade | Of Chile's boundless forests'.

The productions of primitive cultures, including the odes of the early British poet Taliessin, exemplify what Husbands refers to as 'natural poetry'. Such poetry is distinguished by an immediate 'imitation and illustration of things by words', and by being 'lively and affecting' with metaphors varied 'according to the greatness, nature, and quality of the subject'. These attributes, so Husbands claims, are likely to be lost as a poetic culture develops, such development being likely to lead to a specious refinement as poetry becomes encumbered with artificial precepts and conventions. These arguments on behalf of primitive poetry have behind them an ulterior motive, which is to ground a claim for the supposed merit of biblical poetry. But this should not distract from the fact that the claims Husbands makes for primitive poetry in general are startling in their magnitude. He suggests, for instance, that many supposedly barbarous nations have spawned poetic cultures equal to those of Greece and Rome, and that the Welsh odes of Taliessin 'are equal to anything in antiquity'.[104]

Some of the ideas propounded by Husbands were taken up ten years later in the literary historical parts of John Campbell's *The Polite Correspondence*. Letter II of Book IV, 'On the Antiquity of Poetry', written by Leander to Celadon, reasserts the claim for the intrinsic superiority of early poetry: as 'the earliest Science, [it] came soonest to Perfection'.[105] As it did for Husbands,

---

[103] Elledge (ed.), *Eighteenth-Century Critical Essays*, 1: 419–20.
[104] Ibid. 1: 420.
[105] *Polite Correspondence*, 246. The work is discussed in Alan Dugald McKillop, 'A Critic of 1741 on Early Poetry', *Studies in Philology*, 30 (1933), 504–21.

this sentiment ramifies beyond simply the classical cultures and into an application to ancient British literature:

That I may deal no longer in Conjecture, I shall proceed next to inform you, that altho' the Songs of the ancient Druids have been swallow'd up in Oblivion, yet there are still some Remains of *British* Poetry twelve hundred Years old, I mean the Works of Taliesin a *British* Bard, Cotemporary with *Gildas* the Historian; he wrote Odes in various kinds of Verse, not only with great Vivacity and Sentiment, but also with wonderful Regularity, Elegance and Harmony. I do not deliver this upon hear-say, but from my having studied several of his Pieces with great Care; I will give you the Beginning of one, on the Victory gain'd by King *Arthur on Badon-Hill*, in which I have strictly imitated his Measure and manner of Writing.

I

At *Badon* Hill, at *Badon* Hill,
The cruel *Saxons* had their fill
Of Blood, which oft they shed.
The vengeful *Britons*, Thousands slew,
For Thousands came, and but a few,
From the tir'd Victors fled.

II

The *British* Earth drank up their Gore,
And gaping, seem'd athirst for more,
As conscious of the Wrongs,
The num'rous Frauds, and artful Lies,
Deceitful Leagues, and Perjuries,
By which they spoil'd her Sons.

III

All-powerful *Arthur* now pursues,
With eager Haste his hated Foes,
And longs to see his Isle,
Free from this base and barb'rous Race,
Resuming all her wonted Grace,
In Peace and Plenty smile.[106]

Campbell's lines are an expansion of a fragment given in Welsh and Latin, printed in Sir John Price's *Historiae Brytannicae Defensio* (1573) and attributed there to Taliessin. Like Hus-

[106] *Polite Correspondence*, 255.

bands, Campbell invokes the criterion of temporal priority as a means of setting early British poetry on the same footing as that of the classical era and arguing for its possession of cognate artistic principles. The upshot is that he can make such a claim as that Taliessin's odes are no less than '*Pindaricks in Welch*'.[107] Pindar, as well as being noted for his metrical irregularity (or just versatility), was also caricatured in the eighteenth century as the most impassioned and bardic of classical poets, and so was obviously ripe for cross-cultural parallels with primitive poets of the British tradition.

The writings of Husbands and Campbell are, at root, an exercise in cultural nationalism: they demonstrate that British literature, rather than being a thin cultural peninsula jutting out from the classical world, constitutes a territory in its own right: it has its own 'republic of letters'. To say so much *does* reflect an erosion of the status of the classics: it discountenances the notion that for Britain to have a lettered culture, this has necessarily to conform to the template of classical culture. Yet, paradoxically, in claiming that what came earlier was likely to be better, critics such as Husbands and Campbell were actually endorsing one of the arguments that had been used on the ancients' side in the battle against the moderns. If Homer was better than the moderns because he was earlier than them, why should not Caedmon and Taliessin be better for the very same reason? There is, however, one further dimension to this issue. Provenance and morphology are always intertwined: to predicate different beginnings for British poetry is to make British poetry a different thing. It has to be something other than the polite neoclassical confection that writers like Pope had assumed it was, or assumed it could be in its state of most perfect realization. But what is it, then? The resolution of this question is something that I will attempt in Chapter 9.

[107] Ibid. 276.

5

Dryden and the Idea of a Literary Tradition

I

There seems to be no precedent in literary studies for the word 'tradition' being treated with the exactitude with which it is often treated by historians, anthropologists, and students of folk-literature. Even F. R. Leavis's *The Great Tradition* (1948), which one would have thought had much to gain from a translucent definition of its central term, offers little analysis of what is entailed by belonging to a tradition. For the most part, Leavis's notion of tradition takes shape only through scattered remarks on influence and sameness-in-difference: George Eliot learns from Jane Austen; Henry James's *The Portrait of a Lady* re-enacts *Daniel Deronda*; and Conrad is related to Dickens through a shared 'energy of vision'.[1] The only occasion on which he propounds something like a *theory* of tradition is his discussion of Jane Austen's relation to those earlier novelists, chiefly Richardson and Burney, whose works were formative for her own. Glancing back at T. S. Eliot's influential essay 'Tradition and the Individual Talent' (1919), Leavis sees Austen as epitomizing the way that great authors create the antecedent tradition out of which their own writings arise.[2] Tradition, in this account, is retroactive. A great *oeuvre* assimilates, and brings to summation, the body of writings that has preceded it and thus imposes a principle of coherence on the unruliness of the past.

The word 'tradition', as defined by the *OED*, embraces two large meaning clumps. Senses 1 to 4 all relate to 'tradition' as a process: namely as a delivery, handing over or handing down of some legal deed, piece of instruction, set of beliefs, rules, or

---

[1] F. R. Leavis, *The Great Tradition* (London, 1948), 10, 15, 19.
[2] *Great Tradition*, 5.

customs from one generation to the next. One illustration given is from Defoe's *New Voyage round the World* (1725): 'Rivetted in their minds by tradition from father to son.' Senses 5 to 6 meanwhile comprise *objective* versions of the word: 5a relates to 'That which is ... handed down; a statement, belief, or practice transmitted from generation to generation'; and 5b specifies 'any branch or school of art or literature, handed down by predecessors and generally followed'. The origins of both these meaning clumps extend back at least as far as the sixteenth century, and the basic dichotomy occurs in Johnson's *Dictionary* (1755), in which sense 1 concerns the transmission of material 'from age to age', and sense 2 any material being so transmitted.[3] The use of the word 'tradition' in connection with literature comes relatively late, so that none of Johnson's illustrations, for example, concern this specific application. Yet the root perception that writers of later times are the heirs and legatees of those of earlier ones is virtually as old as English literature itself. Probably the first major English author to draw strength from the precedent of an earlier vernacular figure is Lydgate; and his capitalization on the example of his master, Chaucer, could be taken as the starting-point of a principle of tradition operative in English literature.[4]

Traditions are generally understood as events or forms of behaviour that are customary, routine-governed, or that fulfil a commemorative function, the observation of traditions testifying to a communal commitment to honour the past and to be bound by its precedents. The way that a tradition hallows the past is through repetition, so the formula adopted, say, for the state opening of parliament needs to remain invariable if the tradition is to be upheld. But a common factor in traditions is that just as much as entailing remembrance, they often entail an effacement or an act of amnesia. Even though many traditions exist to commemorate past occurrences, it is not unusual for their precise commemorative nature to be forgotten, so that they end up being cherished more on the strength of their own longevity than for the historical event they mark. This scenario

---

[3] See Edward Shils, *Tradition* (Chicago, 1981); and 'Tradition' in Williams, *Keywords*.
[4] For Lydgate's response to Chaucer, see *Chaucer: The Critical Heritage*, ed. Derek Brewer, 2 vols. (London, 1978), 1: 44–59.

holds true, for example, for the adoption in Scotland of the kilt as an item of patriotic and traditional apparel. The wearing of tartan kilts became a fetish among eighteenth-century Scottish gentlemen as a sentimental revival of the dress habits of an earlier Highland peasantry. Around the same time, particular tartan designs were claimed by the different Scottish clans, and the kilt became adopted for ceremonial contexts as distinct from its originally utilitarian function. However, despite kilt-wearing acquiring these new overtones, those who wore them still did so to commemorate the lost Highland peasant culture that first introduced it to Scotland. In our own day, though, this commemorative origin has all but been forgotten, and those who sport kilts do so merely to sustain a tradition of ceremonial dressing stretching back only so far as the eighteenth century.[5]

The phenomenon of the literary tradition, of course, works differently from the sort of traditions I have been describing. Literature is not a nexus of formulaic observances, nor do literary works as a general rule serve to commemorate, though they may witness to, particular historical occurrences. Yet salient points of correspondence still do exist. In the eighteenth century, literature was looked upon as a cultural baton, received from the past and handed on to the future; it was believed to involve acts of formulaic repetition, especially in the somewhat quirkish notion that later writers mirror or even re-enact the achievements of earlier ones; and the birth-point of the English literary tradition, like that of all traditions, can be fixed as when it forgets to commemorate that which has preceded it (namely the classical literary inheritance) and instead starts commemorating itself and its own strength and longevity. The perception of literature as a tradition, as something other and more than simply a concatenation of authors, long predates the English Augustan era. Yet it was in the Augustan period, especially in the person of Dryden, that some of the complexities of literature's being a tradition are first explored. These complexities are mainly metaphoric. In the present chapter, I discuss two related conceits that express how literature is passed down between generations. In the first, tradition is viewed as a process

[5] See Hugh Trevor-Roper, 'The Invention of Tradition: The Highland Tradition of Scotland', in *The Invention of Tradition*, ed. Eric Hobsbawm and Terence Ranger (New York, 1983), 15–41.

of filiation: a great writer of an earlier time, so the conceit goes, stands to one of a later era as a father to his son, and a great work of a previous age can be seen as a sort of familial heirloom passed down from one generation to the next. In the second, the later writer is linked to the former not through figurative parentage but through the Pythagorean transmigration of souls. My argument is that the currency of these strong figures was consistent with literature's for the first time being widely viewed as a *tradition*.

II

Specifically as regards English literature, an influential metaphor has long been one in which the unfolding of tradition is figured as a paternal-filial nexus: the earlier writer uses his influence, as it were, to sire the later one. While this conceit is fairly ubiquitous, it may have sprung originally from a very specific acknowledgement of Chaucer's being the 'founding father' of English literature, so occupying a role relative to the vernacular tradition analogous to that of Homer and Virgil (or Ennius) relative to the classical ones. George Puttenham's *Arte of English Poesie* (1582), for example, refers to Chaucer as the 'father of our English Poets'; Henry Peachum's *The Compleat Gentleman* (1622) says that amongst English poets we should 'esteeme Sir *Geoffry Chaucer* the father'; Dryden calls him 'father of English poetry'; and Samuel Croxall's *The Vision* (1715) addresses him as 'Rev'rend Sire' and 'Parent of *Britannic* Lays'.[6] As the author who was seen as exercising chronological priority over all others in the vernacular tradition, Chaucer's case was naturally unique; but it nonetheless helped to ground a more general analogy between creative influence and paternal authority. This metaphor was given a marked injection of hype in the early seventeenth century as a result of a group of young writers dancing attendance on Ben Jonson, including the likes of Thomas Randolph, Richard Brome, and Nathan Field, who styled themselves 'Sons of Ben'. Jonson's 'sons', moreover, could be fussily

---

[6] *Arte of English Poesie*, cited from Smith (ed.), 2: 17; *The Compleat Gentleman*, cited from Spingarn (ed.), 1: 132; *Of Dramatic Poesy*, 2: 280; *The Vision A Poem. By Mr. Croxall* (1715), 15.

literal-minded in thinking through the ramifications of their elective sonship. So Thomas Randolph marked his receipt of the honour, conferred in about 1630, by composing 'A Gratulatory to Mr. Ben Jonson for his Adopting of Him to Be His Son', a poem in which he enumerates the uncles (as Homer, Ovid, Virgil) and grandparents (as the god Phoebus Apollo) whom he has acquired through his filiation to Jonson. This dogged plying of the conceit would suggest that for Randolph filiation meant something cherished and literal, not merely a vague sort of discipleship.

The conceit of literary paternity has become a standard way of imagining the relations of influence and emulation obtaining between writers in the literary tradition. So much has this been so that, in later times, the desideration of an independent female tradition has sometimes adopted the same accents, with regret being expressed specifically at the absence of literary mothers and grandmothers. In 1845, for instance, Elizabeth Barrett Browning complains that 'I look everywhere for grandmothers and see none'; and in *A Room of One's Own* (1929), Virginia Woolf remarks on the difficulty faced by the nineteenth-century women novelists in writing in the absence of an established female tradition: 'For we think back through our mothers if we are women.'[7] Yet if the parental metaphor traverses periods, and speaks alike of male and female creativity, its popularity may still owe much to the particular use made of it by one writer alone: Dryden.

Dryden, as Christopher Ricks has pointed out, is 'preeminently the critic who conceives of poetic creation and influence as paternal'.[8] Not surprisingly his use of the conceit is uniquely prolific:

Shakespeare was the Homer, or father of our dramatic poets

I had often read with pleasure...those two fathers of our English poetry [Waller and Denham]

---

[7] Letter of 1862, in *The Letters of Elizabeth Barrett Browning*, ed. Frederick G. Kenyon, 2 vols. (in one) (New York, 1899), 1: 232; Virginia Woolf, *A Room of One's Own* (London, 1946), 114.

[8] Christopher Ricks, 'Allusion: The Poet as Heir', in *Studies in the Eighteenth Century III*, ed. R. F. Brissenden and J. C. Eade (Canberra, 1976), 214. I am heavily indebted to Ricks's essay throughout this section.

as he [Chaucer] is the father of English poetry, so I hold him in the same degree of veneration as the Grecians held Homer, or the Romans Virgil

Milton was the poetical son of Spenser, and Mr Waller of Fairfax; for we have our lineal descents and clans as well as other families...[9]

In Dryden's hands, the paternal metaphor escalates into the key paradigm of a theory of literary tradition. One reason for its ascendancy, evident from the illustrations above, is that the conceit allowed for the drawing of easy parallels between classical and vernacular authors. It was widely premised, indeed, that vernacular authors would reproduce the exact same set of interpersonal functions as those attributed to classical ones, so to perceive that Greek literature had a father-figure or fountain-head, a role invariably associated with Homer, was to make it necessary that the same function be performed (usually by Chaucer) in the vernacular canon.

There may have been reasons close to home why Dryden should have been wise to the patrilineal implications of tradition. For one thing, he is one of the few major English poets to have produced sons who also became, if only after a manner, poets. Both were involved in the collaborative edition of Juvenal headed by Dryden himself, Juvenal's 'Satyr' VII being translated by Charles Dryden and XIV by John Dryden Jr. This familial involvement was signal enough for Peter Motteux to have recorded in his journal for February 1692 that

Poetry is it seems hereditary in his Family, for each of his Sons have done one Satyr of *Juvenal*, which, with so extraordinary a Tutor as their Father, cannot but be very acceptable to the world.[10]

But poetry was not exactly hereditary in the family, for the 'son' of Dryden's who stood in direct line of artistic inheritance from him was neither of his biological progeny but an extra-familial son: William Congreve. In his poem 'To my Dear Friend Mr Congreve', Dryden nominates the younger man as his rightful creative legatee. Recalling his removal from the laureateship in 1688, an ignominy made all the worse by its then being conferred on Thomas Shadwell, Dryden expresses regret that the laurel could not have devolved patrilineally to Congreve:

[9] 'Of Dramatic Poesy', in *Of Dramatic Poesy*, 1: 70; 'Discourse Concerning Satire', 2: 150; 'Preface to *Fables*', 2: 280; ibid. 2: 270.
[10] Cited from Ricks, 'Allusion', 225.

> Oh that your Brows my Lawrel had sustain'd,
> Well had I been Depos'd, if You had reign'd!
> The Father had descended for the Son;
> For only You are lineal to the Throne.[11]

Within a year of the performance of Congreve's *The Double Dealer*, in connection with which Dryden had written his commendatory verses, Congreve's role as Dryden's anointed successor was receiving comment; Joseph Addison's 'An Account of the Greatest English Poets' (1694) notes Dryden's growing 'old in rhyme' but also predicts that 'Congreve shall still preserve thy fame alive | And Dryden's muse shall in his friend survive'.[12]

Of course, poets other than Congreve fancied themselves as being in a creative descent from Dryden: Pope and Charles Churchill prided themselves on the same thing. As for Dryden, with a presumption bound to cause offence in a culture in which the comparative merits of classical and modern authors remained sharply at issue, he traced his own lineage from Virgil. According to Dryden, Virgil 'above all poets, had a stock, which I may call almost inexhaustible, of figurative, elegant, and sounding words'; and with a double-edged modesty he conceded that his own lot was to 'inherit but a small portion of his genius'.[13] For those heavily committed on the side of the ancients, such talk was nothing less than an affront; and it accounts for the harsh treatment of Dryden in Swift's *Battle of the Books*. Here Virgil and Dryden confront each other, with the ancient quickly embarassing his shiftless emulator, though not before Dryden makes a futile attempt at mollification:

Dryden in a long Harangue soothed up the good *Antient*, called him *Father*, and by a large deduction of Genealogies, made it plainly appear, that they were nearly related.[14]

What is being attacked here is Dryden's vanity but also his pet habit of portraying the historical relations between writers in paternal terms. That Dryden should have understood literary history as a form of patrimony may have been partly because issues of monarchical and familial inheritance were such central

---

[11] Kinsley (ed.), 853.
[12] *Works*, (ed.), Hurd, 1: 32–3.
[13] *Of Dramatic Poesy*, 2: 250.
[14] Davis (ed.), 1: 157.

preoccupations of his era. Dryden was, of course, one of the period's most eloquent advocates of the indefeasible hereditary right of monarchs, a principle which he addresses in several poems and which lay at the heart of the Exclusion crisis of the late 1670s. Three years after James II did succeed, the Bloodless Revolution of 1688 led to a near-total eclipse of Dryden's cultural and political ambitions and, in particular, to his being ousted, to the furtherance of the hated Shadwell, from his stipendiary position as Poet Laureate and Historiographer-Royal. It goes without saying that the laureateship, being a public office, was not hereditary. Yet, as in the poem to Congreve and his earlier *Mac Flecknoe*, the idea of a familial succession along monarchical lines was something that Dryden found intriguing and congenial. Thus when he recriminates over the loss of the laureateship, the outrage he generates is modelled on the constitutional outrage of a breach of monarchical succession:

> Thus when the State one *Edward* did depose;
> A Greater *Edward* in his room arose.
> But now, not I, but Poetry is curs'd;
> For *Tom* the Second reigns like *Tom* the first.[15]

Christopher Ricks has pointed out that when Dryden's paternal metaphors slant towards issues of inheritance, they also reflect social anxieties supposed to have been allayed by the institution of the so-called 'strict settlement': Dryden's era was the first in which this legal instrument became normative as regards the disposal of family estate.[16] This type of settlement would be drawn up on the occasion of the marriage of the eldest son and would regulate his future finances as well as those of his wife, thus ensuring that the estate would be handed down in its integrity to the eldest son produced by their union. The purpose of the instrument was to prevent the estate being ruined by the excesses of a single generation, and, under its terms, the status of each inheriting individual became reduced in effect to that of a life-tenant. The trepidation allayed by the strict settlement, that of coming into an inheritance only to find that the greater part of it had been spent, paralleled an anxiety to which authors, including Dryden, were beginning to feel themselves incident: that

[15] 'To my Dear Friend Mr. Congreve', in Kinsley (ed.), 853.
[16] See Ricks, 'Allusion', 220–2.

of discovering there was nothing left to say since everything had already been said by earlier writers.

As well as being conversant with the classical tradition, Dryden was probably the earliest major English writer to be capably versed in the writings of an antecedent vernacular tradition. Moreover, as W. J. Bate has argued, he may have been the first author of first rank to be strongly affected by a sense of writing in the immediate aftermath of a series of great creative achievements, as those of Shakespeare, Jonson, and Milton.[17] This sensitivity to being a latecomer made Dryden prey to a particular set of anxieties. He was sympathetic to Horace's complaint in *Epistles* II. i about how an indiscriminate reverence for writers of the past could prejudice the case of modern authors. In a dedicatory epistle to Lord Radcliffe, he protested against those cultural pundits who 'By a seeming veneration to our fathers...would thrust out us, their lawful issue, and govern us themselves, under a specious pretence of reformation'.[18] This anxiety that the merits of modern authors might be overlooked as result of an excessive deference to earlier ones was less unsettling, though, than the suspicion that those earlier writers might indeed have stolen all the best creative opportunities. As Harold Bloom has argued, it tends to be the nature of all major creative achievements to inhibit or dismay future creativity along the same lines. Dryden remarked of Milton, for whom he had an equivocal admiration, that '*This Man...Cuts us All Out, and the Ancients too.*'[19] Elsewhere, he describes the legacy of Shakespeare, Jonson, and Milton in terms of its intimidatory magnitude: 'Strong were our Syres...Theirs was the Gyant Race, before the Flood.'[20] However, the readiest metaphor for expressing the queasiness that authors sometimes felt towards their predecessors was that of a dissipated inheritance. Dryden was of the opinion that even if Shakespeare, Jonson, and Fletcher could 'rise and write again', they would be hard put to repeat their earlier greatness, for though 'We acknowledge

---

[17] W. Jackson Bate, *The Burden of the Past and the English Poet* (London, 1971), 31.
[18] *Of Dramatic Poesy*, 2: 159.
[19] Recorded by Jonathan Richardson; cited by Ricks, 'Allusion', 232.
[20] 'To my Dear Friend Mr. Congreve', lines 3–5, in Kinsley (ed.), 852.

them our fathers in wit...they have ruined their estates themselves before they came to their children's hands'.[21]

It is Dryden, more than any other figure, who provides the
basis for envisioning English literature as a 'tradition', as a baton
to be passed on, or handed down, between authors of different
epochs. He was the first, if not to use, then to popularize the idea
that past and present writers are linked together through a
paternal–filial nexus, each generation occupying a place within
an unfolding genealogy of creativity. To succeed as a writer is to
turn oneself into the offspring of the great writers of the established tradition. This understanding that the literary tradition is
formed genealogically becomes so commonplace as, like many
other Augustan concepts, to spawn its own serio-comic anti-
thesis. Both *Mac Flecknoe* and *The Dunciad*, for example, explore the possibility of a nexus of uncreative inheritance
exclusive to bad authors; and even before *The Dunciad*, Pope
had explored the idea of genealogies of ignominy in *Peri Bathous*
(1728): 'Who sees not that De Foe was the poetical son of
Withers, Tate of Ogilby, E. Ward of John Taylor, and Eusden
of Blackmore?'[22] To understand the full weight of derision
heaped on Flecknoe and Shadwell, Settle and Theobald, Withers
and Defoe, and so on, you have to see the act of genealogical
succession uniting them as a grisly negation of the very principle
of literary tradition.

III

In 1685 Dryden published in the miscellany *Sylvae* five translations from Lucretius's *De Rerum Natura*, including the entirety
of Book IV, 'Concerning the Nature of Love'. Lucretius describes the act of lovemaking in combative terms, the outcome
of the combat, which of the competitors prevails in the wrestle
of their passion, determining whether the child will take the
mother's or the father's likeness. Only in those instances 'When
both conspire, with equal ardour bent' and 'When neither party
foils, when neither foild' will the child's physiognomy be

---

[21] *Of Dramatic Poesy*, 1: 85.
[22] Cited from *The Prose Works of Alexander Pope II*, ed. Rosemary Cowler
(Oxford, 1986), 203.

blended from those of both parents. One further possibility is that the child's image will revert back atavistically to the likeness of a grandparent or ancestor, in which instance 'the genial Atomes of the seed | Lie long conceal'd e're they exert the breed'.[23] These Lucretian ideas about sexual generation flicker to life elsewhere in Dryden's writing. In *Absalom and Achitophel*, David's preferred son is the illegitimate Absalom, whom he loves with an excessive partiality. But what clinches the King's love is not just the fineness of Absalom's general parts but also that, looking at Absalom, David sees 'His Youthfull Image in his Son renew'd'. Dryden, moreover, tells us that what accounts for Absalom's carrying his father's imprint is the vigour with which David performed the act of conception: 'His Father got him with a greater Gust.'[24] The same technicalities of biological inheritance surface once more in the dedicatory epistle addressed to the Duke of Ormond affixed to *Fables Ancient and Modern* (1700):

'Tis observ'd by *Livy* and by others, That some of the noblest *Roman* Families retain'd a resemblance of their Ancestry, not only in their Shapes and Features, but also in their Manners, their Qualities, and the distinguishing Characters of their Minds: Some Lines were noted for a stern, rigid Virtue... Others were more sweet, and affable...[25]

Dryden's *Fables* came out in the year of his death, by which time he had been on familiar terms with three generations of the Ormonds, and the dedication is intended to blandish the hereditary virtues of the family. But if Dryden believed that certain likenesses could descend biologically within families, should we expect them also to be passed down in the lineal relation between poetic fathers and their sons, poetic ancestors and their scions?

Dryden's Flecknoe, like his David, is a father 'blest with issue of a large increase'. Unlike David, however, he is not bound by constitutional rules governing succession, for his elective poetic son is simply the one who bears the stamp of physical likeness to his father. This turns out to be Shadwell, whom Flecknoe recognizes 'alone my perfect image bears'.[26] Such a recourse to

---

[23] 'Lucretius: the Fourth Book', lines 216, 218, 222–3, in Kinsley (ed.), 419.
[24] 'Absalom and Achitophel', lines 32, 20, ibid. 217.
[25] Ibid. 1439–40.
[26] 'Mac Flecknoe', lines 8 and 15, ibid. 265.

physical resemblance as a means to bind together monarch and successor also occurs in a poem lineally descended from *Mac Flecknoe*: Pope's *Dunciad*. When the Goddess Dulness envisions a tradition of ancient city bards, imagined as a sequence of debased father–son combinations, she notes that parents and progeny are conjoined by physical uniformity: 'Each sire imprest and glaring in his son.' 'Imprest and glaring', here, may be a gross parody of Milton's statement of the physical similarity between God and the Son, the latter in whom 'all his Father shone | Substantially expressed'; but, as I will come to, Pope *did* harbour the notion that poetic filiation could issue in systematic congruities between father and son.[27]

This idea that a nexus of creative inheritance between poets will become demonstrable through similarities of physical appearance or life-history reappears in contexts less ironic than those of *Mac Flecknoe* and *The Dunciad*. On 28 July 1667, Abraham Cowley's remains were interred in Westminster Abbey close to those of Chaucer and Spenser. The event was commemorated in Sir John Denham's elegy 'On Mr. Abraham Cowley's Death and Burial Amongst the Ancient Poets' in which Denham traces the rise of a native literary tradition from 'Old Chaucer' through Spenser, Shakespeare, Jonson, and Fletcher until it comes to an apex in Cowley, the author who reconciles the two creative opposites, traditionally associated with Jonson and Shakespeare, of art and nature. But Cowley was an exponent of Latin as well as of English composition, and for this reason Denham identifies his true poetic father as none of the aforementioned authors but, instead, as Virgil. Furthermore, this compliment of association is reinforced by an auxiliary claim of actual physical resemblance. Such was Cowley's congruity with his poetic ancestor that 'Of that great portraiture, so true | A copy pencil never drew'; and speaking on behalf of his own poetic muse Denham confesses that 'Two twins she never saw so like'. These physical resemblances are backed up as well by duplication of *curricula vitae*. Both Virgil and Cowley produced works alike in being 'chaste, moral, and divine', conducing to 'profit and delight'; both were patronized by enlightened

[27] *Dunciad Variorum* (1729), line 98, in Butt (ed.), 5: 71; *Paradise Lost*, III. 139–40, in *Poems*, 151.

rulers (Caesar Augustus and Charles II); and both their lives were issueless and their deaths untimely.[28]

A similar moment occurs in Dryden's 'To the Pious Memory of Anne Killigrew' where he describes 'the double sacrilege' inflicted on Killigrew by the smallpox: facial disfigurement and then death. But Dryden is quickly able to introduce a note of consolation by drawing a parallel with the earlier female poet, Katherine Philips:

> But thus *Orinda* dy'd:
> Heav'n, by the same Disease, did both translate,
> As equal were their Souls, so equal was their Fate.[29]

Killigrew and Philips ('Orinda') were both poets (though perhaps of differing levels of ability); both died young; and both fell victim to the ravaging effects of smallpox. Already by this time Philips stood unrivalled as the pre-eminent female author in the literary canon: Langbaine's entry on her in his *Account of the English Dramatick Poets*, five years after Dryden's poem, eulogizes her as 'honour'd of all men that are Favourers of Poetry' and as one 'who...has equall'd all that is reported of the Poetesses of Antiquity'. No less than comparing a male writer to Chaucer, to identify in another female poet the signature of Philips's life and death was to consecrate her to the female literary tradition.

But why, still, the curious flourishing of parallels? Probably there are two distinct tiers of argument: first that Cowley's and Killigrew's status can only be truly accredited if their careers are seen as running in tandem with or re-enacting those of their illustrious forebears; and, second, that this relation, be it filiation or atavistic return, can only be vouched for by the appearance of signs of resemblance. Certainly, where statements of resemblance are made between classical and vernacular poets, these are normally proffered in the service of some claim about the latter's canonical status. This principle holds, for example, for Dryden's comparison of Ovid and Chaucer in the 'Preface' to *Fables Ancient and Modern* (1700), this being the only occasion in Dryden's work on which he compares at length a classical with a vernacular author. The rationale given for this paralleling

[28] Cited from Anderson (ed.), 5: 679.   [29] Kinsley (ed.), 1: 464.

of the two authors is that of congruity: 'having done with Ovid for this time, it came into my mind that our old English poet, Chaucer, in many things resembled him.' Dryden enumerates several grounds of congruity: both poets were 'well-bred, well-natured, amorous, and libertine'; both were students of philosophy and philology; and both were wont to acquire rather than to invent their stories. Against this some undeniable differences also get noted: for one thing, Ovid's career falls at the end of a golden age of the Roman tongue whereas Chaucer inaugurates the long process of the purification of the English language, a difference reflected in Chaucer's characteristic style being naive and simple as distinct from Ovid's more intricate, conceitful one. The specifying of analogues, however, allows that Chaucer's career be seen as a sort of re-enactment of that of Ovid, and it is through this re-enactment that the vernacular author's canonical credentials are established.[30]

One further example might be added to the foregoing ones. Tucked away as Appendix VI of Pope's *Dunciad Variorum* (1729) is a strange addendum to the work as originally published, entitled 'A Parallel of the Characters of Mr. Dryden and Mr. Pope'.[31] Dryden, of course, stalks the pages of *The Dunciad* as the originator of the two satiric ploys most crucial to Pope's poem: the concept of dulness and the topos of a mock-coronation. The 'Parallel' is a compilation of slanders directed in common against the two writers. These include the slurs of their being unpatriotic, of being mere versifiers rather than true poets, of being suspect translators from Greek and Latin, and of having tricked their subscribers. Pope evidently pursued this idiosyncratic project with some zeal, for each slander is traced to source, with a page number scrupulously supplied. The 'Parallel', in one sense, merely exhibits Pope pluming himself on the strength of his association with Dryden. But such a meticulous statement of congruity between the two authors, as I have hinted, also implies filiation; and the noble succession from Dryden to Pope stands as an implicit rebuff to the ignominious succession depicted in the poem: in 1729, from Settle to Theobald. The 'Parallel' between Pope and Dryden does, however,

---

[30] See *Of Dramatic Poesy*, 2: 271, 277.   [31] Butt (ed.), 5: 230–5.

admit one factor also governing the lineages of duncery: namely, that the sire be 'imprest and glaring in his son'.

IV

If during the English Augustan era, the conceit of literary paternity was a generic one, then it also spawned a more arcane metaphor for imagining the workings of tradition: this specified that a later writer was linked to an earlier, not through figurative parentage, but through sharing the same transmigratory soul. Moreover, just as the paternal metaphor is popularized by Dryden, so it is the same author to whom the metaphor of spiritual transmigration, as applied to literary tradition, also owes its greatest debt. I have already cited a passage in which Dryden claims that major writers belong within 'lineal descents and clans', but I omitted to cite the sequence immediately following:

Milton was the poetical son of Spenser, and Mr Waller of Fairfax; for we have our lineal descents and clans as well as other families: Spenser more than once insinuates that the soul of Chaucer was transfused into his body; and that he was begotten by him two hundred years after his decease.[32]

The initial mention of 'lineal descents and clans' admittedly conjures up an image of biological generation, but in the second half of the sentence the metaphor is modulated. Spenser's engendering by Chaucer is not detailed purely as an act of filiation, for Chaucer's very soul has supposedly incarnated itself in the body of the later writer. The auxiliary metaphor, in other words, is that of 'metempsychosis': the Pythagorean transmigration of souls.

The use of metempsychosis to analogize links between authors is perhaps unsurprisingly not of Dryden's own devising. The earliest such application of which I am aware is that to which Dryden himself alludes, occurring in Spenser's *Faerie Queene* IV (1596). The passage restates Spenser's sense of poetic discipleship to Chaucer, a discipleship that had earlier been promulgated in his *envoi* to *The Shepheardes Calendar* (1579). The relevant stanza runs as follows:

[32] *Of Dramatic Poesy*, 2: 270.

> Then pardon, O most sacred happie spirit
>   That I thy labours lost may thus reuiue,
>   And steale from thee the meede of thy due merit,
>   That none durst euer whilest thou wast aliue,
>   And being dead in vaine yet many striue:
> Ne dare I like, but through infusion sweete
>   Of thine owne spirit, which doth in me surviue,
>   I follow here the footing of thy feete,
> That with thy meaning so I may the rather meete.[33]

Spenser has the self-possession here to announce that the pretext on which he can 'revive' Chaucer's labour is 'through infusion sweete | Of thine owne spirit.' The invocation of the conceit at this juncture has different levels of application. For one thing, Spenser was a fastidious reviver of Chaucerian poetic phraseology, and so the idea of a metempsychotic union between the two expresses the particular intimacy of their poetic relationship. But because Chaucer stood as the generic 'father' of English literature, for Spenser to claim filiation to him was, in a wider sense, for him to announce his own membership of the native literary tradition. Even in the seventeenth and eighteenth centuries, when Chaucer's reputation was far from unassailable, affiliation to tradition was often marked by possession of a soul identified almost exclusively as his. In 1636, Stephen Haxby, for example, pays the poet Charles Fitz-Geffry the bloated compliment that his lines demonstrate the Pythagorean paradox that 'dead mens soules . . . | Are not extinct', for 'Old *Geffry Chaucers* soule reviu'd in thee'.[34] Ten years later, E. G. [Edward Gray?] records that where poets are concerned only their 'grosse Bodies' die, for their souls translate from one to another. Nor is this transmigration arbitrary, for the spirit of a great poet will repair only to another of similar stature. So, we are told, '*Chaucers* learned soule in *Spencer* sung', this same soul then taking up residence in Jonson ('It fill'd up *Ben*').[35]

---

[33] *The Faerie Queene*, IV ii. 34, in *Spenser: Poetical Works*, ed. J. C. Smith and E. de Selincourt (London, 1970), 223. Book IV appeared in 1596.

[34] Stephen Haxby, 'Clarissimo viro Domino Carolo Fitz-geodfrido, Steph. Haxby Cantabrigiensis. S.P.D.', in Charles Fitz-Geffry, *The Blessed Birthday*, 2nd edn. (1636); cited from Caroline F. E. Spurgeon, *Five Hundred Years of Chaucer Criticism and Allusion 1357–1900*, 3 vols. (Cambridge, 1925), 1: 216.

[35] E. G., 'To the Author', in M[artin] Ll[uelyn], *Men-Miracles. With Other Poems*, 2nd edn. (1656). Partially reprinted in Spurgeon, 1: 225.

The theory of spiritual transmigration, in so far as it is relevant to the present chapter, was transported to England from ancient Greece, and attributed to the sixth-century BC moralist and visionary, Pythagoras. None of Pythagoras's writings survived beyond his own era, but his teachings were and are known to the modern world through various Latin sources, including Ovid's *Metamorphoses* XV and biographies by Diogenes Laertius, Porphyry, and Iamblichus.[36] Probably the fullest account is in Diogenes who records that Pythagoras traced the descent of his own soul through Aethalides, Euphorbus, Hermotimus, and Pyrrhus, and through plant and animal incarnations prior to all of these.[37] That he could recollect this chain of transmigrations was because Aethalides (his first embodiment) had specifically requested such a gift from Hermes. Overall, the itinerary of Pythagoras's soul can be seen to figure an ascent from low forms of life to the highest echelon of human embodiment, the 'wise man'.

It falls outside the scope of this chapter to offer a general overview of the reception of Pythagorean ideas in England during the seventeenth century. It suffices to say that his ideas were broadly at large, though mostly in a frivolous and slightly bastardized form. The story told by Xenophanes that Pythagoras once asked an acquaintance to stop beating his dog because in its cries he recognized the voice of a deceased friend occasioned a rather facetious orthodoxy that Pythagorean transmigration entailed a decline from human to animal. This provides the matter of all of Shakespeare's several references to the topic, and is instrumental in Faustus's famous invocation of the possibility of transmigration at the end of Marlowe's play:

> Ah *Pythagoras Metemsycosis*; were that true,
> This soule should flie from me, and I be chang'd
> Unto some brutish beast.[38]

[36] See Peter Gorman, *Pythagoras: A Life* (London, 1979). Spiritual transmigration was reported by Julius Caesar to be a belief of the Druids, a fact (or fiction) widely known in the 18th cent. However, where the concept is applied metaphorically to poetic interrelations, Pythagoras seems to be the sole source.

[37] Diogenes Laertius, *The Lives and Opinions of Eminent Philosophers*, trans. C. D. Yonge (London, 1905), 339–40.

[38] *Doctor Faustus*, 1966–8, in *The Complete Works of Christopher Marlowe*, ed. Fredson Bowers, 2 vols. (Cambridge, 1973), 2: 226. See also William Shakespeare, *Twelfth Night*, ed. M. M. Mahood (London, 1968), IV. ii. 49–59.

This excitable interest in downward migration was probably the main conduit through which Pythagoras's ideas entered the popular imagination. But where spiritual transmigration was used as a metaphor for literary tradition, the relationship indicated between the earlier and later figure was necessarily one of creative equality.[39]

Dryden seems to have been interested in transmigration independently of its potential application as a metaphor. During his career, he translated three classical works in which the idea is documented. Most important amongst these is his rendition late in life 'Of the Pythagorean Philosophy From Ovid's Metamorphoses Book XV', printed in *Fables Ancient and Modern* (1700). Consisting of some seven hundred lines in Dryden's translation, this is one of the main texts in which Pythagoras's ideas have been preserved: Dryden interestingly labels it as 'the most learned and beautiful Parts of the whole Metamorphoses'.[40] It provides a conspectus on the sweep of Pythagoras's moral and natural philosophy, including his appeal for a vegetarian diet and his belief that the soul transmigrates between bodies:

> Nor dies the Spirit, but new Life repeats
> In other Forms, and only changes Seats.

Thus being born is merely 'to begin to be | Some other Thing we were not formerly', and to die is not to perish but merely to transmogrify.[41]

While *Metamorphoses* XV propounds the Pythagorean doctrine of transmigration, Dryden was indebted to another classical work for a vivid depiction of transmigration in action: Virgil's *Aeneid*. When he published his translation of the *Æneis* in 1697, he was inevitably called upon to render a passage in Book IV where Aeneas descends to the underworld to visit his father Anchises (953–1247). This tryst with his parent makes Aeneas privy to a strange pageant in which multitudes of souls throng on the bank of the river Lethe waiting to be immersed in its waters. This immersion guarantees their forgetfulness of the past, this being a precondition if they are to be equipped with

---

[39] One literary endorsement of an upward migration of the soul is John Donne's whimsical and satiric poem, 'Metempsychosis: The Progress of the Soul' (wr. 1601).

[40] Kinsley (ed.), 1718.

[41] Lines 229–30, 390–1, ibid. 1723, 1728.

new bodies and restored to a further mortal existence. The scene is also one of filial initiation (echoed in Dryden's ironic poem on the same theme, *Mac Flecknoe*), in which Anchises reveals the immortality of the soul and directs Aeneas's attention to souls which, in the mortal life into which they are about to be born, will play a part in the great destiny of Rome.

The third classical work translated by Dryden and touching on transmigration is the sixth satire of Persius, addressed 'To Caesius Bassus, a Lyrick Poet'. Dryden's translation (1693) predates his renditions of Virgil and Ovid, but I cite it third as being the invocation most connected with the present topic. In the poem, Persius praises Ennius

> Who, in a Drunken Dream, beheld his Soul
> The Fifth within the Transmigrating roul:
> Which first a Peacock, then *Euphorbus* was,
> Then *Homer* next, and next *Pythagoras*;
> And last of all the Line did into *Ennius* pass.[42]

What Dryden translates as the 'Transmigrating roul' is a creative and intellectual roll of honour, establishing Ennius's pedigree as of the highest distinction. The last three embodiments mentioned make for a telling combination: Homer stood unchallenged as the begetter of the Greek literary tradition; Pythagoras was the begetter of the concept of metempsychosis; and Ennius was often seen as the originary figure or 'father' of Roman literature. What is allegorized is no less than the emergence of a Roman literary tradition from the precedent of the earlier Greek one, this emergence being figured as the flight of a creative soul from the Greek Homer to the Roman Ennius.

The metaphor of transmigratory descent was obviously ripe for the purposes of overblown panegyric, and Dryden's earliest recourse to the conceit in an original poem occurs unsurprisingly in an elegy, 'Upon the Death of Lord Hastings' (1649), the earliest of all his published works. The relevant passage, which bears affinities to the one just quoted from Persius, comes in a section extolling the range of Hastings's abilities:

> O had he di'd of old, how great a strife
> Had been, who from his Death should draw their Life?
> Who should, by one rich draught, become what ere

---

[42] Lines 22–6, ibid. 783.

Seneca, Cato, Numa, Caesar, were:
Learn'd, Vertuous, Pious, Great; and have by this
An universal *Metempsuchosis*.
Must all these ag'd Sires in one Funeral
Expire?[43]

Hastings's soul, so Dryden encourages us to believe, has previously frequented four Roman worthies: Seneca, Cato, Numa, and Caesar. But Dryden departs from the strict logic of metempsychosis to suggest that this transmigratory nexus has been cumulative, in that Hastings subsumes all the virtues possessed by the previous incarnations of his soul, thus representing 'An Universal *Metempsuchosis*'. Also mooted is the related idea that the soul, as it were, assimilates its own genealogy, so that Hastings's death entails another dying for all the parental and ancestral figures who have preceded him: 'Must all these ag'd Sires in one Funeral | Expire?'

The point of the compliment is to stress the roundedness of Hastings's abilities, seen as having been realized through the diverse nature of his transmigratory heritage, but such diversity also militates against his being seen as the beneficiary of a unified tradition. However, in his most meditated invocation of the conceit, occurring in the second stanza of another elegiac poem, the ode 'To Mrs Anne Killigrew', Dryden uses the figure in a regard exclusive to the literary tradition. The stanza speculates in somewhat technical fashion on the origin of the young lady's talents, setting the doctrine of transmigration against a rival version of human geniture:

If by Traduction came thy Mind,
    Our Wonder is the less to find
A Soul so charming from a Stock so good;
Thy Father was transfus'd into thy Blood:
So wert thou born into the tuneful strain,
(An early, rich, and inexhausted Vain.)
    But if thy præexisting Soul
    Was form'd, at first, with Myriads more,
It did through all the Mighty Poets roul,
    Who *Greek* or *Latine* Laurels wore,
And was that *Sappho* last, which once it was before.[44]

---

[43] Lines 67–74, ibid. 2. [44] Lines 22–33, ibid. 460.

By 'mind', Dryden means what Robert Burton and others called the 'rational soul': a sort of animate life-force variously construed as mortal or immortal and equally variously located in the brain, heart, or blood. In the first six lines, Dryden explores the possibility that Anne Killigrew received her soul through 'traduction' or by a process of direct transmission from father to daughter. 'Traduction' was the unorthodox notion, entertained by Hippocrates amongst others, that the parent engenders not just the child's body but its soul as well. The alternative offered to this scenario is that Anne's soul might instead have pre-existed, and might have transmigrated through a sequence of great classical authors including the Greek Sappho, before taking up lodging in Katherine Philips, the English 'Sappho', and migrating thence to the person of Anne Killigrew herself. Under this regime of transmigration, Anne's talent supposedly brings to culmination an entire poetic tradition. The overall compliment is as if to say that Anne's achievement renders the antecedent tradition so coherent and indisputable that you could surmise that 'tradition' were in fact no more than the successive transmigrations of a single illustrious soul. This blandishment of identifying someone as the embodiment of the soul possessed by some earlier luminary works as a sort of short-circuiting simile: what is implied is that the later avatar is so *like* the former as actually to *be* that person. This indeed is the riddling logic of the last line quoted: 'And was that *Sappho* last, which once it was before'. So well did Katherine Philips live up to the precedent set by Sappho that the two have, as it were, become one.

Although Dryden uses transmigration to express the creative descent of Spenser from Chaucer (in doing so falling back expressly on Spenser's own adoption of the conceit), there is some evidence that the metaphor did most sterling service as a means of figuring a nexus specifically of cross-cultural inheritance: as of Roman from Greek literature or of English literature from the classics in general. The exploitation of the topos nearest in time to Spenser's inaugurative usage seems to be in Francis Meres's *Palladis Tamia, Wits Treasury* (1598), which conjoins a vernacular with a classical author: 'As the soule of Euphorbus was thought to liue in Pythagoras: so the sweete wittie soul of Ouid liues in mellifluous and hony-tongued Shakespeare.'[45] The

---

[45] Cited from Smith (ed.), 2: 317.

invocation of metempsychosis for the purpose of an aggrandizing cross-cultural parallel is also apparent in two commendatory poems written to Dryden himself in 1693 by his young disciples, William Congreve and Joseph Addison. The same year had seen the appearance both of Dryden's translations of Juvenal and Persius and of his miscellany *Examen Poeticum*, consisting in significant part of translations from Ovid. It is Dryden's translation of Persius that Congreve's poem is specifically intended to praise. The gist of his compliment is that formerly Persius had languished obscure, only admired on account of his antiquity, whereas Dryden's translation has opened up the possibility of his at last being appreciated on his own merits:

> For still obscure, to us no Light he gives;
> Dead in himself, in you alone he lives.[46]

This conceit of Persius living in Dryden is arrived at from a conflation of translation with transmigration: Dryden revives Persius by translating him but also (so it is hinted) by being the recipient of Persius's transmigratory soul. Much the same conceit, with one further twist, is exploited in Addison's poem 'To Mr. Dryden', in connection with the latter's translation of Ovid. Addison, himself, was later to translate Ovid, and his poem encouraged Dryden to continue to pursue the Ovidian project:

> O mayst thou still the noble task prolong,
> Nor age, nor sickness interrupt thy song:
> Then may we wondering read, how human limbs
> Have water'd kingdoms, and dissolv'd in streams;
> Of those rich fruits that on the fertile mould
> Turn'd yellow by degrees, and ripen'd into gold:
> How some in feathers, or a ragged hide,
> Have liv'd a second life, and different natures try'd.[47]

The last couplet refers to *Metamorphoses* XV, which contains an exposition of Pythagorean philosophy and which Dryden was eventually to translate for *Fables Ancient and Modern*. In the next two lines, ones concluding the poem, Addison cleverly knits together metamorphosis, translation, and spiritual transmigration:

---

[46] Cited from *John Dryden: The Critical Heritage*, ed. Helen and James Kinsley (London, 1971), 206.
[47] Hurd (ed.), 1: 4.

> Then will thy *Ovid*, thus transform'd, reveal
> A nobler change than he himself can tell.

These lines acknowledge how 'transformation' (or metamorphosis) figures as the central topos of Ovid's great work and how Dryden, by undertaking its translation, has executed upon it his own transformative act. But coming hard upon the allusion to metempsychosis ('some… I Have liv'd a second life, and different natures try'd') the 'transformation' of Ovid also hints at nothing less than his having been spiritually reincarnated in his modern avatar, Dryden.

V

The persistence of the metaphor of transmigration, and its life outside the immediate circle of its originator, Dryden, can be seen from two poems written some eighty-five years apart. The first of these is John Denham's elegy 'On Mr. Abraham Cowley', composed on the occasion of Cowley's grand funeral and interment in 1667. Because Cowley was distinguished as an exponent of Latin no less than of English poetry, Denham identifies his most relevant ancestor as a Roman poet, Virgil; and he lists various points of correspondence between the two writers (to which I have already referred). Yet Denham has still further to go in his conviction of Cowley's being a reborn Virgil:

> 'Twas taught by wise Pythagoras,
> One soul might through more bodies pass:
> Seeing such transmigration there
> She [Denham's Muse] thought it not a fable here.
> Such a resemblance of all parts,
> Life, death, age, fortune, nature, arts.[48]

Denham is here running together two distinct protocols for praising authors. The first is where one adduces parallels between two authors with a view to this reflecting particular merit on one of them: this is evident, for example, in Pope's enumeration of parallels between himself and Dryden in a section of the *Dunciad Variorum* already discussed. The second protocol is the one with which I have been expressly concerned, in which

---

[48] Cited from Anderson (ed.), 5: 679.

a later writer is praised as bearing the transmigrated soul of an earlier, illustrious one: so here Denham eulogizes Cowley as the bearer of Virgil's soul. These two protocols are presented as a causal sequence: Cowley's likeness to Virgil is so great as to be explicable only in the terms of a single transmigratory nexus.

The pairing up of classical and modern figures on grounds of affinity was a common scholarly amusement in the Augustan era. Its spirit can be detected in Dryden's comment that 'Spenser and Milton are, in English, what Virgil and Horace are in Latin', and from his reference to Chaucer as 'our English Ennius'.[49] An interesting poem in which this paralleling of authors is assimilated to the conceit of spiritual transmigration is Thomas Cooke's *Pythagoras. An Ode* (1752).[50] The poem is dedicated to 'His Grace THOMAS Duke of NEWCASTLE' who, close to the end, is paid the rather hackneyed compliment of being the '*Mecaenas* of this later Age'.[51] This compliment, however, acquires intelligibility through falling as part of a whole series of parallels between classical and modern figures, in which each pair is united through possession of a shared transmigratory soul. The first section alone is given over predominantly to literary figures. It depicts Pythagoras, 'Surrounded by the philosophic Youth', forecasting 'the transmigrated Sons of Rhyme'. These are sandwiched between philosophers such as Shaftesbury (whose 'pure capacious Breast | Shall be by *Plato*'s soul possess'd') and actors, the relevant lines beginning with Homer's relation to his modern avatar, Milton:

> Old *Homer* shall revive again
> In *Milton*'s bold and sacred Strain.
> The daring *Æschylus* shall sing
> And soar aloft, on *Shakespear*'s Wing;
> Wild as the Lark, but sweet and strong,
> The pleasing Notes shall float along.
> Majestic *Sophocles* appears,

[49] *Of Dramatic Poesy*, 2: 242, 259.

[50] For other works in which paralleling of classical and modern authors takes place, see Samuel Cobb, 'Of Poetry', in *Poems on Several Occasions* (1710), 172–3; Henry Felton, *A Dissertation on Reading the Classics and Forming a Just Style* (1709); and Colley Cibber, *A Rhapsody upon the Marvellous* (1751), esp. 6–7.

[51] Thomas Cooke, *Pythagoras An Ode. To which are Prefixed Observations on Taste and on Education* (1752), 15.

To bathe the Charmer's Cheeks with Tears,
When *Gwendolen* for Succour calls,
When *Yvor* weeps, or *Pyrrhus* falls.
The *Mantuan* Swain, in manhood ripe,
Once more shall wake the rural Pipe,
When *Philips* with his Oaten Reed
Makes Glad the Grove and flow'ry Mead.
Plautus and *Terence*, Sons of Mirth,
Shall give to *Steele* and *Congreve* Birth.[52]

Elsewhere in the poem, Cooke develops the idea of a transmigratory chain, with a soul going through successive re-embodiments; but in dealing with authors he simply enumerates one-to-one correspondences between earlier and later figures. The effect of what he does is to repristinate a general idiom for speaking of the relation of earlier to later authors that since Dryden's day had lapsed into abstraction. His metaphors for literary influence are ostensibly conventional: Homer 'shall revive again | In Milton'; Aeschylus shall 'soar aloft, on *Shakespear*'s Wing'; Virgil shall wake the 'rural Pipe' when Philips takes up his 'Oaten Reed'; and Plautus and Terence 'give . . . Birth' to Steele and Congreve. Yet for all their unprepossessing appearance, they are given renewed vitality by being keyed to the master-theme of metempsychosis.

What status did the metaphor of transmigration have, then, in seventeenth- and eighteenth-century attempts to conceptualize the literary past? The answer to this question must regrettably remain downbeat: in the early Augustan era, the sort of writings, such as 'progress-of-poesy' poems and verse catalogues of poets, that were most instrumental in generating an idea of a literary heritage, generally have no recourse to it—and this contrasts with the broader currency of the alternative metaphor, in which literary history is figured as a paternal nexus or genealogy. Yet the idea of transmigration does lurk covertly in numerous idioms used to describe authorial interrelations, to whose exact purport readers nowadays have become insensitized. It is this conceit that appears fairly nakedly in the praise of Matthew Prior ('The soul of Chaucer is restor'd in thee') in Thomas Tickell's 'Poem on the Prospect of Peace' (1712) but that also

---

[52] *Pythagoras. An Ode*, 8.

peeps out more shyly in Addison's flattering observation that Dryden's 'lines have heighten'd Virgil's majesty, | And Horace wonders at himself in thee', and in John Gay's similarly worded remark on George Granville's discipleship to Waller that 'Waller in Granville lives'.[53]

It matters to literary people in the eighteenth century, perhaps as it does in all periods, not just that a literary tradition exist but that it possess a quality of animateness, that there be a principle of living reciprocation between writers of the past and present. The way that the Augustans made this principle of mutuality vivid to themselves was through the related metaphors of literary paternity and transmigration. Both metaphors fostered an appreciation of how an earlier author could provide the pretext for the success of a later one; and both also had the effect of circumscribing literary success by suggesting that all creativity must take place within the tradition, beneath the aegis of its illustrious company. These metaphors now seem overstrained and potentially restrictive; and it is true that during the eighteenth century their conceptual base gradually gets eroded. What such metaphors imply is a developmental model under which English literature is fathered by the literatures of Greece and Rome and under which the aspiration of vernacular literature is reduced to re-enactment of the splendours of those antecedent cultures. Yet as the grip of the classics is loosened (as happens over the century), the principle of serial re-enactment begins to seem less convincing as a motor of literary tradition; while the belief that writers in tradition are linked through a principle of atavistic return also comes to seem less tenable and, perhaps, less desirable. In our own time, tradition has sometimes been seen not as a force that provokes creativity in later writers but rather as one deterring it, as a malign force bearing down on all who come beneath its shadow. For Harold Bloom, for example, the great writer comes into his creative inheritance only through vanquishing an earlier one whose precedent would otherwise be stifling and incapacitating.[54] But this sort of savage authorial

---

[53] For Tickell, see Anderson (ed.), 8: 413–14; Addison, 'To Mr. Dryden', in Hurd (ed.), 1: 4; Gay, 'On a Miscellany of Poems. To Bernard Lintott' (1708) in *John Gay: Poetry and Prose*, ed. Vinton A. Dearing and Charles E. Beckwith, 2 vols. (Oxford, 1974), 1: 40.

[54] See Harold Bloom, *The Anxiety of Influence: A Theory of Poetry* (London, 1973).

individualism stands at a long remove from the Augustans' own milder ways of conceiving the tradition, through the strong metaphors pioneered by Dryden, those of creative geniture and metempsychosis.

6

Teaching English Literature

I

This book is about attitudes to the literary past in circulation among members of educated society during the long eighteenth century. What interests me is how this past came to be unearthed or made up, and the discourses (of antiquarian recovery, of tradition and canonicity) through which it was ordered. To put it pithily, my book addresses itself to the production of English literary culture not to its consumption; in this respect it differs, for example, from John Brewer's imposing book on *The Pleasures of the Imagination* (1997) which investigates the venues, events, and markets through which the products of high culture are consumed by an expanding audience. The present chapter, however, presents something of an exception to the rest of the volume. For I am interested here, not in the drafting of the literary past, but in the ways through which versions of the past ripple out and become available to a wider constituency of consumers: to the poor and poorly-educated and to the young in the process of their education.

This chapter concentrates, then, on the *permeation*, rather than the construction, of ideas about English literature. It poses the question of how far-flung, outside the metropolitan literati and the higher ranks of society, cognizance of high literature actually was. Recent critics who have described the 'rise of English' have rightly attached significance to the way English literature was bolstered by its accession to the status of an educational subject. This is mostly taken to occur between the 1860s, when the first professorships of English Literature were instituted in British universities, and 1921, when the Newbolt report elevated English literature to its (since unchallenged) position as a compulsory element of secondary educational syllabuses.[1] The rôle played by education in the cultural fortification of English literature

---

[1] For treatment of English as an educational subject, see Richard Foster Watson, *The Beginnings of the Teaching of Modern Subjects in England* (1908; East Ardsley, 1971); Stephen Potter, *The Muse in Chains: A Study in Education* (London, 1937);

seems indubitable, but one of my arguments is that this process gets under way as early as the eighteenth century, therefore appreciably earlier than is generally assumed. Ample evidence exists of the incursion of English literature into eighteenth-century classrooms, yet this has mostly been given scant attention. One reason for such an oversight is the assumption that English literature only acquires educational significance once it becomes furnished with its own syllabus, and once the ends to which it is taught resemble those in whose service it is taught nowadays.

This chapter will trace the incursion of English literature (in the sense of the élite imaginative texts of the language) into syllabuses of education; much of it, indeed, will consist of a march through a sequence of different types of educational institution, up a slowly ascending curve from the elementary school to the university. But as well as noting how literary works come to play an expanding exemplary role in school and university teaching, I am especially concerned with the sort of pedagogic agendas that are furthered by this phenomenon. In the first instance, literary examples are introduced into the classroom as a means of teaching spelling, rhetoric, and verse composition; but from the mid-eighteenth century onwards, a rise in the educational importance of elocution leads to a different call on literature to provide an appropriately elevated sort of practice material. Moreover, the provision of literary *exempla* for the reasons mentioned above gradually mingles with a larger educational project, that of inculcating that brand of mental judiciousness and sensory refinement known as 'taste'.

The teaching of literary material under the particular aegis of 'taste' represents a key moment in the reification of English literature as an educational subject: for it associates the material of literature with a precise mental aptitude necessary to its proper consumption—an aptitude that might itself be termed 'literary'. Yet even though the idea of taste places weight on mental and sensory sophistication, those who most proselytize about it in educational circles remain firmly committed to an

D. J. Palmer, *The Rise of English Studies: An Account of the Study of English Language and Literature from its Origins to the Making of the Oxford English School* (Oxford, 1965); Chris Baldick, *The Social Mission of English Criticism: 1848–1932* (Oxford, 1983); Jo McMurtry, *English Language, English Literature: The Creation of an Academic Discipline* (Hamden, Conn., 1985).

essentially pragmatic or utilitarian view of what is to be achieved through its being taught. In recent times, the rise of English literature, both as an educational subject, and even as a concept in the round, has been linked with the rise of aesthetics, a particular mode of apprehending literary works (and other objects) which, so it has been claimed, emphasizes and even makes a virtue of their lack of utility. Only the absurd function-lessness of literature, and the whole realm of the literary, allows it to possess social value. Yet this chapter concludes by substantiating a very different claim, namely that English literature gains ground as an educational subject in direct proportion to the extent to which its champions find it to be *useful*: it is, as we shall see, the intellectual birth-child of pragmatists not of aesthetes.

II

Two main features governed the likelihood of someone in the eighteenth century becoming conversant with English literature: his or her literacy level and the availability of polite reading matter at affordable prices. As regards the latter, the eighteenth century saw a marked increase in the number of bookselling outlets, both in London and in the provinces.[2] For the most part, retail booksellers, even those far from the metropolis, would be supplied from London, a policy that was facilitated by the increasing efficiency of freight transport and by the commercial agreements regularly taken out between retail booksellers and their London wholesalers. Provincial book retailing was further boosted by the growth of the newspaper industry, for newspapers provided an ideal means through which booksellers could advertise the availability of particular books. By the mid-eighteenth century, many quite small rural centres, such as Lichfield where Johnson's father conducted business, were supporting their own bookshop. Probably the main impediment to the livelihoods of those trading in books was the vogue for

---

[2] See F. A. Mumby, *Publishing and Bookselling: A History from the Earliest Times to the Present Day* (London, 1930); Marjorie Plant, *The English Book Trade: An Economic History of the Making and Sale of Books* (London, 1939); Terry Belanger, 'Publishers and Writers in Eighteenth-Century England', in *Books and their Readers in Eighteenth-Century England*, ed. I. Rivers (Leicester, 1982), 10–13.

circulating libraries, both inside and outside London. In 1758, for example, Joseph Wilson proposed opening a circulating library in Leeds, appealing for subscribers in an advertisement placed in the *Leedes* [sic] *Intelligencer* of 27 November. His gambit for arousing interest was to bruit the benefits of a 'well-regulated Circulating Library', these institutions having been 'universally approv'd' elsewhere.[3] That circulating libraries could allow for familiarity with books, especially novels, on the part of those not normally gaining it (including women) is hinted at in Sheridan's *The Rivals* (1775), where the misogynistic Sir Anthony Absolute declares that a 'circulating library in a town is an evergreen tree of diabolical knowledge'.[4]

If works of poetry and fiction were becoming widely available, who, then, might have read them? The picture painted by an earlier generation of scholars, including Richard Altick and Peter Laslett, was that lower-class reading competence remained, throughout the eighteenth century, only very patchy.[5] This conclusion has since come under attack; but one conundrum bedevilling the whole matter is by what criteria literacy should actually be measured.[6] One necessary distinction is whether 'literacy' is taken as equating with proficiency at reading or at writing, but a further ambiguity concerns what degree of fluency at either activity should be deemed necessary to qualify as literate. The most useful body of hard data derives from Hardwick's Marriage Act

---

[3] Cited from R. M. Wiles, 'Middle-Class Literacy in Eighteenth-Century England: Fresh Evidence', in *Studies in the Eighteenth Century I*, ed. R. F. Brissenden (Canberra, 1968), 52.

[4] *The Rivals*, I. ii, in *The Dramatic Works of Richard Brinsley Sheridan*, ed. Cecil Price, 2 vols. (Oxford, 1973), 1: 85. See also Henry Mackenzie, *The Lounger* 20, 18 June 1785, in *Novel and Romance 1700–1800: A Documentary Record*, ed. Ioan Williams (London, 1970), 331: 'I have purposely pointed my observations, not to that common herd of novels (the wretched offspring of circulating Libraries)...'.

[5] See Richard Altick, *The English Common Reader: A Social History of the Mass Reading Public* (Chicago, 1957); and Peter Laslett, *The World We Have Lost* (London, 1965). A more upbeat estimate of lower-class literacy levels is given in Victor E. Neuberg, *Popular Education in Eighteenth Century England* (London, 1971), 93–113.

[6] For an overview of the issue, see R. S. Schofield, 'The Measurement of Literacy in Pre-Industrial England', in *Literacy in Traditional Societies*, ed. Jack Goody (Cambridge, 1968), 311–25; and David Cressy, 'Literacy in Context: Meaning and Measurement in Early Modern England', in *Consumption and the World of Goods*, ed. John Brewer and Roy Porter (London, 1993), 305–19. Also Neuberg, *Popular Education*, 93–113, 170–4.

of 1754, which established that all marriages had to be validated by an entry in the parish register, to which bride, groom, and two witnesses had to affix their signatures. Those unable to sign instead made a mark. The evidence thrown up by marriage registers shows that, between Hardwick's Act and the end of the century, male illiteracy remained stable at 40 per cent; female illiteracy, meanwhile, which stood at more than 60 per cent in 1754, had fallen ten points by the 1830s, the beginning of state involvement in education.[7]

Such statistics are indicative, but only if not taken at face-value. One problem is that one marriage-partner may well have opted not to sign so as to spare the blushes of his or her illiterate spouse. But a more fundamental quandary is precisely what weighting, amidst the range of literacy indicators, should be given to the ability to sign one's name. In the eighteenth century, reading and writing were seen as distinct skills: they were, for example, taught sequentially (reading naturally coming first); and writing was to a large extent seen as a supernumerary skill for those toiling in the lower employments of society. This sharp demarcation of the skills of reading and writing, somewhat blurred to us today, is indicated by Johnson's initially startling remark that *Gulliver's Travels* was read by both 'the learned and illiterate', 'illiteracy' here being reserved solely for the inability to write.[8]

Evidence extrapolated from the nineteenth century, but applicable to the eighteenth, points to a series of rule-of-thumb correlations between the ability to sign and other facets of literacy.[9] It might be surmised that those who could sign were probably a larger group than those who could write with some degree of fluency; on the other hand, they were certainly less numerous than those who possessed the lowest level of reading skill, i.e. the bare ability to decipher words. The number who could sign was probably roughly equal to the number who could read with serviceable fluency, though not with a fluency that would necessarily have got them through a book of history, philosophy, or *belles lettres*. By the mid-eighteenth century, then, 60 per cent of

[7] David Vincent, *Literacy and Popular Culture: England 1750–1914* (Cambridge, 1989), 3, 53.
[8] 'Life of Swift', in *Lives*, 3: 38.
[9] See Schofield, 'The Measurement of Literacy', 324; Cressy, 'Literacy in Context', 313–14.

the male population could probably read tolerably well, and this perhaps surprising figure does seem to be corroborated by details of readerly consumption. One source of early eighteenth-century social anxiety was that the poor were equipping themselves with educational adornments wholly superfluous to their allotted station as useful drudges. Mandeville, for example, believed that national greatness rested on maintaining a multitude of ignorant poor, and suggested that where people's livelihoods did not obviously call for reading, writing, and arithmetic, such skills were 'very pernicious'.[10] Similarly, the *Grub-Street Journal* no. 247 (19 September 1734) speaks of a 'national *Insania*' caused by many people in low stations being 'more intent upon cultivating their Minds than upon feeding and cloathing their Bodies'.[11]

Anecdotal evidence also suggests reading to have been firmly established at all levels of society. The writer and radical politician, Thomas Holcroft, for instance, spent some of his early years accompanying his parents as they peddled small wares around the Berkshire villages in the 1750s. One of his enduring impressions was the diversity of reading matter to be found in the houses even of poor people: 'Even the walls of cottages and little alehouses would do something; for many of them had old English ballads, such as Death and the Lady, and Margaret's Ghost, with lamentable tragedies, or King Charles's golden rules, occasionally pasted on them.'[12] For much of the populace, whose education would have taken them only so far as a rudimentary reading competence, this was their cultural realm. It was a realm populated not by bound volumes (with the exception of the Bible) but by chapbooks and broadsides purchased from itinerant hawkers. Its 'blockbusters' consisted of ballads, including ones of old vintage such as 'Chevy Chace' and 'Guy of Warwick', popular stories like 'Jack the Giant Killer', 'Saint George and the Dragon', and superstitious tales such as 'Mother Shipton's Legacy'.[13] This material formed the imaginative world of both adults and children, for children's literature as such was

[10] See 'An Essay on Charity and Charity Schools', in *The Fable of the Bees: or Private Vices, Publick Benefits. By Bernard Mandeville*, ed. F. B. Kaye, 2 vols. (Oxford, 1924), 1: 288.
[11] Cited from Wiles, 'Middle-Class Literacy', 51.
[12] Cited from Vincent, *Literacy and Popular Culture*, 198.
[13] See ibid. 54–66.

still an underdeveloped genre, what books there were remaining largely beyond the means of lower-class families.

It was not only the literate, though, who could tap into this imaginative culture: ballads and stories would regularly be recited, either from memory or from the page. The key point, though, is that this culture was very different from that which belonged to the polite classes; and while opportunities for crossover existed, these seem not to have been exploited. A very few eighteenth-century works that enjoyed success within polite circles were rendered into chapbook form, thereby becoming available to a larger, popular audience.[14] Chief amongst these were Defoe's *Robinson Crusoe* and *Moll Flanders*: *Crusoe*, practically from its first appearance, went through numerous abridged versions, several of which, where the retrenchments were most severe and simplificatory, were obviously aimed at the less-educated market. With Defoe, though, cultural exchange flowed both ways: while his work was popularized in abridged formats, even in original form it possessed many traits drawn from 'impolite' literature, including strong, uncluttered plot-lines, a brisk economy of style and, particularly in *Moll Flanders*, an alluring moral seaminess. It is no great surprise, then, that these novels could successfully straddle the divide between popular and polite constituencies, but few other works could boast the same achievement. Such prolific books as *Gulliver's Travels* and *Tom Jones*, works in which the eponymous heroes achieve an independent, quasi-mythical status, fail to make it into chapbook form during the eighteenth century, though the former had its fair share of popular abridgements.[15]

The obstacles to the way of a popular readership for English literature were those of penury, ignorance, indifference, and limited reading competence. Yet there were still many, even in unlikely places, who were minded to read good books. The diary of Thomas Turner (1729–89), a shopkeeper in East Hoathly, Sussex, records that his diverse reading interests took in Pope's translation of Homer, Addison's *Spectator*, Shakespeare, Boyle's

---

[14] See Margaret Spufford, *Small Books and Pleasant Histories: Popular Fiction and its Readership in Seventeenth-Century England* (London, 1981); Pat Rogers, 'Classics and Chapbooks', in Rivers (ed.), *Books and their Readers*, 27–45; and Neuberg, *Popular Education*, 115–25.

[15] Rogers, 'Classics and Chapbooks', 27–9.

Lectures, and the sermons of Tillotson, Gibson, and Sherlock.[16] A shopkeeper, of course, would have tolerable means, but even those of very humble origin were sometimes able to lay their hands on books. Stephen Duck, the working-class Wiltshire poet, probably owned few, but he was lucky enough to be befriended by a man who had been in service in London and who returned to the country with a small collection of books. An early biography of Duck records that his friend 'had learn'd a little which were good Books to read', and the use of this friend's library gave Duck access to the Bible, Milton, *The Spectator* as well as Greek translations.[17]

This general scenario holds also for Mary Leapor, the cook–maid turned poet, who grew up in the Northamptonshire village of Brackley.[18] Both her parents could evidently read, and her father's well-formed script has been preserved in local records. The weakness of Mary Leapor's own hand, though, might suggest that her early education, probably at Magdalen Free School, was orientated towards reading. Notwithstanding her death at 24, Leapor's poetry demonstrates that her reading must have been capacious. Her avidness was probably satisfied through a variety of channels: she became close friends with Bridget Freemantle, a local woman whose background was bookish, her father having been an Oxford fellow; she would have been known to, and perhaps encouraged by, the local vicar Thomas Bowles, author of a grammar, *A Compendious and Rational Institution of the Latin Tongue* (1740); and her career in service included a stint at Weston Hall, which had a library. Whatever her incidental access to books owned by others, we also know that Leapor possessed some of her own; Bridget Freemantle recorded that 'Mrs. LEAPOR's whole Library consisted of about sixteen or seventeen single Volumes, among which were Part of Mr. *Pope's* Works, *Dryden's* Fables, some Volumes of Plays, &c.'[19] Leapor and Duck would, no doubt, have recognized a distinction between popular literature, that of chap-

---

[16] Wiles, 'Middle-Class Literacy', 53.
[17] J. Spence, *A Full and Authentick Account of Stephen Duck the Wiltshire Poet* (1731); cited from Neuberg, *Popular Education*, 39.
[18] The authoritative account of her life is Richard Greene, *Mary Leapor: A Study in Eighteenth-Century Women's Poetry* (Oxford, 1993), see 9–11, 165–85.
[19] Cited from Greene, *Mary Leapor*, 10.

books and oral recitation, and the category of 'good books', but this hierarchical leap would have been lost on all but a few. People of humble origin would probably have heard of polite authors (principally Shakespeare) yet not necessarily have understood the difference between these and the stuff of their own reading. In 1825, Clare could report that the common people know 'the name of Shakespeare as a great play writer because they have often seen him nominated as such on the bills of strolling players', but he thought this conversancy availed little if people remained indifferent to the relative merits of Shakespeare and their own customary reading fare.[20]

A summary might, then, be given of the wider eighteenth-century dissemination of English literature. Across the populace, 60 per cent of males may have been 'literate' in the sense of being competent readers, though the figure falls off in relation to poverty and provinciality. Those who did read availed themselves of an imaginative world, stocked with chapbooks, broadsides, newspapers, and cheap, abridged classics. The small minority whose reading habits were aspirational would no doubt have come by more elevated reading matter, made available by the spread of bookshops and (to some extent) circulating libraries. Yet, although books were becoming more widely disseminated, their numerousness remained of a different order from nowadays. A provincial denizen who owned twenty bound volumes would probably have possessed a 'library' of parochial renown; this pettiness of scale, though, was partly redressed by the fact that a book would often be shared around so as to be read by many more than just the one owner. An overall conclusion must, inevitably, though be downbeat: English literature, conceived as the imaginative reading matter of the cultured classes, would have made little impact on the lives, or even reading habits, of the overwhelming majority. Only for those raised out of the ordinary by cultural aspiration or education would English literature have become reified. And the implications of education are what I now want to discuss.

---

[20] John Clare, 'Essay in Popularity', in *The Prose of John Clare*, ed. J. W. and A. Tibble (London, 1951), 207.

III

There is no state involvement in education until the nineteenth century, before which time educational provision was grossly unsystematic. Some children, no doubt, fell through the educational net (such as there was one) altogether; others may have benefited from a solid rudimentary education, delivered both at school and at home; others, not necessarily from a different social stratum, might have progressed beyond elementary level and attended the local grammar school.[21] The function of the lowest educational rung, the elementary school, was to teach reading, but many also taught writing and the more advanced skill of arithmetic, as well as doling out religious and moral instruction. The schoolmaster in Goldsmith's *The Deserted Village* (1770), for example, is described as being able to 'write and cipher [i.e. do arithmetic] too'.[22] Non-charitable schools acquired the slightly sneering cognomen of 'dame schools': they were, as a rule, run by a single teacher (normally female) who, for a small charge, provided rudimentary education to local children. Establishments of this sort are described in several eighteenth-century poems, most notably Shenstone's *The School-Mistress* (1737). It is probably indicative that Shenstone tells us practically nothing about what actually got taught and learnt, his interest being mainly in the daily drama of classroom restraint and punishment.[23] Probably, indeed, many dame schools provided little more than regimented child-minding. Those who taught in them were, as a rule, unblessed of any credentials beyond their own literacy, and textbooks would have been in short supply. Shenstone's poem does document, though, the use of the horn-book, which was the most popular method of teaching reading: it consisted of a single sheet of paper, on which were printed the alphabet, the nine digits, and

---

[21] The ensuing discussion draws on Nicholas Hans, *New Trends in Education in the Eighteenth Century* (London, 1951); Richard S. Tompson, *Classics or Charity? The Dilemma of the Eighteenth Century Grammar School* (Manchester, 1971); and Neuberg, *Popular Education*.

[22] 'The Deserted Village', line 208, in *The Poems of Gray, Collins and Goldsmith*, ed. Lonsdale, 685.

[23] The earliest version of the poem (1737) is available in *The New Oxford Book of Eighteenth Century Verse*, ed. Roger Lonsdale (Oxford, 1984), 305–7. Lines 3–4 describe 'A matron old, whom we school-mistress name, | Who wont unruly brats with birch to tame'.

the Lord's Prayer, which was covered with transparent horn and locked into a frame.

Dame-schools like Shenstone's were increasingly to be supplanted by charitable or endowed ones. These were traditionally founded from the proceeds of property held in trust: the education they provided, accordingly, was free at the point of delivery, and those who delivered it were appointed and therefore vetted. Such schools might also have aspired to take their pupils beyond simple reading and may even have broached the rudiments of Latin grammar. For most pupils, this would be the point at which their brush with education would finish, but a few would take a further upward step into grammar school. These institutions delivered their instruction in Latin, the term 'grammar' signifying so much, many being enjoined to do so by the precise articles of their foundation. Ages of admission to these schools varied from 7 to 9; pupils who were to be apprenticed probably left them at between 12 and 14; and the rest would have gone through to the age of Oxbridge entrance which in the eighteenth century was normally at around 17.[24] Grammar school education represented a considerable advance on what came prior to it: the schoolmaster would customarily possess a university degree and would be able to call upon appropriate textbooks.

This latter fact about the provision of textbooks is important here, since it is only from the survival of printed books that we can surmise what might actually have been taught in particular schools. Even here the territory is muddy: merely knowing that a textbook must have been widely in use, since it was being regularly reissued, tells us nothing about which age-groups in which schools would have been exposed to it. One source of obscurity is that distinctions of function and practice between schools were often very blurred: the best teaching in the best endowed elementary schools, for instance, probably covered much the same educational ground as the more lowly grammar schools and academies. Yet one thing that can be asserted is that from 1660 onwards, pupils attending schools munificent enough to provide textbooks would have had *some* chance of encountering excerpts from vernacular literary works, and through this means have gleaned some awareness of the English literary

---

[24] See Tompson, *Classics or Charity?*, 33.

tradition. The main sorts of book that afforded these possibilities were anthologies of poetic *exempla*, rhetorical handbooks and spelling primers.[25]

An early example of the first is Joshua Poole's *The English Parnassus: or a Helpe to English Poesie* (1657) which was intended as a crib-book for embryonic poets. It supplied lists of rhyme-words, 'choice' epithets or phrases, as well as a vast assortment of poetic sentiments on a host of subjects. These sentiments are not made up but culled from English poets, yet their sources are not identified and the individual excerpts are run together nearly seamlessly. What is clear is that the opportunity to realize a sense of English literature—if only as a chronological progression of named authors—is entirely overshadowed by the pedagogic task in hand: the coaching of pupils in their own poetry-making. A half-century later, however, a close replica of Poole's project, Edward Bysshe's *The Art of English Poetry* (1702), shows how things have changed. By its third edition, the work boasted three sections, the first and last of which were concerned with versification and rhyme. The middle section, however, comprised a self-standing anthology, called 'A Collection of the most Natural and Sublime Thoughts...that are in the best English poets'. The excerpts are organized by subject-matter but, unlike those in Poole, they are attributed and, moreover, a full authorial list is printed on the title-page reverse. Yet the most revealing aspect of the exercise is that Bysshe felt a need to justify the pattern of his inclusions and omissions. So, for example, he gives the 'obsolete' nature of Shakespeare's language as the reason why he 'is not so frequently cited in this Collection, as he would otherwise deserve to be'.[26] Bysshe's 'Collection', in other words, if not meant to be an anthology of English literature, was still intended to give a faithful portrayal of it: otherwise, he would not have felt a need to defend himself against the charge of infidelity.

The shift from Poole to Bysshe is towards deploying compositional examples in a way that has the indirect effect of reifying a concept of English literature, and a similar tendency can be found if one looks at rhetorical handbooks. The study of rhetoric had

---

[25] I am indebted hereabouts to Ian Michael, *The Teaching of English: From the Sixteenth Century to 1870* (Cambridge, 1987).

[26] Edward Bysshe, *The Art of English Poetry* (3rd edn., 1708), 'Preface'.

long formed a major part of school and university curricula, and the many handbooks of tropes traditionally drew their examples from Greek and Latin sources. Yet, from the late seventeenth century, authors are increasingly inclined to procure their illustrations from English writings. Ralph Johnson's *The Scholar's Guide* (1665) is one case in point. The work was concerned to tutor pupils in Latin composition, principally through getting them to imitate Latin originals. But where Johnson cannot find a Latin equivalent for the compositional form he is trying to recommend, he then resorts to English sources. So, for example, he illustrates the 'essay' form by reference to Hall, Bacon, and Felltham.[27] There is scant evidence that Johnson's practice had an immediate impact, and sixty years pass before the appearance of Anthony Blackwall's *An Introduction to the Classics* (1728), a much more influential work reinstating the same method. The work consists of two parts: the first, a disquisition on why one should read the classics: the second, an enumeration of the different rhetorical tropes, each one illustrated by a passage from some acclaimed English author, as Roscommon, Tillotson, Prior, Milton, Dryden, Shakespeare, and so on.

In 1767 appeared a rhetorical primer adopting the same policy of extensive quotation as Blackwall and acknowledging him as its pioneer, Thomas Gibbons's *Rhetoric; or a view of its Principal Tropes and Figures* (1767).[28] Indeed, so thick are the illustrations that the compiler seems embarrassed by his own profuseness:

If the quotations... [are]... more than are needful for the purpose, his apology must be, that it was difficult for him to deny the insertion of apposite and elegant passages from writers of the first reputation; that those passages may enliven as well as embellish his work; and [the young people may learn to imitate the examples].[29]

The book is divided into two sections: the first devoted to tropes, the second to figures: and each trope or figure is illustrated by copious quotations. The device of *prosopopoeia*, for example, is exemplified by excerpts from Silvius Italicus, Ovid, Virgil, Cicero,

---

[27] See Michael, *Teaching of English*, 144.
[28] Thomas Gibbons, *Rhetoric, or a View of its Principal Tropes and Figures* (1767), facs. repr. (Menston, 1969). Gibbons's 'Preface' refers to 'THE Ingenious and Reverend Mr ANTHONY BLACKWALL'.
[29] Gibbons, 'Preface', sig. A4ᵛ.

Spenser, Milton, Blackmore, Young, and Pope. Gibbons is entirely candid that the intention behind this excessive doling out of illustrations is more radical than merely to press home a cognizance of rhetoric. His purpose, instead, is twofold: to lend his work a literary attractiveness, and to impart to the pupils a taste for fine writing, in the hope that they will acquire a polished style of their own. The overt educational agenda, in other words, seems to mask a 'literary' or appreciative one.

This general shift towards citing *exempla* drawn from vernacular literature, and moreover citing them with their aesthetic potential clearly in mind, is further replicated by the changing format of spelling books. One technique the spelling books adopted was to illustrate correct spellings not merely by listing words but by supplying passages of reading-matter. Before 1700, this material is, as a rule, doctrinal, but in 1694 *A Play-book for Children* became the first to contain nothing but secular reading-matter. In 1714, Harland's *The English Spelling-book revis'd* registered another first, becoming the earliest such primer to be furnished with an extensive anthology of literary passages, including extracts from Quarles, Waller, Garth, Dryden, Blackmore, Cowley, Prior, and Shakespeare. These passages seem to be designed for children at an advanced stage of development and, indeed, so Harland suggests, 'may be of use to older people'. Harland's rationale for providing these excerpts lies in the susceptibility of children to being influenced by what they read: it is this factor that makes imperative the provision of high quality material. Harland, so Ian Michael asserts, harbours few aspirations to be seen as an innovator, but he has all the same grasped the critical fact that there could be aesthetic ramifications even in the mere supplying of school pupils with routine pedagogic *exempla*.[30]

IV

It has become something of a truism of educational history that during the eighteenth century the grammar schools went into decline. This contention is not obviously borne out by the statistics of the operational schools, though some schools may have felt the

[30] Michael, *Teaching of English*, 159.

pinch as a result of the growth of dissenting academies (discussed below), which ate into their potential market. Yet there was one trend, not unrelated to the rise of the academies, which may have set the grammar schools on the defensive: this was an increasing scepticism about the usefulness of a classical education. Just what would-be reformers were seeking to deviate from can, perhaps, be exemplified by taking one singular work of 'old-style' educational theory. In 1753 appeared Henry Wotton's *An Essay on the Education of Children in the First Rudiments of Learning*, a work which had actually been written some eighty years earlier (around 1672). Being published so belatedly did Wotton's work no favours, ensuring in fact that his ideas became aired at just the time when their anachronism would have been most apparent. The book charts the educational development of Wotton's own son William who, under a tutorial regime that his father tries to advance for general usage, became a child prodigy of barely credible proportions. By the time he was 6, the young Wotton had not merely made a quick mastery of his own tongue but had also become proficient in Latin, Greek, and Hebrew. The educational programme recommended is not in fact draconian, and Wotton's pedagogic rhetoric stresses the need to tap into children's innate enthusiasm for knowledge (as evidenced in unparalleled fashion by his own son) rather than to subject them to stern bouts of force-feeding. Yet what strikes one as odd is the author's serene assumption that, granted you have a highly gifted child, the best way you can exploit this giftedness is to gorge him on dead languages. Wotton's conviction is so untroubled that he bothers to state its merit only in passing: his reasoning being that knowledge of old languages will give children more access to 'ancient Authors'; and from this source they will come to 'more Prudence in their Conduct, [and] to more Humility, Peaceableness, and Order in their Conversation'.[31]

William Wotton grew up, not surprisingly, to be a scholar: the specific education he underwent could hardly have prepared him for anything else. Yet Wotton senior almost certainly never viewed his educational programme as comprising training for any particular profession, for it was advanced as a scheme of universal education, or as a scheme that could aspire to univer-

[31] Henry Wotton, *An Essay on the Education of Children in the First Rudiments of Learning* (1753), v. Wotton's educational programme is discussed in Levine, *The Battle of the Books*, 31.

sality amongst the relatively narrow ranks of the educated class. The irony, though, is that by the time the book reached its public, systems of universal education were on their way out. Cynicism about the irrelevance or, indeed, injuriousness of a purely classical education was surprisingly widespread during the seventeenth and eighteenth centuries. Milton's 'Of Education' (1644), for example, bemoans the 'seven or eight years [spent] meerly in scraping together so much miserable Latine and Greek'; and *Spectator* 157, ostensibly an attack on the cruelty of schoolmasters, associates this brutality with the forcible inculcation of Latin, from which boys devoid of the remotest intellectual aptitude were not exempted.[32]

Increasing industrialization and the utilitarian ethos nurtured by the Royal Society probably played some part in fostering resistance to the conventions of a purely classical education, yet the drive towards educational 'realism' (as it became known) emanated most strongly from the dissenting community. The Interregnum was probably the first period in English history in which debate about the orientation and purpose of education took place close to the helm of national policy-making. The philosophy of educational pragmatism was pioneered on the continent by Comenius, who visited England in 1641 possibly at the behest of parliament and whose ideas were popularized in England by such as John Milton and Samuel Hartlib. The essence of the realist philosophy was that education should be practical and utilitarian rather than universal. The agenda, moreover, stressed the usefulness of scientific learning; it encouraged conversancy with modern languages; it was critical of traditional school and university curricula in which a paramount place was given to the study of classical languages and culture; and it encouraged a more humane delivery of education, through nurturing the understanding rather than subjecting pupils to mechanical routines of rote learning.

In the eighteenth century, the implementing of reformed education was most fully realized in the dissenting academies but the general project fanned out more widely: at its heart was a drive to place foremost in the syllabus the systematic study of the

---

[32] *The Works of John Milton*, ed. Frank Allen Patterson *et al.*, 18 vols. (New York, 1931–8), 4: 277; No. 157 [by Steele], 30 Aug. 1711, in *Spectator*, 2: 114–17.

mother tongue. One of the most successful textbooks written with this objective in view is Joseph Priestley's *Rudiments of English Grammar* (1761). Priestley accounts for the perverse neglect of the subject in terms of the inflated regard accorded to classical languages: 'not much above a century ago...our native tongue seemed to be looked upon as below the notice of a classical scholar.'[33] What he sees himself vying against is an educational system geared almost solely to the interests of scholarship, for which the natural language of interchange was Latin. But he is also sensitive to the increasing diversification of trades and occupations, the effect of which was to reduce the Latin language to an advanced state of irrelevance:

The propriety of introducing the *English grammar* into *English schools*, cannot be disputed; a competent knowledge of our own language being both useful and ornamental in every profession, and a critical knowledge of it absolutely necessary to all persons of a liberal education.[34]

One precedent for studying the English tongue was provided paradoxically by the example of classical culture. John Buchanan's *The British Grammar* (1762) cites the proficiency of Greek youths at writing their own language as a backdrop to his own lament: 'Who thinks it of Use to study correctly that Language which he is to use every Day of his Life, be his Station ever so high, or ever so insignificant?'[35]

The methods by which students could acquire good English were broadly three-fold: they could read through general expositions of grammatical rules; they could learn through prepared question-answer routines; and they could be presented with selected passages of English composition, either ones exemplifying grammatical rules (or errors) or exhibiting qualities of style. Priestley's *Rudiments*, for example, sets out by involving its readers in the grimmest form of rote-responding: 'Q. WHAT IS GRAMMAR? A. GRAMMAR is the art of using words properly'; but a later section provides an anthology of extracts from English composition, drawing on the words of Swift, Pope, Hume, Addison, Johnson, Shakespeare, and others. The rationale behind

---

[33] Joseph Priestley, *Rudiments of English Grammar* (1761), 'Preface', ix.
[34] Ibid. viii.
[35] James Buchanan, *The British Grammar* (1762), facs. repr. (Menston, 1968), xviii.

this provision is set down at the start: 'THE following pieces are collected from our most celebrated English Writers, for the exemplification both of the rules of *Grammar*, and of the *Observations on Style*.'[36] Yet the passages were not to be perfunctory aids to the pupils' study of grammar and style, for Priestley admits that they have been chosen so as to impress upon them good taste and (more vaguely) to instil in them 'what is rational, useful and ornamental in their temper, and conduct in life'.[37] Literary examples, then, are useful to illustrate precepts about grammar and style but, in introducing them, Priestley is also keen to coax his students towards acts of specifically 'literary' appreciation. So the pupils are invited to align their taste with that embodied in the excerpts, and to allow themselves to be improved morally by this fragmentary experience of literary works.

As one travels from 1650 to 1750, the likelihood of exposure to vernacular literature at elementary level or grammar school progressively increases. Yet, because schools could only deliver syllabuses for which they could afford to buy textbooks, actual classroom practice probably always lagged a little behind the emergence of a revisionary ethos. More explicit evidence of continuity between a reformed education and the teaching specifically of literature comes from two sets of proposals, one drawn up by the American Benjamin Franklin and the other by the Irishman Thomas Sheridan, father of Richard Brinsley, for an idealized public education. Franklin's *Idea of a New School* (1751) was motivated by a reformist zeal for a revised syllabus that would equip pupils for an active career, notionally in the professions or in business. Its most striking feature is the absence of tuition in the classical languages, though this deficit was to be more than compensated for by the mastery pupils would gain over their own language, 'which is of more immediate and general use'. Franklin anticipates that even the most basic reading skills will be acquired through contact with 'literary' works, conceived as texts that are notable for style as much as content. So 'second class students' will understand simple grammar from 'some of the easier *Spectators*'; pupils in the fourth class will acquire letter-writing skills through adopting as models the letters of Sir William Temple,

---

[36] The anthology of compositional extracts occupies 65–92.
[37] Ibid. 65.

Pope, and such like; and in the final year, alongside the study of 'history, rhetoric, logic, moral and natural philosophy, the best English authors may be read and explained; as Tillotson, Milton, Locke, Addison, Pope, Swift, the higher papers in the *Spectator* and *Guardian*, the best translations of Homer, Virgil, and Horace'. At no stage of Franklin's model curriculum would literature be a supernumerary element. Yet the syllabus culminates with students progressing to consider literature seemingly *for its own sake*: a radical departure.[38]

Thomas Sheridan's 'Plan of a Public School' forms part of his *A Plan of Education for the Young Nobility and Gentry of Great Britain* (1769). Sheridan was probably the most public and indefatigable spokesman for the utilitarian viewpoint in education, his guiding principles being that education should be vocationally relevant, and that at its core should be proficiency in English, for 'all that is got by the present complete system of English education, is a smattering in two dead languages'.[39] Sheridan also endorses the idea that pupils envisaging entering specific professions should be 'fast-tracked' by following a syllabus modified to their precise needs. Younger boys in Sheridan's envisaged school will be set to study the language chiefly in 'books of religion or morality', though they will also have 'to read and repeat some of the purest and most elegant passages, extracted from the best English writers'. For his 'Upper School', despite advancing that students should 'read a few, a very few of our English poets', Sheridan recommends a capacious syllabus, taking in Milton, Shakespeare, John Philips, Thomson, Mason, and Armstrong. In spite of the presence of literature on the syllabus, Sheridan stops short of claiming that the study of literary works possesses intrinsic value. Literature's role is as a medium for the study of language, for a sort of mental relaxation, 'to unbend their minds', and for the acquisition of taste. Even when recommending a range of literary works, Sheridan is keen to safeguard against the injury that could result from pupils coming into contact with

[38] Benjamin Franklin, 'Sketch of an English School; for the Consideration of the Trustees of the Philadelphia Academy', in *The Complete Works in Philosophy, Politics and Morals of the Late Dr. Benjamin Franklin*, 3 vols. (London, 1806), 2: 370–8.
[39] Thomas Sheridan, *A Plan of Education for the Young Nobility and Gentry of Great Britain* (1769), 16.

188 TEACHING ENGLISH LITERATURE

literary works marked by falseness or irregularity. So he enjoins that a teacher presenting Shakespeare's tragedies should draw attention as much to their faults as to their beauties. This admonitory approach will supposedly ensure that pupils acquire a correct taste—a taste that will reveal itself in good composition and in the making of true critical judgements.[40]

Conclusions to be drawn from the texts considered in this section can only be tentative. However, it is likely that between 1660 and 1730 some elementary and grammar school pupils would have made an incidental acquaintance with the concept of a vernacular literary canon through learning to spell and compose in verse and through studying the classics. One index of this trend is provided by Vicesimus Knox's anthology of *Elegant Extracts* (1784) which sought to round up 'a great number and variety of such pieces ["of English Verse"] as were already in use in schools'.[41] The key thing is not *that*, or *when*, English literature was encountered but that it would have been encountered in spite of not being, in any express sense, taught. And this should caution against the casual assumption that English literature only exists in the educational realm once it has been furnished with its own syllabus. Where literary works (or bits of them) appeared on proposed or actual syllabuses, they, for the most part, served different ends from those we customarily associate with the subject. There is no sense that conversancy with literary texts was thought useful as regards bringing children to an acquaintance with their own cultural heritage. Perhaps surprisingly, considering the strong patriotic tendency in much Augustan literary criticism, there is no sense of literature serving as a rallying-post for a spirit of corporate nationhood. Generally, then, literature gets taught in the service of ends that are not primarily 'literary', though pupils were sometimes encouraged, in a secondary way, to respond to works or gobbets in ways that could be construed as 'aesthetic'. Ian Michael has suggested that James Greenwood's school anthology *The Virgin Muse* (1717), which the author claimed was suitable 'for the *Teaching to Read Poetry*' may have been the first educational textbook to express

---

[40] Ibid. 101.
[41] Vicesimus Knox, *Elegant Extracts: or Useful and Entertaining Pieces of Poetry, Selected for the Improvement of Youth, in Speaking, Reading, Thinking, Composing, and in the Conduct of Life* (1784?). The date of the first edition is uncertain.

the idea that an understanding of poetry could be nurtured as a skill worthwhile in itself.[42] But there is little evidence that this premise soon catches on in the educational realm.

V

The English dissenting academies came into being as a more or less direct result of the aggressive conformity legislation of the 1660s.[43] The Act of Uniformity stipulated that all public or private schoolmasters make a formal declaration of their allegiance to the Anglican liturgy and obtain a licence to teach from their relevant church authority. The effect of this programme of legislation, however, was mostly other than intended: while making it more difficult for non-conformists to set up or be employed as teachers, the fact that students at the two great universities were also required to subscribe to the Uniformity Act actually accelerated the demand for an educational system outside the reach of the state. Thus the need for academies was created even by the legislation that sought to ensure their suppression. The state's desire to clamp down on educational dissidence was, in any event, rebuffed by a series of adverse legal judgements, as in Bates's case of 1670, which recorded that if a schoolmaster was the nominee or the founder of a school, he could not be ejected even in the absence of a church licence. By 1730, nearly a thousand dissenting academies had been established and as these, unlike the Oxbridge universities, did not insist on any doctrinal allegiance, they were free to receive students from both dissenting and Anglican communities alike.

The academies educated pupils across a broad age-range. Warrington Academy, for example, initially received boys as young as 14 and then educated them through to graduation level: doubling up, in other words, as both grammar school and

---

[42] Michael, *Teaching of English*, 171.

[43] For the history of these institutions, I am indebted chiefly to H. McLachlan, *English Education under the Test Acts: Being the History of the Non-Conformist Academies 1662–1800* (Manchester, 1931); and Irene Parker, *Dissenting Academies in England: Their Rise and Progress and their Place among the Educational Systems of the Country* (New York, 1969). See also Thomas P. Miller, *The Formation of College English: Rhetoric and Belles Lettres in the British Cultural Provinces* (Pittsburgh, 1997), 86–116.

university. This idea of a foundation 'at once both School and University, not needing a remove to any other house of scholarship' is explicitly advocated in Milton's 'Of Education'.[44] Yet, as well as straddling this traditional educational divide, a more radical contribution of the academies was to define anew the purpose and content of education. Although grammar schools were adjusting to the new educational ethos by increasingly offering non-classical tuition, they were in many cases tied to an old style curriculum by their very articles of foundation. The academies, on the other hand, were entirely free to implement syllabuses that accorded with the prevailing pedagogic wisdom. As the nation's commercial life became ever more complex, it was increasingly obvious that no single scheme of education could prepare young people for employment in all the walks of professional life that were available to the educated: as the church, the military, the law, commerce, and the world of public affairs. The academies accordingly offered an education that was slanted towards the needs of a professional and business culture rather than towards those of scholars or the more nebulous educational requirements of those destined to hold public office.

As I have said, opposition to universal education had by the middle of the century taken firm root. Joseph Priestley, for example, begins *An Essay on a Course of Liberal Education* (1765) by desiderating 'a proper course of studies . . . for Gentlemen who are designed to fill the principal stations of active life, distinct from those which are adapted to the learned profession'; four years later, Thomas Sheridan can be found regretting that young noblemen 'are all trained in one and the same course, which fits them for no one employment upon earth'.[45] Although the mission of the academies always had been to provide a more practical education than had previously been available, a further need was still felt for the education of each pupil to be tailored to his likely subsequent occupation. Sheridan's treatise, accordingly, recommends that students looking towards careers in medicine, Holy orders, law, the army, commerce, or estate ownership (most of them unavailable to dissenters) should pursue syllabuses

---

[44] *Works*, 4: 280.
[45] Priestley, *An Essay on a Course of Liberal Education for Civil and Active Life* (1765), 1; Sheridan, *A Plan of Education*, 16.

slightly different one from another. Evidence exists that some targeting of educational provision did, indeed, go on in the academies, as at Warrington. Here the full course was one of five years, the fourth year being devoted to moral philosophy and the fifth to exercises that would prepare pupils for 'a proper Discharge of ... [a] Public Office'. Yet for students 'intended for a life of Business and Commerce' a truncated three-year course was laid on, so as not to involve them in studies superfluous to their needs.[46]

Amongst all the academies, Warrington was unparalleled in terms of the distinction of its tutors and in the general reputation it won for itself. In an era in which the Oxbridge universities have been accused of intellectual sluggishness, Warrington acquired the heady cognomen of the 'Athens of the North'. The institution's lifespan was short: it opened its doors in 1757, ceased to admit students from 1783 and was officially wound up three years later. Yet in its brief period of existence, those employed as tutors in *belles lettres* included John Aikin, editor of the *Monthly Magazine*; William Enfield, author of two prodigiously successful elocutionary primers, *The Speaker* (1774) and *Exercises in Elocution* (1780); Gilbert Wakefield, energetic scholar and religious polemicist, and author of *Silva Critica*, a work that sought to reconcile theological and classical learning; and Joseph Priestley, an intellectual polymath who achieved distinction variously as a scientist, linguistician, theologian, and educationalist. The line-up represents a convergence of intellectual talents in the humanities unmatched other than by the universities of the Scottish Enlightenment. Inaugurated in 1757, Warrington was one of the later academies to be founded, and many of its staff moved from, or were educated in, other dissenting establishments. John Aikin, for example, spent time at Kibworth under its head Philip Doddridge, an educational pioneer credited with being the first to establish the vernacular as the language of the lecture-room throughout all stages of education.[47] Warrington, in other words, was not a pioneering institution so much as a paragon of what had become best practice in reformed education.

[46] McLachlan, *English Education under The Test Acts*, 210. For a treatment specifically of Warrington Academy, see P. O. Brien, *Warrington Academy 1757–86: Its Predecessors and Successors* (Wigan, 1989).
[47] McLachlan, *English Education under the Test Acts*, 21.

What, then was taught at Warrington? And to what extent did the syllabus enable students to become acquainted with English literature? Most of the evidence unfortunately is oblique and anecdotal, but some of it retains an indicative value. The library catalogue printed in 1775 shows, as one might expect, extensive holdings in the more modern subjects, history faring especially well with eighty-one titles as against seventy in classics. A further category is called 'Miscellanies' and while it does include some actual miscellanies, most of the titles relate to (mainly English) literature: authors represented include Shakespeare, Swift, Bacon, Gray, and Prior.[48] The actual integration of literature into the syllabus, however, was probably minimal. The educational 'Plan', published in 1760, shows first-year students taking language studies and elementary mathematics; in the second year, logic, natural history, and 'natural philosophy' are added to the curriculum; the third year has the students progressing to moral philosophy and theology; and the final year promises studies relating uniquely to each student's envisaged vocation.[49] We would expect literature to be entertained beneath the auspice of *belles lettres*, yet what was covered in this syllabus slot remains obscure. We do know, though, that John Aikin ran a series of Saturday morning classes in which he addressed himself to passages from some of the finest English poets such as Milton, Pope, Thomson, Young, and Akenside. Having read out some passages, he would then hear his students read in turn, pointing out their mistakes.[50]

Aikin's Saturday morning sessions are indicative in more than one sense. While Saturday teaching was not uncommon in academies, the non-weekday slot suggests a course of study lacking mainstream curricular status. It is apparent, moreover, that literature was being introduced in subordination to the training of students in elocution. During the eighteenth century, elocution came to bulk large as a component of reformed syllabuses. One part of the general elocutionary project I want to consider later:

[48] The library catalogue originally drawn up in 1775 is reprinted in Parker, *Dissenting Academies*, 'Appendix IV', 154–9.

[49] See McLachlan, *English Education under The Test Acts*, 210. Useful information about the workings of the Academy is contained in Robert E. Schofield, *The Enlightenment of Joseph Priestley: A Study of his Life and Work from 1733 to 1773* (Pennsylvania, 1997), esp. 87–158.

[50] Parker, 111.

this is the attempt to create a standard of correct elocution, especially by rationalizing Scottish, Irish, and English provincial pronunciation to the supposed norm of the home counties. The odour of linguistic imperialism here is unmistakable but, in a more general way, good elocution was valued as an indispensable adjunct of gentlemanly polish and practical social competence. Thomas Sheridan, a driving force in the elocutionary movement, recalled a conversation he had with Swift shortly after having matriculated at college. Swift asked whether he was being taught 'how to speak', and when Sheridan replied in the negative, the great man's retort was peremptory: 'Then...they teach you *Nothing*.'[51]

A celebrated elocutionary primer that made liberal use of literary excerpts was William Enfield's *The Speaker: or, Miscellaneous Pieces Selected from the best English Writers...with a View to Facilitate the Improvement of Youth in Reading and Speaking* (1774). The work ran through innumerable editions until the middle of the nineteenth century as well as being subject to imitation and plagiarism, and Enfield followed up with a work of almost identical make-up *Exercises in Elocution* (1780). It has been suggested by Margaret Weedon that in its hey-day Enfield's *Speaker* would have been known to 'almost every English schoolboy with any pretensions to education'.[52] It figures, for example, in the lists of recommended books at the end of Clara Reeve's *The Progress of Romance* (1785) and Erasmus Darwin's *A Plan for the Conduct of Female Education in Boarding Schools* (1797). Its breadth of educational catchment is all the more interesting because the work, far from being some lumpen classroom manual, offered a vivid conspectus of the field of 'English literature'. Enfield's choice of material was imaginative and even original. The first edition included gobbets drawn from admittedly predictable figures such as Butler, Prior, Pope, Thomson, Addison, and Gray, but also found room for a figure of more unresolved reputation, Sterne; and the 1792 edition chalked up a particular first by providing the first printing in book form of nine poems by William Cowper, including 'On the Death of Mrs.

[51] The anecdote is quoted from Howell, *Eighteenth-Century British Logic and Rhetoric*, 216.
[52] Margaret Weedon, 'Jane Austen and William Enfield's *The Speaker*', *British Journal for Eighteenth-Century Studies*, 11 (1988): 159–62.

Throckmorton's Bulfinch'.[53] Moreover, like Priestley in his *Rudiments of English Grammar*, Enfield was attuned to the aesthetic potential held out by literary excerption. This is especially clear in the 'Advertisement' of *Exercises in Elocution* where he specifies that besides merely providing 'exercises', he has chosen 'a large number of . . . passages from the most approved literary productions of our own country, as might serve to lead young persons into some acquaintance with the most valuable writers, and assist them in forming a taste for the beauties of fine writing'.[54]

The anthology of extracts contained in *The Speaker* was offered with a view to its helping pupils practise their elocution, but the work gives the firm impression that the literary agenda has in fact outstripped, or at least come to vie with, the strict elocutionary one. Prefixed to the anthological section are two essays: the first on elocution, the second 'On Reading Works of Taste'. The second of these attempts to find objective grounds for distinguishing its own subject-matter from 'Works of Knowledge', these being writings in which language serves as a 'vehicle of instruction', and in which the primary objective is lucidity or (to use the eighteenth-century term) 'perspicuity'. However, in works of taste 'the writing itself becomes a principal object of attention', to be judged only in terms of its fidelity to the author's imaginative conceptions.[55] Such works, in other words, remain recalcitrant to simply mimetic criteria of worth. In the context of its own time, Enfield's analysis is critically strenuous and far-sighted, and in a way that might seem out of place in an elocution manual. What its inclusion demonstrates, though, is just how insistent the literary agenda has now become. Enfield's excerpts are drawn from celebrated writers not so as to avoid the injurious influence that might be the result of citing bad ones, but so that students, in a positive way, can be apprised of the most approved literary productions of their own country. We cannot say that literature is yet being 'taught' exactly, but the phenomenon of literature, and of a vernacular literary inheritance, is being forcefully urged on the attention of pupils.

[53] Ibid.
[54] William Enfield, *Exercises in Elocution Selected from Various Authors and Arranged under Proper Heads* (1780), 'Advertisement'.
[55] *The Speaker or Miscellaneous Pieces Selected from the Best English Writers* (1774), xxix.

Enfield's *Speaker* is indicative of the hospitable attitudes that many of the academies had to literature, and also of how literature sometimes crept on to syllabuses under the guise of elocutionary instruction. When Philip Doddridge was studying at Kibworth Academy, he set down in a letter details of the institution's syllabus. Regarding the oratorical exercises prescribed for the second half-year, he recorded: 'Bacon's Essays often used... and our exercises were a kind of comment upon some remarkable sentences they contained.'[56] The remark illustrates how easy the slide was from pronouncing extracts to subjecting them to criticism. What part Enfield, himself, played in elocutionary training at Warrington remains unclear, but his colleagues John Aikin and Joseph Priestley both regarded it as indispensable to a balanced education. Priestley's own elocutionary lectures were published in 1777, a decade after their original delivery, as *A Course of Lectures on Oratory and Criticism*. The critical section was modelled on Alexander Gerard's *Essay on Taste* (1758) and Lord Kames's *Elements of Criticism* (1762), addressing what was becoming a standard repertoire of critical issues: the pleasures of imagination, the sublime, compositional originality, the nature of true taste, and so on. As well as enumerating literary genres and rhetorical figures, the work is also profuse with exemplary quotations drawn from English literature. That literature could be annexed to elocutionary training allowed its appearance on the syllabus to remain consistent with the utilitarian ethos dominant in reformed education: it made familiarity with literature seem like a necessary and practical competence.

It is a paradox that the institutions in England that did most to propagate the concept of English literature were ones existing outside the mainstream of education and society. While one thinks of English literature as nowadays being central to national culture, its educational emergence in the eighteenth century served the end of a marginal and radical agenda. To deliver the paradox in its crudest form: the enshrinement of literature as one of the icons of English nationhood was first undertaken by those who probably had most to lose by (and were already losing out from) a totalizing view of what 'Englishness' entailed. For they were already outside the strict pale of Englishness in as much as

---

[56] McLachlan, *English Education under The Test Acts*, 136.

they practised a religion that diverged from that of the state.[57] There are ways, however, that this paradoxical state of affairs can be rationalized. Groups are often driven to embrace the trappings of national identity not so much to consolidate their position, or to employ exclusionary tactics against other groups, as to over-come a perceived disadvantage, to grasp status that lies beyond their immediate orbit. Because the academies sought to prepare their students for an active role in society as professionals and businessmen, a high premium was placed on social ease and mobility. Having been educated on the fringe, these students were destined thence to move to the professional and commercial centre, and their passport to this new station was a portfolio of skills both practical and patriotic: an advanced grasp of English grammar, elocutionary correctness, and an acquaintance with English literature. Knowledge of English literature was part of the insignia of the dissenting student's readiness for full immer-sion into the life of the English commercial state.

VI

These generalizations about the rise of English literature as a teachable subject within a marginal community in England also hold true for its rise in the universities of the Scottish Enlighten-ment. It has become a paradoxical truism that English literature was, in fact, invented by the Scots; and while it follows from what I have already said that this is to overstate the case, the overstate-ment is not altogether a gross one.[58] Nor perhaps should this necessarily surprise us, given that those groups feeling the strong-est need to proclaim their national assimilation are likely to be the ones most conscious of their own marginality. The situation that Scotland found itself in during the eighteenth century ensued from

---

[57] For comment on the non-conformist contribution to 'mainstream' culture, see Donald Davie, *A Gathered Church: The Literature of the English Dissenting Inter-est, 1700–1930* (London, 1978).

[58] For the Scottish contribution to the dissemination of English literature, see Robert Crawford, *Devolving English Literature* (Oxford, 1992); Franklin D. Court, *Institutionalizing English Literature: The Culture and Politics of Literary Study, 1750–1900* (Stanford, Calif., 1992); *The Scottish Invention of English Literature*, ed. Robert Crawford (Cambridge, 1998). Also Miller, *The Formation of College English*, 144–252.

the Act of Union of 1707. The effect of the political unification of Britain was to incite the weaker nation of the union, Scotland, to try to equal the perceived commercial and cultural success of the stronger member. The incorporation of Britain thus entailed a process of Anglicization. The eighteenth century also witnessed numerous Scottish works, such as Adam Smith's *Wealth of Nations* (1776) and Adam Ferguson's *Essay on the History of Civil Society* (1767), analysing the way societies developed and 'improved'. Improvement, as it was understood, consisted of more efficient agricultural techniques, increased commerical activity, refinement of culture, and the adoption of 'politeness' as a social standard. What became obvious to eighteenth-century Scottish intellectuals was that their nation still lagged at the primitive end of the developmental scale. So much, indeed, was this the case that comparisons between 'primitive' Highland culture and that of the American Indians became an anthropological fashion.[59] It was evident, in any event, that if Scotland were to achieve the state of social civility, it would need to acquire many of the accoutrements of its more developed southern neighbour. Indeed, unless Scotland could haul itself up commercially and culturally, it risked sacrificing many of the potential benefits of the union.

The scramble to Anglicize is a striking feature of the Scottish Enlightenment.[60] One manifestation of it is the vogue north of the border for *The Spectator*: the periodical's moralizing exerted an influence on the university teaching of ethics, and the decorous modern life-style it represented was widely appreciated as a model for the would-be civilized society.[61] But another area in which Anglicization proceeded apace was in the reformation of the language. It was believed by many that a necessary means of consolidating the union was through the establishment of a common language. This would entail creating a common linguistic stock purged of dialect terms (or 'provincialisms') and nurturing a uniform pronunciation. North of the border, this linguistic ideal was accompanied by a good deal of solemn breast-beating

---

[59] Crawford, *Devolving English Literature*, 16–17.

[60] On the broad issue of Anglicization, see Nicholas Phillipson, 'Politics, politeness and the Anglicization of early eighteenth-century Scottish culture', in *Scotland and England 1286–1815*, ed. R. A. Mason (Edinburgh, 1987), 226–47.

[61] For the influence of *The Spectator* on Scottish élite culture, see for example Miller, *The Formation of College English*, 152, 173 and *passim*.

to the effect that the Scottish tongue was peculiarly barbaric and vicious. This dilemma over language should not be seen as purely a general matter, to do with how Scotland could best play its part in the union, for it also impinged on the individual predicament of many Scots (including James Boswell) who, having been educated in Scotland, then trekked southwards in the hope of gainful employment in London. For were these aspirants not to be able to speak and write 'correctly', they would inevitably be disqualified from the professional advancement they were seeking. This matter received wide comment as, for example, from the expatriate novelist Smollett. When Roderick Random, the eponymous hero of his novel, comes to London, he hears that a London schoolmaster would be prepared to teach him 'the pronunciation of the English-tongue, without which (he says) you will be unfit for business in this country'.[62]

The leader of the elocutionary movement was, as I have mentioned, the somewhat improbable figure of Thomas Sheridan. His first career had been as an actor in Dublin, but, after retiring from the boards, he gave his energies to two interlinked projects: first, to remedy deficiencies in Irish higher education, especially by instituting a new model academy; second, by leading a crusade for a uniform standard of correct English. In this last ambition, Sheridan remained determinedly unfazed by his own rasping Irish brogue which made him a conspicuously poor advert for the pronunciatory standards he was trying to champion. His *British Education* (1756), a cardinal statement of his beliefs, floats several arguments as to the virtue of a standardized language. A uniform elocution is necessary in order to unite citizens into allegiance to the British state; a fixed and pure language is the best hope that a nation's cultural achievements can triumph over the ravages of time; and the liberal arts can be brought to a high pitch of accomplishment only in the context of a widespread 'study and practice of oratory'.[63] These arguments, though, represent a grandiloquent defence of a project whose immediate ends were probably more narrowly pragmatic. Elocutionary training would allow

[62] Tobias Smollett, *The Adventures of Roderick Random*, ed. P. G. Boucé (Oxford, 1981), 96.
[63] Thomas Sheridan, *British Education: or the Source of the Disorders of Britain* (1756), Scolar Press reprint (Menston, 1971), 214, 257–8, 388.

the upwardly-mobile from the outposts of the union to acquire court speech, and so to enjoy the enhanced status that came from having divested themselves of their linguistic provinciality.

Sheridan's ideas chimed with educated sentiment in Scotland. In 1761, he lectured in Edinburgh to an audience of 'three hundred nobles, judges, divines, advocates, and men of fashion'. Sixteen lectures were delivered in total, divided between 'Elocution' and 'The English Tongue', 'with considerable enlargements concerning those points with regard to which Scotsmen are most ignorant, and the dialect of their country most imperfect'. Awareness of issues surrounding Scottish English was especially focused amongst members of the Select Society, an élite philosophical club set up in Edinburgh in 1756 and numbering Hume, William Robertson, and James Boswell among its members. At the end of his lecture series, Sheridan enjoined the society to carry on 'the study of the English tongue in a regular and proper manner'.[64] Such an exhortation was unlikely to have fallen on deaf ears, since many amongst the Edinburgh literati were already bearers of the linguistic flame. Hume rather notoriously compiled a list of 'Scotticisms'—those traits that most sharply identified Scottish linguistic usage—which were printed in the *Political Discourses* (1752) and subsequently in the *Scots Magazine* (1760).[65] The list was originally prepared for private use, but it testifies to a touchiness about the barbarism of native Scots idiom that was shared by other intellectuals such as Robertson, Hugh Blair, and James Beattie. Boswell addressed himself to the issue and projected a dictionary of Scottish words, an enterprise in which he was encouraged by Johnson. Johnson, in his turn, was wont to adopt a slightly sardonic posture: a letter to Boswell requests 'Please to return Dr. Blair thanks for his sermons. The Scotch write English wonderfully well.'[66]

[64] Ibid. See Miller, *The Formation of College English*, 152–7.
[65] For 'Scotticisms', see Pat Rogers, 'Boswell and the Scotticism', in *New Light on Boswell: Critical and Historical Essays on the Occasion of the Centenary of The Life of Johnson*, ed. Greg Clingham (Cambridge, 1991), 56–71; and James G. Basker, 'Scotticisms and the Problem of Cultural Identity in Eighteenth-Century Britain', *Eighteenth-Century Life*, 15 (Feb. and May 1991), special issue on *Sociability and Society in Eighteenth-Century Scotland*, ed. John Dwyer and Richard B. Sher, 81–95.
[66] Johnson, *Letters*, 3: 19.

Some ambiguity persisted as to whether speaking with a Scottish accent was as bad as speaking conventionally accented English, only with the insertion of Scottish words and idioms. Boswell records conversing with Burke on just this matter:

I said to Burke, 'You would not have a man use Scotch words, as to say a *trance* for a *passage* in a house.' 'No,' said he, 'that is a different language.' 'But,' said I, 'is it not better, too, to try to pronounce not in the broad Scotch way and to say *passage* and not *pawssage*.' 'Yes,' said Burke, 'when once you're *taught* how they pronounce it in England; but don't *try* at English pronunciation.' Said Richard Burke, 'Better say *pawsage* than *pissage*.' And indeed some Scotsmen, such as Rae, the advocate, make blunders as bad as this.[67]

The passage makes clear how Scottish speakers courted social disapproval if they affected an English accent without genuinely having one, and particular hostility seems to have been reserved for Scots whose acquisition of English speech traits was so avid that they gave the impression of disowning their national origins. The Scottish poet David Mallet, for example, who moved to London in his twenties, Anglicized his name (from Malloch) and spoke with reputedly flawless English pronunciation. For his pains, he was reviled by other expatriate Scots.

Self-improvement in speech was part of a broader mission of cultural advancement. The eighteenth century saw a proliferation in Scotland of intellectual and convivial clubs, whose members tasked themselves with the betterment of style and taste. It was in the context of this cultural serious-mindedness that in 1748 an important event in the development of English literature occurs. A young academic, an intellectual product of Glasgow and Oxford, was prevailed on to deliver a course of public lectures in Edinburgh: the lecturer was Adam Smith and his course was given under the title of 'Rhetoric and *Belles Lettres*'. Smith's lectures were laid on for an audience of citizens but in 1751, when he moved to Glasgow to take up the Chair of Logic, they were for the first time assimilated into a university curriculum.

Smith's lectures were never published, and no manuscript version is known to exist, but what has survived is an almost complete set of student notes derived from the lecture course

---

[67] Cited from Rogers, 'Boswell and the Scotticism', 63.

given by him in 1762–3: these lectures comprise a developed version of the earlier public discourses delivered in Edinburgh.[68] Smith lectured in English, itself a point of significance, and took as his subject the general topic of communication. His lectures range across a wide variety of written kinds, dealing at a general level with narrative and descriptive composition but also considering historical and didactic discourses as well as oratory. Their main aim is to advise students on how to deliver themselves eloquently in speech and how to achieve a felicitous writing style with regard to appropriate rules. Smith takes a considerably more generalized approach to good writing than was customary in the older-style rhetorical handbooks. These presented good writing as consisting of a narrow acquaintance with rhetorical tropes and figures, whereas Smith enumerates a set of free-ranging practical nostra for polite composition. For instance, at the beginning of the fifth lecture, he cautions his audience against constructing sentences that give the impression of tailing off:

It is a great defect in the arrangement of a sentence when it has what they call a tail coming after it, that is, when the sense appears to be concluded when it is not really so. This is always avoided by placing the terminative and circumstantial term before the attributive.[69]

This gives a flavour of Smith's eminent practicality, and his emphasis throughout on the merit of stylistic plainness and transparency is in keeping with a broadly utilitarian ethos. But his exhortations towards correct style need also to be seen in the context of the Anglicizing movement in Scotland, for correctness is clearly understood (if not explicitly stated) to mean conformity to English standards. So in his fourth lecture, he praises the 'harmonious and sonorous pronunciation of the English nation' and warns of the difficulty faced by non-native speakers in trying to emulate it.[70]

---

[68] See Adam Smith, *Lectures on Rhetoric and Belles Lettres*, ed. John M. Lothian (Edinburgh, 1963). For discussion of Smith's lectures, see Howell, 536–76; and Crawford, 28–33.
[69] Smith, *Lectures*, 18.
[70] Ibid. 14.

Smith's lectures, then, are a contribution to the mission of Scottish self-improvement, this improvement being indistinguishable from an assimilation of English traits. The Anglicizing urge is perhaps most evident from the authors chosen to exemplify compositional virtues. Where the examples are modern, they are drawn exclusively from English authors. Although Smith was conversant with the work of many Scottish authors, including Allan Ramsay, these are totally unrepresented: it is clear that he felt that no Scottish writer could provide an auspicious compositional model. Because the virtue that Smith is recommending amounts to something as diffuse as 'good writing', the authors whom he chooses to illustrate it together trace out a sort of canon. At its heart, though, is not Shakespeare but Swift, to whom Smith pays the crowning compliment that 'his language is more English than any other writer that we have'.[71]

Two premises underpin Smith's course of lectures, the first a very old one, the second more novel. The first is that no literary triumph can occur unless the language is in a state of development sufficient to allow it to happen. This belief that the fortunes of the national language and literature are intertwined only disappears once a progressive notion of language change loses tenability. The second of his premises is that the 'improvement' of the language is inseparable from its convergence with a standard of authentic Englishness. Exactly the same premises are at work in a course of lectures originally delivered at the University of Edinburgh by Hugh Blair, and published as his *Lectures on Rhetoric and Belles Lettres* (1784). Unlike Smith's lectures which languished unpublished, Blair's became a popular textbook of *belles lettres* and criticism, running through umpteen editions between their original appearance and the end of the following century. The lectures make for a hotch-potch, containing philology, grammar, stylistic analysis, and the literary historical treatment of classical and modern genres. In spite of the innumerable literary examples included, Blair's objective was not principally to inculcate techniques for the analysis of literature. His book was designed instead to appeal on a general level to those 'employed in composition, or in public speaking' as well

---

[71] Ibid. 2.

as to those desirous 'to acquire principles which will enable them to judge for themselves in that part of literature called the Belles Lettres'.[72] Though I want to return later to some of the issues raised by Blair's *Lectures*, it still might be stressed here just how pragmatic were his motivations. Those envisaged as benefiting from his book are those in quest of a practical linguistic competence, moreover a competence that will be exercised in the specific context of their professional employments.[73]

Blair shares the same fervour for linguistic improvement and the same utilitarian outlook evident in works such as Joseph Priestley's *Rudiments of English Grammar*. His hope to see study of the vernacular language raised in educational importance is expressed in Lecture IX:

> Whatever the advantages or defects of the English language be, as it is our own language, it deserves a high degree of our study and attention, both with regard to the choice of words which we employ, and with regard to the syntax, or the arrangement of these words in syntax.[74]

Blair believed that the English language, like all languages, had received its 'predominant tincture' from the national character of its speakers. This was not so much to deny that a language would adjust to reflect ephemeral changes in habit or fashion as to suppose that it would contain an 'original stock of words' passed down across generations, and that this would remain the bed-rock of a nation's speech 'throughout many ages'.[75] To be versed in one's national tongue, therefore, would be to be acquainted with this core vocabulary comprising its essential character. From this premise Blair draws out a distinction between purity and propriety of linguistic usage (Lecture X): 'purity' refers to the use of words and idioms native to a language as opposed to those having been imported into it; 'propriety' meanwhile denotes the use of a select vocabulary of words in a language that have become consecrated through a tradition of

---

[72] Hugh Blair, *Lectures on Rhetoric and Belles Lettres*, 5th edn., 3 vols. (Edinburgh, 1793), 1: 6.

[73] The extent of Blair's pragmatism has met with disagreement. Franklin Court, for example, sees Blair as departing from Smith's 'pragmatic and political concerns' to introduce a new emphasis on taste and sensibility.

[74] Blair, *Lectures*, 1: 229.

[75] Ibid. 1: 220.

polite usage. Predictably, Blair maintains that for English style to be pure, it must be purged of 'Scotticisms' and 'Gallicisms'; and he praises Swift, his favourite stylist along with Addison, for 'using no words but such as were of native growth'.[76] When he turns to Addison, the author to whom he devotes most attention, the aspect of good style that he finds manifested is 'perspicuousness' or clarity. And although he does accord a role for ornament, 'those graces which a flowery imagination diffuses over writing', his principle of style remains broadly utilitarian.[77]

In the past few years, the universities of the Scottish Enlightenment have been accorded a prominent role in the origination of English literature. The theory goes that literature grows out of a discourse of polite cultural interchange, of conversational civility, that is sustained by the establishment of various discursive institutions: the club, coffeeshop, printed periodical, and so on.[78] Crucial, though, in terms of providing a suitable discursive space for literature, were the Scottish universities, which have been identified as the first such institutions in which English was taught as an academic subject. Douglas Lane Patey, for example, in claiming that all radical alteration to a canon must run parallel with a 'rearrangement' in the social structure of canonical authority, points to the establishment in the later part of the century of the first academic chairs of 'poetry', 'belles lettres', and 'fine arts'—a clear reference to the new trends in Scottish university education; the exact association seems also to be made in an article by John Guillory; while Robert Crawford, in two separate books, has linked the same developments in Scottish education with the arresting claim that the Scots invented English literature.[79]

It is certainly the case that the admission of vernacular writers on to educational syllabuses in Scotland is an important mile-

---

[76] Ibid. 1: 236, 237.   [77] Ibid. 2: 60.

[78] See Jürgen Habermas, *The Structural Transformation of the Public Sphere: An Inquiry into a Category of Bourgeois Culture*, trans. Thomas Burger (Oxford, 1989); Terry Eagleton, *The Function of Criticism: From The Spectator to Poststructuralism* (London, 1984), 9–43; Peter Stallybrass and Allon White, *The Politics and Poetics of Transgression* (London, 1986), 80–124.

[79] Patey, 23; John Guillory, 'Canonical and Non-Canonical: A Critique of the Current Debate', *English Literary History*, 54 (1987), 483–527, esp. 494–503; for Crawford, see *Devolving English Literature*, and *The Scottish Invention of English Literature*.

stone in the reification of English literature; but as I have suggested already, the syllabi that Smith and Blair were instituting, and the pragmatic ends to which these were dedicated, are very different from what we nowadays associate with the teaching of English. Smith's and Blair's educational curricula were designed to promote professional competence among people whose employment entailed that they compose or speak publicly, and to encourage a rationalization of the diverse linguistic habits of the countries composing the Union of Great Britain into one integrated tongue. In so far as we can talk about an educational syllabus as equating with a canon (an equation that university teachers are perhaps over-fond of making), the canons furnished by Smith and Blair bear little relation to the sort of canons and genealogies of literature discussed elsewhere in this book. Smith and Blair privilege expository prose over poetry and drama as the medium most compatible with their students' practical concerns while also, and for the same reason, favouring more recent over earlier writing. Thus Chaucer, Spenser, and Ben Jonson recede into invisibility, Shakespeare finds himself vying for preeminence with the likes of Sir William Temple and the Earl of Shaftesbury, and lodged at the very heart of the pedagogic canon are Addison and Swift. Moreover, the enshrinement even of Swift is on terms that might confound the modern reader: Blair's sole lecture exclusive to the author is devoted, not to what we might consider a canonical work, but to his treatise 'A Proposal for correcting, improving, and ascertaining the English Tongue'.

The lectures of Smith and Blair are the beginning of a process, one from which the writer (and probably the reader) continues to benefit, by which English literature enters into the academy; but the degree of continuity of the sort of literature they privilege, and their reasons for privileging it, with our own modern-day practices is apt to be exaggerated. Furthermore, the project pursued by Smith and Blair can easily be seen as a retrograde step, for it involved the resurrection of the old category of *litterae humaniores*, cultivated writing taken as a generality. What supposedly lends unity to this generic field, however, has now changed from a vague notion of 'knowledge' to 'communication', seen as the animating principle of speech and writing across all boundaries. Yet in so far as the overriding supposition of Smith and Blair is that English literature be taught because it is *useful* to

206 TEACHING ENGLISH LITERATURE

do so, one aspect of this usefulness has so far gone unmentioned. This is the idea, which I will go on to discuss, that literature could have an important social rôle in inculcating 'taste'.

It has been claimed by Douglas Lane Patey among other critics that an important factor in the emergence of literature is the rise of aesthetics: during the eighteenth century, the term 'literature' picks out, indeed becomes synonymous with, those writings that are deemed the appropriate objects of 'aesthetic appreciation'. Patey suggests that one effect of the advent of aesthetics is that a restricted grouping, the 'arts of the beautiful', becomes cordoned off from what previously was a much larger and more various confederation of kinds of 'making'; and as proponents of this new theory of art, he cites the German critic Alexander Baumgarten, whose *Aesthetica* came out in 1735, and the English writers Joseph Addison and Francis Hutcheson. Yet there are certain difficulties arising from this scenario, some of them acknowledged by Patey himself. For one thing, whether there actually was during the eighteenth century a British philosophy of aesthetics or 'aesthetic movement' is highly debatable. Moreover, even if we hazard that such a movement *did* occur, it seems hardly to have been much influenced by Continental theorists such as Baumgarten. On the whole, it makes more sense as regards the British scene to speak not so much of a philosophy of aesthetics as of a 'theory of taste': for taste becomes the key concept, especially from the mid-century onwards, under whose aegis debates concerning the appreciation of art works are conducted.[80]

Even if a 'cult of taste' as such belongs only to the middle part of the century, the roots of taste's conceptual ascendancy can be traced back to the vogue, beginning some decades earlier, for the ancient rhetorician Longinus and the French critic Bouhours.

---

[80] A useful anthology of 18th-cent. writings on taste is *Taste and Criticism in the Eighteenth Century*, ed. H. A. Needham (New York, 1952, 1969). See also R. L. Brett, 'The Aesthetic Sense and Taste in the Literary Criticism of the Early Eighteenth Century', *Review of English Studies*, 20 (1944), 199–213; and Engell, *Forming the Critical Mind*, 103–25.

Both figures stimulated a departure from the dogmatic brand of neo-classicism, epitomized by the writings of Thomas Rymer, in which literary merit was judged against what were seen as inviolable rules of good composition. In the early eighteenth century, a revised critical method was formulated around two precepts. First, it became accepted that literary works might be successful in ways other than through mere conformity to some fixed set of literary regulations. Thus in Pope's famous line from the *Essay on Criticism*, it is allowed that writers can '*snatch a Grace* beyond the Reach of Art'—or, in other words, achieve felicities which rather than being conditional on the observance of literary rules can arise directly from their being flouted.[81] Second, it was felt to behove critics to adopt a conciliatory attitude towards the works they criticized; instead of carping at a work's shortcomings, the critic should ideally try to pinpoint both its strengths and weaknesses. Once critics were required to be 'appreciative', and once the literary felicities subject to such appreciation became seen as subtle and rarefied, a specialized brand of discernment was required: this was taste.

What distinguishes eighteenth-century theorizing of taste is an equivocation over whether taste belongs with the senses or the reason. One vein of thinking allocated it unreservedly to the senses, even to the extent of viewing it as a sense individual to itself: Leonard Welsted, for example, asserts that 'To have what we call *Taste*, is having, one may say, a new Sense or Faculty superadded to the ordinarily [*sic*] ones of the Soul'.[82] A natural corollary of this position was that taste should be seen as spontaneous in its operation, and as indifferent, or opposed, to the injunctions of reason. The influential discussion in Lord Shaftesbury's 'Advice to an Author', for instance, stresses how taste has no truck with 'any Knowledge of principles, proportions, causes, or of the Usefulness of the Object'; and John Gilbert Cooper's *Letters concerning Taste* (1755) contains a vivid description of taste in terms of 'that instantaneous Glow of Pleasure which thrills thro' our whole Frame, and seizes upon the Applause of the Heart, before the intellectual Power, Reason, can descend from the Throne of the Mind to ratify its Approbation'.[83]

[81] 'Essay on Criticism', line 155, in Butt (ed.), 1: 256.
[82] Welsted, 'The State of Poetry' (1724), in Durham (ed.), *Critical Essays*, 366.
[83] John Gilbert Cooper, *Letters concerning Taste* (1755), Letter 1, 3.

Those who argued for taste's being purely or largely a sensory phenomenon, however, were opposed by an equal band for whom the reason was the faculty to which it predominantly belonged. Of this party was Charles Rollin, whose influential textbook, rendered into English as *The Method of Teaching and Studying the Belles Lettres*, says that taste 'is less the effect of genius than judgement'.[84] Similarly, Edmund Burke in his essay 'On Taste' (1759) supposes that taste is 'no other than a more refined judgment', though he expands this into a more complex definition in which taste amalgamates the 'primary pleasures of sense', the 'secondary pleasures of the imagination' and 'the conclusions of the reasoning faculty'.[85] Much the same reasoning is to the fore in Alexander Gerard's *An Essay on Taste* (1759), published the same year as Burke's essay. Gerard suggests that judgements of taste depend, in the first instance, on the raw data of sense impressions, so that nobody can possess a reliable taste unless all their senses are working in an effective union. But even this, Gerard suggests, will be insufficient to compose 'good taste', unless the senses are 'aided with *judgement*, the faculty which distinguishes things different, separates truth from falsehood, and compares together objects and their qualities'.[86] This muddying of the water between the senses and the reason seems to me to be the cardinal feature of eighteenth-century discussions of taste, evident, for example, in Hugh Blair's equivocation that while 'Taste is not resolvable into any such operation of Reason', it nonetheless remains the case that reason 'assists Taste in many of its operations'.[87] It was this blurring of the categories, in effect the sensualizing of the concepts of the understanding, that led Kant to deny the British theory of taste the title of a philosophy.

This quibbling over the precise seat of human taste might seem arcane, but it had implications for whether the tastes of individuals could ever be reconciled to a common standard, and for whether it was feasible to inculcate taste through formal

---

[84] Rollin, *Method of Studying the Belles Lettres* (5th edn, 1759), 1: 50.

[85] Published in the 2nd edn. of his *Philosophical Enquiry*. Cited from *A Philosophical Enquiry into the Origin of our Ideas of the Sublime and Beautiful*, ed. James T. Boulton (Oxford, 1958, 1987), 23.

[86] Alexander Gerard, *An Essay on Taste*, facs. repr. of third edn. (1780), introduced by Walter J. Hipple (New York, 1978), 83.

[87] Blair, *Lectures*, 1: 20, 21.

education. If the seat of taste was taken as being the human sensory apparatus, then taste could be assumed to be a faculty common to everyone. On the other hand, if one were to stress the rôle of the rational intellect in the exercising of taste, then this might suggest inequalities between different people's endowments of taste. Blair, for example, whose premise is that taste is 'ultimately founded on a certain natural and instinctive sensibility to beauty', suggests that although no standard of perfect taste can ever be set up, we can fall back on a vaguely conceived common standard of good nature.[88] Lord Kames's influential earlier work, *The Elements of Criticism* (1762), is a bolder development of the same idea. The backdrop to Kames's theories of taste and the fine arts is an awareness of the fissiparous nature of society, which separates people according to 'birth, office, or occupation'. Kames believes that for a society to remain stable a countervailing principle of social integration is required, and this principle he associates with what he terms a 'republic of taste'. People from different classes and employments can be expected to agree on what are pleasant or disagreeable objects and images, and this phenomenon points to a shared, communal taste. The existence of this shared standard moreover makes for a beneficial principle of social cohesion.[89]

The two rival theories, that taste was a form of sensory activity and, on the other hand, that it arose from the intellect, conduced in different ways, but in equal measure, to the belief that it could be inculcated through education. Charles Rollin, for example, an early espouser of the teaching of taste, declares it to be 'a kind of natural reason wrought up to perfection by study'.[90] Lord Shaftesbury, even while defining taste in terms very different from Rollin, is another convinced of its educational scope. In his *Soliloquy: or Advice to an Author*, he asks 'If a natural *good* TASTE be not already form'd in us; why shou'd not we endeavour to form it, and become *natural*?'[91] In a similar vein, Burke declares that

---

[88] Ibid., 1: 21, 19–45.

[89] Henry Home, Lord Kames, *Elements of Criticism* (1762), 11th edn. (1839), ch. XXV, 'STANDARD OF TASTE'.

[90] Rollin, *Method*, 1: 50.

[91] Anthony Ashley Cooper, 3rd Earl of Shaftesbury, *Characteristics of Men, Manners, Opinions, Times*, ed. Philip Ayres, 2 vols. (Oxford, 1999), 1: 174.

It is known that the taste (whatever it is) is improved exactly as we improve our judgment, by extending our knowledge, by a steady attention to our object, and by frequent exercise.[92]

This view that taste could be inculcated was not contingent on its being seen as a rational faculty, since it was apparent that the human senses were also susceptible to education in the sense that nowadays we sometimes speak of someone having an 'educated palate'. Moreover, in the same way that someone acquires such a palate by exposing it to a range of different tastes, a person's taste could be improved, so it was thought, through exposure to a wide range of 'objects of taste'. As Gerard puts it, 'HABITUAL acquaintance with the objects of taste, not only thus supplies a stock of knowledge, but also wonderfully *improves* the judgment'.[93]

It should be stressed that although those entities most commonly cited as 'objects of taste' were literary works, the operation of taste actually transcended the limited ambit of literature. Most commentators allow for it to be exercised in connection with both cultural and natural phenomena, with the effect that taste gets held up as a regulatory principle for the entire field of sensory existence. This having been conceded, the vogue of taste, especially as it was proposed as an element of reformed education, still had the effect of thrusting literature into a key exemplary rôle. Joseph Priestley's *Rudiments of English Grammar*, for example, contains a large number of 'Examples of English Composition', provided ostensibly for their exemplification of grammatical and stylistic rules. Priestley, however, is aware that such examples could also serve the valuable purpose of leading young people towards 'a just and manly taste in composition'.[94] There is a reversal here of what we might be inclined to expect. Nowadays, we regard an aptitude for making critical discriminations as contributing towards the larger purpose of our gaining knowledge about literature. But in the eighteenth century, it was the other way about: becoming versed in literature was a corollary, or by-product, of the primary agenda of teaching taste.

The presentation of literature to pupils with a view to their acquiring 'taste' represents an advancement on its being used merely to assist children's spelling improvement, their recogni-

[92] *Philosophical Enquiry*, 26.
[93] Gerard, *Essay on Taste*, 109.
[94] Priestley, *Rudiments of English Grammar*, 65.

tion of tropes, or their mastery of elocution. This difference lies in literature's coming together with a technique of consumption that can loosely be called 'critical', in the sense of having to do with appreciation and judgement. Literary works are being taught, or at least being brought to the notice of pupils, in the context of values that themselves seem 'literary'. Yet in so far as the eighteenth-century theory of taste attaches value to literary works, this value continues to be regulated by larger pragmatic and utilitarian concerns—as such it differs in a crucial way from the sort of value which recent critics have claimed to be conferred on literary works by the discourse of aesthetics, or at least by that discourse as understood in the precise way that has become popular among some critics. Moreover, the failure to recognize this has given rise to a high-level misconception about the construction of English literature. It is this misconception that the final section of this chapter will explore, and try to correct, doing so moreover with some due acknowledgement of the building in which much of my book has been composed, the library of the Newcastle upon Tyne Lit and Phil.

VIII

On 7 March 1793 a group of liberal gentlemen assembled in Newcastle for the first 'regularly constituted' meeting of a new society: the Literary and Philosophical Society of Newcastle upon Tyne. Its founder was the Reverend William Turner who had already addressed the prospective membership on the advantages of such a society, these likely advantages being suggested by societies of the same kind which were already providing 'excellent helps to the improvement and spread of knowledge'. Turner lists a number of reasons why the establishment of this sort of society in Newcastle would be especially auspicious. For example, being on the road between London and Edinburgh and being a major trading port 'Newcastle is peculiarly well situated for procuring *Literary Intelligence*'. But he also points out that the 'two great natural products of this part of the country', namely coal and lead, provide particular opportunities for scientific investigation that might improve their extraction and utilization. In this connection, moreover, Turner can turn to the precedent of the society previously founded in Manchester which had already contributed to the 'improvements of its extensive manufactures'.[95]

The first piece of business for Turner's society was to arrange a programme of speakers; and in the first twelve months after its inauguration, members were subjected to a series of useful and serious-minded expositions. Reverend Dr Thorburn of South Shields aired some 'Conjectures on Light as an Object of Chemistry'; Reverend J. Walton delivered 'A Letter on some Ancient Pigs of Lead'; and Mr Hind regaled his audience with 'An Essay on the Fire and Choke Damp of Coal Mines'. Yet, curiously, the first paper delivered to the society was by the educational reformer William Enfield, one time of Warrington Academy, and entitled 'An Essay on the Cultivation of Taste, as a proper Object of Attention in the Education of Youth'.[96]

In the paper, Enfield admonishes traditional forms of gentlemanly education, studies which 'have had no other object than to furnish the head with stores of learning and science'. What he proposes instead is education of the whole person, an education that will help the recipient 'feel' and 'act'. Enfield's conviction is that schemes of education, rather than aiming to '*exercise the Understanding and Judgment*' should instead aim 'to *cultivate the Taste*', an objective that can be achieved by the exposure of pupils to 'objects of taste' as they are to be discovered in nature or art. The benefits that Enfield envisages flowing from his curriculum of taste would be twofold: people of developed taste or 'sensibility' (a word that he conflates to an unusual degree with 'taste') will possess a more stringent moral character; but also 'a cultivated taste' will 'introduce[] a man with great advantage to the notice of the world'.[97]

---

[95] See 'Speculations on the Propriety of Attempting the Establishment of a Literary Society in Newcastle', in *The Reports, Papers, Catalogues, &c of the Literary and Philosophical Society of Newcastle upon Tyne* ('Hedley' papers).

[96] It was under this title that the lecture was printed and circulated privately in 1818. It is included in 'Hedley' papers.

[97] Thomas Miller (*The Formation of College English*, 109) actually sees Enfield's work as a move away from the strict utilitarianism of earlier dissenting lecturers like Doddridge and Priestley in the direction of sensibility and belletrism. There is certainly a modulation of tone, and Enfield does seem more influenced by Scottish literati like Kames. But it remains that he is invited as the inaugural speaker to a society overtly dedicated to utilitarian ends.

The signal compliment paid to Enfield of his being the first speaker to address the newly-founded society may have owed to his prominence in the literary societies of Warrington and Norwich (where he was then living) but also to his reputation as an educationalist. He had already made a case for the reading and study of polite literature in his 'On Reading Works of Taste' incorporated into *The Speaker*, his argument being that works of polite literature are 'calculated for the improvement of taste' and provide an opportunity for exercising the judgement 'in determining ... [their] ... degree of merit'.[98] These same propositions also underpin the provision of literary examples in Enfield's other elocutionary primer, *Exercises in Education*. For Enfield, literary works deserve inclusion on educational syllabuses because exposure to them can nurture pupils' taste; and the possession of an advanced or 'correct' taste will facilitate young people going out into the world, where the ability to mix fluently, and moreover to undertake useful activity, will be indispensable to their future fortunes. It is Enfield's belief in the *usefulness* of acquiring good taste that accounts for why he should have been invited to speak to a society that had overtly dedicated itself to practical and utilitarian ends.

The above needs to be emphasized all the more because of one of the rogue narratives that has gained ground in connection with the invention of literature and the formation of the national canon. The story goes something like this. For English literature to come into being, a discourse has to emerge capable of picking out literary or 'creative' works from the larger mass of educated writings, this discourse being 'aesthetics'. What defines the category of the aesthetic is its privileging of the sensory over the rational in its response to stimuli, and also the antithetical relation in which it stands to all discourses of function. The rise of aesthetics allows for the first time for a group of writings to gain value on the basis of their uselessness: to say a piece of writing lends itself to an aesthetic response is to propose it to be autotelic, self-justifying, a servant to no canon of function other than its own.

Perhaps the most ebullient and eloquent statement of this argument comes in Terry Eagleton's *The Ideology of the Aesthetic* (1990):

[98] *The Speaker*, xxxii–xxxiv.

As a form of value grounded entirely in itself, without practical rhyme or reason, the aesthetic is at once eloquent testimony to the obscure origins and enigmatic nature of value in a society which would seem everywhere to deny it, and a utopian glimpse of an alternative to this sorry condition. For what the work of art imitates in its very pointlessness, in the constant movement by which it conjures itself up from its own inscrutable depths, is nothing less than human existence itself, which (scandalously for the rationalists and Utilitarians) requires no rationale beyond its own self-delight.[99]

The idea in this passage has proved very influential: Trevor Ross, for example, in his recent *The Making of the English Literary Canon* (1998), asserts that the consolidation during the eighteenth century of the modern notion of literature had the effect of taking 'the reader out of a public world and into a personally enriching yet radically private encounter with difference'.[100]

This view of things seems to me to be in its essentials not true, or at best only partially so. For one thing, the principal aegis beneath which literary works are spoken about and dissected during the eighteenth century is not 'aesthetics' as such but 'taste': it is worth noting that notwithstanding Baumgarten's *Aesthetica* of 1735, the word 'aesthetics' does not enter the English language at all before the nineteenth century and continues to be rare even to the middle of that century. 'Taste' as a mode of appreciation of literary works, is very different from the category of aesthetics. In the eighteenth century, 'taste' was generally seen as a mobilization of the senses aided and moderated by the reason; moreover, far from ushering literature into an enclave of the non-functional, taste stresses that the perusal of literary works can have highly practical applications. To have exposure to 'objects of taste', and thereby to acquire a 'correct taste', is to gain the wherewithal of mixing and acting in a society in which mixing and acting, as distinguished from gentlemanly retirement and spectatorship, are becoming increasingly valued.

It would be wrong to suggest that the construction of the aesthetic proposed by Eagleton and others, as a private realm of the sensual and subjective, has no support in writing of the period. The point is rather that those who espouse it form one party among a larger contingent of those who speak very differ-

[99] Eagleton, *The Ideology of the Aesthetic*, 65.
[100] See Ross, *The Making of the English Literary Canon*, 300.

ently. Moreover, the 'autonomization' of literature, to use an expression of Ross's, does not address the way in which literary works were gaining ground on educational syllabuses in schools, dissenting academies, and the Scottish universities. For this phenomenon was premised explicitly on an understanding that literature was indeed *useful*, that conversancy with it could qualify a person for a more successful absorption into public life and commercial society. Experience of literature might facilitate a degree of personal self-cultivation, but there was a strong belief, entertained by Enfield and other educational reformers, that this would always ultimately redound to the improvement of the state. Personal improvement and public improvement were conterminous with each other.

7

Johnson's *Lives of the Poets*

On 3 May 1777, Johnson wrote to his friend James Boswell, alerting him to the fact that 'I am engaged to write little Lives, and little Prefaces, to a little edition of the English Poets'.[1] Johnson's stress on the diminutiveness of the project was calculatedly mock-modest: he himself was going to scoop £300 from an edition being undertaken by a coalition of 'almost all the booksellers in London'. The object of the exercise was to reassert the same booksellers' possession of literary copyrights in the face of the incursions being made into their domain in Scotland. At its inception, the edition was to have begun with Chaucer, but because the battles over copyright were being joined most fiercely in connection with more recent writers, a decision was made to start proceedings only so late as Milton. It should be stressed that such issues relating to the book's contents were decided, not by Johnson, but by the cartel of booksellers; of the fifty-six poets eventually included, Johnson himself proposed only five: Watts, Blackmore, Pomfret, Thomson, and Yalden. The *Works of the English Poets* is now utterly overshadowed by Johnson's *Lives*, which, printed independently as early as 1781, have long since acquired their own autonomous identity. But it should not be forgotten that Johnson's original rôle was rather that of a humble factotum, indispensable, but also strictly subservient, to a larger enterprise. So little involved in the planning of the verse collection was he, and so sensitive to this fact, that on one occasion he complained to the principal publisher John Nichols that 'your Edition...is very impudently called mine'.[2] Even today, the supposed inadequacies or partial-

---

[1] To Boswell, 3 May 1777, in Johnson, *Letters*, 3: 20.
[2] To Nichols, *c.* April 1780, ibid. 3: 226. See Robert Demaria, Jr., *The Life of Samuel Johnson: A Critical Biography* (Oxford, 1993), 275–94, 277.

ities of the *Works*, such as their exclusion of female poets and of all writers prior to Milton, are routinely laid at Johnson's door.

If Johnson's proprietorship of the *Works* is one common literary historical fallacy, then another myth about the *Works* has been propagated by a surviving letter from Edward Dilly, one of the publishers involved in the enterprise, to Boswell. The latter had written seeking clarification of the general aspirations of the edition and of Johnson's rôle in it; what he received back from Dilly included the following:

The first cause that gave rise to this undertaking, I believe, was owing to the little trifling edition of the Poets, printing by the Martins, at Edinburgh, and to be sold by Bell, in London. Upon examining the volumes which were printed, the type was found so extremely small, that many persons could not read them; not only this inconvenience attended it, but the inaccuracy of the press was very conspicuous. These reasons, as well as the idea of an invasion of what we call our Literary Property, induced the London Booksellers to print an elegant and accurate edition of all the English Poets of reputation, from Chaucer to the present time.[3]

Dilly's measured puffing of his own edition has tended to be put down as a true report, if not as the last word, on the respective merits of the *Works* and the edition which it was intended to rival. But, owing to a superb piece of research by Thomas Bonnell, modern critics now have the advantage of knowing that little of what he says can be accepted at face value.[4] For one thing, Dilly's remark about the 'trifling' nature of Bell's edition, as well as its vitiation by textual inaccuracies and printing errors, these shortcomings justifying the provision of a new edition, is hard to square with the chronological facts. For the decision by the coterie of London booksellers to undertake their collaborative edition was actually taken before any of Bell's volumes were published: the likelihood is, so Bonnell argues, that the proprietors had merely got wind of the imminent

---

[3] *Life of Johnson*, ed. G. B. Hill, rev. L. F. Powell, 6 vols. (Oxford, 1934–50), 3: 110.
[4] Thomas F. Bonnell, 'John Bell's *Poets of Great Britain*: The "Little Trifling Edition" Revisited', *Modern Philology*, 85 (1987), 128–52. See also Bonnell's 'Speaking of Institutions and Canonicity, Don't Forget the Publishers', *Eighteenth-Century Life*, 21: 3 (1997), 97–9.

appearance of Bell's edition and were badmouthing it for obvious commercial reasons.

Even the deprecation of Bell's volumes as a 'little trifling edition' is at variance from the facts. Bell proclaimed that the object of his undertaking was no less than 'to furnish the public with the most beautiful, the correctest, the cheapest, and the only complete uniform edition of the British Poets'. His aspiration was to place at the disposal of the reading public a library of 'English classics' that was, at the same time, domiciled within a single printed edition. By its completion, fifty poets had spread themselves over the one hundred and nine volumes printed. Dramatists were omitted, and only Chaucer, Spenser, and Donne are included of poets writing prior to Milton; the latest born of all Bell's entrants is Charles Churchill, whose name also facilitates a pleasing alliteration in the work's title: 'from Chaucer to Churchill'.[5] Nor does Bell skimp in his mode of treating individual authors. The work of each author is accompanied by a biographical preface, taken from an existing source; in addition, a critical essay (again taken from some existing source) accompanies the works of a select group of poets; and, finally, Bell's edition is illustrated with title-page vignettes and engravings of individual poets.

All this underlines the calculated defamation done to Bell's project in Dilly's letter to Boswell. Yet not only were its aspirations expansive, its execution was also sound. Contrary to Dilly, Bell reproduced his copy-texts with, as judged against the standards of the time, a respectable degree of fidelity; and the print quality of the volume is high. Indeed, Bell could finance these high production standards precisely because his was not a 'cheap' edition at all. His set of volumes, retailing at £8.8s, represented in fact a more hefty purchase than the £7.10s *Works* designed to drive it out of the market. Moreover, Bell branched out into even more *de luxe* editions, as with calf leather, gilding, and marbling. That Bell could have been branded as offering 'cheap' merchandise owed purely to one single, but crucial, fact. As well as selling his edition in complete sets, he also offered his wares in individual volumes priced at 1s 6d each.[6] It was this publishing ruse that allowed him to corner

[5] See Bonnell, 'John Bell's *Poets of Great Britain*', 130.
[6] Ibid. 139–40.

the cheap end of the market, a territory over which the London-based *Works* never even attempted to offer competition. The same ruse, moreover, accounts for why Bell's edition was able to become such a publishing phenomenon. Looking back on the whole vexatious business of his commercial war with the London publishers, Bell congratulated himself on having at the cost of £10,000 printed 378,000 volumes in fulfilment of his enterprise. By doing so, he, more than any predecessor, deserves to be seen as having been responsible for bringing literary culture to the masses.

II

There is no doubt that Johnson's *Lives* are a significant contribution to the scripting of the English poetic past: they are discussed in this light by both René Wellek and Lawrence Lipking. Latterly, however, there has been a tendency for their impact to be distorted or overstated. Martha Woodmansee, for example, has claimed not untypically that the '*Lives of the Poets* contributed decisively to the differentiation of "authoring" from ordinary literary labour by establishing a pantheon of great authors whose "works" differ qualitatively from the sea of mere writing'.[7] Not just is their impact a 'decisive' one, but the *Lives* also get credited with putting in place a construct that had not previously existed ('establishing a canon...'). As will become clear, my understanding of the role of the *Lives* is not merely distinct from Woodmansee's but more nearly the opposite of it. What this chapter will do is explore the context and achievement of Johnson's *Lives*, by taking note of their appearance in accompaniment to a serial anthology, by considering the cultural rôle of such large-scale poetic anthologies, and by addressing Johnson's particular contribution to the genre of literary biography.[8]

---

[7] Martha Woodmansee, 'On the Author Effect: Recovering Collectivity', in *The Construction of Authorship: Textual Appropriation in Law and Literature*, ed. Martha Woodmansee and Peter Jaszi (Durham, NC, 1994), 15–28, 18.

[8] For a general treatment of literary anthologization in the period, see Barbara Benedict, *Making the Modern Reader: Cultural Mediation in Early Modern Literary Anthologies* (Princeton, 1996).

As I have said, the extent to which Bell's edition provided the immediate catalyst for the *Works* of 1779–81 may have been overstated. For one thing, the idea of a multi-volume collection of English poets had established itself long before Bell came on to the scene. Indeed, three such works had come out in the ten years or so before Bell's began appearing, all of them, it might be noted, printed in Scotland: *The English Poets*, in forty-nine volumes (1765–76), *The British Poets*, in forty-four volumes (1773–6), and *A Collection of the English Poets*, in twenty volumes (1776–7). These works represent the earliest compendious gatherings of English poetry, but preceding them was a long tradition of poetry being exhibited in more slender, anthologized form.

As we glance back at earlier attempts to anthologize a canon of English poetry, one essay by the antiquarian William Oldys, and supplied as preface for Thomas Hayward's compilation *The British Muse* (1738), bulks large as a signally important document. Hayward remains an obscure figure: he was probably born in 1707, but practically no evidence exists concerning his edition, the events of his life, or the year of his death.[9] All that can be said is that the three-volume anthology that came out under his name in 1738, subtitled 'A Collection of Thoughts, Moral, Natural, and Sublime of our English Poets who Flourish'd in the Sixteenth and Seventeenth Centuries', was hugely successful and was hailed as setting a new standard in compilations of its kind. What it sought to do was make available a thesaurus or printed commonplace-book of choice sentiments that that could assist, albeit in a rather formulaic manner, the writing of new poems: Thomas Warton, for example, praises it as 'the most comprehensive and exact COMMON-PLACE of the works of our most eminent poets throughout the reign of queen Elizabeth, and afterwards'.[10] Oldys's preface, presented as an 'Historical and Critical Review of all the Collections of this Kind that were ever published', is probably the earliest history of what we might loosely call English poetic 'anthologization', though the collections he elects to survey, much in the manner

[9] See Norman Hidden, 'Thomas Hayward and "The British Muse"', *English*, 37 (1988), 217–22.
[10] Warton, *History*, 3: 281. See Ann Moss, *Printed Commonplace-Books and the Structuring of Renaissance Thought* (Oxford, 1996).

of Hayward's own one, are assemblages of poetic 'beauties' or 'sentiments', often arranged or 'digested' alphabetically as in a dictionary. Oldys's essay, understandably given its role as a puff for Haywood's volume, finds an assortment of general faults in all previous excursions into the territory. Some anthologists have selected poetic sentiments in reality undeserving of the compliment; others have fallen into partiality, either excluding lyrical poems or omitting dramatic verse; others have ended up citing 'the worst parts of their author'; and a further group has arbitrarily privileged modern writers over earlier ones.[11]

The earliest works equating with Oldys's concept of a poetic anthology appear at the very beginning of the seventeenth century. In the year 1600, for example, appear *Belvedere, or, The Garden of the Muses* compiled by John Bodenham and also a work entitled *England's Parnassus; or, The Choicest Flowers of our Modern Poets*, both these being marred, so Oldys claims, by having had available for anthologization only poets of fairly limited merit.[12] Only with John Cotgrave's *The English Treasury of Wit and Language* (1655), which was able to call on the achievements of the great Jacobean dramatists, was this disadvantage entirely overcome. But Cotgrave's performance is vitiated, to Oldys's mind, on several other accounts: its extracts are painfully abridged; authors' names are detached from the extracts given; and many of the sentiments included do not qualify as the most illustrious that might have been selected.[13]

The next work falling beneath Oldys's harsh consideration is Joshua Poole's *The English Parnassus* (1657), an 'elaborate piece of poetical patchwork', consisting of 'an alphabet of monosyllablic rhymes', 'an assemblage of epithets' and 'an heap of phrases and ends of verse'.[14] This pronounced sense of the work's being a hotch-potch is borne out by the omission, as from Cotgrave's, of authorial names—a neglect that sharply reduces the potential for the book to reify a sense of the literary tradition. Edward Bysshe's *The Art of English Poetry* (1702), though otherwise modelled on Poole's earlier work, upgrades it

[11] Thomas Hayward, *The British Muse* (1738), 'Preface', iv–vi.
[12] Ibid., 'Preface', vi–ix. Johnson defines 'Anthology' 1 as 'A collection of flowers'. Sense 3 is 'A collection of poems'.
[13] Ibid., 'Preface', vi–xiii.
[14] Ibid., 'Preface', xiii.

in respect of this particular issue, even providing a full list of the excerpted authors. To this extent, it moves in the direction of being an anthology of authors rather than of excerpts (and therefore more addressed to canon-formation), but Bysshe falls foul of Oldys in his turn by giving conspicuously short shrift to older authors. For 'when he says our best *English* poets' complains Oldys, 'he means only the *modern*'; indeed, Bysshe had hardly chosen to skirt controversy when accounting for the limited coverage given to the likes of Spenser and Shakespeare on the grounds that 'their language is now become so obsolete, that most readers, of our age, have no ear for them'. When Oldys turns to the final work of which he takes notice, Charles Gildon's *The Complete Art of Poetry* (1718), he finds this one deficiency remedied, but still thinks the work blighted by a different set of shortcomings. Although Gildon is approved for his enthusiasm for Shakespeare, Oldys is dismissive about the anthologist's more general credentials: 'he was not very extensively read in our poets...and was not industrious enough in extracting from those he had.'[15]

The defects that Oldys uncompromisingly attaches to these older anthologies he sees as being supplied by Hayward. Yet much hard work has to be done to make what might be seen as the limitations of Hayward's work count as blessings. That Hayward, for example, excludes such notable poets as Milton, Cowley, Waller, Dryden, Otway, Lee, Prior, and Congreve is put down to his having 'chosen rather to devote himself to neglected and expiring merit'; and that he declines to include any material prior to the sixteenth century is defended by the argument that readers will need to have consumed the present volume before being ready to appreciate the beauties of any earlier poetry.[16] Despite its celebrated status, Hayward's collection does something less than break the mould: rather he adopts the format of the printed commonplace-book, though dedicating to its service an unaccustomed amount of antiquarian scholarship. Moreover, the premises on which Hayward operates are identical with those of several earlier works whose shortcomings are reprimanded in Oldys's preface. Hayward, rather than seeing literature as a field made up of notable authors and works, still sees it,

[15] Ibid., 'Preface', xv–xviii.   [16] Ibid., 'Preface', xx.

in the older way, as a portfolio of free-floating sentiments and images, these susceptible to being digested along stricter lines in the sort of anthology that Hayward set out to compile.

That Hayward's *British Muse* should be seen as less a literary 'anthology' (an arrangement of poetic flowers plucked for their particular loveliness) than a dictionary of poetic sentiments accounts for why Oliver Goldsmith, in his *The Beauties of English Poesy* (1767), can state that he has undertaken the work after having been told by his publisher 'that there was no collection of English Poetry among us, of any estimation'.[17] Goldsmith intended to supply this deficiency in a work that, though scarcely celebrated in its time, has a much juster claim than Hayward's of thirty years earlier to be seen as a pioneering effort. His is probably the earliest anthology in which works are not merely selected but also assorted and prefaced in such a way as to enunciate an unambiguous canon of English poetry. Moreover, Goldsmith is acutely conscious that the act of anthologization involves a process of selection: before this time poetic anthologizers had happily picked apart the inclusions and omissions of predecessors but had scarcely felt any need to apologize for, or to theorize, their own choices. Principles of selection, in the process of their being applied, were always invisible.

Goldsmith's description of the selection process, though interesting, is crucially at variance from itself. On the one hand, he admits to the subjective nature of his selections, an admission standard to modern-day anthologies but one which in Goldsmith's day was unusually concessive: he offers his own collection as 'to the best of my judgement... the best collection that has yet appeared: though, as tastes are various, numbers will be of a very different opinion'.[18] But while he leaves it open for his readers to demur on the constitution of his volume, he also fortifies himself that he has in fact 'run but few risques' since 'every poem here is well known, and possessed, or the public has been long mistaken, of peculiar merit'. Indeed, so much do the contents of his edition dictate themselves that Goldsmith feels

[17] *The Beauties of English Poesy. Selected by Oliver Goldsmith. In two vols.* (1767), vol. 1, 'Preface', i.
[18] Ibid., ii.

abashed about claiming merit for his own individual selections, given that 'in all languages the best productions are the most easily found'.[19]

Ultimately, Goldsmith falls back, in a rather Johnsonian way, on an appeal to the aggregative judgement of the reading public. But even if judging the public's mind is perhaps less of an exact science than Goldsmith lets on, the more important point here is his acceptance that it behoves an anthology to come to some formulation of the basis on which its selections have been carried out. This acceptance seems all the more pertinent in Goldsmith's case, given that his anthology is so nakedly adjudicatory in tone and organization. It scarcely stretches the point to say that the ordering of poems across Goldsmith's two volumes inscribes a pecking order of English literature, this sense of hierarchy being underscored in the short introductory paragraphs that preface each poem. Stationed at the front of the first volume, for instance, is *The Rape of the Lock*, of which Goldsmith writes, as if conscious to justify its foremost position, that it 'seems to be Mr. Pope's most finished production, and is, perhaps, the most perfect in our language'.[20] Next follow Milton's 'Il Penseroso' and 'L'Allegro', which the introductory note encourages us to think of as more perfect expressions of Milton's style than *Paradise Lost*. Other works making an early appearance are Gray's 'Elegy', Johnson's 'London', Shenstone's 'The School-Mistress' and Denham's 'Cooper's Hill'; but by the time we get to the later stages of the second volume, Goldsmith's powers of approbation have exhausted themselves, and his critical comments are mainly grudging or dismissive. The boundaries of the project are defined in somewhat quixotic fashion: eighteenth-century poets dominate, making the anthology in large part one of contemporary verse. Goldsmith has, however, reached back to 'Cooper's Hill', Dryden's 'Mac Flecknoe', and Waller's 'On the Death of the Lord Protector', and has retreated back even further to include two early poems by Milton. Yet there is no sense of a balance of coverage across the whole chronological spectrum taken in by the anthology; the work instead presents itself more as a trove of Goldsmith's favourite poetic things.

[19] Ibid. iii.   [20] Ibid. 1: 1.

The onus felt by some anthologists to spell out the grounds on which their selections were made owed much to the mid-century vogue of the idea of 'taste': the idea, that is, that people's judgemental faculties are to some degree subjective and for this reason potentially idiosyncratic. Vicesimus Knox, for example, notwithstanding that his *Elegant Extracts* (1784?) is largely aimed at schoolchildren feels a need to go through the same rigmarole of theorizing his principles of inclusion, the more so since 'tastes will for ever differ'. Much as with Goldsmith before him, what results is a piece of logical tail-chasing. Most suitable, so he determines, for pedagogic use are the more well-known pieces of poetry, in the selection of which, it might be thought, 'Private judgment...must often give way to public'. Yet this principle of divergent tastes having been proposed, it soon gets obliterated by Knox's conviction that one might speak of the absolute merit of a literary work, a merit that will normally disclose itself through popular consensus. As for Goldsmith, so for Knox also, popularity is held up as 'the least fallible test of merit', since the 'best pieces are usually the most popular'. So Knox's anthology ends up being presented to the reader in a double way as an expression of his own taste and as a statement of the settled preference of the reading public.[21]

The serial collections of the late eighteenth century, of which the *Works* of 1779–81 comprise one, built upon practices of anthologization long pre-dating them. The particular lesson that modern-day students of Johnson's *Lives of the Poets* stand to learn from the nearer efforts of Goldsmith and Knox has to do with evaluation. What kind of value, or how much value, the fact of anthological selection bestows depends inevitably on the criteria of selection adopted. Moreover, in a collection like Goldsmith's *Beauties*, with each poem fastidiously stationed in an aesthetic pecking-order, a strongly differentiated scheme of value emerges. When Martha Woodmansee, as cited earlier, claims that Johnson's *Lives* establish 'a pantheon of great authors', she omits to acknowledge any scheme of value other than the bare fact of selection. But in Johnson's own time, it was as much the terms of an author's incorporation as the fact of his incorporation that conferred value. This, indeed, accounts for

[21] Vicesimus Knox, *Elegant Extracts* (1784?), 'Preface', iv–v.

the paradox that while modern critics like Woodmansee tend to view Johnson's *Lives* as enshrining a pantheon of great authors, Johnson's contemporaries were more inclined to wax indignant over the degrading, even assassinatory, treatment meted out in them to many of the authors so 'fortunate' as to be selected.

III

Johnson's *Lives*, looked at simply as a compilation of authorial biographies, inevitably stand on the foundation of a great deal of earlier biographical endeavour. Indeed, their accomplishment lies not so much in original research as, so J. P. Hardy has stated, in 'the skill and relevance with which their author has reworked and compressed available material'.[22] The reconstructive task posed by each biography was necessarily individual: in some instances, Johnson had to compress down a superfluity of biographical data; on other occasions, he had to amplify a much more meagre stock of information. Moreover, for many of his biographees, Johnson was juggling three distinct categories of source-material. These categories are enumerated by Pat Rogers as (i) 'single lives' of authors, like Tickell's biography of Addison in 1721; (ii) 'authorial lives', or the entries on writers in collections exclusively of authorial biography, like Phillips's *Theatrum Poetarum* (1675) and Winstanley's *Lives* (1687); and (iii) what Rogers calls general lives, or accounts of writers in national or universal dictionaries of biography, especially Thomas Fuller's *History of the Worthies of England* (1662), Thomas Birch's *A General Dictionary, Historical and Critical* (1734–41) and the two eighteenth-century editions of the *Biographia Britannica*. Of these three categories, I am principally interested here in the latter two.[23]

Johnson was familiar with Langbaine's and Winstanley's collected authorial lives of the late seventeenth century, but the two

[22] *Johnson's Lives of the Poets: A Selection*, ed. J. P. Hardy (Oxford, 1971), 'Introduction', xi. Hardy's observation is quoted at the start of Pat Rogers's authoritative treatment of 'Johnson's *Lives of the Poets* and the Biographic Dictionaries', *Review of English Studies*, NS 31 (1980), 149–71. I am heavily indebted here to Rogers's essay.

[23] See Rogers, 'Johnson's *Lives of the Poets*', 150.

works in this category to which he had most frequent recourse both belong to his own century. Giles Jacob's *Poetical Register* came out in two volumes in 1719–20, the first volume treating 'The Lives and Characters of the English Dramatick Poets', the second providing 'An Historical Account of the Lives and Writings of our most considerable English Poets'. Both volumes carry a frontispiece consisting of miniature poetic engravings arranged so as to form an icon of the literary canon. In the first, small portraits of Jonson, Fletcher, Wycherley, Dryden, Otway, and Beaumont encircle a larger, central one of Shakespeare; in the second, an image of Chaucer is ringed by the smaller canonical satellites of Milton, Cowley, Butler, and Waller. Jacob's *Poetical Register* stands apart from most previous and subsequent works of the same kind in as much as it includes living authors; for most previous works, death provided the most elementary condition of inclusion, partly for reasons of diplomacy and partly because the activity of collecting authorial biographies took place under a general rubric of 'fame', in which the rescuing of deceased authors from post-mortal oblivion was of paramount importance.

Given the inclusion of living authors, given, that is, that the compilation presented itself as something other than mortuary homage, it was inevitable that it would bruise sensibilities and rattle egos. These unavoidable dangers become apparent even in the work's advance publicity, Jacob's second volume being puffed in the *Daily Post* on 13 July 1720 in the following terms:

An Historical Account of the Lives and Writings of all our English Poets, whether Epick, Lyrick, Elegiack, Epigrammatists, &c including the living Authors, viz. the D. of Buckingham, Archbishop of York, Bishop of Rochester, Mr. Prior, Mr. Pope, Major Pack, Sir Richard Blackmore, Mr. Tickell, Mr. A. Phillips, Mr. Yalden, Mr. Sacheverall, Mr. Croxall, Mr. Fenton, Mr. Gay, Mr. Sewell, Dr. Young, &c. To which is prefix'd, An Essay on the Rise, Progress, and Beauty of all Kinds of Poetry...[24]

As James McLaverty has pointed out, the listing of contemporary authors inevitably raised to prominence uncomfortable questions of rank. Just as a duke precedes an archbishop, whose

[24] Cited from J. McLaverty, 'Pope and Giles Jacob's *Lives of the Poets: The Dunciad* as Alternative Literary History', *Modern Philology*, 83 (1985), 25.

skirts are then followed by a mere bishop, so Prior and Pope head up the list of contemporary authors. But what are we to make of the fact that Prior actually precedes Pope, and that Gay is pushed down the list by the likes of Sir Richard Blackmore, Ambrose Philips, and Samuel Croxall? The sorts of objection, captious or otherwise, that might arise from the 'Advertisement' propose themselves on a grander scale in connection with Jacob's project as an entirety, especially in its general portrayal of the Augustan literary scene and adjudications on individual authors. Probably it was Jacob's dismissive account of the comic play *Three Hours after Marriage* in which Pope had a hand that triggered the most withering retaliation against the work. In the notes to Pope's *Dunciad Variorum*, Jacob's approving comments on authors are liberally quoted—especially at junctures where the same authors are being held up to ridicule in the poem itself.[25]

Jacob's *Poetical Register* is succeeded somewhat later by a five-volume *Lives of the Poets* published by R. Griffiths in 1753, the name appearing on the title-page being that of Theophilus Cibber.[26] The actual compiler, however, was a friend of Johnson's, Robert Shiels, though Cibber was hired to 'revise, correct, and improve it', and to supply the greater lustre of his name.[27] The entries are characteristically longer and more considered than those which had appeared in earlier works of the same kind, but remain nonetheless in large part pieced together from antecedents, the works of Winstanley, Langbaine, Jacob, and Elizabeth Cooper being liberally cross-referenced. What Shiels has added to the endeavours of his predecessors, as well as some fresh matter, is a greater scrupulosity in attending to, and acknowledging, earlier sources.

Shiels's *Lives* was the earliest work of collected authorial lives to benefit from, if not exactly a new genre, then one that was taking rapid strides forward: national or universal biography. In 1734 appeared the first volume of *A General Dictionary, Historical and Critical*, an enterprise modelled on the work of the

[25] See ibid. 26–9.
[26] See William R. Keast, 'Johnson and "Cibber's" *Lives of the Poets*, 1753', in *Restoration and Eighteenth-Century Literature: Essays in Honour of Alan Dugald McKillop*, ed. Carrol Camden (Chicago, 1963), 89–101.
[27] Ibid. 90.

'Celebrated Mr. BAYLE', and compiled by a team of biographers and translators amongst whom Thomas Birch played the leading role. The *General Dictionary* was the first attempt to apply inductive principles to the composition and collection of biographies. The editors laid out the task to which they had appointed themselves in the following terms:

The new Articles are drawn up from the original Authors, (who are quoted every where in the most exact manner) without any regard to other Historical Dictionaries, unless to correct their errors; and entirely in Mr. Bayle's manner, that is, with critical Remarks, printed under the Text, which will render the Work less voluminous; and these Remarks we have endeavoured to render agreeable by a variety of reflections of a miscellaneous kind.[28]

The essence of the method was to base each life-history only on a primary source whose authenticity lay beyond dispute; and to expose all secondary accounts to whatever procedures of verification the particular instance allowed. The methodology is one that expresses itself through a distinct *mise-en-page*: the main text appears suspended above and between an apparatus of bibliographical notes, 'critical remarks', and longer discursive notes; and a further set of notes is keyed not to the main text but to the annotative remarks themselves. In practical terms, the technique allowed for sources to be played off against each other, as, for example, in this note attached to the entry on Denham:

[A] Went to Lincoln's-Inn.] Mr Langbain (1) and Sir Thomas Pope-Blount (2) tell us that *he followed the Study of the Civil Law there*; but this appears to be a mistake, for Mr Wood assures us (3) that he studied the *Common Law*.

Referred to here are Langbaine's *An Account of the English Dramatick Poets*, Sir Thomas Pope Blount's *De Re Poetica* and Anthony à Wood's *Athenae Oxonienses*.

Since James Osborn's researches published in 1938, it has become possible to identify the prime mover and principal architect of the *General Dictionary* as the clergyman and antiquarian Thomas Birch (1705–66), who not only took responsibility for the whole oceanic project but penned fully six hundred

---

[28] *A General Dictionary, Historical and Critical* (1734–41), 'Preface', iii.

new biographies as his own individual contribution, including virtually all the literary ones. Birch, indeed, born into Quaker stock and without a university education, deserves more than anybody else the title of the father of literary biography in English.[29] In 1747, six years after the appearance of the final volume of the *General Dictionary* appeared the first volume of a new work building on its precedent, the *Biographia Britannica: or the Lives of the most Eminent Persons who have Flourish'd in Great Britain and Ireland*. Its general editor is unknown, but William Oldys and John Campbell both contributed to the enterprise. It was predicated on the old ethos of 'fame', proposing the erection of 'a kind of generous MONUMENT' to 'the most deserving of all ages' as 'an expression of gratitude due to their services'. Interestingly, when the editors surveyed the field of existing biographies, what they desiderated in particular were biographies of authors:

The Lives of our POETS have been often, but never well, written; LANGBAIN is too concise, and his follower [Jacob], who pretends to have improved him, has much mistaken his talent, and done very little honour to those he has attempted to celebrate.[30]

The *Biographia Britannica* came out in six volumes, the last divided into two parts, between 1747 and 1766. Only twelve years later, a second edition of the work, which was to peter out after only six volumes and having got only so far as the letter 'F', began to appear, the editors being able to supply themselves with a large body of materials left by William Oldys, a contributor to the earlier edition. For the most part, the second edition of the *Biographia Britannica* emerged too late to have had much bearing on the *Lives*, though, as Pat Rogers has pointed out, Johnson's entry on Akenside is clearly based on the entry on the poet in the first volume of the *Biographia*'s second edition.[31]

Rogers has provided the most meticulous general scrutiny of Johnson's sources and his patterns of reliance on them. What he

[29] See James Marshall Osborn, 'Thomas Birch and the *General Dictionary* (1734–41)', *Modern Philology*, 36 (1938), 25–45.
[30] *Biographia Britannica: or the Lives of the most eminent Persons who have flourished in Great Britain and Ireland*, 7 vols. (1747–66), 1, 'Preface', xi–xii. Nominally in six vols. but the final 'volume' is divided into two parts, each separately bound.
[31] Rogers, 'Johnson's *Lives of the Poets*', 155.

resolves is that the extent of his reliance on single lives may in the past have been exaggerated. Because Johnson often had to work harder to bring such works into his possession, on several occasions soliciting friends for a loan of them, he tends to mention them more frequently; but Rogers still maintains his greater indebtedness to have been to the collections of authorial or national biography that he had closer to hand.[32] If we simply address the latter two categories of biography, then the picture is confused by the fact that entries to which Johnson made himself indebted may have already built up debts of their own. So that while, in general terms, Johnson may have consulted source 'a' and not source 'b', what he procured from 'a' may be what 'a' had already taken from 'b'. Rogers ends up making the following surmises: that the *General Dictionary* and the *Biographia Britannica* are the sources to which Johnson most often refers, with the latter being perhaps the more prolific fund of material; that the *Lives* compiled by Shiels under Cibber's name are his immediate port of call where the two previously mentioned works lack entries; and that Jacob's *Poetical Register* acts as a lender of last resort when no information can be gleaned elsewhere, especially as in instances where Johnson is dealing with near contemporaries (Jacob's being the only collection to include living writers). Only in connection with nine of the writers does Johnson appear to use a single life as opposed to an entry in one or more biographical collections, or indeed to a receding sequence of such entries, as the primary source for his own biographical treatment.[33]

IV

Johnson's is the first work of specialized literary biography to be strongly influenced by the sceptical scholarship of Pierre Bayle.[34] One of his main sources, as I have already suggested, was

---

[32] Ibid. 151–2.

[33] See ibid. 152–6.

[34] For Johnson and Bayle, see Martin Maner, *The Philosophical Biographer: Doubt and Dialectic in Johnson's 'Lives of the Poets'* (Athens, Ga., 1989), see ch. 3, esp. 43–56. For Johnson's method as a biographer, see Robert Folkenflik, *Samuel Johnson: Biographer* (Ithaca, NY, 1978), see esp. ch. 2, '"Trifles with Dignity": The Task of Johnsonian Biography', 29–55.

Thomas Birch's *General Dictionary*, closely modelled on Bayle's *Dictionnaire historique et critique* (1697), and he confided to Boswell that 'Bayle's Dictionary is a very useful work for those who love to consult the biographical part of literature, which is what I love most'.[35] The Baylean method depended on the painstaking accreditation or rejection of sources, and on a high degree of candour about the processes of inference on which a biography relied. It would be wrong to say that Bayle rejected narrative, but he maintained that all the life details underpinning a given narrative should be properly vouched for and authenticated.

Johnson's *Lives* attest to his appreciation that constructing a literary past always depends on discriminating between sources, and accordingly much of the labour involved must consist of generating criteria against which this discrimination can take place. A typical passage of Johnsonian reasoning on this point comes, for example, at the very beginning of his 'Life of Butler':

> OF the great author of *Hudibras* there is a Life prefixed to the later editions of his poem by an unknown writer, and therefore of disputable authority; and some account is incidentally given by Wood, who confesses the uncertainty of his own narrative: more, however, than they knew cannot now be learned, and nothing remains but to compare and copy them.[36]

It is noteworthy, here, that Johnson does not begin with his biographical subject, who is only introduced in the following paragraph: 'SAMUEL BUTLER was born in the parish of Strensham...'. The first paragraph is instead set aside for details even more foundational than those of Butler's birth: the availability and status of textual records. To some extent, Johnson is merely acknowledging, with due propriety, the reliance of his biography on two earlier works, one anonymous and the other Wood's *Athenae Oxonienses*; but he also finds it an opportune moment for some general reflection on the principles against which sources should be judged and their comparative status ascertained. So he resolves that a text by an unknown hand can only ever be of 'disputable authority'; he asserts it as a binding law of scholarship that no subsequent enquirer can ever know more than is contained in contemporaneous records; and he

---

[35] *Life*, 1: 425.   [36] *Lives*, 1: 201.

proposes that the way to negotiate between rival historical sources is through a process of collation ('compare and copy them').

This transition, from citing a source or reporting an incident to uncovering the principles against which its authenticity should be judged, is common in Johnson's *Lives*. In his 'Life of Roscommon', for example, he recounts how when the poet was a little boy he experienced a vivid premonition of his father's death, an event that was to occur only a fortnight later. Johnson had come across this story in John Aubrey's *Miscellany*, and, having cited it, he proceeds to muse on the larger issue of reliable testimonies:

The present age is very little inclined to favour any accounts of this kind, nor will the name of Aubrey much recommend it to credit: it ought not however to be omitted because better evidence of a fact cannot easily be found than is here offered, and it must be by preserving such relations that we may at last judge how much they are to be regarded. If we stay to examine this account, we shall see difficulties on both sides: here is a relation of a fact given by a man who had no interest to deceive, and who could not be deceived himself; and here is, on the other hand, a miracle which produces no effect: the order of nature is interrupted to discover not a future but only a distant event, the knowledge of which is of no use to him to whom it is revealed. Between these difficulties, what way shall be found? Is reason or testimony to be rejected? I believe what Osborne says of an appearance of sanctity may be applied to such impulses or anticipations as this: Do not wholly slight them, because they may be true; but do not easily trust them, because they may be false.[37]

As ever with Johnson, the conundrum elicits a response of sternly attentive reasoning. The issue at first sight presents itself as a conflict between testimony and reason. Johnson is sceptical that such an event *could have* occurred, not because premonitions are impossible, but because a premonition serving no purpose, in that the baleful event prefigured could not in any case have been prevented, is a useless phenomenon. And since he assigns premonitions to the category of divinely ordained miracles, to lend credence to the story would be to suppose that God sometimes intervenes in the human world in ways that turn out

---

[37] Ibid. 1: 230–1.

to be futile. Yet set against the implausibility of the event having occurred is the fact that it is vouched for by a reputable authority. It is true that Aubrey's story is not authenticated by other sources, but at the same time he had no reason to fabricate it. Moreover, if we are minded to doubt Aubrey's testimony, what grounds exist for accepting any testimony on past events, even where these are less overtly unlikely? Eventually, Johnson, having picked over and pried into the matter, puts it to rest with a piece of marmoreal equivocation as to how we should approach such problematic events: 'Do not wholly slight them, because they may be true; but do not easily trust them, because they may be false.'

Examples of this kind are legion in the *Lives of the Poets*. In the 'Life of Addison', Johnson reflects on the particular diplomacy involved in reporting testimony on the recently deceased, given the inevitability of causing a 'pang' to 'a widow, a daughter, a brother, or a friend'.[38] Johnson may have felt all the more acutely the biographer's responsibility to weigh evidence, simply because he was so drawn to anecdotes (they are his métier), and particularly to anecdotes concerning a person's private actions, where any inaccuracy was likely to be defamatory. Anecdotes were, so Johnson believed, not just the grist of a good biography as the whole purpose of the biographical form. When Boswell announced his intention to write a book about Corsica, Johnson told him to include 'as many anecdotes as you can'; and after reading Joseph Warton's *Essay on the Writings and Genius of Pope*, he recommended the book on the grounds that 'The facts, which he mentions, though they are seldom anecdotes, in a rigorous sense, are often such as are very little known, and such as will delight more readers than naked criticism.'[39] The 'rigorous sense' Johnson has in mind is where the word refers to a 'secret history' as opposed to what was becoming its modish sense of 'a minute passage of private life'.[40]

The sorts of anecdote that most fascinated Johnson were those that vouchsafed a private understanding of a public person, that revealed the hidden idiosyncrasies and fallibilities that even the

[38] Ibid. 2: 116.
[39] *Life*, 2: 11; Johnson's remarks about Warton cited from Folkenflik, *Samuel Johnson*, 43–4.
[40] See *Dictionary*.

great possess. In *Rambler* 60 he lays down that 'the business of the biographer is often to pass slightly over those performances and incidents, which produce vulgar greatness, to lead those thoughts into domestick privacies, and display the minute details of daily life, where exterior appendages are cast aside'. It is in accordance with this principle, for example, that he praises Sallust for including in his account of Catiline that Catiline used to slow and quicken the speed of his walking in synchrony with the thought processes going on in his head.[41] Such unobtrusive pathologies of everyday living occupy an unusually pronounced position in the *Lives*. Perhaps nowhere does this side of Johnson's biographical practice come more into its own than in his 'Life of Swift', Swift's being of all his biographees the one whose behaviour seems most involved in patterns of psychological compulsion. Johnson records, for example, that Swift, notwithstanding being a good raconteur, would fastidiously pause, after having spoken for a minute, to give an opportunity to another speaker; that he in all circumstances refrained from laughter; and that he had a compulsive zealotry in counting up his own household expenses.[42]

The point of anecdotal material of this kind is not that it reveals much about, or is causally linked to, aspects of the writer's craft. In his 'Life of Thomson', Johnson, in fact, mocks the very idea of easy correlations between the life and work, instancing the case of a lady who deduced from Thomson's poems that their author was a 'great lover, a great swimmer, and rigorously abstinent', none of which was actually the case.[43] Yet Johnson's love of anecdotes reflects something more than just a propensity for gossip or prurience. Its basis is a conviction that the true understanding of a life lies in its unstated domestic minutiae rather than in its official or public actions. It is on account of their misunderstanding of this that he criticizes previous biographers in *Rambler* 60:

biography has often been allotted to writers who seem very little acquainted with the nature of their task, or very negligent about the performance. They rarely afford any other account than might be collected from publick papers, but imagine themselves writing a life when they exhibit a chronological series of actions or preferments;

[41] *Yale*, 3: 321.   [42] *Lives*, 3: 56, 58–9, 60.   [43] Ibid. 3: 297–8.

and so little regard the manners or behaviour of their heroes, that more knowledge may be gained of a man's real character, by a short conversation with one of his servants, than from a formal and studied narrative, begun with his pedigree, and ended with his funeral.[44]

The moments in Johnson's *Lives* that seem most quintessential to his practice are ones where his savouring of anecdotes clashes with the stalwart rigour which he had taught himself to apply to biographical source material. Such a moment occurs, for example, in his 'Life of Dorset' where he repeats the anecdote that the poet's celebrated song 'To all you Ladies now at land', was composed on the very eve of a mighty naval battle. Initially, Johnson cites this tale as a remarkable instance of 'tranquillity of mind and promptitude of wit'; yet this is barely left to lie before he interposes a sceptical counterpoint: 'Seldom any splendid story is wholly true.' And he then cites the conflicting testimony of the Earl of Orrery that Dorset had spent a week working up the poem. Yet even now Johnson's position is not that the anecdote should be jettisoned, but rather that we should still retain (to Dorset's credit) the aspects of it that remain untouched by Orrery's adverse testimony. So that although Orrery debunks Dorset's 'facility', his report still 'leaves him his courage'.[45]

Matters to do with the probity of anecdotal material nearly always touch on the morality and pathos of lives. The anecdote is the medium by which the individual life, entrammelled by its own mediocrity, can momentarily be aggrandized; and it is nearly always the case that Johnson's debunking of anecdotes coincides with the puncturing of an inflated reputation or pre-tension. One such occurrence, for example, is his arithmetical disproof of the story that William King, in the course of eight years' study at Oxford, had not just read but annotated fully 'twenty-two thousand odd hundred books and manuscripts'.[46] On the other hand, Johnson occasionally records an anecdote that, for reasons of compassion and humanity, one might wish not to be true. Such a one concerns Thomas Otway:

[Otway] died April 14, 1685, in a manner which I am unwilling to mention. Having been compelled by his necessities to contract debts, and hunted, as is supposed, by the terriers of the law, he retired to a

---

[44] *Yale*, 3: 322.   [45] *Lives*, 1: 305.   [46] Ibid. 2: 26.

publick house on Tower-hill, where he is said to have died of want; or, as it is related by one of his biographers, by swallowing, after a long fast, a piece of bread which charity had supplied. He went out, as is reported, almost naked, in the rage of hunger, and, finding a gentleman in a neighbouring coffee-house, asked him for a shilling: the gentleman gave him a guinea; and Otway going away bought a roll, and was choaked with the first mouthful. All this, I hope, is not true; and there is this ground of better hope, that Pope, who lived near enough to be well informed, relates in Spence's memorials that he died of a fever caught by violent pursuit of a thief that had robbed one of his friends. But that indigence and its concomitants, sorrow and despondency, pressed hard upon him has never been denied, whatever immediate cause might bring him to the grave.[47]

Johnson keeps in view the strictly conjectural nature of the story of Otway's choking through a running series of interpolations: 'as is supposed...is said to have...as it is related...as is reported'. The scrupulosity of these insertions suggests a mind bent on a clear distinction between testimony and truth; but, at the same time, the passage gives due weight to the desire we might feel for one version of the truth to prevail over another. The story of Otway's unlucky death is one which Johnson is initially 'unwilling to mention', and which he can but 'hope is not true'; and the rival report originating from Pope and preserved in Spence's *Memorials* (or *Observations*) provides 'ground of better hope'. But much as one might wish in the circumstances for Pope's testimony to be true, and Johnson found it easy to harbour strong feelings of this sort, he is still at pains to see it exactly for what it is. For even allowing for the accuracy of Pope's report, it remains no less the case that 'indigence and its concomitants, sorrow and despondency, pressed hard upon [Otway]'. The movement of mind through the passage quoted is one instinct with a siege of contraries: Johnson's commitment to deliver the truth as faithfully and objectively as possible wins out only narrowly, and only after a struggle, over an opposite inclination of making the past comply with his own sentimental desires. This conflict between the two opposite promptings is at the heart of Johnson's biographical practice.

[47] Ibid. 1: 247.

V

Johnson's *Lives* employ a basic tripartite structure: a chronological life, a pithy character sketch and then a section on the
author's works. It is true that these distinct phases on occasions
blur into each other, but they can be seen in sharp relief in a
short, uncomplicated 'Life' like that of Gray. The biography
begins, in the traditional way, *ab ovo*: 'Thomas Gray...was
born in Cornhill, November 26, 1716'; and takes us through to
Gray's final illness, a gout which fastening on his stomach 'produced strong convulsions, which (30 July 1771) terminated
in death'. In the next section, Johnson embarks, with an unsym-
pathetic abruptness, on a general sketch of Gray's personality, largely taken from a secondary source: 'His character I
am willing to adopt...from a letter written to my friend Mr.
Boswell by the Rev. Mr. Temple.' This section then gives way to
a further one considering Gray's literary achievement: 'GRAY's
poetry is now to be considered.'[48]

This tripartite structure was not of Johnson's own creation;
traces of it show up in several of his biographical predecessors
such as Giles Jacob, Elizabeth Cooper, and Robert Shiels.[49]
However, Johnson's use specifically of the character sketch
seems at a remove from that of the earlier literary biographers.
In the seventeenth-century collections of biography by Phillips,
Winstanley, and Langbaine, the drafting of lives is based on the
genre of the Theophrastan character sketch, the paramount
technique being that of portraying each biographee as having
been shaped by a single, ascendant 'ruling passion' or psychological compulsion. It is in accordance with this technique, for
example, that Shakespeare and Jonson become seen as incar-
nating strongly opposite character principles, with Shakespeare
being the poet of nature, Jonson that of learning. Johnson, on
the whole, resists this simplificatory casting of character, though
he does not always pass up the opportunities it offered; one of
his most celebrated passages, the set-piece comparison between
Dryden and Pope in the 'Life of Pope', stands in an atavistic

[48] Ibid. 3: 421, 429, 433.

[49] See Martine Watson Brownley, 'Johnson's *Lives of the English Poets* and earlier
Traditions of the Character Sketch in England', in *Johnson and his Age*, ed. James
Engell, Harvard English Studies 12 (Cambridge, Mass., 1984).

relation to this earlier tradition. Yet in the very same 'Life', Johnson delivers his sternest rebuke to the 'ruling passion' school of biographical characterization:

It must be at least allowed that this 'ruling Passion', antecedent to reason and observation, must have an object independent on human contrivance, for there can be no natural desire of artificial good. No man therefore can be born, in the strict acceptation, a lover of money, for he may be born where money does not exist; nor can he be born, in a moral sense, a lover of his country, for society, politically regulated, is a state contradistinguished from a state of nature, and any attention to that coalition of interests which makes the happiness of a country is possible only to those whom enquiry and reflection have enabled to comprehend it.

This doctrine is in itself pernicious as well as false: its tendency is to produce the belief of a kind of moral predestination or overruling principle which cannot be resisted: he that admits it is prepared to comply with every desire that caprice or opportunity shall excite, and to flatter himself that he submits only to the lawful dominion of Nature in obeying the resistless authority of his 'ruling Passion'.[50]

Given that Johnson did not have to hand the psychoanalytical tools that might have helped him understand adult behaviour in light of the formative experiences of childhood, he is relinquishing here the most obvious technique available to him for construing a biographical life. Indeed, it is a feature of Johnson's *Lives* that they display a deep scepticism about whether individual lives can ever be sufficiently causal and consistent to yield themselves to the shaping hand of the biographer. Far from life occurrences, or naunces of personality, being shown to be predestined, Johnson's *Lives* constantly dwell on the fortuitous or chance-ridden elements in human development. He reports, for instance, that when Cowley was a small boy, a copy of Spenser's *Faerie Queene* was wont to lie on the window of his mother's apartment; and it was through seizing on this that Cowley became 'irrecoverably a poet'. Cowley's chance induction into his vocation leads Johnson to the generalization that 'Such are the accidents which produce . . . that particular designation of mind, and propensity for some certain science or employment, which is commonly called Genius.' For Johnson, the particular mode of

[50] *Lives*, 3: 174.

expression of human genius is always a matter of serendipity: 'The true Genius is a mind of large general powers, *accidentally* determined to some particular direction' (my emphasis).[51]

These accidental determinations of genius are not something that Johnson detects in connection with every life, though a pronounced feature of the *Lives* is his interest in the education of his biographees, this being the phase of life in which he believed that the complexion of a person's genius was normally decided. Much as Johnson believed that a whole life, the entire temper of a person's genius, could be accounted for through a single happenstantial event, so he reasons along similar lines in connection with the genesis of works of literature. Tracing the origins of *Paradise Lost* from Milton's earlier play *Adam Unparadised*, for example, he reflects on the 'delightful entertainment' emanating from tracing how 'great works' are 'suddenly advanced by accidental hints'.[52] Exactly the same reflection, moreover, is brought on by consideration of Pope's *Rape of the Lock*, which bears out in similar fashion how 'performances, which strike with wonder, are combinations of skilful genius with happy casualty'.[53]

The biographies narrated in Johnson's *Lives* invariably observe a pattern of a great design or predestinated arrangement being overriden by chance or contingency. No life traverses a preordained route; no character is devoid of some principle of inner contradiction; no talent lends itself to a predictable outcome; not even the greatest works bear witness to a smooth transition from genesis to outcome untouched by hazard or, in Johnson's word, 'casualty'. Even though, then, the *Lives* have affinities with the earlier tradition of authorial biography beginning with the likes of Phillips, Winstanley, and Langbaine, and although they bring this tradition to its fulfilment, they are shaped uniquely by a set of very distinctive Johnsonian attitudes.

VI

The *Lives* were to prove Johnson's most controversial work. As distinct from any of his other writings, their critical reception,

---

[51] *Lives*, 1: 2.   [52] *Lives*, 1: 124.   [53] *Lives*, 3: 104.

given Johnson's death in 1784, was in large part a posthumous one; and the biographies themselves seemed to many to epitomize the most dislikable traits of Johnson's personality. What stood out most in the *Lives* was the sheer censoriousness of Johnson's dealings with other poets, one that seemed to some to be coloured by his uncompromising Tory politics. As early as 1782, the *Monthly Review* pointed out his habitual predisposition to criticize rather than praise his subjects:

> Through the whole of his performance the desire of praise, excepting in the case of some very favourite author, is almost always overpowered by his disposition to censure; and while beauties are passed over 'with the neutrality of a stranger and the coldness of a critic,' the slightest blemish is examined with microscopical sagacity.[54]

This cruel attention to deficiency is not spared even to writers who were Johnson's contemporaries, whose treatment at his hands is bereft of 'brotherly kindness'.

Johnson's candour is not everywhere condemned: Robert Anderson, in his 'Preface' to *The Works of the British Poets* (1795), who applauds the *Lives* as Johnson's 'most perfect production', speaks with kindly understatement of the author's 'valuable detached opinions'.[55] But the majority of commentators were ruffled by, and sometimes virulent about, the sharpness of his tone. Writing under the pseudonym of Benvolio, Anne Seward, who nursed a longstanding grudge against Johnson, attacked him in a series of letters to the *Gentleman's Magazine* in 1786 and 1787. In the second of these, she regretted that he had not died 'before the publication of the "Lives of the Poets"', for 'injustice and malice are too apparent in that work'; in another contribution of 1787, she modulated her idiom only slightly in declaring that 'it cannot be malevolent to say he [Johnson] was *malignant*'.[56] Moreover, the sorts of asperity for which Johnson was castigated were not narrowly literary critical ones, as for example his notorious distaste for lyric poetry, but also took in his more general reflections on conduct and character. Writing in 1783, for instance, Robert Potter

---

[54] *Monthly Review* 66 (1782), 126; cited from Donald A. Stauffer, *The Art of Biography in Eighteenth-Century England* (Princeton, 1941), 392.
[55] Anderson (ed.), 1, 'Preface', 3.
[56] *Gentleman's Magazine* (1786), 302; G. M. (1787), 685.

rebukes Johnson for broadcasting unfounded allegations about Addison's rapaciousness over the profits of *The Spectator*; and also for giving out that it was Lord Lyttelton's habit, when in the position of showing visitors around William Shenstone's garden at the Leasowes, to take them around in the reverse route so that they would form a poorer impression of it.[57]

Probably the most fervid antagonist to the *Lives* was the highly strung and irascible critic Percival Stockdale. Stockdale had for several years sent out admiring gestures towards Johnson, as when, in his *Enquiry into the Nature, and Genuine Laws of Poetry* (1783), he borrowed from *Rambler* no. 156 in criticizing Joseph Warton's strictures on Pope.[58] But his affections turned sour when he came to believe that he had been the London booksellers' original choice to write the biographies accompanying their new serial collection of English poetry, and that only late in the genesis of the project had he been supplanted by Johnson. Moreover, whereas Stockdale hoped that Johnson's *Lives* would refer favourably to his own critical and biographical writings, Johnson consented to do nothing more than in his 'Life of Waller' to give 'a very transient, and anonymous notice' to Stockdale's earlier biography of the same poet.[59] Stockdale's revenge was sharp though leisurely: disparaging comments on Johnson are a feature of several of his later works and letters. In 1793, a letter to Edward Jerningham includes a denunciation of Johnson almost apoplectic in its fury:

[Johnson's] mind was extremely defective in Taste; when he wrote the Lives of the Poets, his Faculties were extremely on the Decline; his arrogance had arisen to an insufferable pitch; his high-church and rank Tory-Principles and Prejudices contaminated most of his Criticisms; what, then, were we to expect from him but such Lives as would, in fact, be a *Disgrace to English Literature*? To Milton, both as a Man, and a Poet, he is often grossly unjust:—he treats Pope's Essay on Man with unqualified, and sovereign Contempt, though it's *Poetry* is beautiful:—he insults the memory of Hammond, of Swift, of Akenside, of

---

[57] Robert Potter, *An Inquiry into some Passages in Dr. Johnson's Lives of the Poets: Particularly his Observations on Lyric Poetry and the Odes of Gray* (1783), 5–8.

[58] See Howard D. Weinbrot, 'Samuel Johnson, Percival Stockdale, and Brick-bats from Grubstreet: Some Later Response to the *Lives of the Poets*', *Huntington Library Quarterly*, 56 (1993), 105–34, 113.

[59] Ibid. 114.

Gray:—and I have said that his Lives of the English Poets would, in proper Time, be found to be a *Disgrace to English Literature.*—[60]

In the course of this single letter, Stockdale four times rinses his mouth out with the phrase that Johnson's *Lives* should be considered a 'Disgrace to English Literature'. Yet the full exaction of his revenge was to come only with his *Lectures on the Truly Eminent English Poets* (1807), which is spattered with ungenerous reflections on Johnson's earlier work, and each of whose two volumes is preceded by a short set of verses in which Stockdale announces himself as taking up the 'cause of truth' against the 'prejudices' which he discovers too often to 'Corrupt, debase, mislead thy [Johnson's] noble mind'.[61]

Yet it was not just the tone, but also the content of Johnson's observations to which exception was taken. In particular, it was felt that his lives often demeaned themselves by peddling minutiae, paltry biographical details that had no relevance to the actual writing careers of the subjects under scrutiny. Potter, for example, confesses himself sorry

to see the masculine spirit of Dr. Johnson descending to what he perhaps in another might call 'anile garrulity.' In reading the life of any eminent person we wish to be informed of the qualities which give him the superiority over other men ... Can it be of any importance to us to be told how many pair of stockings the author of the Essay on Man wore?[62]

The nub of this is the aspersion that the retailing of anecdotes is unmanly: Johnson's dignified expatiations have given way to womanish gossip. Moreover, a sense of the critical emasculation of the *Lives* crops up elsewhere. In a curious contribution to the *Gentleman's Magazine* in March 1787, 'General Remarks on Writings of Old Men', R.O.P. regrets the misguided publication of the *Lives* and sees the work as evidence of the onset of mental

---

[60] Letter of 30 March 1793, ibid. 128; see also 116.

[61] See also Joseph Warton's aggressive remark about Johnson in his 1797 edition of Pope's poetry, cited in Joan Pittock, *The Ascendancy of Taste: The Achievement of Joseph and Thomas Warton* (London, 1973), 161: 'His Lives of the Poets are unhappily tinctured with this narrow, prejudiced, and confined notion of poetry, which has occasioned many false or spurious remarks, and many ill-grounded opinions, in a work that might have been, and was intended to have been, a manual of good taste and judgment.'

[62] Potter, *An Inquiry*, 4.

impotence, such that if Johnson had undertaken the work earlier he would 'have adduced more sound and manly reasons' for his critical judgements.[63]

It is fitting that Johnson, the great purveyor of anecdotes about others, has had his memory consecrated to posterity in similarly large part through the force of anecdote. That Johnson's own life was in process of being received and formulated anecdotally is apparent as early as 1786 when John Wolcot ('Peter Pindar') published his mock-eclogue *Bozzy and Piozzi, or the British Biographers, A Town Eclogue*. The poem imagines the two zealous Johnsonians vying for the 'palm of anecdote' before Sir John Hawkins, subsequently the editor of *The Works of Samuel Johnson*, who sits in arbitration. The two competitors attempt to outdo each other in issuing a stream of absurd anecdotes and bland inconsequentialities concerning Johnson's life.[64] Of course, in the first instance, the satire is directed less at Johnson than at the rhetoric of his adulators; but it is difficult not to suspect Wolcot's conversancy with the negative reception that had greeted Johnson's own brand of anecdotalism.

Yet these cavils about the censorious tone of Johnson's *Lives*, and their repeated recourse to anecdote, still perhaps played a lesser part in the overall reception of the *Lives* than the particular constitution of the literary canon that the *Works* were seen as enshrining. Of course, in as much as the *Works do* enunciate a canon, it should be remembered that this is scarcely Johnson's, since he only added five authors to the lengthy list drawn up by the consortium of booksellers. But this was a fact that, naturally enough, Johnson's detractors were all too ready to ignore. Within a year of the completion of the *Works*, for example, Vicesimus Knox had published his essay 'On the Prevailing Taste in Poetry' (1782) attacking the obsolescence of many of the poets incorporated in the edition:

The late collection of poets has restored to temporary life many a sickly and dying poet, who was hastening to his proper place, the tomb of oblivion. Why was any more paper wasted on Dorset, Halifax, Stepney, Walsh and Blackmore? How can a work pretend to the comprehensive

---

[63] *G.M.* (1787), 227.
[64] See *Parodies of the Romantic Age*, ed. Graeme Stones and John Strachan, 5 vols. (London, 1999), 2: 11–38.

title of the Body of English Poetry, in which the works of Spenser and Shakespeare are omitted to make room for such writers as King or Ambrose Philips?

Knox is sufficiently principled to concede that, given his limited hand in selection, the peccadilloes of the *Works* are not fairly to be placed at Johnson's own door, but he still ungraciously accuses him of a dereliction of responsibility in throwing 'the blame from himself on the compilers, whom he was not permitted, or did not endeavour, to control'.[65]

Even if the *Works* do not compose a *Johnsonian* canon as such, they do constitute a canon of sorts, and one to which, however non-committedly, Johnson was prepared to lend his name; and several attempts to revise or dethrone this canon are made in the following twenty years or so.[66] Johnson's friend John Scott, for example, who predeceased him by a year, responded with *Critical Essays on Some of the Poems of Several English Poets* (1785), in which he slashed down Johnson's file of names to produce a canon consisting of Denham, Milton, Pope, Dyer, Collins, Gray, Goldsmith, and Thomson. Moreover, Johnson's friend or not, Scott criticizes the constitution of the *Works* for the arbitrariness of its selections and proposes that a scheme of 'rational, impartial criticism' would have much reduced in number the writers who genuinely accede to the 'name of English Classicks'. So he queries why Rochester, Roscommon, Sprat, Halifax, Stepney, and Duke all make it into the *Works*, whereas Carew, Sedley, and Hopkins have been omitted. However, the greatest oversight he spots in the booksellers' list, and one which it remains surprising that Johnson did not rectify, concerns Goldsmith, who according to Scott 'certainly had a just claim to admission'.[67] Scott's reservations were to strike a chord with Robert Anderson who regurgitates this passage in the 'Preface' to volume 1 of his *Works of the British Poets*. He confesses himself at a loss why 'the managers of this edition

---

[65] Vicesimus Knox, *Essays, Moral and Literary* (1778), 2 vols. (1822), 2: 215.

[66] For a different sort of argument about Johnson as a canonizer, see Anne McDermott, 'Johnson's *Dictionary* and the Canon: Authors and Authority', *Yearbook of English Studies*, 28 (1998), 44–65. See also Alvin Kernan, *Samuel Johnson & the Impact of Print* (Princeton, 1987).

[67] John Scott, *Critical Essays on Some of the Poems of Several English Poets* (1785), see essay VIII (on Goldsmith), 247 ff.

admitted some authors, while others of similar character were rejected' and complains that 'where Pomfret, Yalden, and Blackmore, are preferred to Eusden, Welsted and Hill, it is not easy to account for the preference'.[68]

The flame of canonical revisionism is taken up, not surprisingly, by Stockdale in his *Lectures on the Truly Eminent English Poets* (1795). Stockdale sees his mission as being to set down his opinions on the 'Writings and Characters of our great Poets', and his work was expressly intended as an antidote to Johnson's *Lives*, 'for amongst the Poets of Dr. Johnson, there are names which have not the least pretensions to eminence'.[69] To this end, Stockdale renders down Johnson's supposed 'canon' to a mere nine poets: Spenser, Shakespeare, Milton, Dryden, Pope, Young, Thomson, Chatterton, and Gray. What most stands out, however, is that of Stockdale's twenty bulky lectures, no less than six are assigned to Thomas Chatterton, an author unrepresented in the *Works* of 1779–81, who is saluted in the initial lecture on the poet as an 'astonishing genius' and 'truly wise, and good', whose reputation is a matter of such moment as to touch on the 'honour of our country' and 'the eternal glory of the republick of letters'.[70]

Probably the most influential attack on Johnson's *Lives* and on the version of the national canon supposedly enshrined in the *Works of the British Poets* comes in Wordsworth's 'Essay, Supplementary to the Preface' (1815). Wordsworth addresses himself to the *Works* in the context of a critique of what he took to be Johnson's misguided elevation of the reading public as sole arbiters of literary value. Johnson, so Wordsworth believed, was guilty of understanding canonicity purely as an expression of mass opinion, a procedure that Wordsworth felt especially keen to repudiate since his own poetry was in process of falling victim to just that body of opinion. Wordsworth is wrong hereabouts to believe that Johnson's judgements placidly concur with a wider public opinion, but he is right to think that the consortium which produced the *Works* had an obvious financial interest in erecting a canon specifically of familiar and best-selling poets: the publishers, so he states, 'decided upon the claim of authors

[68] Anderson (ed.), 1, 'Preface', 3.
[69] Percival Stockdale, *Lectures on the Truly Eminent English Poets*, 2 vols. (1795), 1: vii–ix.
[70] Ibid. 2: 147–8.

to be admitted into a body of the most eminent, from the familiarity of their names with the readers of that day, and by the profits, which, from the sale of his works, each had brought and was bringing to the Trade'. This criterion of popular appeal had led the booksellers to incorporate into their canon only writers from Cowley onwards, a commercial decision that aroused Wordsworth's scorn:

What is become of the morning-star of English poetry? Where is the bright Elizabethan constellation? Or, if names be more acceptable than images, where is the ever-to-be-honoured Chaucer? where is Spenser? where Sidney? and, lastly, where he, whose rights as a poet, contra-distinguished from those which he is universally allowed to possess as a dramatist, we have vindicated,—where Shakespeare?

Instead of such luminaries, the *Works* can only boast Roscommon, Stepney, Philips, and a crowd of 'other reputed Magnates—metrical writers utterly worthless and useless'.[71]

It is easy to deflect some of Wordsworth's opprobrium from Johnson. He did not set the parameters of the collection; his criteria of appraisal are not universally collusive with public opinion, as is evident, for example, when he tries to unseat Granville from an inappropriately high level of public regard; and his entries on several lesser poetic figures are so severe as to be belittling. What the responses to Johnson by Stockdale and Wordsworth perhaps really testify to is an intolerance directed towards 'minor' poets. By the appearance of the *Lives*, the status of the minor author was becoming a topic of literary discussion. In 1782, as part of his expanded edition of *Essays Moral and Literary*, Vicesimus Knox penned some 'Cursory Remarks on some of the minor English Poets'. The idea of the minor writer is conveyed at the start by the images of the 'sweet warblings of the linnet and the red-breast' compared with the full-throated lark, and by the pretty violet or primrose compared with the 'lofty cedar'. The point of his essay, as well as to acknowledge that the 'first dignities in the poetical commonwealth are pre-occupied by such writers as Spenser, Milton, Dryden, and Pope', is to draw attention to 'the numerous subaltern stations' that are

---

[71] 'Essay, Supplementary to the Preface', in *The Prose Works of William Wordsworth*, ed. W. J. B. Owen and Jane Worthington Smyser, 3 vols. (Oxford, 1974), 3: 79.

frequently filled 'with honour'. Knox has clearly been impressed by works like Richard Hurd's *Discourse on Poetical Imitation* (1753) and Edward Young's *Conjectures on Original Composition* (1759), for he frames the distinction between the major and minor figure in terms of originality and derivativeness: writers who display 'great merit', but whose merit is a product of imitation, constitute the 'middle ranks' of literary authorship, neither major nor insignificant but 'minor'.[72]

The Works of the English Poets now look like an heroically laboursome compilation of essentially minor writers. Johnson himself seems to acknowledge the category of materials he is dealing with in a couple of places: in the 'Life of Pope', he mentions the name of Walsh as one 'yet preserved among the minor poets' and later refers to Paul Whitehead as 'a small poet'. But although the locution of the 'minor writer' was relatively new, collections of authorial lives as far back as Phillips's and Winstanley's had been sensitive to the inevitable stratification of authorial ability and achievement, only they had formulated the issue in a different way. Their older differentiation had not been between 'major' and 'minor' writers but between those authors who were secure and those who were vulnerable in the after-life of their fames. It is, moreover, a differentiation that continues to be invoked in the eighteenth century: William Oldys, for example, defends the selection of authors in Hayward's *The British Muse* by arguing that

he has chosen rather to devote himself to neglected and expiring merit; conceiving it more useful and meritorious to revive and preserve the excellencies, which time and oblivion were on the point of cancelling for ever, than to repeat what others had extracted before...

The point is an ethical one: the anthologist and collector should stand guarantor of the fames of those writers who are incorporated into his project, but the greater responsibility is that to 'neglected and expiring merit', to the less lustrous bodies in the firmament of authors, to the category of authors subsequently to be branded as 'minor'.

The hostility of the reception greeting Johnson's 'canon' amounts to an attack on the category of the minor author (one

---

[72] *Essays, Moral and Literary*, 2: 454, 456.

in some degree anticipated by Johnson's own sometimes hostile reflections in the *Lives*); and that this attack should take place testifies to the approaching extinction of the honourable old idea of 'literary fame'. In Chapter 3, I argued that fame was a key idea in the attempt of seventeenth-century antiquarians to recover a literary heritage, but by the 1780s and 90s, the ethical scholarship of Weever and Fuller and of the likes of Oldys and Hayward in the eighteenth century, with its devotion to 'neglected and expiring merit', will no longer suffice. Critics of Johnson's *Lives* instinctively respond to it as to a work of canon-formation, as an attempt to institute a literary pantheon, and then end up condemning the work because the policy of admission into this pantheon is so indiscriminate. Yet Johnson's project, though it does not actually speak in the accents of fame, incorporates much of its old ethic: in its rudiments, the project is inclusive not selective, recuperative not discriminatory. Nothing so much bespeaks the emergence of a new mentality than the jaunty iconoclasm of Vicesimus Knox's remark already quoted about 'sickly' poets being hastened to their proper resting-place, 'the tomb of oblivion'. This attitude contrasts grimly and plangently with the visual image I painted in Chapter 3 of the indefatigable John Weever traipsing through innumerable graveyards, poring over the faded letters on crumbling monuments, salvaging the dead from the inevitability of their oblivion. Knox's comment represents nothing so much as the death of that tradition for which Weever and others had honourably stood.

VII

In February 1767, there occurred 'one of the most remarkable incidents of Johnson's life'. Johnson was in the habit of visiting the extensive library of Buckingham House in London, the residence of Queen Charlotte. Coming to hear of these visits, the King asked that he be informed when Johnson next used the library; and when this happened, the King came down from his apartment to speak to the great man. Boswell records one part of the conversation as follows:

His Majesty expressed a desire to have the literary biography of this country ably executed, and proposed to Dr. Johnson to undertake it. Johnson signified his readiness to comply with his Majesty's wishes.[73]

Whether Johnson had a mind to, or indeed ever did, 'comply with his Majesty's wishes' is a moot point: in the event, the composition of the *Lives* complied, more humbly, with the requirements of a consortium of London booksellers. In this chapter, I have stressed the continuity of Johnson's undertaking with what had gone before it. The biographies were written to accompany a serial collection of English poetry, for which there were several antecedents, and in the process of writing them Johnson borrowed extensively from existing sources.

In addressing Johnson as a literary historian, a literary biographer of his country, it is inevitable to find that his reputation goes before him. It is culturally engrained that we think of him as a cultural legislator, a dogmatist. His involvement with the *Works* of 1779–81 all too quickly gets translated into his institution of a high-cultural pantheon. Yet Johnson was, in reality, a reluctant canonist. His approach is intellectually sceptical not hagiographical. Rather than stressing the serene and inevitable processes through which genius arrives at its own expression, he concentrates on the quixotic and happenstantial. He scratches beneath the surface and official appearance of the public person to reveal the human idiosyncracies and fragilities lying beneath.

The brief handed to Johnson was one that he was in fact poorly qualified to execute. The *Works* were envisaged as a large-scale, inclusive project, eschewing literary, as opposed to commercial, discrimination. In his biographical treatments, Johnson, however, proved unable to stifle the discriminations naturally arising to his own judgemental intellect. In this sense, the *Lives* as a part of the project run counter to the rest of it: the one sifting and evaluating, the other blankly incorporating. As a result, in the aftermath of its publication, Johnson found himself pincered between two wholly opposite forms of criticism: condemned for a lack of discrimination in incorporating into the *Works* so many underserving, minor figures, and condemned for an excess of discriminatory zeal in criticizing individual writers. These contradictory assaults have much, of course, to do with Johnson's relation to the rival constituencies of his

[73] *Life*, 2: 40.

admirers and detractors, but they have equally as much to do with an increasing gulf between aesthetic and antiquarian ideals. The terms of Vicesimus Knox's attack on the *Works*, for setting itself up as a haven from oblivion for sickly and infirm talents, shows how much literary history has now unshackled itself from its origins as a mortuary discourse. In the seventeenth-century authorial dictionaries of Phillips and Winstanley all writers were welcome alike since all were seen as possessing an equal entitlement to the perpetuation of their reputations beyond the grave. The implicit case made against Johnson by Knox, Wordsworth, and others, however, is that henceforth the glorious dead should live, but their inglorious siblings should be consigned to their sleep.

8

Making the Female Canon

I

The final quarter of the eighteenth century sees the appearance of the first multi-volume compilations of English poetry, including John Bell's *The Poets of Great Britain Complete from Chaucer to Churchill*, running to 109 volumes (Edinburgh, 1776–82) and its English rival *The Works of the English Poets* (1779–81), boasting biographical prefaces by the hand of Samuel Johnson. In the following decade, amidst other lesser compilations, appeared Robert Anderson's *Works of the British Poets* (1792–5), itself fifteen years later to be succeeded by a nearly identical production in Alexander Chalmers's twenty-one volume *Works of the English Poets from Chaucer to Cowper* (1810). What was new about these works was their combination of rhetoric and performance: they advertised themselves on the grounds of completeness, and came in sufficient bulk to make this claim seem convincing. Their promise was to deliver into the possession of their readership the entire corpus of English poetry. It is in this context that one fact about them leaps out as incontestable and egregious: not one of the works mentioned above admits even a solitary female writer.[1]

It has not taken until our own time for this fact to be greeted with consternation and dismay. In 1825, Alexander Dyce, for example, tried to do his bit to remedy the deficiencies of his predecessors by collecting together *Specimens of British Poetesses*, complaining in the work's 'Preface' that

---

[1] I have relied on a number of reference items in addition to the *DNB*. These are *First Feminists: British Women Writers 1578–1799*, ed. Moira Ferguson (Bloomington, Ind., 1985); *A Dictionary of British and American Women Writers 1660–1800*, ed. Janet Todd (London, 1984); *Eighteenth-Century Women Poets: An Oxford Anthology*, ed. Roger Lonsdale (Oxford, 1989); and *The Oxford Guide to British Women Writers*, ed. Joanne Shattock (Oxford, 1993). The appearance of all names is standardized against Shattock ed. whenever applicable, otherwise against Todd (ed.).

Of the Selections which have been made from the chaos of our past Poetry, the majority have been confined almost entirely to the writings of men; and from the great Collections of the English Poets, where so many worthless compositions find a place, the productions of women have been carefully excluded.[2]

The exclusion of women poets from the 'great Collections', the more so for these having been a phenomenon of the closing decades of the 1700s, has helped propagate the notion that such, in totality, was the eighteenth-century's verdict on women's poetry. The period, so it might be generalized, simply did not countenance the possibility of female membership of the literary canon. This rather damning deduction is certainly one that has been arrived at by some recent commentators. Dorothy Mermin, for example, has spoken of the 'almost total absence of women poets from the central literary tradition in England before the nineteenth century', this anomaly being attributable to a 'cultural suppression of female voices'; and Elizabeth Eger singles out the anthologies of Anderson and Chalmers for particular blame as contributing to 'our cultural forgetting of women writers'.[3] Andrew Ashfield, moreover, in his recent anthology of women poets of the Romantic era, goes so far as to ponder whether it might be a 'law of literary history that the characterisation of women's literature—be it as perversely masculine, "unsex'd", or sweetly feminine—ensures that it can never be canonical and survive as a persistent object of attention'.[4] One purpose of this chapter is to challenge this line of argument on two principal accounts. First, multi-volume anthologies of English poets are not, nor were ever, the sole form of literary production to stand in material relation to national canon-formation;

---

[2] Alexander Dyce, *Specimens of British Poetesses* (1827), 'Preface', iii.

[3] Dorothy Mermin, 'Women Becoming Poets: Katherine Philips, Aphra Behn, Anne Finch', *English Literary History*, 57 (1990), 335; Elizabeth Eger, 'Fashioning a Female Canon: Eighteenth-Century Women Poets and the Politics of the Anthology', in *Women's Poetry in the Enlightenment: The Making of a Canon, 1730–1820*, ed. Isobel Armstrong and Virginia Blain (London, 1999), 206–7.

[4] *Romantic Women Poets 1770–1838*, ed. Andrew Ashfield (Manchester, 1995), 'Introduction', xii. For discussion of Romantic women poets and the canon, see Stuart Curran, 'Romantic Poetry: The I Altered', in *Romanticism and Feminism*, ed. Anne K. Mellor (Bloomington, Ind., 1988), 185–207; and Marlon B. Ross, *The Contours of Masculine Desire: Romanticism and Women's Poetry* (New York, 1989), esp. ch. 6, 'The Birth of a Tradition: Making Cultural Space for Feminine Poetry', 187–231.

second, it distorts the picture to allow texts (of whatever kind) of the 1780s and 90s to speak for the eighteenth century as a whole. What I will argue here instead is that the process of women writers' accession to their own canon, as well as their incorporation into the larger poetic tradition, occurs somewhat earlier than is apt to be supposed.[5]

No one doubts that female poets and dramatists made great strides from the late seventeenth century onwards.[6] Aphra Behn's success, mixed as it was with notoriety, has perhaps obscured the fact that during her life she was the sole female dramatist to enjoy high profile, but in the season of 1695–6, labelled by two different critics as 'crucial' and 'magic', seven new plays by women, including ones by Catharine Trotter, Mary Pix, and Delarivier Manley, as well as Aphra Behn's posthumous *The Younger Brother*, are premièred on the English stage: in a further four years, moreover, there occurs the first première of another female dramatist, Susanna Centlivre. In this remarkable season, more than a third of all new plays performed are either by women or adapted from women's writings; and Trotter, Manley, and Pix fortify their resolve by penning supportive prefaces to each other's plays, through which they create 'a discernible sorority'. The flagrancy and concertedness of this female self-assertion, indeed, is such as to provoke a misogynistic retaliation in the form of a play entitled *The Female Wits: or the Triumvirate of Poets*, written by W. M.[7]

If the season of 1695–6 launches women writers as a significant presence in the English theatre, female progress in non-dramatic poetry is less spectacular, though assured all the same. Roger Lonsdale has pointed out that in the first decade of the eighteenth century only two women published collections

[5] For discussion of women's incorporation into the literary tradition during the eighteenth century, see Margaret J. M. Ezell, *Writing Women's Literary History* (Baltimore, 1993), 66–131.

[6] On the rise of women writers in the 18th cent., see Robert Halsband, '"The Female Pen": Women and Literature in C18 England', *History Today*, 24 (Oct. 1974), 702–9; and Roger Lonsdale's 'Introduction' to his anthology of *Eighteenth-Century Women Poets*.

[7] See Paula R. Backscheider, *Spectacular Politics: Theatrical Power and Mass Culture in Early Modern England* (Baltimore, 1993), 71; and Jacqueline Pearson, *The Prostituted Muse: Images of Women Dramatists 1642–1737* (New York, 1988), 169. Pix and Trotter contributed to Manley's collection of poems on the death of Dryden, *The Nine Muses* (1700).

of verse, whereas in the last one this figure has mushroomed to more than thirty.[8] Moreover, far from there being a sectarian antipathy between female poets and their male counterparts, many of the leading male writers, including Pope, Swift, and Johnson had associations with, and encouraged and mentored, female poets. During the period, women achieve an increasing visibility in miscellany volumes like *The Flower-Piece* (1731) and *The Flowers of Parnassus* (1736), as well as penetrating into the most successful and high-prestige verse anthologies like Dodsley's *Collection* (1748–58) and Woty's and Fawkes's *Poetical Calendar* (1763). Furthermore, some of the more zealous verse correspondents to the influential *Gentleman's Magazine* also happen to be women.

The Female Wits mentioned above is probably the earliest complaint in English about the supposedly undue profile and success being enjoyed by female writers. Voiced specifically about dramatists, it could not have been made at this time about female poets. But by the middle of the eighteenth century, complaints of this kind, addressed towards non-theatrical writings by women, become more common. In 1762, for instance, Elizabeth Carter's *Poems on Several Occasions* elicit a sarcastic response in the *Critical Review*, attacking the 'fashion' for women to acquire or affect learning: 'There never was an age wherein the fair sex made so conspicuous a figure with regard to literary accomplishments as in our own'.[9] This disdainful response to the high visibility of female writers may have been influenced by some remarks made a few years earlier by Samuel Johnson in his *Adventurer* 115 (1753):

In former times, the pen, like the sword, was considered as consigned by nature to the hands of men; the ladies contented themselves with private virtues and domestic excellence, and a female writer, like a female warrior, was considered as a kind of excentric being, that deviated, however illustriously, from her due sphere of motion, and was, therefore, rather to be gazed at with wonder, than countenanced by imitation. But as the times past are said to have seen a nation of Amazons, who drew the bow and wielded the battle-axe, formed

[8] Lonsdale (ed.), *Eighteenth-Century Women Poets*, xxi.
[9] *The Critical Review* 13 (1762); cited from Lisa A. Freeman, '"A Dialogue": Elizabeth Carter's Passion for the Female Mind', in Armstrong and Blain (eds.), *Women's Poetry in the Enlightenment*, 58.

encampments, and wasted nations; the revolution of years has now produced a generation of Amazons of the pen, who with the spirit of their predecessors have set masculine tyranny at defiance, asserted their claim to the regions of science, and seem resolved to contest the usurpations of virility.[10]

Taken out of context, Johnson's remarks read like a straightforward attack on female literary pretensions, but their anxiety is in reality a more general one, to do with what he saw as a rising floodtide of feckless scribblings threatening to inundate literary culture, for which male and female writers were responsible alike. It is this phenomenon that he descries as the '*universal* eagerness of writing' (my stress). Moreover, Johnson's comments on the militarism of female writers may have been calculated to amuse or pique authors like Elizabeth Carter, Anna Seward, and Charlotte Lennox with whom, in one way or another, he was associated.

Whether or not they criticize it, Johnson's comments do reflect the higher profile being enjoyed by women writers in the mid-eighteenth century, but there were some areas where the picture was less reassuring. As I have said, women authors were getting into print in the sort of anthology that published contemporary verse or that of the recent past (though it should be admitted that favouritism still sometimes gets given, as in Dodsley's *Collection*, to writers who had links with leading male poets or male coteries).[11] But when we turn to verse collections that express English poetry in its historical dimension, female representatives become noticeably thinner on the ground. Elizabeth Cooper's *The Muses Library*, a cross between a verse anthology and a collection of authorial lives, for example, comes out in 1737, promising its readership 'a Series of English Poetry, from the Saxons to the Reign of King Charles II' and containing also the 'Lives and Characters of all the Known Writers in the Interval'. While it should be remembered that the project was cut short, only one volume of the proposed two actually appearing, it remains a salient fact that Cooper, assisted by the formidable literary antiquarian William Oldys, failed to find grounds on

[10] *Adventurer* 115, 11 Dec. 1753, in *Yale*, 2: 457–8.
[11] Prominent are Lady Mary Wortley Montagu, once closely associated with Pope, Swift, and Gay; Lady Luxborough, who formed a coterie with Shenstone, Graves, and Somervile; and Elizabeth Carter, associated with Samuel Johnson.

which to admit a single female author. A year later, Thomas Hayward's popular (and three-volume) *The British Muse*, which concentrated on the sixteenth and seventeenth centuries, admits Elizabeth Cary as its sole female representative. And even in the second-half of the century, it is easy to find anthologies like Goldsmith's *Beauties of English Poesy* (1767), the same editor's *Poems for Young Ladies* (1767), and the anonymous *Poetical Miscellany* (1789) that have no scruples about dispensing with women altogether.

The absence of women from historical anthologies should not, however, be taken as the case across the board. A notable exception, for example, is Elizabeth Elstob's *The Rudiments of Grammar for the Anglo-Saxon Tongue* (1715) in which the author set out to demonstrate the rootedness of the English language, and indeed of a whole English poetic idiom, in the Saxon tongue. For this purpose, Elstob compiled a curious short anthology of poetic excerpts, in which a succession of canonical English poets are shown diversifying their lines with monosyllables, these being taken as a touchstone for Saxon linguistic influence. Having progressed through a sequence of predictable male poets such as Denham, Cowley, Waller, and Dryden, Elstob remarks that 'After so many Authorities of the Gentlemen, these few Instances from some of our Female Poets, may I hope be permitted to take place', and goes on to cite from Katherine Philips, Anne Wharton, and Anne Finch, Countess of Winchilsea.[12]

Though Elstob's anthology of English poetic monosyllables remains something of a curiosity, its contribution to a discourse of canon formation should certainly not be dismissed. A work more explicitly dedicated to this end, however, and which also proves hospitable to female authors, is James Greenwood's *The Virgin Muse, Being a Collection of Poems from our Most Celebrated English Poets* (1722). Addressed to several named ladies, and soliciting 'the protection of . . . [their] . . . Virtue and Innocence', the anthology takes its name from Katherine Philips's poem 'The Virgin', which is stationed at the front.[13] Greenwood's anthology was aimed in significant part at a schoolchild

[12] *Rudiments of Grammar*, xxvii–xxviii.
[13] James Greenwood (ed.), *The Virgin Muse* (1722), iii.

audience, being proposed as 'a compleat Book for the *Teaching to Read Poetry*', though probably also at a narrower circle of petticoat scribblers and readers.[14] It anthologizes mostly post-1660 verse, though a few pieces by Chaucer are also thrown in, and gives especially ample coverage to Waller, Cowley, and Milton's *Paradise Lost*. But mixed in with this essentially conventional drafting of the post-1660 verse canon, Greenwood squeezes in four pieces by Philips, and solitary ones by Anne Wharton and Anne Finch.

The evidence of Elstob and Greenwood points two ways: women are represented but only perhaps as a result of *parti pris* in the first instance and cultural chivalry in the second. Elstob had already become something of a feminist champion. Given the subject-matter, and given the state of female education, it is an extraordinary fact that of 260 subscribers to her *English-Saxon Homily* in 1709, almost half were women; and the assimilation of Philips, Wharton, and Finch into her anthology of monosyllables is very explicitly a feminist statement.[15] For Greenwood's part, the representation allowed to female poets owes much to the dedicatees of his volume being female. For women poets to achieve a healthy representation in an historical anthology where factors of this sort do not apply, we probably have to wait for more than another half-century.

A slight improvement in the fortunes of female poets is registered in Vicesimus Knox's *Elegant Extracts: or Useful and Entertaining Pieces of Poetry. Selected for the Improvement of Youth* (1782) which admits a handful of familiar female writers, including Elizabeth Carter, Anna Barbauld (née Aikin), Elizabeth Pennington, Anna Seward, and Elizabeth Rowe. But, even so, given the crowdedness of Knox's anthology, their representation still remains grudging. A decade later Joseph Ritson's *The English Anthology* (1793–4) is notably more hospitable, allowing space to Philips, Behn, Lady Chudleigh, Anne Killigrew, Elizabeth Rowe, Laetitia Pilkington, Mary Leapor, Anne Finch, Lady Mary Wortley Montagu, Mary Masters, and Mary Jones. Yet even here a caveat is required. The anthology consists of four parts spread across three volumes. The first part contains

[14]   Ibid., v.
[15]   The subscription figure for Elstob's *English-Saxon Homily* is given in Halsband, 'The Female Pen', 704.

the main body of the anthologized material; Part III consists of poems of uncertain authorship; Part IV is made up of extracts of long poems, such as *The Faerie Queene and Paradise Lost* whose bulk would have made it impossible to accommodate them in Part I; 'Part the Second', however, is set aside for Ritson's female poets, where they reside securely quarantined from the rest of the volume. While Ritson accepts the existence of, and is prepared to furnish his readers with, a canon exclusive to women's poetry, he still remains unconvinced that such poetry constitutes part of the English literary canon *per se*. Only perhaps as late as Robert Southey's three-volume *Specimens of the Later English Poets* (1807) do we see the work of a large number of women poets not just being recognized but actually being *incorporated* as constitutive of canonical English verse. Here, rubbing shoulders with their brother eminences, are the likes of Mary Chandler, Lady Chudleigh, Catharine Trotter, Anne Finch, Anne Killigrew, Mary Leapor, Mary Monck, and Lady Mary Wortley Montagu.[16]

The general picture that has emerged so far is one of female writers struggling to gain assimilation into the anthologized literary tradition until the very close of the eighteenth century. But there are two sorts of partiality that lie behind this conclusion. For one thing, the evidence from anthologies should be tempered by an understanding that most eighteenth-century anthologies still belonged to the old 'collections of beauties' genre, their objective being to assimilate literary fragments, choice sentiments and phrases, rather than to illustrate or canonize individual authors. Moreover, to suppose that such works, in the nature of their selections and omissions, *necessarily* indicate a canon is to impose modern assumptions and reasonings on texts which, in some instances at least, stand in defiance of them. But even if one asserts, without pausing too much to consider what such an assertion is worth, that female authors fail to achieve canonization in seventeenth- and eighteenth-century historical anthologies, then might they not have been canonized in other forms of literary or scholarly production: as, for example, in collections of authorial biography?

[16] See Eger, 'Fashioning a Female Canon', 213–14.

II

It might surprise that even from the inception of dictionaries of authorial lives, female authors were seen as meriting inclusion. In Edward Phillips's inaugurative *Theatrum Poetarum* (1675), for example, they are gathered in a section at the back of the volume dubbed 'Women among the Moderns Eminent for Poetry', this section being paired with a preceding one entitled 'Women among the Ancients Eminent for Poetry'. Phillips's file of female poets, much in the spirit of the rest of the book, is an ill-considered ragbag. It includes entrants like Lucretia Marinella, dubbed an 'Italian Lady'; Lady Jane Grey; 'Arabella', described as 'an English Lady, in the time of King James'; and Anne Askew, the main criterion of whose admission is having been burnt at the stake under Queen Mary. Yet dispersed amongst the more wayward figures cited are names which will gradually coalesce into a distinct female tradition: for instance Aphra Behn, Elizabeth Cary, Margaret Cavendish, and Lady Mary Wroth. And already at the centre of this embryonic canon of female authors, there is 'Catherine Philips', described as 'the most applauded at this time, Poetess of our Nation, either of the present or former Ages'.[17] It was probably because Phillips had cordoned off his female poets from the rest of the volume that Winstanley, in his *Lives of the most Famous English Poets* (1687), which relied heavily on the earlier work, could choose to dispense with them *en bloc*. But this gesture seems like the last stand of a particular brand of chauvinism. Gerard Langbaine's *Account of the English Dramatick Poets* (1691) takes note of six female playwrights: 'Astraea' Behn, Frances Boothby (author of just one identifiable play, *Marcelia or The Treacherous Friend*), Elizabeth Cary, the Countess of Pembroke, Katherine Philips, and Margaret Cavendish.

Notwithstanding the neglect of women writers in Winstanley's *Lives*, by the beginning of the eighteenth century, their inclusion in collections of authorial biography is standard practice. In 1719–20, Giles Jacob's two volumes of authorial lives, for instance, contain entries, even if on occasions very skimping ones, on Behn, Boothby, Cary, Centlivre, Manley,

---

[17] Phillips, *Theatrum Poetarum*, 235–61.

Pembroke, Philips, Pix, Trotter, Finch, Mary Davys, Chudleigh, Martha Fowke, Rowe, and Wharton. Similarly, the 1753 compilation of *Lives* put together by Robert Shiels, but published under the name of Theophilus Cibber, lets in a roughly equal-sized and fairly duplicatory cast of figures: Philips, Cavendish, Killigrew, Behn, Chudleigh, Monck, Finch, Manley, Centlivre, Elizabeth Thomas, Rowe, Constantia Grierson, Trotter, Pilkington, and Chandler. Clearly, the naturalization of female authors in collections of authorial biography helps raise their canonical status, but the evidence of such texts needs to be balanced against that supplied by an adjacent group: collections of general biography.

In 1734 appeared the first volume of *A General Dictionary, Historical and Critical*. Containing about nine hundred biographical entries, it is the earliest ancestor of the *Dictionary of National Biography*, and under the general editorship of Thomas Birch, it pioneered in English the method of inductive biography. Birch and his colleagues raised biography for the first time to the level of scholarship, and did so on the basis of a dense apparatus of textual keys and multiple categories of footnotes which serve to cradle the main text. In the eleven volumes of the *General Dictionary*, unfolding themselves over eight years (1734–41), only five women writers are seen as meriting treatment under this fastidious regime of scholarship: Behn, Finch, Philips, Rowe, and Wharton. Yet, much as only five are included, the treatment of these figures can reasonably be thought of as constituting the first scholarly biographies of female authors. John Lockman, for example, in his biography of Behn narrates as best he can her life-story; considers the nature of her literary works; addresses her moral character and examines the appropriateness (as he sees it) of her ideas; records some lengthy testimonials on her by contemporaries; and acknowledges earlier biographical efforts by the likes of Phillips, Langbaine, and Jacob.

Birch's *General Dictionary* establishes the format and ground-rules for scholarly biography: the *Biographia Britannica*, whose first volume came out in 1747 and which was brought to completion in seven volumes only in 1766, follows its method so laboriously that its *mise-en-page* is nearly identical. Here, however, the cause of women's poetry goes backwards since only

Rowe and Behn make it in: out go Philips, Finch, and Wharton. This whittling down of female representatives seems all the more ungenerous given that the *Biographia* draws specific attention to poetry as one vocation in which 'our countrymen...have been eminent', and moreover desiderates any good biographies of writers: 'The Lives of our POETS have been often, but never well, written.'[18] Yet it may be that the curtailing of female entrants, as a result of suppression or negligence, was seen as having been misguided, for the 'Supplement' of 1766, a section designed to rectify oversights and to accommodate influxes from the recent past, welcomes in Manley, Cavendish, Trotter, and Lady Chudleigh. This more inclusive attitude towards women writers passes into the revised edition of the *Biographia Britannica* initiated by Andrew Kippis in 1778. Though his edition only staggered through to letter 'F', Kippis's team had by this point accommodated Behn, Juliana Berners, Cavendish, Centlivre, Chudleigh, and Trotter (as Catharine Cockburn), suggesting a more hospitable attitude towards women writers than had been maintained in either of the work's two predecessors. In the same spirit, James Granger's *A Biographical History of England, from Egbert the Great to the Revolution* (1769–74) finds room for nine women writers without even reaching the eighteenth century, a much stronger showing than in either Birch's *Critical and Historical Dictionary* or the first edition of the *Biographia*.

These collections of authorial and general biography, even allowing for spasmodic resurgences of misogyny, are more accommodating of female writers than the historical anthologies. Even the earliest of all English authorial dictionaries, Edward Phillips's of 1675, includes them, though admittedly under terms of quarantine at the back of the volume. Yet merely to enumerate inclusions and omissions, as I have done so far, tells us nothing at all about the rhetorical tone in which women authors get addressed. A particularly revealing test-case, in this regard, one that should caution us against assuming that mere inclusion in such works provided a guarantee of flattering treatment, is provided by Margaret Cavendish, the story of whose posterity is one unusually assailed by reputational vicissitudes. Her achieve-

---

[18] *Biographia Britannica* (1747–66), I: xi.

ment is acknowledged in Phillips's originary list of 'Women among the Moderns Eminent for Poetry', but the earliest significant biographical coverage comes with Langbaine's *Account of the English Dramatick Poets*. Here the generosity of treatment borders on gallantry, with Cavendish being described as

A Lady worthy the Mention and Esteem of all Lovers of Poetry and Learning. One, who was fit Consort for so Great a Wit, as the Duke of *Newcastle*. Her Soul sympathising with his in all things, especially in Dramatick Poetry; to which she had a more than ordinary propensity.[19]

Langbaine acknowledges that, as he puts it, 'there are some that have but a mean Opinion of her Plays', but he finds reason to discount this objection on the grounds that she always aspires to be original: 'the Language and Plots of... [her plays]... are all her own'.

Langbaine contributes two ingredients to the mix of Cavendish's characterization: her writings are original, this compliment being the more forceful given the zeal with which he inculpates numerous other authors of plagiarism, a charge indeed that had already cast a shadow over the reputation of Aphra Behn; and her abilities, though self-standing, are also to some degree complementary to those of her husband: 'so Great a Wit'. A further character-note is added by Giles Jacob in 1719, that of the extreme prolificity of her writing ('she was the most voluminous writer of all the female poets'); and this fact, a potentially disreputable one, along with Langbaine's commendation of her originality, feeds into the entry on the Duchess in Cibber's *Lives* of 1753.[20]

The major travails of Cavendish's post-mortal reputation, however, are to be played out not in the authorial dictionaries but in the oddly vexed treatment she elicits in the *Biographia Britannica*. In the *Biographia*'s first edition, she pays the ultimate price of the perceived complementarity of her own literary talents with those of her husband: that of being relegated to the level of one of his footnotes, with no individual entry of her own. In this subordinate form, a thumbnail history is supplied of her life, in which the doubtful nature of her abilities, and their

[19] *Account of the English Dramatick Poets*, 390–4.
[20] *Lives of the Poets of Great Britain*, 2: 162–9.

expression in different forms of association with those of her husband, are the main features dwelt on:

a woman of great wit, and some learning, for besides the life of the Duke and her own, she wrote a great number of folio's, and published six and twenty plays; in several of which, there are scenes and songs written by the Duke. It must be owned, that in many of these pieces there is much extravagance, and more of fancy than of judgement in them all.[21]

There are a number of stealthy contaminations at work here: the fervour of Cavendish's imagination is contaminated by a sense of the weakness of her judgement; the inter-involvement of her abilities with those of her husband is twisted into an intimation of creative reliance, in as much as there are 'scenes and songs' in her plays written by him; and the sheer numerousness of her productions is polluted by the hint being dropped about their low quality.

In 1766, in the 'Supplement' to the *Biographia*'s first edition, redress was given to those wrongly overlooked first time around, and Cavendish became one of its 'beneficiaries'. She now gets a self-standing entry of her own but one lethally laced with misogynistic venom. She is introduced sarcastically as a lady 'famous for her voluminous writings', and after details of her early life, the biographer sums up her literary endeavours thus:

She continued abroad with her Lord till the restoration of K. Charles II after which, returning to England, she spent much of the remaining part of her life upon productions of literature in various ways; and had a teeming genius in producing such brats of the brain, but brought her consort no other issue, for the want of which, she made the best atonement that lay in her power, by writing *An account of his life*.[22]

The prolificity of her productions, her 'brats of the brain', is set in inverted relation to her failure to bear her husband a child; moreover, this injury done to her husband, and to the continuation of his seed, could only be atoned for, we are told, by her writing his biography, through which means she would be able to perpetuate his memory if not his line. It is hardly surprising

[21] *Biographia Britannica* (1747–66), 2: 1214.
[22] Ibid., 'Supplement', 6, Part 2, 128–9.

that in the second edition of the *Biographia*, the general editor Andrew Kippis should feel it incumbent on himself to rewrite Cavendish's entry pretty much from scratch. His biography takes pains to document the high regard in which she was held by her peers, even reproducing some of the more flattering notices; but he remains balancedly sceptical about her true literary ability, the tone of his adjudication being notably qualificatory and subjunctive:

If her fancy had been enriched by information, restrained by judgment, and regulated by correctness of taste, she might probably have risen to considerable excellence.[23]

III

The evidence of the authorial dictionaries and the collections of national biography points to a cultural acknowledgement of women writers well before the nineteenth century, but one period in which women's writing seems to be given especially rapid advancement is the third quarter of the eighteenth century. I have already commented on the very hospitable attitude towards women writers shown in the Cibber–Shiels collection of lives published in 1753, fifteen women in all being included, from Katherine Philips to Mary Chandler. What I did not mention, however, was that in his treatment of literary women, Shiels was indebted to a book published the previous year, one that broke new ground in its scholarly recuperation of women writers: George Ballard's *Memoirs of Several Ladies of Great Britain who have been Celebrated for their Writings or Skill in the Learned Languages, Arts and Sciences* (1752).

Ballard was born, and lived the greater part of his life, in Chipping Campden, a small Gloucestershire market town, where he seems in his early days to have been apprenticed as a tailor. Yet his real love and lifetime pursuit was for antiquarian learning; and, supplied through correspondence with a dozen or so friends, numbering among them some of the most assiduous antiquarians in the country, he set out to compile, as Thomas Rawlins dubbed it, 'a Short History of the Lives of the Learned

---

[23] *Biographia Britannica* (1778–), 3: 340.

among ye Female Sex'.[24] Ballard's searches were remarkably wide and pertinacious. Ruth Perry, to my knowledge the only modern historian to have tried to recover his memory, describes his endeavours thus:

He rifled the choicest libraries of rare books, went through bales of unsorted manuscripts, interviewed living relatives or acquaintances of learned women where that was possible, read through bundles of old letters, and legal deeds and wills, copied the inscriptions from tombstones and monuments almost effaced by time, checked parish records, and noted every hitherto published mention of the learned women he included in his volume.[25]

In spite of living in a small country town, Ballard belonged to a close-knit social network of like-minded scholars. He was located only forty miles from Oxford, which facilitated both visits there and a humming line of scholarly correspondence; the famous Anglo-Saxonist Elizabeth Elstob lived only ten miles away in Evesham; and Richard Graves, a gentlemanly scholar and subsequently the author of *The Spiritual Quixote* (1773), to whose sons Ballard left his entire collection of old coins, lived barely three miles away in the village of Mickleton. As well as plying Ballard with scholarly tit-bits, his friends also recommended subjects to him. Thomas Rawlins wrote to remind him of 'the matchless Orinda'; and Francis Wise, keeper of the Radcliffe Library, encouraged him not to forget 'the famous Mrs. Julian Barns'.[26] Though Ballard pledges himself to memorializing 'those who have distinguished themselves in the republick of letters', he recognizes the achievements of a loose grouping of accomplished and illustrious women, including Lady Jane Gray and the English Queens Mary and Elizabeth. But his gathering of female writers in particular must have been thought-provoking at the time: he mentions Juliana Berners (variously 'Barns' or 'Barnes'), the fifteenth-century author of a treatise on hunting contained in *The Book of St. Albans*, Philips, Wharton, Cavendish, Pembroke, Killigrew, Chudleigh, Monck, Finch, and Grierson. By the time that Kippis and his team set out

[24] Ruth Perry, 'George Ballard's Biographies of Learned Ladies', in *Biography in the 18th Century*, ed. J. D. Browning (New York, 1980), 85–111. Rawlins cited from ibid. 87.
[25] Ibid. 86.
[26] Ibid. 88.

to revamp the first edition of the *Biographia Britannica*, Ballard's *Memoirs* had assumed the status of principal source-book for this specialized category of biographies. The *Biographia*'s entry on Mary Astell, for example, is squarely based on his; and the appearance for the first time in a work of collected biography of the little-known Berners owed entirely to his authority.

Ballard is an unlikely hero in the history of women's recognition as writers and scholars; but in so far as the *Memoirs* impressed itself on successor biographers like Kippis, his achievement in memorializing the lives of learned women was appreciable. But another male hero of the same era, equally unlikely and hardly more sung, is John Duncombe. Duncombe was not an antiquarian so much as a literary networker, whose web of illustrious friends and contacts placed him in a situation of great influence in the literary world of the mid-century. He was familiar with Johnson, Richardson, and other major writers; he dabbled in poetry and *belles lettres*; he contributed essays to the periodicals the *Connoisseur* and the *World*; he involved himself in Kippis's revamp of the *Biographia Britannica*; and he wielded the greatest part of his cultural influence through being a prolific contributor to the *Gentleman's Magazine*, and in particular through presiding over its book review section.[27]

In 1754 Duncombe published the only poem of his to achieve wide dissemination in his own day and to survive through to ours, 'The Feminiad'. It was published separately in 1754 and 1757, but gathered momentum through inclusion in several popular anthologies such as Dodsley's *Collection* (vol. IV (1755)), Fawkes's and Woty's *Poetical Calendar* and *The Lady's Poetical Magazine* (1782). Although the '-iad' suffix normally suggests a mocking diminution of a subject, Duncombe's intentions were in good faith: he wanted to enumerate the female literary geniuses of England. The poem falls clearly into two parts, lines 1–103 and 104 to the end. In the first, Duncombe reprimands the lazy prejudice of discounting women's intelligence and admiring them purely for their physical attractions,

[27] John Duncombe, *The Feminiad. A Poem.* (1754), in Augustan Reprint Society no. 207, ed. Jocelyn Harris (Los Angeles, 1981), 'Introduction', iii–iv.

enjoining the reader to '*Admire* the person, but *adore* the mind'. Indeed, traditional male scepticism about women's abilities is all the more intolerable, he declares, since 'Our *British* nymphs' have shown a particular aptitude for cultivating their minds as well as their appearances, turning themselves into a 'blooming, studious band' of whom some 'led by Contemplation, soar on high' while others 'The canvas tinge, or touch the warbling lyre'.[28] Yet though Duncombe tries gallantly to dispel some prejudices about women, there are others he is happy to endorse. Much as it is wrong for men to doubt women's intellectual capacities, it remains appropriate for them to suspect that learning in women can sometimes be counter-productive,

> Since letter'd nymphs the knowledge may abuse,
> And husbands oft experience to their cost
> The prudent housewife in the scholar lost.[29]

Female intellectual gifts are only to be welcomed in so far as they remain in fruitful coexistence with the traditional skills of housekeeping.

In the second part of the poem, Duncombe recites the names and extols the merits of the notable chantresses of English poetry, beginning with the 'chaste ORINDA' and ranging through Finch, Trotter, Rowe, the Countess of Hertford, Viscountess Irwin, Mehetabel Wright, Judith Madan, Mary Leapor, Elizabeth Carter, Martha Ferrar, Elizabeth Pennington, Hester Chapone, Susanna Highmore, and Frances Brooke. Although Duncombe begins the poem by eulogizing women's intellectual capacities, his inclusion of particular authors has more to do with their exemplification of useful and pious living. Katherine Philips, for example, gets praised for the way her lines glow with 'Fair Friendship's lustre'; the entry on Catharine Trotter foregrounds her writings on 'philosophical, and sacred subjects'; and Duncombe dwells, as biographers of her habitually did, on the pious resignation of Elizabeth Rowe's 'wish'd for' death.[30]

But as well as the female luminaries mentioned so far, the poem also contains a sort of apocrypha or anti-canon of writers who remain irreconcilable with the particular image of female literariness that the poem is intent on celebrating. First appear

---

[28] Ibid. 6–9.   [29] Ibid. 10.   [30] Ibid. 12, 14, 16.

Delarivier Manley, Susanna Centlivre, and Aphra Behn, the three of them hissed at as 'Vice's friends and Virtue's female foes'. Their offence lies in the scandal attending Manley's *New Atalantis* (1709) and the supposed indecency of the plays of Centlivre and Behn, no wittiness or dramatic craft being allowed to redeem 'The dang'rous sallies of a wanton Muse'.[31] Next are introduced Teresia Phillips, Laetitia Pilkington, and Lady Frances Vane, all of whom wrote memoirs or autobiographies capitalizing on the inherent scandal of their lives.[32] The issue rests in part as a moral one: the authors whom Duncombe chooses to demonize are ones who have stained themselves with immoral behaviour or scandalous writings; but his poem also seems biased against female professionalism *per se*, against women who have been guilty of pursuing a career whose effect would be to eclipse or usurp their more fundamental responsibility towards a husband and home. In particular, he gives short shrift to women, like Behn and Centlivre, who prostitute their talent by writing for the stage; even in the flattering entry on Trotter, for example, it is noticeable how little acknowledgement he gives to the fact that in her early career she had written plays.

In spite of Duncombe's poem being devoted to the celebration of female talent, its presiding genius remains a male one: Alexander Pope. The poem is composed throughout in the sort of neatly antithetical couplets that characterize Pope's verse, but it also contains echoes of and allusions to particular of his poems. Duncombe seems to have taken especially to heart the message in Pope's *Epistle to Arbuthnot* about the need for all writers to reconcile their literary abilities with a life of all-round ease and attractiveness:

> Peace to all such! but were there One whose fires
> True Genius kindles, and fair Fame inspires,
> Blest with each Talent and each Art to please,
> And born to write, converse, and live with ease...[33]

---

[31] Ibid. 14–15.

[32] The three were often reviled. In his *Amelia*, Fielding omits to describe his hero Booth sleeping adulterously with Miss Matthews but, as a means of conveying the general idea of this event, refers the reader instead to 'the apologies with which certain gay ladies have been pleased to oblige the world'. *Amelia* (1751), bk. IV, ch. I.

[33] Butt (ed.), 4: 109–10.

The 'One' who combines these indispensable virtues is Addison, whose shortcomings in other areas Pope then goes on cruelly, and famously, to dissect. These lines, their sentiments, and in a fainter way, their phraseology, seem to have come to Duncombe's mind in connection with his belief that even literary-minded women should maintain a proper balance between domestic responsibility and the pursuit of writing or learning:

> But lives there one, whose unassuming mind,
> Tho' grac'd by nature, and by art refin'd,
> Pleas'd with domestic excellence, can spare
> Some hours from studious ease to social care,
> And with her pen that time alone employs
> Which others waste in visits, cards and noise;
> From affectation free, tho' deeply read,
> 'With wit well natur'd, and with books well bred?'[34]

Duncombe's notion of the rota of female responsibilities is very revealing. Study and writing are founded on 'domestic excellence'. Only when a woman has her household chores thoroughly taken in hand should it become permissible for her to address herself to other matters; moreover, the time that study might be allowed to replace in her calendar is that which would otherwise be spent on the social frippery of 'visits, cards and noise'. This is the time, as Duncombe rather strictly puts it, that women should 'alone' give over to the development or expression of their intelligences.

It should be noted how far Duncombe is from countenancing the idea that women should write professionally, that women's writing should be used to advance them in a sphere outside their own domesticity. At points such as this, his rhetoric seems, if not exactly infused by, then complicit with, a wider anti-feminist rhetoric counselling the dangers of female wit and learning. Such a rhetoric appears in blatant form, for example, in *The Art of Knowing Women* (1730), where the author leaves the library of the learned lady Clorinda convinced in his head that '*Learning in Women* is nothing but an extravagant *Self-Conceit*.'[35] This depression of female education and literariness to the level of an

---

[34] *The Feminiad*, 11.
[35] Cited from Felicity Nussbaum, *The Brink of All We Hate: English Satires on Women, 1660–1750* (Lexington, 1984), 148.

incongruous vanity went hand in hand with the assumption that learning could have no possible utility for a woman. That a woman's intellectual development was likely to prove detrimental to proper domestic governance was a generic male phobia, evident in the story circulated about Elizabeth Elstob, the distinguished Anglo-Saxonist, who spent her last years living in the Cotswolds, that she kept a dirty house.[36]

Most of Duncombe's poem is voiced by a narrator figure, but from line 342 this voice gives way to an 'Aönian maid' who addresses herself admonitorily to the band of female poets: 'our sister choir'. This concluding passage is modelled on the speech by Sarpedon to Glaucus in the *Iliad*, book XII, but more particularly on Pope's parody of the same passage in the 1736 edition of *The Rape of the Lock*, a passage that was inserted into the poem, so Pope's early editor William Warburton claimed, possibly on the poet's own authority, as a means of drawing out its moral.[37] Both the Homeric original and the spoof passage in the *Rape* concern the justification of forms of social privilege: how does a warrior repay, or at least be seen to deserve, the gift of social and military seniority bestowed on him? And how, in Pope's *Rape*, does a society belle 'earn', or recompense, the amorous adoration directed towards her? In both cases, these issues arise expressly in connection with, and are intensified by, forebodings of death or physical deterioration. The warrior pays for his privileges through his preparedness for an early death; the belle, on the other hand, needs to justify the attention lavished on her by displaying 'good Humour', a down-to-earth philosophicality, part of which has to do with cultivating virtues of character resistant to the ageing process. These general themes Duncombe seizes on avidly for his own purposes. The 'Aönian maid' encourages the choir of female poets to reconcile domesticity and learning ('Employ by turns the needle and the pen') and to cultivate in themselves virtues that will prove imperishable:

> These lasting beauties will in youth engage,
> And smooth the wrinkles of declining age,
> Secure to bloom, unconscious of decay,
> When all Corinna's roses fade away.

[36] The story is recorded in *Biographia Britannica* (1778–), 5: 585.
[37] See Butt (ed.), 2: 195.

> For ev'n when love's short triumph shall be o'er,
> When youth shall please, and beauty charm no more,
> When man shall cease to flatter; when the eye
> Shall cease to sparkle, and the heart to sigh,
> In that dread hour, when parent dust shall claim
> The lifeless tribute of each kindred frame,
> Ev'n then, shall Wisdom for her chosen fair
> The fragrant wreaths of virtuous fame prepare;
> Those wreaths which flourish in a happier clime,
> Beyond the reach of Envy, and of Time.
> While here, the immortalizing Muse shall save
> Your darling names from dark Oblivion's grave;
> Those names the praise and wonder shall engage
> Of every polish'd, wise and virtuous age;
> To latest times our annals shall adorn,
> And save from Folly thousands yet unborn.[38]

In her edition of Duncombe's poem, Jocelyn Harris responds to these lines by remarking breezily that 'The dangerous ironies of Clarissa's very similar speech... are entirely absent.'[39] Yet most noticeable about these lines is their reticence about what women's literary production is actually for. The main encouragement given here for women to cultivate learning is that they might diversify their attractions to men. Once a woman's looks become ravaged by age—'When man shall cease to flatter'—a more 'lasting', interior set of beauties is called for to supply their place, ones that will procure for their owners a reputation beyond the grave. What is discounted once again is a notion that women's self-development and attainments in writing and studying are valuable for their own sake, or can be expected to reap any dividend in this mortal world.

Duncombe's poem may have pointed out a gap in the literary market, for a year after its appearance two acquaintances of his, George Colman the younger and Bonnell Thornton, gathered together a collection of verses in two volumes, published as *Poems by Eminent Ladies* (1755).[40] Though an exercise in

---

[38] *The Feminiad*, 30–1.
[39] Ibid., 'Introduction', vi.
[40] For a discussion of the anthology, see Benedict, *Making the Modern Reader*, 160–5; Ezell, *Writing Women's Literary History*, 90–2; and Eugene R. Page, *George Colman the Elder: Essayist, Dramatist and Theatrical Manager 1732–1794* (New York, 1935), 38–9.

opportunistic hackney, Colman's and Thornton's is a landmark publication, the first historical anthology of women's poetry.[41] As regards the selections, the editors were happy to repose themselves on an already received canon, one that was easily to hand, for example, in the Cibber–Shiels *Lives* of 1753: the *Monthly Review*, indeed, criticized the work on just this account, that the poems anthologized are 'very common'.[42] The first edition of the anthology offered selections from eighteen women authors between the Restoration and the mid-eighteenth century (Barber, Carter, Jones, Behn, Chudleigh, Cockburn, Grierson, Madan, Masters, Pilkington, Killigrew, Lady Mary Wortley Montagu, Cavendish, Philips, Finch, Leapor, Monck, and Rowe), but by the time the volume reached its fourth edition in 1780, this number had swollen to thirty-three with a more rounded representation of contemporary authors being achieved through some thinning out among the works of the original eighteen. Much as in their selection policy, when they came to penning the biographical notices prefatory to each author's poems, the editors fell back, with due acknowledgement, on the earlier labours of Cibber–Shiels and Ballard.

The 'Preface' presents the collection as a demonstration of the equality of women's writing with men's, as a 'standing proof that great abilities are not confined to the men, and that genius often glows with equal warmth, and perhaps with more delicacy, in the breast of a female'. Moreover, as an authentication of this, the edition calls attention to the fact that many of the selected poets have received praise from estimable male figures like '*Cowley, Dryden, Roscommon, Creech, Pope,* or *Swift*'.[43] The ostensible worthiness of Colman's and Thornton's project, however, seems tarnished by the way they went about puffing it, especially through use of an issue (22 May 1755) of their own journal, *The Connoisseur*. The issue's narrator describes how, on visiting a great lady of taste, he finds placed in his hands a work

[41] Alexander Dyce in his *Specimens of British Poetesses* (1827) states that 'The present volume was planned, and partly executed, before we were aware of the existence of perhaps the only similar publication in the language,—viz. *Poems by Eminent Ladies*'. He then goes on to criticize the work on the grounds that 'It contains . . . no extracts from rare books'. See 'Preface', v.

[42] *Monthly Review* 12 (1755): 512; cited from Benedict, *Making the Modern Reader*, 163.

[43] *Poems by Eminent Ladies*, 2 vols. (1755), 'Preface', 1: iii.

entitled 'POEMS by EMINENT LADIES' containing 'a great number of very elegant pieces ... which cannot be surpassed (I had almost said, equalled) by the most celebrated of our male-writers' and which prompts a confession that 'I never imagined, that our nation could boast so many excellent Poetesses'. When he goes to bed the same night, these 'excellent Poetesses' start to run in his head, and he dreams of a great debate held in the Court of Apollo, the motion being 'whether the *English* ladies, who had distinguished themselves in poetry, should be allowed to hold the same rank, and have the same honours paid them, with the men'. The matter can only be settled by the conducting of a trial in which Pegasus, the winged horse of the muses, is saddled up to be ridden by a succession of female poets: the Duchess of Newcastle, Katherine Philips, Anne Killigrew, Aphra Behn, Mary Leapor, Mary Barber, Constantia Grierson, and finally Laetitia Pilkington. The matter at issue is whether the various female authors can ride the horse in a way that demonstrates their equality with, or supremacy over, their male counterparts, but the essay quickly loses sight of this gender contest. What replaces it is a bout of visual punning, in which methods of riding are equated with writing styles. So Margaret Cavendish, for example, is shown riding with a loose rein, much as her poetic outpourings were often seen as unrestrained; the decorous Katherine Philips, on the other hand, 'never ventured beyond a canter or an hand-gallop'; while the forthright Aphra Behn disdains to ride side-saddle and insists instead on mounting Pegasus 'astride'. When it comes to the notorious Laetitia Pilkington, who was divorced by her husband after having been caught in *flagrente delicto*, Thornton and Colman record with a puerile wink that 'despising the weak efforts of her husband to prevent her, she boldly jumped into the saddle'.[44]

Although the efforts of Duncombe and Colman and Thornton help to further consolidate a canon of female authors, the terms on which this occurs are not wholly favourable or flattering for women. But it would be wrong to account for this entirely on the grounds that these are canons drawn up and promulgated by men. Exactly twenty years after Duncombe's *Feminiad*, for example, appeared a poem that sought both to respond to, as

[44] *The Connoisseur*, 69 (22 May 1755), 260–7.

well as update, it: Mary Scott's *The Female Advocate; A Poem. Occasioned by Reading Mr. Duncombe's Feminead* (1774). Scott, whose life-details remain sketchy, though she lived in Somerset and seems to have been dogged by ill-health (as she complains in the poem), asks that her muse 'Tell what bright daughters BRITAIN once could boast, | What daughters now adorn HER happy coast', and the poem, in the manner of Duncombe's, unfolds as a series of thumbnail sketches or 'characters' of female authors.[45] Her poem rounds up several writers who appeared too late for Duncombe to take account of them; she finds room for some literary figures who were not strictly, or principally, poets, such as Sarah Fielding, Charlotte Lennox, and Elizabeth Montagu; and she broadens the remit of Duncombe's original poem to include women of notable learning, such as Elizabeth Tollett who, while she composed poetry in both English and Latin, is praised specifically for speaking 'fluently and correctly the *Latin, Italian,* and *French* languages'.[46]

Though, in a dedicatory epistle, Scott expresses regret that 'it was only on a small number of Female Geniuses that Gentleman [Duncombe] bestowed the wreath of Fame', she still stops short of claiming that 'every woman is formed for literature'.[47] Rather those who have the attributes, and congenial personal circumstances, should feel it incumbent on them to acquire as much learning as possible. But even such muted exhortations to learning take second place to the poem's overriding encouragement of female virtue, since, as Scott puts it, 'True pleasure dwells with ev'ry virtuous mind'.[48] Much as the poem praises female learning, it also admonishes any sense that learning can form an end in itself, or that 'Honour, Fame, or Fortune' can stand in the stead of true virtue. The poem ends with some autobiographical lines in which Scott mentions her own 'faded health' and

---

[45] *The Female Advocate; A Poem. Occasioned by Reading Mr. Duncombe's Feminead* (1774), in Augustan Reprint Society 224, ed. Gae Holladay (Los Angeles, 1984), 2. There are thumbnail biographies in Todd (ed.), *Dictionary of British and American Women Writers*, and Lonsdale (ed.), *Eighteenth-Century Women Poets*. The most detailed discussion of her life and principal poem is by Moira Ferguson in her *Eighteenth-Century Women Poets: Nation, Class, and Gender* (New York, 1995), 27–43.
[46] *The Female Advocate*, 23.
[47] Ibid., 'To a Lady', v–viii.
[48] Ibid. 12.

'unceasing pains'; and implicitly recommends herself as a paragon of her own principles in as much as 'next to virtue, science
charms my eye'.[49] But her curiously frank depiction of her own
trying life and sense of self-defeat (she mentions her own 'un-
availing sigh' and the 'remnant hours' of her life) also becomes
enshrined as an ideal image of the female writer. This ideal seems
to be upheld in the poem by the early deaths of Katherine Philips
and Anne Killigrew; in the grieving widowhood of Lady Rachel
Russell whose husband was executed during the reign of Charles
II; and in the 'pathetic epistle' composed on her death-bed by
Mary Monck. The association between female literary prowess
and a form of spiritual martyrdom had surfaced before, most
notably in the apotheosis in several earlier works of that pious
literary talent, Elizabeth Rowe, and the idea continues to be
important to Scott.

The two decades from Ballard's *Memoirs of Several Ladies of
Great Britain* (1752) to Mary Scott's *The Female Advocate*
(1774) witness a growing sensitivity to the existence of a female
literary tradition. Between these two dates fall the Cibber–Shiels
Lives (1753) with its notably hospitable attitude towards female
writers, Duncombe's *The Feminiad* (1754), the Colman and
Thornton compilation of *Poems by Eminent Ladies* (1755),
and the 'Supplement' (1766) to the first edition of the *Biographia Britannica* which introduced biographies of Margaret
Cavendish, Delarivier Manley, and Lady Chudleigh, as if in
penance for their original oversight in the edition itself. Of
course, this development did not remove the pretext, or even
the need, for further protestations about the obstacles standing
in the way of female literary talent: as late as 1782, for example,
William Hayley in his *Essay on Epic Poetry* (1782), complains
about how the voice of 'braggart' Prejudice has often forbidden
'Female hands to touch the lyre':

> Deny'd to Woman, Nature's fav'rite child,
> The right to enter Fancy's opening wild![50]

Yet for all that might still remain to be done in the acceptance of
women's abilities as writers, it would be wrong to discount the

[49] Ibid. 22, 41.
[50] William Hayley, 'An Essay on Epic Poetry', Ep. IV. 84–6, in *Poems and Plays
by William Hayley Esq*, 6 vols. (1788), 3: 83.

progress that by this stage has already been made—and more wrong still to brand the whole of the eighteenth century as conspiring in the 'cultural suppression of female voices'.[51]

Yet, notwithstanding this, the gains being achieved by female writers have mainly to do with their enshrinement within a gender-specific canon, a canon seen as distinct, and dispensable, from the literary tradition constituted by the most celebrated male authors. That this should be so reflects a change between the seventeenth and eighteenth centuries in the attitudes that feed into the recognition of women's literary success. Up until the early eighteenth century, the tendency remained strong for skill in writing to be expressed in intrinsically masculine terms. Abraham Cowley, for example, praises the writing of Katherine Philips as 'manly', as incorporating the natural 'strength' of men with the sweetness of women.[52] Meanwhile, Dryden acknowledges the achievement of Elizabeth Thomas's poems with the disconcerting flattery that they were thought 'too good to be a woman's'; and in 'To the Pious Memory', he accounts for the miraculous genesis of Anne Killigrew's literary talents on the grounds that 'Thy Father was transfus'd into thy Blood'.[53] However, of all female writers, it is perhaps Aphra Behn, partly as a result of the independent nature of her lifestyle, who most often elicits praise in terms of the manly vigour of her writing: she 'did at once a Masculine wit express'.[54] What the eighteenth century adds to female canon formation is essentially its feminization. An image of the canonical female author is engendered that circumvents the need to suggest that authorial success by women can only be arrived at through the adoption of masculine traits and the replication of masculine forms of literary prowess. But the price that is paid for understanding female literary success in essentially feminine terms is that women writers

---

[51] See Mermin, 'Women Becoming Poets', 335.

[52] 'On *Orinda*'s Poems', in *The English Writings of Abraham Cowley*, ed. A. R. Waller, 2 vols. (Cambridge, 1905), 1: 405.

[53] Ward (ed.), *Letters*, 126; Kinsley (ed.), 1: 460. See Ezell, *Writing Women's Literary History*, 70–8.

[54] Anonymous, 'A Pindarick To Mrs *Behn*', cited from *Kissing the Rod: An Anthology of 17th Century Women's Verse*, ed. Germaine Greer *et al.* (Virago, 1988), 261. For a discussion of the positive connotation of 'manly' as used in a literary context, see Laura L. Runge, *Gender and Language in British Literary Criticism 1660–1790* (Cambridge, 1997), 1–39.

become identified with, and confined within, a canon seen as exclusive to their own sex—the canon gallantly or affectionately compiled by the likes of Duncombe and Scott.

IV

Canons are often shaped by a process of dialectic. The elevation of Shakespeare and Jonson in the late seventeenth century as the two most hallowed English dramatists had much to do with their appearing to incarnate authorial characteristics not merely distinct from each other but actually opposite: Shakespeare becomes the author of mercurial wit, Jonson the one of stately learning. And the relation between the two figures creates the parameters in which subsequent canonical achievement can occur. At much the same time, the canonization of women writers begins to be shaped by a similar dialectical logic, with two very contrary figures, Katherine Philips and Aphra Behn, entering into an association that comes to delineate the rival possibilities of female literary accomplishment.

The legend of Philips's 'incomparability' dates to the 1664 edition of her collected works, whose title-page puffs her, rather in fairground fashion, as 'The matchless Orinda', and whose Preface, written by Lord Orrery, states that 'We might well have call'd her the English Sappho, she of all the female poets of former Ages, being for her verses and her virtues both, the most highly to be valued'.[55] Philips's legend may have been engendered by Orrery and also Abraham Cowley, who praised her lavishly in some verses stationed at front of the 1667 edition of her works, but it is also nurtured protectively by a succession of literary antiquarians. In 1675, she gains admission to Edward Phillips's 'Women among the Moderns Eminent for Poetry' as 'the most applauded at this time, Poetess of our Nation, either of the present or former Ages'. In 1691, Gerard Langbaine inflates even this ample praise by eulogizing her as 'A Lady of that admirable Merit, and Reputation, that her Memory will be honour'd of all Men that are Favourers of Poetry', and as one

---

[55] Cited from Katherine Philips, *Poems*, in vol. 1 of *Minor Poets of the Caroline Period*, ed. George Saintsbury, three volumes (Oxford, 1905), 1: 492.

'who...has equall'd all that is reported of the Poetesses of Antiquity'; and in 1694, she is the only female writer included in the section entitled 'Characters and Censures' ('censure' meaning a judgement and not implying condemnation), a collection of biographies of canonical English authors, incorporated into Sir Thomas Pope Blount's *De Re Poetica*.[56]

A particular mark of her unique status is that Philips quickly assumes the role of canonical gatekeeper: the basis on which other women can enter the female literary tradition is alone through some sort of professed, or imaginatively conceived, association with her. In his elegy of 1686, 'To the Pious Memory of Mrs Anne Killigrew', for example, Dryden describes a transmigratory soul passing through a chain of great poets, including Sappho, before installing itself in Katherine Philips, Sappho's English embodiment. Next he details a parallel, canonizing in implication, between the lives and untimely deaths through smallpox, of Philips and Anne Killigrew:

> thus *Orinda* dy'd:
> Heav'n, by the same Disease, did both translate,
> As equal were their Souls, so equal was their Fate.

That Killigrew should fall victim to the same disease as Philips is cited as evidence that she can expect to sit beside her in the great pantheon of female poets. This conceit in which the ravaging of smallpox is interpreted as a canonical signature also impresses itself on Lady Mary Wortley Montagu, who was struck down with the same disease in 1715–16. In a letter to Pope of a year later, she quotes, with slight modification, the lines in Dryden's poem that brought together Killigrew and Philips, 'As equal were our Souls, so equal were our fates', and then remarks glumly that 'I dispair of ever having so many fine things said of me as so extrodinary [*sic*] a Death would have given Occasion for'.[57]

But though Philips's star twinkled the brightest, it was not the only one to occupy a place in the firmament of women's writing.

---

[56] *Account of the English Dramatick Poets*, 403; *De Re Poetica*, 168–9. The section on 'Characters and Censures' is separately paginated.

[57] Kinsley (ed.), 464; letter to Alexander Pope, 1 April 1717, in *The Complete Letters of Lady Mary Wortley Montagu*, ed. Robert Halsband, 3 vols. (Oxford, 1965), 1: 330–1. See Isobel Grundy, *Lady Mary Wortley Montagu* (Oxford, 1999), 200.

The other bright meteor was that of Aphra Behn. Behn extracts a rather tainted compliment from Edward Phillips in his *Theatrum Poetarum* as 'a Dramatic writer, so much the more considerable as being a Woman'; but she gets a glowing posthumous tribute from Langbaine who, while not omitting to mention that 'she has borrowed very much', reports that she won eminence 'not only for her Theatrical Performances, but several other Pieces both in Verse and Prose'. Her combined efforts, so he concludes, 'gain'd her an Esteem among the Wits, almost equal to that of the incomparable *Orinda*, Madam *Katherine Phillips*'.[58] Philips and Behn are not writers who in any strictly literary terms invite comparison or association: their names link together only in so far as they become, in different ways, the two most obviously canonizable female writers. Behn, herself, was sufficiently versed in the lore and rhetoric of self-canonization to understand that her own consecration to tradition depended on an appropriate obseisance towards her predecessor. In a late poem of 1689, for example, imploring that her own verses be touched with immortality, she uses the petition 'Let me with Sappho and Orinda be...'.[59]

Philips's eminence was always understood as to some degree a factor of her supposed virtue and decorum. Lord Orrery's Preface to the 1664 edition had drawn attention to the admirability of her 'verses and virtues both'; and her prominence as a moral paragon, as much as a literary one, was evident to supporters and detractors alike. In 1696, for example, Mary Pix writes a prefatory poem for Delarivier Manley's *The Royal Mischief* in which she encourages Manley to preserve the momentum of her rapid literary rise. But her words are also chosen to imply endorsement of Manley's own hostility to Philips and her legacy:

> Your infant strokes have such Herculean force,
> Your self must strive to keep the rapid course;
> Like *Sappho* Charming, like *Afra* Eloquent
> Like Chast *Orinda* sweetly Innocent... [60]

---

[58]　*Account of the English Dramatick Poets*, 17.
[59]　Cited from Mermin, 'Women Becoming Poets', 350.
[60]　'To Mrs. Manley, upon her Tragedy', in *The Royal Mischief* (1696), sig. A3. For the way that Trotter and Manley coveted Behn's mantle, see Rosemary Foxton, 'Delariviere Manley and "Astrea's Vacant Throne"', *Notes and Queries*, NS 33 (1986), 41–2.

Here 'Orinda' is not merely 'Chast' and 'Innocent' but also 'sweetly' so: her moral virtues threaten to dissolve in their own sugariness. For Behn, however, the case was entirely opposite: the immorality of her lifestyle and the indecorousness of some of her writings was always liable to attract adverse comment. *A Journal from Parnassus* of 1688 goes so far as to call into doubt her sexuality on account of her having been guilty of a 'Lewdness' that 'no Woman could have been Author of'; and in Anne Finch's 'The Circuit of Appollo', Behn is admonished by the eponymous god for her inability to represent love 'without blushes, or faults'.[61] Throughout the following century, the notoriety of her life and writing proves an endless source of embarrassment and shuffling for her biographers. In 1753, Robert Shiels, for example, quotes from the *Biographia Britannica*'s complaint that her comedies 'are full of the most indecent scenes and expressions', but then rather desperately tries to retrieve her reputation by claiming that this shortcoming has less to do with a laxity of morals than with a failure of artistic control: 'Mrs Behn perhaps, as much as anyone, condemned loose scenes, and too warm descriptions; but something must be allowed for human inadvertency... '.[62]

The contrarieties existing between the 'chaste' amateur poet, Philips, and the licentious, professional writer, Behn, are ones that shape eighteenth-century attempts to fashion a female canon. This conflict is not so much between Philips and Behn as between the kind of writer each represents: and out of this struggle it is the model of the chaste Orinda that emerges triumphant.[63] It remains impossible throughout the following century to fashion a publicly palatable canon of female writers in

---

[61] Anon., *A Journal from Parnassus*, ed. Hugh MacDonald (1937), 26; 'The Circuit of Appollo' cited from Ferguson (ed.), *First Feminists*, 250–2. For a discussion of the latter, see Carol Barash, *English Women's Poetry, 1649–1714: Politics, Community and Linguistic Authority* (Oxford, 1996), 284–7.

[62] *Lives of the Poets of Great Britain*, 3: 26.

[63] See Backscheider, *Spectacular Politics*, 74: 'By 1696, Philips was firmly established as what men wanted in a woman writer.' For a general discussion of Philips and Behn as canonical rivals, see ibid. 74–104; Mermin, 'Women Becoming Poets', 335: 'Philips's unblemished reputation offered singular encouragement to women writers, while Behn's notoriety survived into the nineteenth century as both example and warning'; Marilyn Williamson, *Raising their Voices: British Women Writers 1650–1750* (Detroit, 1990), 18–22 and *passim*; and Barash, *English Women's Poetry*, 5.

which women's strictly literary credentials do not end up becoming entwined with their moral ones. Moreover, the fact that many well-known writers were tainted with sexual scandal (Behn, Centlivre, Manley, and Pilkington amongst others) exerts an influence on female canon-making for which there is no real counterpart in male canon formation. Its effect is especially marked in the mid-eighteenth century, when the preliminary excavation of female authors gives way to more conscious processes of ordering. So much is evident in Ballard's *Memoirs*. Though he includes the likes of Philips and Anne Killigrew, he finds no place for the likes of Behn, Susanna Centlivre, Delarivier Manley, and Elizabeth Thomas (who ended up in prison). Duncombe's *Feminiad* conducts itself in much the same vein, breaking off from its roll-call of female eminences publicly to scold the 'unblushing mien of modern Manley, Centlivre, and Behn' as well as (in a line lifted from Richard Graves's antifeminist poem *The Heroines: or, Modern Memoirs* (1751)) the decadent scandal-mongerers of 'Phillips, Pilkington and V[ane]'. Similarly, the first edition of the *Biographia Britannica* seems to have exercised a specifically moral censorship in deferring inclusion of Delarivier Manley until the 'Supplement' of 1766, and then admitting only a deprecatory entry drawing attention to the 'intire ruin of her virtue'. It should be admitted that a not dissimilar prudery had ensured that two scurrilous male authors, Rochester and Wycherley, had also been locked out of the first edition, but moral censorship still remained more of a hazard for female writers than for male ones.

The derogation of female authors on the grounds of their licentious lifestyles easily blurred into a suspicion of all women who were professional, and so had a monetary interest in the wide circulation of their writings. The touting of one's literary wares for money could easily be seen in women as a form of immodesty, even cultural harlotry. Ballard, for example, as well as excluding disreputable women, is also meticulous in excluding women who wrote commercially. Under his scheme of things, Anne Killigrew, a young lady of unremarkable attributes, gets classed as an 'Eminent Lady', whereas Aphra Behn does not. The animus of male canon-formers against female professionals is especially evident in Duncombe, with his championing of 'the needle and the pen', and his tendency to discuss women's literary prowess in the context of issues of marital eligibility and responsible housekeeping. It is true that Behn continues to possess a canonical intransigence: nobody in the eighteenth century could realistically recite a canon of female authors (as opposed to vaguely 'Eminent Ladies') which could dispense with her altogether, but, even so, throughout much of the eighteenth century she stands in opposition to the dominant logic of female canon-formation. Of those who secured advantage from that logic, the two great beneficiaries were Katherine Philips and Elizabeth Rowe.

The myth of Katherine Philips, the 'matchless Orinda', seduced the eighteenth century and has held her devotees in thrall as late as our own century. Philips wrote a body of poetry, translated two plays by Corneille and wrote correspondence to the Earl of Orrery which was published after his death. The canonizing myth that has built up around her life is one in which she is seen (in Elaine Hobby's words) as 'a model lady poetess, dabbling in versification in a rural Welsh backwater, confining her attention solely to the proper feminine concerns of love and friendship'.[64] To this congenial image of apparent reticence and modesty needs to be added her early death at the age of 32, and still more crucially the belief, only subject to challenge in the last ten years or so, that she never sought to publish her work and never coveted literary eminence. The theory of Philips's authorial reticence owes much to her agonized response (her 'sharp Fit of Sickness') to a supposedly pirated version of the poem that appeared in London in November 1663, and which has been put down as evidence of her aversion to having her writings published. But as Maureen Mulvihill has pointed out, her response, rather than being one of abashment, is more likely to have been an acute form of pique at not being able to control the first public appearance of her works.[65]

In spite of being, in Mulvihill's words, 'a young, underdeveloped writer of slight life experience and cloying sentimentality',

[64] Elaine Hobby, *Virtue of Necessity: English Women's Writing 1649–88* (London, 1988), 128.

[65] Maureen E. Mulvihill, 'A Feminist Link in the Old Boys' Network: The Cosseting of Katherine Philips', in *Curtain Calls: British and American Women and the Theatre 1660–1820*, ed. Mary Anne Schofield and Cecilia Macheski (Athens, Oh., 1991), 71–104. Mulvihill emphasizes how the myth of Orinda was fashioned by powerful male backers. See also Hobby, *Virtue of Necessity*, 130.

Philips became the centrepiece of the emergent female canon.[66] That she did so was less because of her intrinsic literary worth than because her career, and the wider perception and mytho- logization of it, defined the terms of consecration to the female canon. It is on the basis of Philips's canonizing model that Anne Killigrew can be puffed up into a literary eminence; and it is probably Philips's precedent that underlies the extraordinary canonical vogue in the middle of the eighteenth century of Elizabeth Rowe.[67] Rowe's most famous work *Friendship in Death: in Twenty Letters from the Dead to the Living* appeared in 1728, consisting of a series of epistles by pious-minded ghosts intended to edify their recipients and instruct them in the ways of the celestial world. It encourages its readers to despise the corrupt state of the mundane world and eagerly to anticipate their transportation to the next one. After her death in 1737, the pious resignation of her final days acquired an exemplary status similar to that of Addison's famously serene death and is com- pulsively harped on by her biographers. The sharp contrast between the exemplary piety of Rowe's writing and the scan- dal-mongering of other female writers, especially diarists and autobiographers like Teresia Phillips and Frances Vane, is evi- dent in Duncombe's *Feminiad* where Rowe is introduced in a shower of moral luminescence immediately after the lines re- proving 'Manly, Centlivre and Behn', and also in the Cibber– Shiels *Lives* where her comportment is described as such as 'might put some of the present race of females to blush'.

The main burden of this chapter has been to take issue with the commonplace that the eighteenth century can be character- ized in part by its suppression of female literary voices, that the era witnesses an 'almost total absence' of women poets from the recognized tradition. The true state of affairs is in reality very different from this. The eighteenth century sees the earliest attempts of consequence to assemble and draft a female canon; moreover, it sees the first efforts being made, even if somewhat unzealous ones, to understand how women writers might figure within the established canon, the canon of male authors. Yet for

---

[66] See Mulvihill, 'A Feminist Link', 100.
[67] Rowe's career and its significance is discussed in John Richetti, *Popular Fiction Before Richardson: Narrative Patterns 1700–1739* (Oxford, 1969), 239–61.

all the means through which female authors become consecrated to tradition, the terms of this consecration need to be seen for what they are. For women writers to meet with success remained a different cultural event from the successes being achieved by male authors. Female creativity is ringed around by ethical assumptions and stereotypes that figure much less in connection with their male peers. It has been suggested, indeed, that the female author seen as most ripe for canonization is a kind of Clarissa figure, sternly moral-minded, but also isolated and beleaguered, whose literariness is counterpart with, or even an expression of, her essential victimhood.

9

Classicists and Gothicists:
The Division of the Estate

I

In December 1818, an essay was printed in *Blackwood's Edinburgh Magazine* 'On the Revival of a Taste for our Ancient Literature': appearing anonymously, it had been penned by the magazine's most prolific contributor, John Wilson. Wilson took as his subject-matter the 'strong disposition that has of late discovered itself in this and other literary countries of Europe, to recover the vestiges of earlier times and especially to restore its ancient literature'.[1] This antiquarian revival Wilson associates with a 'great change' in the general 'poetic temper of the country', and he speculates about how such a change has come about. His explanation is that as a people slowly emerges 'from a condition of barbarism into civilization', it will feel compelled to distance itself from and perhaps disown its own rude ancestry; but once this process of deliverance has been safely accomplished, feelings of aversion will be supplanted by those of nostalgia, with a 'returning admiration of [the] people for the memory of their forefathers'.[2]

The period of English literature most guilty of spurning its ancestry is, so the author observes, 'our Augustan age'; and the reversal of this tendency he sees as setting in during the later decades of the eighteenth century and carrying through until the moment of the essay's composition.[3] This periodization of the issue, however, is profoundly inadequate. The English Augustans were not uniformly indifferent or hostile to the vernacular literary past: indeed, as this book has shown, the recovery of several distinct bodies of native literary historical material can

[1] *Blackwood's Edinburgh Magazine* 4 (1818), 264–6, 264.
[2] Ibid. 264–6.   [3] Ibid. 264.

be dated to the late seventeenth and early eighteenth centuries. Moreover, nearly all cultural eras pride themselves on an enthusiasm for, and a deference towards, their own literary ancestry. In 1782, for example, Vicesimus Knox had included in the second edition of his *Essays, Moral and Literary* a piece entitled 'On the Prevailing Taste for the Old English Poets', this vogue for older writing being detected nearly forty years before it gets reported on approvingly in *Blackwood's*. Similarly, in 1759, the author of an anonymous pamphlet entitled *An Impartial Account of Mr. Upton's Notes on the Fairy Queene* stops off to urge that 'Every reader of taste must congratulate the present age, on the spirit which has prevailed of reviving our OLD POETS'.[4] It is less the level of inclination to resurrect and venerate the literary past that distinguishes one period from another than of what that past is thought to consist.

This chapter tells the story of the literary historiographical legacy that the eighteenth century left to the early nineteenth, and indeed, though more distantly, to our own day: this is a bifurcated tradition. Just as the idea of a native literary tradition is born out of an act of severance from the classical literary inheritance, so the eighteenth century witnesses the emergence of a similar sort of dichotomy. This is not between the classical and the vernacular *per se* as between writings that affiliated themselves to the classical literary tradition and its values and those which incorporated a different set of principles, these being grouped in the mid-eighteenth century under the cognomen of 'gothic'.[5] This rivalry between the classical and gothic still animates our own perception not just of our literary past but

---

[4] Anon., *An Impartial Account of Mr. Upton's Notes on the Fairy Queene* (1759), 1.

[5] In the 18th cent., the word 'Gothic' could be used to refer specifically to the early Germanic tribe, the Goths; to the characteristic attitudes and cultural forms of the medieval era; or to a vaguely defined 'rudeness' or 'barbarity' of taste. The term was often defined against the 'classical', as in Dryden's remark in his *Observations on The Art of Painting* (1795): 'All that has nothing of the ancient gusto, is called a barbarous or Gothic manner, which is not conducted by any rule, but only follows a wretched fancy, which has nothing in it that is noble.' Cited from *The Works of John Dryden*, ed. Sir Walter Scott, rev. George Saintsbury, 18 vols. (London, 1881–92), 17: 327. For discussion of 'gothic', see Robert Kiely, *The Romantic Novel in England* (Cambridge, Mass., 1972), 27–30; and Nick Groom, 'Celts, Goths, and the Nature of the Literary Source', in *Tradition in Transition: Women Writers, Marginal Texts, and the Eighteenth-Century Canon*, ed. Alvaro Ribiero, SJ, and James G. Basker (Oxford, 1996), 275–96, esp. 276–7.

also of our present-day literary possibilities, though the space of the non-classical has since been lost to gothic and has instead been commandeered by the upstart term 'Romanticism'. This new understanding of English literature as an estate divided unhappily between the classic and the gothic represents a loss of cultural innocence, as the native literary heritage has for the first time to encompass the fact of difference and relativism.

II

One way of approaching developments in literary history in the mid-eighteenth century is through the fortunes of the Renaissance poet, Edmund Spenser.[6] Spenser had acceded, even as early as in the writings of the Elizabethan critics, Webb, Meres, and Puttenham, to a revered position in the pantheon of English poetry. This position, though, had always been attended by reservations, which were to become more insistent in the post-Restoration era. An expression of them can be found, for example, in the following lines of Joseph Addison's 'Account of the Greatest English Poets' (1694):

> Old Spenser, next, warm'd with poetic rage,
> In ancient tales amus'd a barb'rous age;
> An age that yet uncultivate and rude,
> Where'er the poet's fancy led, pursu'd
> Thro' pathless fields, and unfrequented floods,
> To dens of dragons, and enchanted woods.
> But now the mystic tale, that pleas'd of yore,
> Can charm an understanding age no more;
> The long-spun allegories fulsome grow,
> While the dull moral lyes too plain below.
> We view well-please'd at distance all the sights
> Of arms and palfries, battles, fields and fights,
> And damsels in distress, and courteous knights.

[6] For a general discussion of the recovery of Elizabethan literature, see Earl Reeves Wasserman, 'The Scholarly Origin of the Elizabethan Revival', *English Literary History*, 4 (1937), 213–43. For Spenser's status in the eighteenth century, see Greg Kucich, *Keats, Shelley, and Romantic Spenserianism*, (University Park, Pa., 1991), esp. 11–64; and (voicing opinions different from my own), see ch. 4, 'The Cultural Logic of Late Feudalism: Or Spenser and the Romance of Scholarship, 1754–62', in Jonathan Brody Kramnick, *Making the English Canon: Print-Capital-*

But when we look too near, the shades decay,
And all the pleasing landscape fades away.[7]

Spenser probably died in 1599, only seventy-three years before
Addison's own birth, but Addison's lines are impregnate with a
sense of chronological removal; Spenser here is 'Old'; he belongs
to an 'age' clearly and abruptly discontinuous from Addison's
own era; his fictions, moreover, are 'ancient' and 'barb'rous'. Of
course, there is a doubleness in some of these remarks. Spenser is
so inveterately 'old' partly because his poetry revived and sustained a poetic style long predating that of his own day, making
him a Renaissance poet who was also a medievalist; but
Addison's primary concern remains that of blandishing the
chaste and regular productions of his own culture by labelling
as 'uncultivate and rude' those of an earlier one.

Spenser affronts Addison's Augustan sensitivity because of the
alien nature of his aesthetic. His writing is animated by an
uncouth frenzy or 'rage', provoked by a vagrant imagination
('Where'er the poet's fancy led'); his stories merely tickle or
'amuse' us; and the drawn-out allegories, with their ponderous
moralizings, pall on the reader. What Spenser's poem defiantly
fails to offer the reader is any form of intellection; it omits the
sort of rational conversation so beloved of the Augustans. Moreover, it is not just the general complexion of Spenser's aesthetic
that offends Addison, for his plot-lines, with their repetitive
interchange 'Of arms and palfries, battles, fields, and fights'
only serve to dismay. All of these reservations build into Addison's summative verdict that Spenser's writings ultimately fall
short. The insubstantial pageant dissolves when subjected to rational scrutiny, and to an 'understanding age' his 'mystic tale'
remains charmless.

Addison's treatment of Spenser is perhaps perplexing. His
poem enrols him as one of the 'Greatest English Poets', yet at
every turn his remarks are patronizing, ceaselessly dwelling
on how Spenser, perhaps justly celebrated against the dubious

ism and the Cultural Past, 1700–1770 (Cambridge, 1998). For the idea that Romanticism should be seen as 'a renaissance of the Renaissance', see ch. 2, 'The Second
Renaissance', in Stuart Curran, *Poetic Form and British Romanticism* (New York,
1986), 14–28.

[7] Addison, *Works*, I: 29–30.

aesthetic criteria of his day, is found wanting against the loftier standards of Addison's own time. This paradox, however, is less pert than it might at first seem. The literary canon has always been driven by a strong internal logic of self-perpetuation that tends to override the transitory trends and foibles of aesthetic judgement. Addison is happy to reaffirm Spenser's canonical status even at the same time as unsparingly belittling him. He is familiar with a convention of canonizing Spenser's achievement and similarly aware of an equally conventional way of critiquing that achievement. Moreover, we can be sure that Addison was working from unalloyed convention and hearsay, given his confession to Pope, recorded by Spence, that at the time of writing his 'Account' he had never in fact read a single line of Spenser's verse.[8]

When Addison got around actually to reading Spenser's poetry, his understanding of it changed. *Spectator* 419 is devoted to what Dryden had earlier designated as '*the Fairie way of Writing*', which is where the poet 'entertains his Readers Imagination' with figmentary characters such as 'Fairies, Witches, Magicians, Demons, and departed Spirits'. Addison is now happy to consecrate this as 'a kind of Writing', where the word 'kind' carries a stamp of conceded legitimacy; and those who demur at such 'Fairie' compositions he dismisses as men of 'cold Fancies'. Moreover, the way that Addison comprehends Spenser's work has turned towards anthropology, with the 'Fairie way of Writing' being seen as a natural emanation from the superstitious culture of the medieval period when barely a village existed in England 'that had not a Ghost in it'. Of the purveyors of this form of writing, Shakespeare is held up as the most illustrious, but Addison also pays homage to Spenser 'who had an admirable Talent in Representations of this kind'.[9] In admitting so much, Addison has not discovered aspects of Spenser's craft that he failed to notice in his 'Account' of 1694: his characterization of the poet's aesthetic remains largely intact. He has merely found a means of turning to Spenser's praise qualities in his writing that he had earlier cited to his discredit.

The rehabilitation of Spenser in the eighteenth century, to a point at which Addison's dismissive remarks of 1694 seem them-

---

[8] Spence, *Observations*, no. 170.
[9] No. 419, 1 July 1712, in *Spectator*, 3: 570–3.

selves to inhabit a bygone critical era, is furthered by no work so much as John Hughes's 1715 edition of Spenser's works, to which were appended two influential essays 'An Essay on Allegorical Poetry' and 'Remarks on the Fairy Queen'. Hughes sees Spenser as a poet animated by a 'boundless Fancy', as not just an imaginative poet but as a poet who 'writes to' the imagination.[10] Moreover, if the imagination is itself a kind of supernature, Spenser's imagination is one peculiarly peopled by magical apparitions. So far Hughes is in sympathy with Addison's 1712 *Spectator* paper: Spenser is the poet of imagination *par excellence* and the imagination is held up as the spark from which poetry in general is kindled into life. But, at the same time, Hughes advances an argument, to prove enormously influential in subsequent criticism of Spenser, the effect of which is to qualify his enthusiasm for the Spenserian imagination. This is that although Spenser passes as a poet of exuberant imagination, his imaginings are in a paradoxical sense rational ones. That this can be so is due to the allegoric nature of the poem, which allows its fabulous events to simulate a 'real Action or instructive Moral'.[11] Were this not the case, and were Spenser's pageant of exorbitant adventures and his entourage of knights, giants, and wizards not susceptible to being construed allegorically, they 'wou'd indeed appear very trifling'.[12]

Hughes's appreciation of the poem's allegoric technique helps him to construe it as realistic, and so too does his understanding of the historical period in which Spenser wrote. He maintains that in Spenser's age, the 'Remains of the old *Gothick* Chivalry were not quite abolish'd': in other words, the dominant motif in the *Faerie Queene* of knights errant undertaking acts of derring-do does not so much emanate from an over-frothed imagination as reflect in idealized form the behaviour and manners of the poet's own time.[13] The enthusiasm with which Hughes is prepared to canonize Spenser as a poet of fancy is in exact proportion to his ingenuity in making the imaginative square with the realistic and reasonable.

[10] 'An Essay on Allegorical Poetry. With Remarks on the Writings of Mr. Edmund Spenser', in *The Works of Mr. Edmund Spenser*, ed. John Hughes, 6 vols. (1715), I: xxvii.

[11] Ibid., xxviii.

[12] 'Remarks on the Fairy Queen', ibid., lxii.

[13] Ibid., lxiii.

What underlies the entirety of Hughes's discussion of *The Faerie Queene* is an observation, serenely innocent in its actual formulation, which was to have a marked impact on subsequent responses to Spenser: namely that his most celebrated work is 'a Poem of a particular kind'.[14] What he means is that the poem possesses a compositional logic specific to itself, and any response to it must be aware of this and take it fully into account. For example, it would be totally inapt to compare the *Faerie Queene* with classical works, these being constituted by a different logic: this would be no less inappropriate than 'drawing a Parallel between the *Roman* and the *Gothick* Architecture'.[15] To assert the particularity of the *Faerie Queene* is by implication to accept the ultimate relativeness of all critical and aesthetic judgements: one ought not to assess all cultural artefacts against the same criteria because the criteria of judgement should be dictated by, and be in harmony with, the particular object that is under scrutiny.

This heresy of relativeness, as it appeared to its detractors, is something to which I will return later; but it is worth recording here merely that the doctrine enabled Hughes and other writers of the time to generate a critical sympathy towards Spenser entirely absent from a work such as Addison's 'Account of the Greatest English Poets'. Partly as a result of this critical warming towards him, Spenser undergoes a pronounced vogue in the mid-eighteenth century. The formidable antiquarian Thomas Birch edited his work in 1751 as did John Upton in 1758, the latter being anticipated in the same author's *A Letter Concerning a New Edition of the Faerie Queene* (1751); a number of celebrated imitations of Spenser are produced by the likes of James Ralph, Mark Akenside, James Thomson, and William Shenstone; and in 1734 John Jortin published a set of *Remarks on Spenser's Poems*. This sudden access of enthusiasm for Spenser matters to this book because understanding his special achievement is increasingly seen as a prerequisite for understanding English literature in general. The case of Spenser in particular raised questions about the different sorts of writing, and their respective merits, of which English literature was constituted and also the dating of a pivotal transitional point. The writer,

[14] Ibid., lx.   [15] Ibid.

moreover, in whom questions to do with Spenser's posthumous standing cohere most closely with this raft of general issues is the celebrated eighteenth-century literary historian, Thomas Warton.[16]

Warton is an awkward writer about whom to make generalizations. His work is unusually porous to influences from outside, so that for all his unrivalled scholarship, the conclusions he comes to on the basis of it are apt to be diffident, provisional, or derivative; furthermore, he possessed a quality of split-attentiveness that allows him to endorse, sometimes in close proximity, ideas of completely contradictory complexion. His engagement with Spenser's achievement begins in 1754 with his *Observations on the Faerie Queene*, in the first chapter of which he tries to characterize the literary historical moment from which Spenser's poetry emerged. He defines this period very fastidiously: it postdates the restoration of learning in Europe, when works of classical antiquity started being translated and studied, but it still precedes the point at which the culture of the anterior age, that of 'gothic ignorance and barbarity', had been fully dispelled.[17] It is a work situated on a cusp: gothic barbarism is about to give way to the classical and enlightened. Yet in spite of the inherently transitory nature of Spenser's 'moment', Warton, in 1754, takes a sharply unfavourable, even withering, view of it. It was, as he bluntly puts it, in 'the midst of this bad taste' that 'Spenser began to write his FAERIE QUEENE'.[18] Moreover, some of the criticisms that Warton makes against Spenser are ones that those secure in the polished classicism of their own culture were particularly wont to make against the cultural productions of supposedly less enlightened times. One section, for example, simply details 'Spenser's "Inaccuracies"' (of style and versification), and elsewhere Spenser is criticized for having used but also abused the classics, having been guilty of 'misrepresentation of the fables of antiquity'.[19]

[16] For a general discussion of Warton as a literary historian, see René Wellek, *The Rise of English Literary History* (Chapel Hill, NC, 1941), ch. 6, 166–201; and Pittock, *The Ascendancy of Taste*. See also David Fairer's long and excellent introduction to his facsimile edn. of *Thomas Warton's History of English Poetry* (London, 1998), 1–70.
[17] Thomas Warton, *Observations on the Faerie Queene of Spenser* (1754), 1.
[18] Ibid. 3.
[19] Ibid. 44.

The *Observations* of 1754 do contain sentiments that are much more sympathetic towards Spenser than the opening attack on his 'bad taste' would seem to promise. But even so, the most marked feature of Warton's revised 1762 edition of the work is the mollification of his earlier censoriousness, and a new radicalism in the arguments he is prepared to muster on Spenser's behalf. At the very outset, he retracts and smooths over the asperity of the earlier edition: reference to Spenser's having written in the midst of 'bad taste' is replaced by the anodyne comment: 'Such was the prevailing taste, when Spenser projected the Fairy Queen.'[20] Similarly, at the end of the first section of 1754, Warton had noted that Spenser's poem lacked the visible sense of plan that one would generally expect from an epic poem, though he tempered the remark by admitting that a loose structure was probably a precondition for the imaginative exuberance for which Spenser was chiefly noted. In 1762, however, this observation about Spenser's strengths and weaknesses is expanded into a more generalized credo about the relativity of all critical judgements:

It is absurd to think of judging either Ariosto or Spenser by precepts which they did not attend to. We who live in the days of writing by rule, are apt to try every composition by those laws which we have been taught to think the sole criterion of excellence. Critical taste is universally diffused, and we require the same order and design which every modern performance is expected to have, in poems where they never were regarded or intended. Spenser... did not live in an age of planning.[21]

That Warton should protest here against the fact that 'Critical taste is universally diffused', against, that is, the complacency of judging works of all ages against the same rule, suggests the extent of his recoil from his remark of 1754 about Spenser's having written in an era of 'bad taste'.

The 1762 *Observations* do not mark a closure in Warton's thinking about Spenser, for the same poet was to have an important rôle in his *History of English Poetry* (1774–81). Moreover, it is probably in the latter work that his examination of the

[20] Thomas Warton, *Observations on the Fairy Queen of Spenser... A New Edition*, 2 vols. (1807), 1: 5.
[21] *Observations* (1807), 1: 21.

circumstances of Spenser's *Faerie Queene* abuts most closely on larger questions about the very nature of native literary history. By this stage, Warton's understanding of Spenser has undergone more subtle modification. In the *Observations*, the *Faerie Queene* is assigned to an interim historical era between the revival of learning and the full extinction of gothic barbarism: a period that is technically not gothic but in which the old vitiations of gothic can still be felt. In the *History*, the era is characterized quite differently, as one of equilibrium, in which classical and gothic energies enter into fruitful coexistence: 'the Gothic romance', so Warton notes (with seeming gladness), 'although somewhat shook by the classical factions... still maintained its ground'.[22]

In this confrontation between classical and gothic there would only ever be one winner; and Warton notes that even in Spenser's day the vogue for 'Greek and Roman learning became universal'.[23] Yet what stands out in Warton's *History* is that the irresistible rise of classicism is not something that he particularly welcomes. For example, discussing the revival of classical learning so much praised in 1754, he remarks that 'This inundation of classical pedantry soon infected our poetry', where not just the curt 'infected' but also the use of 'our' in connection with a verse culture defined against the classical, represents a significant departure from his earlier position.[24] It is the ability of the Elizabethan age to channel into itself both the energies of the gothic and the composure of the classical that allows Warton now to term it 'the golden age of English poetry'.[25]

The migration of Warton's views about Spenser and the Spenserian age from the 1754 *Observations* to the *History* of 1781 owes much to the influence exercised over him by one particular work, Richard Hurd's *Letters on Chivalry and Romance* (1762). No literary historical work previously had defended with such express intent and force of elegance the literature of the gothic (or early medieval) era. Hurd's book begins with what must have seemed an abrupt and arresting statement of its central contention: 'The ages, we call barbarous, present us with many a subject of curious speculation.'[26] This rehabilitation of the

---

[22] *History of English Poetry*, 3: 497.   [23] Ibid. 3: 491.   [24] Ibid. 3: 494.
[25] Ibid. 3: 490.   [26] *Letters on Chivalry and Romance*, 79.

gothic era (much as in the writing of Hughes) will consist not so much of a celebration of cultural 'otherness' but rather of a harmonization of the gothic with what are essentially classical canons of reasonableness, for as Hurd points out 'Nothing in human nature ... is without its reasons.'[27]

Hurd is the first commentator to propose drawing the three greatest English poets, Spenser, Shakespeare, and Milton, into the party of the gothic.[28] Moreover, it is not merely that he sees them as essentially gothic writers, sinking creational tap-roots down into the barbarous culture of the medieval era, for he claims it to be specifically the *best* of each of them that can be attributed to the gothic. So, in connection with Shakespeare, he asserts that 'one thing is clear, that even he is greater when he uses Gothic manners and machinery, than when he employs classical'.[29] That this should be so follows naturally from another of Hurd's startling premises: namely that the gothic age is peculiarly conducive and '*adapted to the ends of poetry, above the classic*'.[30]

Much of this, of course, begs the question of what exactly Hurd took the gothic period, or the literature it spawned, to be. The answer is that he reduces gothic literature to one paramount genre: the metrical romance. This literary form, so he maintained, had issued from, and been counterpart with, a particular historical system of manners and behaviour, known as 'chivalry'; and this Hurd saw in its turn as a cultural emanation from a precise form of social organization, that of feudalism. This very systematic line of thinking helped him to guard both romance and chivalry in general against the accusation of their conventions being arbitrary or facile, divorced from tangible reality. Against any such suggestion, Hurd can counter that 'chivalry was no absurd and freakish institution, but the natural and even sober effect of the feudal policy'.[31] The main properties

---

[27] Ibid. 79.
[28] Though for an earlier identification of Shakespeare as an essentially gothic writer, see Pope's remark that 'one may look upon his works, in comparison of those that are more finished and regular, as upon an ancient majestic piece of Gothic architecture, compared with a neat modern building: the latter is more elegant and glaring, but the former is more strong and solemn'. 'Preface to the Works of Shakespeare', in *The Works of Alexander Pope, Esq*, ed. Joseph Warton, 9 vols. (1797), 9: 458.
[29] *Letters on Chivalry and Romance*, 117.   [30] Ibid. 127–8.   [31] Ibid. 84.

of chivalry are seen as the entertainment of a cult of knighthood, often understood as operating analogously to a religious order; an imperative that knights display valour in the face of trials and adventures; and a rarefied solicitude for women and their well-being. It might be pointed out that hereabouts Hurd's argument is beset by problems of circularity: he knew that medieval romance was a realistic genre because it replicated the mores of chivalric society, but in fact all that Hurd could claim to know about such a society was afforded him by his reading in the very same romances. It was in these works, and in pretty much these alone, that the traces and vestiges of chivalry resided.

From where, and in which era, the romance form emerged was another subject of high speculation. William Warburton, in an essay on the origin of 'books of chivalry', prefixed to Charles Jervas's translation of *Don Quixote* in 1742, had claimed that they had been brought back by the returning crusaders. In 1765, however, Thomas Percy, in his essay 'On the Ancient Metrical Romances' incorporated into his *Reliques of Ancient English Poetry*, directly challenged this thesis. Percy argued that the old 'romances of chivalry' instead descended from the historical songs of the 'Gothic Bards and Scalds'.[32] It was the Scandinavian countries, so he maintained, that longest preserved 'the genuine compositions of their ancient poets', these being, through no coincidence, the countries that were most laggardly in converting to Christianity.[33] From the tenth century, these Northern peoples, or Normans, moved into France, carrying their heroic songs with them, from which the French and English chivalric romances were eventually to be born.

For Percy, then, the origins of chivalry are recessive ones, since to uncover the metrical romances is only to be referred further backwards to the heroic songs of even earlier cultures. Percy even suggests that some metrical romances may have emerged in England not as a result of the Norman invasion but in a direct descent from the heroic songs of the Anglo-Saxons, songs which, while he can claim no substantive knowledge of them, he

[32] Thomas Percy, *Reliques of Ancient English Poetry*, ed. Henry B. Wheatley, 3 vols. (London, 1891), 3: 341. For discussion of the origins of the *Reliques*, see Nick Groom, *The Making of Percy's Reliques* (Oxford, 1999).

[33] Percy, *Reliques*, 3: 348.

surmises must have existed.[34] Percy's theory necessitates seeing chivalry in a slightly different way from Hurd. Hurd comprehends chivalry in a fastidious way as an exacting code of military behaviour and organization whereas Percy sees it as equating with a more generalized martial culture, which only gradually acquires its subsequently distinctive stress on gentility and honour. One scrupulousness, however, that Percy does attribute to chivalry at all times is its spirit of deference and complaisance towards women; and it is this key element that fortifies him, not without a little prejudice, in his conviction that the culture of chivalry cannot have come from the East.[35]

When Warton came to write his *History of English Poetry*, he acknowledged the vexatiousness of this general issue by inserting in his first volume an essay entitled 'Of the Origin of Romantic Fiction in Europe'. Warton's essay is a curious piece of intellectual harmonization. He begins by accepting as normative the position espoused by Warburton that romance was either 'communicated to the western world by means of the crusades' or, that, even slightly before this, it had been carried by the Saracens into Spain at the time of their immigration in the ninth century.[36] Yet Warton could hardly avoid giving some credence to the theory of his friend Thomas Percy that the romantic fables had been known to the scalds long before the crusades. What the force of reason, allied to the imperative of amicable tact, urged on him, then, was a composite theory, namely that even though romance does essentially spring from the east, shortly before the birth of Christ 'a nation of Asiatic Goths' had moved into Northern Europe, carrying the technique of romance fabling with them, and from these migrant peoples had emerged the Scandinavian scalds of the early medieval era.[37]

During the eighteenth century, the unearthing of medieval or 'gothic' literary works goes on apace. Of all the types of material, though, that were susceptible to being recovered, the metrical romances were by some margin the most important.[38] The

---

[34] Ibid. 3: 349.   [35] Ibid. 3: 341.
[36] *History of English Poetry*, 1: sigs a–aᵛ.   [37] Ibid. 1: sig. c4ᵛ.
[38] See Arthur Johnston, *Enchanted Ground: The Study of Medieval Romance in the Eighteenth Century* (London, 1964); and David Duff, *Romance and Revolution: Shelley and the Politics of a Genre* (Cambridge, 1994), see ch. 1. See also Curran, *Poetic Form and British Romanticism*, 128–33.

main reason for this was that the structure and motifs of romance were seen as the building blocks of some of the great achievements of Renaissance culture, notably Spenser's *Faerie Queene*. Hence an understanding of the romances could be thought integral to a rounded appreciation of the Renaissance masters: Thomas Percy, for example, recommends his own collection of romances (and ballads) on the grounds that 'It would throw new light on the rise and progress of English poetry, the history of which can be but imperfectly understood, if these are neglected.'[39] Yet the existence of the romances, as well as explaining the provenance of works such as the *Faerie Queene*, also provided a vindication of them, a sort of aesthetic alibi. What could be laid against Spenser was the sheer exorbitance of his imagination, but such a charge largely evaporated if it could be established that running through his work was a strong vein of realism: metrical romance, in so far as it delineated, and vouched for the authentic existence of, the exotic world of chivalry, held out just this confirmation. Romances, moreover, were widely deemed to comprise the greatest single literary achievement of the gothic world. Percy, indeed, explicitly contrasts the romance with the several other forms of dull and insipid effusions that had been 'grubbed up' by antiquarians. As for romances, on the other hand, these had always (by the same deluded antiquarians) been 'fastidiously rejected' 'because founded on fictitious or popular subjects', even though 'Many of them exhibit no mean attempts at epic poetry' and are 'generally equal to any other poetry of the same age'.[40]

So far I have detailed the upward progress of two bodies of writing, each buoyed by association with the other: the metrical romances and the poetry of Spenser. An awareness of the romances made Spenser respectable by allowing his poetry to be seen as grounded and realistic; and the rise of Spenser made the romances seem venerable, as comprising the building blocks of his achievement. It is in Richard Hurd's *Letters on Chivalry and Romance* that Spenser achieves his full critical apotheosis, being ranked alongside Milton as 'the two greatest of our Poets' and as comparable with Homer.[41] It is, moreover, in Hurd's work that

---

[39] *Reliques*, 3: 354. [40] Ibid.
[41] *Letters on Chivalry and Romance*, 114.

Spenser's achievement is most unequivocally branded as a gothic one: his poetry emanates from the feudal world, being 'rapt with the Gothic fables of chivalry'.[42] The structure of the *Faerie Queene*, or its apparent lack of structure, is explained in terms of its being a piece of 'Gothic architecture', susceptible to being understood only in light of its own non-classical principles.[43] Once the poem is understood truly, as exemplifying the compositional logic of the gothic, it then yields itself to being read as a glorious confirmation of the essential point of Hurd's whole treatise, namely '*The preeminence of the Gothic manners and fictions, as adapted to the ends of poetry, above the classic*'.[44]

The ambiguity surrounding Spenser's achievement owed, as I have suggested, to an historical uncertainty. From what sort of epoch had the *Faerie Queene* emerged? In one sense, it seemed to hail from an era of new-found classicism, the so-called 'revival of learning'; but this still remained a time at which gothic mores and principles were far from extinguished. The *Faerie Queene* comprises the last great work of the medieval period; but its misfortune was to come into the world sufficiently late as to invite evaluation against the principles belonging not to its own epoch but to the following one. Hurd, like Warton, appreciated the teasing nature of the history, but, for him, Spenser's relation to the gothic imagination does not comprise merely a dilemma of historical placement. For he sees the gothic as a code of rules and as a maelstrom of imaginative energies that continue to be available to poets, that poets have never ceased to have at their disposal. The gothic and classical do not so much delineate a narrative (of the one being supplanted by the other) as frame the possibilities of English literary creativity. The elevation of Spenser is tantamount to a bifurcation of the tradition. Spenser will henceforth head up the party of the gothic, as the quintessential champion of gothic creativity; and English literature will be increasingly seen, as I will discuss later, as an estate cruelly and enduringly divided between the gothic and the classical.

---

[42] Ibid.   [43] Ibid. 118.   [44] Ibid. 127–8.

III

In the writings of Hughes, Hurd, Percy, and Warton are distilled a series of practical nostra for how literary history should be conducted. While not exactly originating, these writings helped to popularize, habits of intellectual approach and literary historical practice that continue to our own day. For one thing, it begins to be assumed that a literary work will be intimately linked with, and moreover reflect, the society in which it gets produced. Before this point, a dominant paradigm for explaining the morphology of literature had been, as I explained in Chapter 5, the idea of tradition: the idea, that is, that literature is a sort of creative freight passed on from earlier to later writers. But progressively this notion gives quarter to a conviction of literature's determination by society, its shifts and evolutions being in synchrony with those of society at large. Literature, no matter the magnitude of its debt to the imagination, is still more beholden to quotidian fact. Percy, for example, in his treatment of early romances, needs no encouragement to assume their rootedness in fact: indeed, 'the more ancient they are', so he observes, 'the more they are believed to be connected with true history'.[45] For Percy, poetry begins in all societies with the transmission of fact; and it is only as a sort of aesthetic decadence sets in, and bards feel a need to decorate their sparse narratives, that a place gets belatedly found for fictionality. This is the point at which the original function of romance narratives 'to instruct or inform' gives way to the inclination 'merely to amuse'.[46]

The enthusiasm with which Percy argues for the reunification of poetry and fact is mirrored in other literary historical works of the period. Thomas Blackwell's *An Enquiry into the Life and Writing of Homer* (1735), for example, tries to specify the conditions that make for Homer's genius, and finds them in the auspicious state of the language and of social manners at the time at which he was writing. The assumption is that Homer's works, no matter their imaginative vibrancy, speak frankly about their humble linguistic and social origins. The same logic, as I have already indicated, became applied to Spenser. The ground

---

[45] *Reliques*, 3: 347.　　[46] Ibid.

on which commentators like Hurd could maintain such a high regard for his achievement was that the *Faerie Queene* faithfully documented its time: in particular, it testified to the survival of a chivalrous culture even as late as the 1580s when the poem was composed, a point that commentators often underscored by noting the occurrence of 'medieval' jousting tournaments even up until the same period.[47] This belief in the inextricability of literature and society is also to the fore in Warton's *History of English Poetry*. Here Spenser's genius is seen as dating from a watershed in English literary history, 'the revival of learning', this cultural event being occasioned by a precise governmental policy, the Henrician break from Rome, which impacted indelibly on a set of religious institutions (the monasteries).[48] These facts constitute the social context (to use a modern expression) of the *Faerie Queene*.

As well as relating literary works to the realm of extrinsic fact, critics like Hurd and Warton were also interested in how such works could be seen as relating to each other. It had quickly become a dogma that Spenser's *Faerie Queene*, for example, was causally linked to the earlier metrical romances: these were the raw material out of which it had been compiled. But could this contention actually be proved rather than merely asserted? One answer to this quandary was to view a work's indebtedness to another as reified in the specific form of literary allusion; it is in light of this principle that Percy can state that Chaucer and Spenser are reliant on the metrical romances because their writings 'abound with perpetual allusions' to them.[49] Literary history is increasingly thought to entail uncovering allusions; moreover, the very fabric of the literary tradition becomes seen as woven from the pack-threads of the allusions made by poets to each other.

Kindred with the technique of spotting allusions was that of examining the books that an author might be surmised to have read (to which, of course, he might also be prone to allude); a writer's erudition becomes, as it were, a virgin snowfield through which his steps can be tracked by the fastidious scholar. In his

[47] See e.g. *Works*, ed. Hughes, 1: lxiii: 'Sir *Philip Sidney* tilted at one of these Entertainments...'.
[48] See *History of English Poetry*, 2: 443 ff.
[49] *Reliques*, 3: 355.

Observations of 1754, for example, Warton had encouraged scholars to try to see through the eyes of the authors they were studying, which could be achieved most directly by attending to the books that had been consumed by them. Eight years later, with Warton on the point of bringing out his 1762 edition, he received a letter from Samuel Johnson in which Johnson singled out a particular aspect of the earlier work for special praise:

You have shown to all who shall hereafter attempt the study of our ancient authours the way to success, by directing them to the perusal of the books which those authours had read.[50]

It may be that Warton's head was turned a little by this praise for, in his expanded 1762 edition, he returned to the comments that had won Johnson's approbation, this time placing on them even greater emphasis. He notes in particular that the critic or editor who constantly turns to classical authors in order to explain Renaissance poets like Jonson or Spenser 'will in vain give specimens of his classical erudition' unless he also calls to mind 'those books, which though now forgotten, were yet in common use and high repute' at the time the authors wrote 'and which they consequently must have read'.[51]

This understanding that the works of one author will be touched by, and most probably allude to, those of others, particularly those of contemporaries, yielded up to literary history a discourse of thick description. Writing literary history entailed positioning authors against their most celebrated contemporaries whom, as Warton rather complacently puts it, 'they must have read'. But the injunction that the literary historian should consume the books that had been read by earlier authors was only part of a general imperative that the past should be approached through an act of historical sympathy. This imperative nowadays seems so banal as scarcely requiring to be stated, but prior to the mid-eighteenth century the idea that it might facilitate the understanding of a literary work to study the culture from which it emanated was not widely accepted.

Before considering Warton's particular brand of 'historicism', it might be useful to analyse to what this historicism actually

[50] Johnson to Warton, 16 July 1754, in *The Correspondence of Thomas Warton*, ed. David Fairer (Athens, Ga., 1995), 27.
[51] See *Observations* (1807), 2: 317–18.

stood in opposition. One work that epitomizes the earlier, prevalent notion that literary worth was supra-temporal, that the
achievements of a writer could and ought to be assimilated to
an ahistorical standard, is Mark Akenside's attempt at numerical
criticism, 'The Balance of the Poets'. 'The Balance', consisting of
a short preamble followed by a number grid, appeared in Robert
Dodsley's fortnightly periodical *The Museum* (which Akenside
edited) in 1746. Akenside was by nature an assiduously sche-
matic thinker. Following, but also enlarging on, the precedent of
a 'very curious paper' by the French art historian Roger de Piles
entitled 'The Balance of the Painters', he scores twenty ancient
and modern poets against nine criteria of putative excellence.
These criteria are in large part inherited from de Piles, and are
coloured accordingly by having been applied first to painters
rather than to poets, but Akenside wrestles them into relevance
to his own undertaking.[52]

The categories of literary accomplishment proposed by
Akenside might be set out as follows: (1) the entire structure of
a work; (2) the designing of 'striking situations' and 'moving
incidents'; (3) 'delineation of characters and manners'; (4) expressions of particular passions; (5) 'justness and decorum'; (6) linguistic expression; (7) versification; (8) the morality of the work;
and (9) a 'Final Estimate' of the overall excellence of each poet.
Even allowing for an eccentricity in the very rudiments of the
exercise, Akenside's schema possesses additional singularities.
For one thing, each poet is scored out of a maximum of twenty,
this grade representing the 'degree of absolute perfection'; this
top mark, moreover, easily outstrips the most generous award
that, in any of his columns, Akenside actually feels obliged to
confer, which is eighteen, 'the highest that any poet has attained'.
The schema, in other words, is implicitly Platonic: poets are
scored under the aegis of an unworldly perfection to which even
Shakespeare and Homer can present only a pale semblance. But
another interesting quirk arises from Akenside's tabulation: the
scores acquired against the eight criteria do not add up to, nor
even computationally much influence, the 'Final Estimate', which
seems to stand on its own as a summative impression. In other

[52] *Museum*, 2 (1746): 165–9. For the attribution of 'The Balance' to Akenside, see
Poetical Works, ed. Dix, 36–7 and nn. 53 and 54 (77).

words, in spite of its appearance as an exercise in hard-headed number crunching, the 'Balance' ends up asserting nothing so much as the real incalculability of literary merit.

The exercise undertaken by Akenside is that of settling 'the comparative esteem of the greater *Poets* in the several polite languages'. Included in his 'Balance' are a clutch of classical poets and dramatists as well as more modern French, Spanish, Italian, and English writers; these latter are Milton, Pope, Shakespeare, and Spenser, a file of names from which Dryden, to whom the dissenting Akenside might have felt a natural antipathy, is the only notable absentee. The highest scorers are Homer and Shakespeare who share eighteen points apiece, with Milton and Virgil being awarded seventeen and sixteen respectively; all the others jostle together at between ten and fourteen. The high mark accorded to Milton, especially his vanquishing of Virgil, is a sign of the times, as indeed is Shakespeare's shared eminence with Homer. Moreover, Shakespeare's run of scores already betrays the religious superstition overtaking his reputation. His 'Final Estimate' of eighteen is the numerical outcome most resisting derivation from the run of scores shown in the previous columns: some of these, indeed, are decidedly unflattering, not least the ringing zero awarded to his powers of structural organization. In spite of the multiple criteria built into Akenside's 'Balance', the most engrained premise of the exercise is that writings from very different cultures and periods can be subjected to a common process of adjudication. Poetic worth transcends time; and all poets are equally eligible for measurement against the unworldly perfection of Akenside's '20'.

This belief that it characterizes literary value to transcend, and reach out from, the culture that has narrowly engendered it entered into close league with another one: namely, that greatness in a literary work, rather than merely being confirmed by, is actually *a factor of*, its ability to transcend its time. A work, if it is to achieve greatness, will do so specifically through those ways, and at those moments, in which it sloughs off the particularities of its cultural background. Of course, the difficulty thrown up by this idea is that of differentiating between parts of a work that remain mired in the contingencies of their time and those which float free into the realm of universality. Often invoked as a resolution of this quandary was the notion that what consecrated a work to the status of trans-cultural greatness was its length of endurance, its capacity to stand the 'test of time'.

The test of time, as a standard of literary merit, had descended to English literary culture from Horace, who had proposed influentially, in a passage translated in Pope's *Epistle to Augustus*, that a work whose reputation saw out a full hundred years could be agreed to have rested its case for canonical status:

> If time improve our Wit as well as Wine,
> Say at what age a Poet grows divine?
> Shall we, or shall we not, account him so,
> Who dy'd, perhaps, an hundred years ago?
> End all dispute; and fix the year precise
> When British bards begin t'Immortalize?
> 'Who lasts a Century can have no flaw,
> I hold that Wit a Classick, good in law.'[53]

The hundred years criterion was never taken up as an absolute yardstick: indeed, Pope, in his earlier *Essay on Criticism*, cited as indicative of modern decline that 'Length of *Fame*' had dwindled to 'bare Threescore' years.[54] However, the general idea that merit could be judged by length of public regard coalesced with other characteristic Augustan beliefs, such as that aspects of human existence considered unvarying were of more consequence than those subject to ephemeral fashion, and (maintained by some) that literary taste was educable and capable of sustaining a cultural consensus. These assumptions come together in Johnson's definitive invocation of the 'test of time' at the beginning of his 'Preface to Shakespeare' (1765):

To works, however, of which the excellence is not absolute and definite, but gradual and comparative; to works not raised upon principles demonstrative and scientifick, but appealing wholly to observation and experience, no other test can be applied than length of duration and continuance of esteem. What mankind have long possessed they have often examined and compared; and if they persist to value the possession, it is because frequent comparisons have confirmed opinion in its favour.[55]

---

[53] 'The First Epistle of the Second Book of *Horace*', lines 49–56, in Butt (ed.), 4: 199. See Anthony Savile, *The Test of Time: An Essay in Philosophical Aesthetics* (Oxford, 1982), 33–40.

[54] Lines 480–1, in Butt (ed.), 1: 293.

[55] *Yale*, 7: 59–60.

Johnson asserts here that literary works belong to a category of objects whose value discloses itself under comparative analysis. Just as 'no man can properly call a mountain high or a river deep without knowledge of many mountains and many rivers' (as he says immediately after), so the stature of a particular book can only be ascertained through a lengthy process of comparison with others. A book that has survived the test of time is one that has come triumphantly through this process of accreditation by comparison. To say so much, of course, is to make an assertion both about value as it inheres in literary works and about the nature of human opinionation in general: any opinion entertained by a multiplicity of different people, especially over a span of time, must be well-founded.

It would be foolish to reduce all critical opinion between 1660 and the mid-eighteenth century to complicity with the views represented here of Akenside and Johnson. However, most commentators would have concurred with the belief that the temporal survival of a work was consequential to, or indicative of, its stature; and a tendency existed for literary worth to be considered as unconditional, unaided or unimpeded by factors of culture (or at least by factors above the level of the merely linguistic). Moreover, where conditions governing literary attainment do get proposed, these tend to be too generalized, or are applied too indiscriminately, to meet with the standards of probity that were subsequently to be demanded by scholars and antiquarians. So much might be said, for example, of the factors of climate and cultural chronology sometimes suggested as having a bearing on literary success, as in Milton's anxiety in *Paradise Lost* that 'an age too late, or cold | Climate' would 'damp...[his]...intended wing'.[56]

In the 1750s, however, a new cultural dictum makes itself heard, namely that literary value should be viewed as relative, and that scrupulous judgement of a work should take into account any cultural advantages or disadvantages that have circumscribed the act of its composition. A cardinal statement of this conviction occurs in the 1754 edition of Warton's *Observations*:

[56] *Paradise Lost*, IX. 44–5, in *Poems*, 856–7.

IN reading the works of an author who lived in a remote age, it is necessary, that we should look back upon the customs and manners which prevailed in his age; that we should place ourselves in his situation and circumstances; that so we may be the better enabled to judge and discern how his turn of thinking, and manner of composing were biass'd, influenc'd, and, as it were, tinctur'd, by very familiar and reigning appearances, which are utterly different from those with which we are at present surrounded.[57]

The least questionable point here is simply that the historian should make himself conversant with the mores pertaining in the age in which his chosen author wrote; such a doctrine, though, was hardly original, and had much earlier been assimilated into the historical method of scholars like Richard Bentley and Lewis Theobald. But a more subtle and far-reaching contention is that the very objective of the historical method is to place oneself in the actual circumstances of one's subject, to see the world as it were through his eyes. Only through exchanging his own vantage for that of his chosen subject can the literary historian appreciate what an earlier writer was seeking to achieve, and how much he profited from, duplicated, or outstripped what had been done before.

What Warton is advocating is a form of 'historicism', but historicism lends itself to different shades of radicalism.[58] What he avows in the passage above is that all activities are conditioned by the historical circumstances under which they are undertaken: the intellectual predispositions and the creative aspirations of an age are alike engendered by history. But what might be seen as following from this premise is that opinions held, or judgements passed, in the present about events of the past are themselves, and to no less a degree, implicated in history. The verdict that we reach on Shakespeare, the regard that we hold for his achievement, is, just as much as Shakespeare's genius itself, a product of the historical moment that engenders it. Our most deep-seated opinions are merely expressions of the time in which we live, of little intrinsic relevance to time past or time future. To follow Warton's line of reasoning to its eventual conclusion (which he

[57] *Observations* (1754), 217.
[58] For a discussion of the rise of historicism, see Levine, *Humanism and History*, ch. 8 'Eighteenth-Century Historicism and the First Gothic Revival', 190–213. Also see comments by Earl Reeves Wasserman in 'Scholarly Origin', 235–6.

never quite does), then, is quickly to find oneself sucked into the spiral and free-fall of pure relativism; for if all attitudes and judgements are generated by history, no vantage-point, external to history, can exist from which different opinions or criteria of value can be gauged for their absolute merit. Many in the eighteenth century, though, were coming to the conclusion that little availed other than to reconcile themselves to this disturbing reality. In 1776, for example, Jonathan Richardson brought out a volume of his *Richardsoniana* in which he meditated on the diversity of human manners and customs and the impracticality of reducing them beneath a single judgemental standard. Such are the political, philosophical, and moral disputes that human beings have found themselves embroiled in that he decides 'it would almost incline us to doubt whether [human opinions] have any fixed point in the nature of things, and do not almost depend on accidental convenience, and the various circumstances of time and place'. And if the nature of our most cherished truths, and the disputes that are generated by different versions of the truth, are all historically engendered, then no recourse to a tribunal of arbitration is possible: 'For what criteria can we have? and who shall be the judge?'[59]

Richardson's question is inescapably the nub: it was unavoidable that critical opinion would polarize around it. One school of thought, as I have intimated already, harmonized the issue by deciding it to be the prerogative of a literary work itself to supply the criteria to be used towards its own judgement. True judgement becomes the task of viewing an object against the standard that the object itself incorporates. John Hughes, for example, in his 'Remarks on the Fairy Queen', noted that the whole 'Frame' of Spenser's fable 'wou'd appear monstrous, if it were to be examin'd by the Rules of Epick Poetry'.[60] Similarly, Warton in his 1754 *Observations* cautioned against the mistake of viewing the 'enchantments of Spenser with modern eyes'; and he drew out the idea at greater length in 1762 in berating how absurd it would be 'to think of judging either Ariosto or Spenser by precepts which they did not attend to'.[61] The aberration that

---

[59] Jonathan Richardson, *Richardsoniana* (1776), 2; cited from Levine, *Humanism and History*, 192–3.
[60] Hughes (ed.), 1: lx.
[61] *Observations* (1754), 217; *Observations* (1807), 1: 21.

Warton thought his contemporaries ('We who live in the days of writing by rule') were prone to commit was that of trying 'every composition by those laws which we have been taught to think the sole criterion of excellence'.[62] To run into this fallacy amounted to a form of intellectual grotesquerie, for which the best sorts of analogy were offered by the visual arts. Warton, for example, demonstrates the folly of judging the *Faerie Queene* against aesthetic standards incompatible with the poem by insisting that 'Exactness in...[Spenser's]...poem would have been like a cornice which a painter introduced in the grotto of Calypso'; and in Richard Hurd's *Letters on Chivalry and Romance* the same intellectual absolutism is satirized in its application to architectural styles:

When an architect examines a Gothic structure by Grecian rules, he finds nothing but deformity. But the Gothic architecture has it's own rules, by which when it comes to be examined, it is seen to have it's merit, as well as the Grecian.[63]

Coming together in critics like Hurd and Warton are a simple penchant for literary works of the gothic era and an historicist philosophy that stressed the relativistic nature of aesthetic judgement. This concoction of elements, moreover, was to prove very influential, to be seen, for example, some years later in Percival Stockdale's discussion of Spenser in his *Lectures on the Truly Eminent English Poets* (1807). Stockdale has taken to heart the message of the earlier generation of scholar-critics that a poem, rather than being a sudden irradiation of authorial genius or a representation of the 'eternal objects of nature', 'must as certainly take its complexion from the religion, policy, customs, and manners of the time at which it is written'. This having been conceded, it follows that 'Unless, while we read him, we place, and view him in the midst of these circumstances, we shall be but very partially acquainted with his beauties, or with his faults'. Admiration for Spenser's achievement is again coupled with a relativistic credo dictating that a work can only be measured against the circumstances of its time, these wider contingencies determining what ought to be seen as 'beauties' or 'faults'; and if the sluggish reader has failed to guess the

[62] *Observations* (1807), 1: 21.
[63] *Observations* (1807), 1: 22–3; *Letters on Chivalry and Romance*, 118.

provenance of these ideas, Stockdale proceeds obligingly to quote the key section from the 1754 *Observations* where Warton had spoken about 'reading the works of an authour who lived in a remote age'.[64]

Stockdale's understanding that what Warton, Hurd, and others had bequeathed to the next generation was not so much an idea as a collocation of mutually sympathetic ones was shared by those who were opposed to the doctrine of 'historicism'. One such was the essayist and anthologist Vicesimus Knox, whose counterblast appeared in his *Essays, Moral and Literary* (1782) as a piece entitled 'On the Prevailing Taste for the Old English Poets'. The 'taste' about which the essay is concerned is one for which Knox has failed to develop any relish; and throughout the essay he demonizes it through a series of tart antitheses. Those who entertain this modish taste find themselves reduced to mere antiquarians ('The mere antiquarian taste in poetry...') whose foolish intoxication is set against the settled opinion of all right-thinking people: 'the common reader', 'the lover of poetry', and the 'candid'.[65] Knox's argument takes effect by all but collapsing the distinction between venerating some old books and venerating such books solely because they are old, and then blaming this categorial collapse on antiquarians themselves. For the antiquarian, so Knox intimates, the value of a work resides merely in its chronological removal from and obscurity to the reading public.

Knox appreciates full well the historical reasoning that underpins the antiquarian case, the fallacy of which, so he believes, consists in a confusion between explanation and extenuation. To put oneself in the position of writers from an earlier period may be to understand how and why they came to compose as they did, but this should not in itself amount to a justification of their way of proceeding: what is intrinsically bad in a work will remain bad for all that the origin of its badness can be *understood* by an application to factors of the time. The upshot is that the antiquarian invariably gulls himself into discerning beauties that do not really exist:

---

[64] *Lectures*, 1: 6–7.   [65] *Essays, Moral and Literary*, 1: 246–7.

By an effort of imagination, we place ourselves in the age of the author, and call up a thousand collateral ideas, which give beauties to his work not naturally inherent.[66]

For Knox, the sort of contextual appreciation of a work (with a 'thousand collateral ideas' called up) that had been propounded by scholars like Warton actually did a disservice to cool, impartial judgement. In one sense, of course, he is right: judging a literary work against the same standards that it appears to endorse itself is no more inherently *authentic* than simply judging it straightforwardly by our own lights. And there is nothing inherently simplistic in his insistence that hardly any of 'our relicks of ancient poetry' 'would be tolerated as the production of a modern'.[67] Indeed, nothing so much encapsulated for Knox the waywardness of the historicist position than that a writer such as Chatterton could feel there was less to be gained from trying to write new poems than from pretending to have discovered old ones.

IV

Knox departs from his opponents about the grounds on which aesthetic judgements on earlier literary works should be passed, but he also, perhaps more instinctually, recoils from the dusty writings of the medieval era. His palate simply disrelishes the 'obsolete and uncouth Phraseology' of the medieval style. And while he concedes that the antiquarian is ultimately entitled to the singularity of his taste, he firmly resists the idea that such a taste should be set up in opposition to the settled consensus in favour of the classical tradition, the tradition of Homer, Virgil, Milton [*sic*], and Pope. This is the true current of English literature, to which the gothic writings of Gower, Chaucer, Lydgate, Dunbar, Douglas, and the like provide only a muddy tributary. It might be noted, though, that much as Knox satirizes the antiquarian predilection for older books, it is, of course, only a particular category of old books that he sets his face against: Chaucer and Spenser are to be hailed as through the mists of a remote and barbarous age, whereas Homer is to be saluted as a

<hr>

[66] Ibid. 1: 250.   [67] Ibid. 1: 248.

contemporary. Had Knox been writing fifty years earlier, he would probably have been less sure of where he stood, through being less sure of where the battle-lines were drawn. But by the turn of the nineteenth century the conflict between classicists and gothicists had already reached a point of entrenchment.[68] And the author in whom, in the eighteenth century, this feud between the gothic and the classical most internalizes itself as a psychomachia is Thomas Warton.

The beginning of Warton's dalliance with the gothic seems to lie in the feverish romanticism of much of his early poetry. 'The Pleasures of Melancholy' (1747), for instance, imagines the poet wandering in 'solemn glooms | Congenial with my soul' and conjuring to his eye a succession of melancholy incidents and subjects. This line of development is consummated, close to the poem's end, with a direct apostrophe to 'Melancholy, queen of thought', which then gives way to an invocation of the goddess 'Contemplation':

> Then ever beauteous Contemplation, hail!
> From thee began, auspicious maid, my song,
> With thee shall end; for thou art fairer far
> Than are the nymphs of Cirrha's mossy grot;
> To loftier rapture thou canst wake the thought,
> Than all the fabling Poet's boastful pow'rs.
> Hail, queen divine! whom, as tradition tells,
> Once, in his evening walk a Druid found,
> Far in a hollow glade of Mona's woods;
> All piteous bore with hospitable hand
> To the close shelter of his oaken bower.
> There soon the sage admiring marked the dawn
> Of solemn musing in your pensive thought;
> For, when a smiling babe, you loved to lie
> Oft deeply list'ning to the rapid roar
> Of word-hung Meinai, stream of Druids old.[69]

Warton's attraction to 'solemn glooms' allows him at the same time to take leave from the construction of the poet as a rational,

---

[68] For treatment of the divided canon, see James Chandler, 'The Pope Controversy: Romantic Poetics and the English Canon', *Critical Inquiry*, 10 (1984), 481–509; and Robert Griffin, *Wordsworth's Pope: A Study in Literary Historiography* (Cambridge, 1995).

[69] Eric Partridge (ed.), *The Three Wartons: A Choice of their Verse* (London, 1927), 112.

social being; instead his poet-figure is an outsider, drawing his inspiration from the natural world, from his ghostly prompter, the Goddess Contemplation, and from the ancient authors whom he picks out as his forebears, the Druids of Anglesea. Of course, aligning oneself with the genealogy of the ancient Druids was an implicit endorsement of a non-classical conception of English literature. The Druids had long been famed for their resistance to the Roman occupation of Britain and in the early eighteenth century were increasingly fêted as the founding fathers of the native literary tradition.

Warton's 'Pleasures of Melancholy' drew inspiration from an earlier poem by his brother, Joseph Warton's 'The Enthusiast' (1744), which has the same rudiments of a natural and crepuscular setting and an isolated poet-figure trying to imagine his way into communion with ancient poets: 'The bards of old, | Fair Nature's friends'.[70] The seeds of this poem seem to lie in Joseph Warton's friendship with James Thomson, developing in the 1740s, and his lines seem to be a deliberate reworking of an influential section of *The Seasons* which had originally appeared as part of 'Summer' (1727). Here in a long and entangled passage, Thomson's narrator imagines himself wandering in 'the haunts of meditation... where ancient bards the inspiring breath | Ecstatic felt'. His sensibility roused by his imagination of these things, he suddenly feels the exalting proximity of other-worldly presences:

> Deep-roused, I feel
> A sacred terror, a severe delight,
> Creep through my mortal frame; and thus, methinks,
> A voice, than human more, the abstracted ear
> Of fancy strikes—'Be not of us afraid,
> Poor kindred man! thy fellow-creatures, we
> From the same Parent-Power our beings drew,
> The same our Lord and laws and great pursuit.
> Once some of us, like thee, through stormy life
> Toiled tempest-beaten ere we could attain
> This holy calm, this harmony of mind,
> Where purity and peace immingle charms.
> Then fear not us; but with responsive song,
> Amid these dim recesses, undisturbed

[70] Ibid. 72.

By noisy folly and discordant vice,
Of Nature sing with us, and Nature's God.
Here frequent, at the visionary hour,
When musing midnight reigns or silent noon,
Angelic harps are in full concert heard,
And voices chaunting from the wood-crown'd hill,
The deepening dale, or inmost sylvan glade:
A privilege bestow'd by us alone
On contemplation, or the hallow'd ear
Of poet swelling to seraphic strain'.[71]

Thomson's lines make for a defining statement of the nature of the literary tradition. Tradition, rather than being seen as a legacy passed down, is introjected into the creative act itself: the process of realizing oneself as a poet is seen as involving an imaginative conjuration of one's chosen forebears, projected outwards as an assignation with other-worldly visitors. These 'bards of old', ubiquitously invoked in the poetry we nowadays call pre-Romantic, are shadowy presences. They may correlate in some instances with the originary classical poets Homer and Ennius or with the biblical father-poets Moses and Job; and they are certainly invoked on occasions by poets who were resolutely antipathetic to the claims of gothic culture: Mark Akenside, one such, appeals in *The Pleasures of Imagination* (1744) to the novice poet to place himself under the influence of Nature, so he might 'breathe at large | Ætherial air; with bards and sages old'.[72] This having been allowed, these ancient bards, flitting shadowily in their moon-lit green world, conjured by aspiring poets like Thomson and the Wartons, bear their strongest affinity to the ancient poetic Druids. As such, the topos of their invocation is one that aggrandizes a non-classical tradition, a tradition that would eventually find a name for itself, especially after Richard Hurd's *Letters on Chivalry and Romance*, in a freshly honorific sense of the word 'gothic'.

The origin of Warton's lifetime labour as an investigator of the medieval world can be traced to his early absorption, as well as that of his brother, in the romantic historiography of Thomson.

[71] Thomson, 'Summer' (1746), lines 516–63, in *The Seasons and The Castle of Indolence*, ed. James Sambrook (Oxford, 1972, 1991), 51–2. I prefer this text to the standard, unmodernized edition, also edited by Sambrook.
[72] Lines 41–2, in Dix (ed.), 92.

Similarly, his absorption in Spenser's writing may go back as far as his student days, for in a poem welcoming the appearance of John Upton's edition of the *Faerie Queene* in 1758, and at the same time experimenting with Spenser's style and imagery, he imagines himself as an Oxford student poring over 'romantic Spenser's moral page' but lamenting the faded obscurity of the poet's allegoric meanings. Help is to hand, though, as Upton's edition of the *Faerie Queene*, its editor's hand touched with wizardry, will unlock the 'guarded vale' and 'flowery forest' of the Spenserian imagination, like Britomart battering down the 'castle of proud Busyrane'.[73]

Warton's attitude towards Spenser, and towards gothic creativity as a whole, the best of which Spenser's *Faerie Queene* was thought to epitomize, modulates, as I have already said, through the two editions of the *Observations* and the *History of English Poetry*. In 1782, moreover, he had further occasion to visit the old feud between the gothic and classical in a poem written to mark the installation in the gothic ante-chapel of New College, Oxford of a stained glass window designed by Sir Joshua Reynolds. Reynolds had been commissioned, partly through the intermediary offices of Joseph Warton, to replace the deteriorating fourteenth-century glass of the west window. He duly visited to inspect the window and was introduced to the idea of creating eight smallish figural designs; having surveyed the window, though, he convinced the Fellows that by adjusting the surrounding stonework a more imposing design could be achieved that would allow, in addition to the eight figures, a more developed central image of Christ in the Manger. The altered plan was approved and Reynolds set himself to the task of providing originals in the form of paintings, these to be transferred to the glass by John Jervais. The operation was complete by 1782.[74]

Reynolds and Warton were friends, and Warton was aware that Reynolds, in his illustrious series of Royal Academy lectures, had been advocating the inherent superiority of classical standards of taste over those of the gothic. Yet, even taking this into account, the fervour with which he welcomed Reynolds's

[73] Partridge (ed.), *The Three Wartons*, 161.
[74] The installation of the window is analysed in Levine, *Humanism and History*, 190–213.

classical design, as expressed in the poem he penned after its installation, is remarkable. His 'On Sir Joshua Reynold's [*sic*] Painted Window at New College, Oxford' begins by reconstructing the poet's excited but queasy feelings during the period of the window's construction. He is full of praise for the new window's faultless embodiment of classical principles but also misgiving about the desecration of the earlier gothic image:

> Ah, stay thy treacherous hand, forbear to trace
> Those faultless forms of elegance and grace![75]

What the new window threatened to extinguish was the medieval air of the old building, one characterized by its deep vaulting and elaborate stone tracery, and by its former 'wreathed window' tinged with 'hues romantic'. This dusky solemnity ('By no Vitruvian symmetry subdued') is something from which Warton cannot resist taking a heavy parting. Yet even in the period of the new window's installation, he felt himself thrilling to its aesthetic purity. What Reynolds's stern classicism was in the process of exorcising, however, was not merely the dated medievalism of the old window but also, so it seemed to Warton, his own life-long devotion to the gothic aesthetic. The flawless nature of the finished window had conquered over 'The fond illusions of ... [Warton's] ... mind', and pained him with regret that, 'enamour'd of a barbaric age', he had turned himself into 'A faithless truant to the classic page'. With the installation completed, and the window's full glory revealed, Warton can only capitulate to his friend's 'matchless skill', acknowledging that in the face of the work's 'just proportion' and 'genuine line', the 'Gothic chain' is broken, its charms exposed as fantastic and delusory.[76]

It is important that the terms on which Warton asserts the falsehood of gothic are represented accurately. At the end of the poem, his gaze leaves the window itself and pans around the chapel as a whole; and what he sees convinces himself of the possibility of fusion and reconciliation: the new window, with its classical styling, embellishes the existing building, not desecrating 'this ancient shrine' so much as enabling it 'with purer

[75] Partridge (ed.), *The Three Wartons*, 179.
[76] Ibid. 179–81.

radiance [to] shine'.[77] The classical and gothic are acknowledged as rival tastes, competing aesthetic logics, though the
classical has the added attribute of being able to blend harmoni-
ously with its opposite (not even Warton allows that the mixing
of gothic elements into an essentially classical design can be
wholesome). In an earlier section of the poem, however, he
suggests that this proposed equivalence of gothic and classical
distorts the real picture. For gothic, though an intelligible and
true taste, is true and intelligible only when viewed against the
narrow set of cultural circumstances that give rise to it; the
classical, on the other hand, holds true to immutable precepts
of art, its taste not being 'peculiar' or dictated by 'fashion's fickle
claim'.[78]

This argument against gothic was really an inverted mirror-
image of the chief argument that could be mustered in its favour.
Critics like Hurd had defended gothic against accusations of the
outlandish nature of its aesthetic, by claiming that this aesthetic
was built on an unappreciated realism: if only one viewed gothic
works focusedly against the social factors giving rise to them,
the aptness of the gothic mode would become apparent. But to
argue that gothic works required to be read restrictedly against
their circumstances of production was tacitly to admit that they
lacked the universal appeal of classical works, works which
were, as Warton puts it, 'by no peculiar taste confined'.[79] The
case for the defence actually incorporated the case for the pros-
ecution. Even the enthusiastic Hurd finds himself heavy-footed
in the quagmire of this dilemma. Having announced in Letter
VIII of his *Letters on Chivalry and Romance* '*The preeminence
of the Gothic manners and fictions . . . above the classic*', in the
next letter he has to admit that the gothic code of behaviour will
remain largely incomprehensible to people not living in, or
knowledgeable about, the feudal world; and he contrasts this
situation, implicitly unfavourably, with classical manners, which
arise 'out of the customary and usual structures of humanity'.[80]

What can be said about the attitudes expressed in Warton's
verses on Reynolds's window? Should it be read at face-value as
his renunciation of the gothic aesthetic and acknowledgement of
the intrinsic superiority of the classical taste? What can be said

---

[77] Ibid. 182.   [78] Ibid. 181.   [79] Ibid.   [80] Ibid. 127–8, 148.

with certainty is that the presiding image of the poem is one of the building's sullen interior suddenly being lit up by the effulgence of Reynolds's creation. The window emits a 'new lustre', a 'purer radiance', this seeming to signify more largely the enlightenment principles that have gone into its accomplishment. Yet, on the other hand, it would have been unthinkable for Warton to have composed a poem about how Reynolds's design had vitiated the building (even if he thought it had done); and it may be that the poem was written in a spirit of disingenuous flattery. We know, in any event, from a letter sent by Reynolds to Warton that he himself resisted taking its sentiments at face value:

I owe you great obligations for the Sacrifice which you have made, or pretend to have made, to modern Art, I say pretend, for tho'...you have like a true Poet feigned marvellously well, and have opposed the two different stiles with the skill of a Connoisseur, yet I may be allowed to entertain some doubts of the sincerity of your conversion, I have no great confidence in the recantation of such an old offender.[81]

Reynolds's suspiciousness is understandable: could Warton have been disowning most of his preceding scholarly career, a career dedicated to the recovery and understanding of works of the gothic age? But even if the poem is less a rescension of his previous opinions, might it not still stand as a clarification of them? Might it tell us that for all Warton's enthusiasm for gothic things, this enthusiasm was only ever encompassed within an abiding allegiance to the classical. The issue is the more poignant, since if Warton was less than a whole-hearted champion of gothic, what champion did it actually have?[82]

Some recent scholars seem to me to have been in undue haste to read Warton's verses as a palinode. To deny this to be the case is not merely to suggest that Warton's lines practise some amicable diplomacy (as Reynolds recognized) but also to understand that it cost very little for him to rehearse the standard case against gothic. From his curt remark in the 1754 *Observations* about Spenser's having written in an age of 'bad taste', Warton

---

[81] Fairer (ed.), *Correspondence*, 453.
[82] See Raymond D. Havens, 'Thomas Warton and the Eighteenth-Century Dilemma', *Studies in Philology*, 25 (1928), 36–50. For treatment of Warton's 'divided allegiances', see also ch. 12, 'The Compromises of Thomas Warton and *The History of English Poetry*', in Lipking, *The Ordering of the Arts*, 352–404.

had been perfectly familiar with that case. Like Hurd in his *Letters on Chivalry and Romance*, he appreciated that the primary charge against gothic consisted of the 'peculiarity' of its taste, but he also understood that the case for the universality of aesthetic value could itself fall under critique. In the 1762 *Observations*, for example, he had condemned as a modern folly the practice of judging all works against one 'sole criterion of excellence', and as early as 1754 he had lamented the 'diffusion' of taste (or the reduction of all tastes to a single one). To argue in this way, of course, in denying that all literary works invite judgement against a single criterion of taste, is to oppose the central contention of the classicist position.

The main legacy that Warton and other gothicists were to leave to the following century was to have outlined the way that English literature could be seen as divided estate. The conflict between the classical and the gothic will henceforth circumscribe all attempts to articulate the nature of the canon, just as it will circumscribe the possibilities of future creation within the tradition. In 1782, Knox, for example, can set down as all but incontrovertible that 'the admirers of English poetry are divided into two parties'; and, only three years later, Warton himself, in the 'Preface' to his edition of Milton's minor poems, speaks of the rivalrous nature of the tradition as an established truism: 'the school of Milton rose in emulation of the school of Pope'.[83]

The work that had been mainly responsible for inciting this conflict of poetical faculties had been written by Thomas Warton's brother, Joseph. In his *Essay on the Genius and Writings of Pope* (1756, 1782), Joseph had allotted Pope, a writer 'of the *didactic, moral* and *satyric* kind', a lower canonical status than the 'sublime' and 'pathetic' poets, Spenser, Shakespeare, and Milton. Yet the mere ranking of the authors in this way was not in itself controversial. The controversy lay instead in the way that Warton accused the Popean style of writing, self-disciplined, formally correct and moralistic, of a poetic flightlessness, and claimed to discover much higher elevations of creative transport in some of Pope's supposedly lesser contemporaries, Young, Thomson, and Gray. All the authors

[83] John Milton, *Poems upon Several Occasions*, ed. Thomas Warton (1785), xi.

whom Warton ranks above Pope were susceptible to being thought of as 'gothic', and Warton goes on later to suggest provocatively that it characterizes Pope's devotees that they suffer from an inaptitude to appreciate the beauties of the higher gothic works: 'He who would think the *Faery Queen, Palamon* and *Arcite*, the *Tempest*, or *Comus*, childish and romantic, might relish POPE.'[84]

What a literary tradition constructed along the lines of gothic rather than classical principles would look like is evident as early as Thomas Gray's *Progress of Poesy*, written between 1751 and 1754. Gray's poem recites a poetic tradition based on the single poetic criterion of sublimity, especially as expressed through the voguish Pindaric ode. Such a tradition begins in England with Shakespeare, 'Nature's darling', to whom she unveiled 'Her awful face'; and next comes Milton who 'rode sublime | Upon the seraph-wings of Ecstasy'. It is true that the third poet in Gray's sequence of honour is Dryden, a poet not normally spoken of as possessing gothic credentials, though Gray does hold up for particular praise his irregular odes rather than his more formal works. Yet perhaps more significant than the inclusion of Dryden is the omission of Pope, whose writing in the odic vein Gray dismisses as 'not worthy of so great a man'. And when Gray forlornly asks towards the end of the poem 'Oh! lyre divine, what daring spirit | Wakes thee now?', the only poet he can think to name is himself.[85] The significant point here is not just the identity of the poets enrolled in Gray's canon: after all the lineage of Shakespeare, Milton, and Dryden, even given Gray's temerity in urging his own canonical credentials ahead of those of Pope, would hardly have registered as iconoclastic. Of greater note is the basis upon which these poets qualify for canonical inclusion: their attainment of sublimity.

The cultural conflict that I have been concerned with here, the rise of the gothic aesthetic as a countervailing category to that of

---

[84] Cited from Joseph Warton, *An Essay on the Genius and Writings of Pope*, 5th edn. 2 vols. (1806), 2: 403. The sentence quoted is repeated nearly verbatim, as well as the surrounding sentiments, in 'The Life of Alexander Pope, Esq', in Warton (ed.), *Works of Alexander Pope* (1797), 1: lxix. See Hoyt Trowbridge, 'Joseph Warton's Classification of English Poets', *Modern Language Notes*, 51 (1936), 515–18.

[85] 'Progress of Poesy' cited from Lonsdale (ed.), 176; Gray's dismissive remark, presumably aimed at Pope's 'Ode for Musick, on St. Cecilia's Day' (1713), is cited from 175.

the classical, helps to shape the literary era that we now label 'Romanticism'. Robert Griffin, indeed, has gone so far as to define Romanticism, not as a distinctive poetic style or subject-matter, so much as a rejection of what was seen as 'modern poetry', chief within which was the poetry of Pope. For the early eighteenth century, the key canonical antagonism is that between Dryden, the poet who brings the literary language to a state of full refinement, and Shakespeare, a poet unquestionably great, but one who (many people thought) wrote in an age of linguistic barbarism. For the late eighteenth century, it lies between Pope and the gothic authors, a feud encapsulated by Byron, Pope's most celebrated nineteenth-century admirer, in a dismissive remark on his contemporaries: 'They are also fighting for life; for, if he [Pope] maintains his station, they will reach their own—by falling.'[86]

If Romanticism is the belated revenge of the gothic upon the classical, this revenge is cheaply exacted. The attack on Pope, as an author heedless of the claims of the gothic aesthetic, was always based on a partial reading of him. After all, Pope begins his career by writing imitations of the cardinal gothic authors, Chaucer and Spenser, and in short order goes on to produce a version of the duskily medieval tale of Eloisa and Abelard: Pope, after all, it is who expresses his admiration for Shakespeare by likening his works to 'an ancient majestic piece of Gothic architecture'.[87] The strength of Pope's own gothic credentials was always apt to be overlooked or treated sourly by his detractors, as when Thomas Warton, in the 'Preface' to his edition of Milton's poetry, records his father's opinion that Pope's 'Eloisa' had 'pilfered from COMUS and the PENSEROSO', a 'plagiarism' that Pope apparently believed would lie undetected because Milton's works were 'scarcely remembered'.[88] Yet just as much as the case against Pope as a gothic writer was overstated, the gothic credentials of Spenser and Milton also admitted a similar degree of exaggeration. How, in fairness, could Milton be assigned to a literary camp defined in terms of its antagonism to the classical? The dubiousness of this was not lost on

---

[86] See Griffin, *Wordsworth's Pope*, 24–8; Lord Byron, *Selected Prose*, ed. Peter Gunn (London, 1972), 406.

[87] Warton (ed.), 9: 458. For extended quote, see n. 28 above.

[88] *Poems upon Several Occasions*, viii–ix.

some eighteenth-century commentators: Vicesimus Knox, for example, in his essay 'On the Prevailing Taste in Poetry', approves the cultural ascendancy of the most championed gothic writers but only as a result of denying their credentials to be truly gothic: 'Spenser and Milton drew not from a Gothic model, but from the polished Italians.'[89]

The battle between the gothicists and classicists produced an obvious casualty, Pope: no clearer example exists of a revolution in aesthetic taste leading to a major author being ousted from, or at least being relegated within, the canon. For the most part, however, a change in the criteria governing canonization remains something distinct from a change in the canon's constitution. Writers like Spenser and Milton, though they bulked large in new gothic versions of the canon, had played earlier, and would play again later, an equally stalwart role in canons conceived along more classical lines. So it is with several other canonical figures. While Chaucer is sometimes praised for the rude vitality of his gothic style, on other occasions he gets saluted as the earliest refiner of the English poetic tongue; and while Dryden stands at the head of Joseph Addison's canon of linguistic refinement, sixty years later we find him drafted into Thomas Gray's canon of sublimity. Perhaps what most distinguishes the canonical work is just this sort of mutability, the ability to present a fresh and eligible face to each new revolution in critical taste.

[89] *Essays, Moral and Literary*, 2: 210–16, 213.

Appendix 1: Pope's 'discourse on the rise and progress of English poetry, as it came from the Provincial poets'

AERA I

RYMER, 2d part, pag. 65, 66, 67, 77.
Petrarch 78. Catal. of Provencals [Poets.]

1. School of Provence

  Chaucer's Visions, Romaunt of the Rose,
  Pierce Plowman, Tales from Boccace.
  Gower.

2. School of Chaucer

  Lydgate,
  T. Occleve,
  Walt. de Mapes,
  Skelton.

3. School of Petrarch

  E. of Surrey
  Sir Thomas Wyat,
  Sir Philip Sydney,
  G. Gascoyn, Translator of Ariosto's
    Com.

4. School of Dante

  Mirror of Magistrates,
  Lord Buckhurst's Induction,
    Gorboduck,—Original of good
    Tragedy,—Seneca [his Model]

AERA II

SPENCER, Col. Clout, from the School of Ariosto and Petrarch, translated from Tasso.

5. School of Spencer,
    and
From Italian Sonnets

  W. Brown's Pastorals,
  Ph. Fletcher's Purple Island,
    Alabaster, Piscatory Ec
  S. Daniel,
  Sir Walter Raleigh,
  Milton's Juvenilia. Heath. Habinton.

Translators from Italian

  Golding,
  Edm. Fairfax,
  Harrington.

6. School of Donne
{ Cowley, Davenant,
Michael Drayton,
Sir Thomas Overbury,
Randolph,
Sir John Davis,
Sir John Beaumont,
Cartwright,
Cleveland,
Crashaw,
Bishop Corbet,
Lord Falkland.

{ Carew,
T. Carey,
G. Sandys, in his Par. of Job
Fairfax,

{ Sir John Mennis,
Tho. Baynal.

Cited from Owen Ruffhead, *The Life of Alexander Pope* (1769), 424–5.

Appendix 2: Letter of Thomas Gray to Thomas Warton 15 April 1770

Sr

OUR Friend Dr. Hurd having long ago desired me in your name to communicate any fragments, or sketches of a design, I once had to give a history of English Poetry, you may well think me rude or negligent, when you see me hesitating for so many months, before I comply with your request, and yet (believe me) few of your friends have been better pleased than I to find this subject (surely neither unentertaining, nor unuseful) had fallen into hands so likely to do it justice, few have felt a higher esteem for your talents, your taste, & industry. in truth the only cause of my delay has been a sort of diffidence, that would not let me send you any thing so short, so slight, & so imperfect, as the few materials I had begun to collect, or the observations I had made on them. a sketch of the division & arrangement of the subject however I venture to transcribe, and would wish to know, whether it corresponds in any thing with your own plan, for I am told your first volume is already in the press.

INTRODUCTION

On the poetry of the *Galic* (or Celtic) nations, as far back as it can be traced.

On that of the Goths: its introduction into these islands by the Saxons & Danes, & its duration. on the origin of rhyme among the Franks, the Saxons, & Provençaux. some account of the Latin rhyming poetry from its early origin down to the 15th Century.

P:I

On the School of Provence, wch rose about the year 1100, & was soon followed by the French & Italians. their heroic poetry, or romances in verse, Allegories, fabliaux, syrvientes, comedies, farces, canzoni, sonnets, balades, madrigals, sestines, &c:

Of their imitators the *French*, & of the first *Italian* School (commonly call'd the *Sicilian*) about the year 1200 brought to perfection by Dante, Petrarch, Boccace, & others.

State of Poetry in England from the Conquest (1066) or rather from
Henry 2$^{d's}$ time (1154) to the reign of Edward the 3^d (1327).

P:2

On *Chaucer* who first introduced the manner of the Provençaux improved by the Italians into our country. his character & merits at large;
the different kinds in wch he excell'd. Gower, Occleve, Lydgate, Hawes,
G: Douglas, Lindsay, Bellenden, Dunbar, &c:

P:3

Second Italian School (of Ariosto, Tasso, &c:) an improvement on the
first, occasion'd by the revival of letters the end of the 15th century. The
lyric poetry of this & the former age introduced from Italy by Ld Surrey,
Sr T. Wyat, Bryan, Ld Vaux, &c: in the beginning of the 16th century.
   Spenser, his character. Subject of his poem allegoric & romantic, of
Provençal invention: but his manner of treating it borrow'd from the
Second Italian School. Drayton, Fairfax, Phin: Fletcher, Golding, Phaer,
&c: this school ends in Milton.
   A *third Italian* School, full of conceit, begun in Q: Elizabeths reign,
continued under James, & Charles the first by *Donne*, Crashaw, Cleve-
land; carried to its height by Cowley, & ending perhaps in *Sprat*.

P:4

School of France, introduced after the Restoration. Waller, Dryden,
Addison, Prior, & Pope wch has continued down to our own times.
   You will observe, that my idea was in some measure taken from a
scribbled paper of *Pope*, of w^{ch} (I believe) you have a copy. You will
also see that I have excluded *dramatic* Poetry entirely wch if you have
taken in, it will at least double the bulk & labour of your book.[1]
   I am, sir, with great esteem, your most humble and obedient servant,

THOMAS GRAY

Cited from *Correspondence*, ed. Toynbee and Whibley, 3: 1122–5.

---

[1]Some material was inserted here in the original letter but was not preserved in the
transcript on which the text above is based.

Bibliography

Primary

Place of publication is London where not stated.

ADDISON, JOSEPH, *Works*, ed. Richard Hurd, 6 vols. (1811).
AKENSIDE, MARK, 'The Balance of the Poets', in *Museum*, 2 (1746), 165–9.
——*Poetical Works*, ed. Robin Dix (1996).
ANDERSON, ROBERT (ed.), *The Works of the British Poets*, 13 vols. (1795).
ANON., *An Impartial Account of Mr. Upton's Notes on the Fairy Queene* (1795).
——*A Journal from Parnassus*, ed. Hugh MacDonald (1937).
ASHFIELD, ANDREW (ed.), *Romantic Women Poets 1770–1838* (Manchester, 1995).
BALLARD, GEORGE, *Memoirs of Several Ladies of Great Britain who have been Celebrated for their Writings or Skill in the Learned Languages, Arts and Sciences* (1752).
BEATTIE, JAMES, *Essays* (Edinburgh, 1776).
Biographia Britannica: or the Lives of the most Eminent Persons who have Flourished in Great Britain and Ireland, from the Earliest Ages, down to the Present Times, 6 vols. (1747–66).
Biographia Britannica, 2nd edn, ed. Andrew Kippis, 5 vols. (1778–93).
BIRCH, THOMAS (ed.), *A General Dictionary, Historical and Critical*, 10 vols. (1734–41).
BLAIR, HUGH, *Lectures on Rhetoric and Belles Lettres*, 5th edn., 3 vols. (Edinburgh, 1793).
BLOUNT, THOMAS POPE, *De Re Poetica: or Remarks upon Poetry. With Characters and Censures of the most Considerable Poets whether Ancient or Modern* (1694).
BOSWELL, JAMES, *Life of Johnson*, ed. G. B. Hill, rev. L. F. Powell, 6 vols. (Oxford, 1934–50).
BREWER, DEREK (ed.), *Chaucer: The Critical Heritage*, 2 vols. (1978).
BROWN, JOHN, *The History of the Rise and Progress of Poetry* (1764).
BROWNING, ELIZABETH BARRETT, *Letters*, ed. Frederick G. Kenyon, 2 vols. (in one) (New York, 1899).
BUCHANAN, JAMES, *The British Grammar* (1762), facs. repr. (Menston, 1968).

BURKE, EDMUND, *A Philosophical Enquiry into the Origin of our Ideas of the Sublime and Beautiful*, ed. James T. Boulton (Oxford, 1958, 1987).

BYRON, GEORGE GORDON (Lord), *Selected Prose*, ed. Peter Gunn (London, 1972).

BYSSHE, EDWARD, *The Art of English Poetry*, 3rd edn. (1708).

CAMDEN, WILLIAM, *Remains Concerning Britain* (1870).

—— *Remains Concerning Britain*, ed. R. D. Dunn (Toronto, 1984).

CAMPBELL, JOHN, *The Polite Correspondence: or Rational Amusement; being a Series of Letters, Philosophical, Poetical, Historical, Critical, Amorous, Moral and Satyrical* (1741).

CHAUCER, GEOFFREY, *Riverside Edition*, ed. Larry D. Benson *et al.* (Oxford, 1988).

CIBBER, COLLEY, *A Rhapsody upon the Marvellous . . . Being a Scrutiny into Ancient Poetick Fame, Demanded by Modern Common Sense* (1751).

CLARE, JOHN, *Prose*, ed. J. W. and A. Tibble (1951).

COBB, SAMUEL, *Poems on Several Occasions*, 3rd edn. (1710).

COLMAN, GEORGE (the younger) and THORNTON, BONNELL, *The Connoisseur*, 69, 22 May 1755, 260–7.

—— (eds.), *Poems by Eminent Ladies*, 2 vols. (1755).

COOKE, THOMAS, *Pythagoras An Ode. To which are Prefix'd Observations on Taste and on Education* (1752).

COOPER, ANTHONY ASHLEY, 3rd Earl of Shaftesbury, *Characteristicks of Men, Manners, Opinions, Times*, ed. Philip Ayres, 2 vols. (Oxford, 1999).

COOPER, ELIZABETH, *The Muses Library, or a Series of English Poetry from the Saxons to the Reign of Charles II* (1737).

COOPER, JOHN GILBERT, *Letters concerning Taste* (1755).

COWLEY, ABRAHAM, *English Writings*, ed. A. R. Waller, 2 vols. (Cambridge, 1905).

—— *Poetry & Prose*, ed. L. C. Martin (Oxford, 1949).

COWPER, WILLIAM, *Poems*, ed. John D. Baird and Charles Ryskamp, 3 vols. (Oxford, 1980–95).

CROXALL, SAMUEL, *The Vision. A Poem* (1715).

DAVENANT, SIR WILLIAM, *Gondibert*, ed. David F. Gladish (Oxford, 1971).

DEFOE, DANIEL, *The Compleat English Gentleman*, ed. Karl D. Bülbring (1890).

DENNIS, JOHN, *Critical Works*, ed. E. N. Hooker, 2 vols. (Baltimore, 1939–43).

DRAYTON, MICHAEL, *Complete Works*, ed. Revd. Richard Hooper, 3 vols. (1876).

DRYDEN, JOHN, *Letters,* ed. Charles E. Ward (Durham, NC, 1942).
—— *Poems,* ed. James Kinsley, 4 vols. (Oxford, 1958).
—— *Of Dramatic Poesy and other Critical Essays,* ed. George Watson, 2 vols. (1962).

DUFF, WILLIAM, *An Essay on Original Genius* (1767), ed. John Valdimir Price (1994).

DUNCOMBE, JOHN, *The Feminiad. A Poem.* (1754), in Augustan Reprint Society no. 207, ed. Jocelyn Harris (Los Angeles, 1981).

DURHAM, W. H. (ed.), *Critical Essays of the Eighteenth Century 1700–1725* (Oxford, 1915).

DYCE, ALEXANDER (ed.), *Specimens of British Poetesses* (1827).

ELLEDGE, SCOTT (ed.), *Eighteenth-Century Critical Essays,* 2 vols. (Ithaca, NY, 1961).

ELSTOB, ELIZABETH, *The Rudiments of English Grammar for the English-Saxon Tongue* (1715).

ENFIELD, WILLIAM (ed.), *The Speaker or Miscellaneous Pieces Selected from the Best English Writers* (1774).
—— (ed.), *Exercises in Elocution Selected from Various Authors and Arranged under Proper Heads* (1780).

FELTON, HENRY, *A Dissertation on Reading the Classics and Forming a Just Style* (1709).

FIELDING, HENRY, *Joseph Andrews,* ed. Martin C. Battestin (Oxford, 1967).
—— *The Covent-Garden Journal and A Plan of the Universal Register-Office,* ed. Bertrand A. Goldgar (Oxford, 1988).

FIELDING, SARAH, *The Adventures of David Simple,* ed. Malcolm Kelsall (Oxford, 1994).

FRANKLIN, BENJAMIN, *Complete Works in Philosophy, Politics and Morals,* 3 vols. (1806).

FULLER, THOMAS, *The History of the Worthies of England* (1662).

GAY, JOHN, *Poetry and Prose,* ed. Vinton A. Dearing and Charles E. Beckwith, 2 vols. (Oxford, 1974).

GERARD, ALEXANDER, *An Essay on Taste,* facs. repr. of 3rd edn. (1780), introd. by Walter J. Hipple (New York, 1978).

GIBBON, EDWARD, *Memoirs of My Life,* ed. George A. Bonnard (1966).

GIBBONS, THOMAS, *Rhetoric, or a View of its Principal Tropes and Figures* (1767), facs. repr. (Menston, 1969).

GILDON, CHARLES, *The Lives and Characters of the English Dramatick Poets* (1699).

GOLDSMITH, OLIVER (ed.), *The Beauties of English Poesy,* 2 vols. (1767).
—— *Works,* with a memoir by William Spalding (1858).

GRAY, THOMAS, *Common-Place Book*, 3 vols., Pembroke College Library (unclassified).

—— *Works*, ed. T. J. Mathias, 2 vols. (1814).

—— *Correspondence*, ed. Paget Toynbee and Leonard Whibley, 3 vols. (Oxford, 1935).

GREENWOOD, JAMES (ed.), *The Virgin Muse* (1722).

GREER, GERMAINE, HASTINGS, SUSAN, MEDOLF, JESLYN, and SANSONE, MELINDA (eds.), *Kissing the Rod: An Anthology of 17th Century Women's Verse* (1988).

HAYLEY, WILLIAM, *Poems and Plays*, 6 vols. (1788).

['Hedley' papers] *Reports, Papers, Catalogues, &c of the Literary and Philosophical Society of Newcastle upon Tyne*.

HAYWARD, THOMAS (ed.), *The British Muse* (1738).

HERFORD, C. H., SIMPSON, PERCY, and SIMPSON, EVELYN (eds.), *Ben Jonson*, 11 vols., (Oxford, 1925–51).

HERRICK, ROBERT, *Poetical Works*, ed. L. C. Martin (Oxford, 1956).

HORACE, *Odes and Epodes*, ed. and trans. C. E. Bennett, rev. edn. (Cambridge, Mass., 1966).

HURD, RICHARD, *Letters on Chivalry and Romance with the Third Elizabethan Dialogue*, ed. Edith J. Morley (1911).

JACOB, GILES, *The Poetical Register or the Lives and Characters of the English Dramatick Poets* (1719).

—— *An Historical Account of the Lives and Writings of our most Considerable English Poets* (1720) [usually referred to as *Poetical Register* vol. 2].

JOHNSON, SAMUEL, *Dictionary of the English Language*, 2 vols. (1840).

—— *Lives of the English Poets*, ed. George Birkbeck Hill, 3 vols. (Oxford, 1905).

—— *Yale Edition* (New Haven, 1958–).

—— *Lives of the Poets: A Selection*, ed. J. P. Hardy (Oxford, 1971).

—— *Letters*, ed. Bruce Redford, 5 vols. (Oxford, 1992–4).

KNOX, VICESIMUS (ed.), *Elegant Extracts: or Useful and Entertaining Pieces of Poetry, Selected for the Improvement of Youth* (1784?).

—— *Essays, Moral and Literary*, 2 vols. (1822).

LAERTIUS, DIOGENES, *The Lives and Opinions of Eminent Philosophers*, trans. C. D. Yonge (London, 1905).

LANGBAINE, GERARD, *An Account of the English Dramatick Poets* (1691).

LL[UELYN], M[ARTIN], *Men-Miracles. With Other Poems*, 2nd edn. (1656).

LONSDALE, ROGER (ed.), *The Poems of Thomas Gray, William Collins, Oliver Goldsmith* (1969).

——(ed.), *The New Oxford Book of Eighteenth Century Verse* (Oxford, 1984).

——(ed.), *Eighteenth-Century Women Poets: An Oxford Anthology* (Oxford, 1989).

MADAN, JUDITH, *The Progress of Poetry* (1783).

MANDEVILLE, BERNARD, *The Fable of the Bees: or Private Vices, Publick Benefits*, ed. F. B. Kaye, 2 vols. (Oxford, 1924).

MARLOWE, CHRSTOPHER, *Complete Works*, ed. Fredson Bowers, 2 vols. (Cambridge, 1973).

MILTON, JOHN, *Works*, ed. Frank Allen Patterson *et al.*, 18 vols. (New York, 1931–38).

——*Poems*, ed. John Carey and Alastair Fowler (1968).

MONTAGU, LADY MARY WORTLEY, *Complete Letters*, ed. Robert Halsband, 3 vols. (Oxford, 1965).

NEEDHAM, H. A. (ed.), *Taste and Criticism in the Eighteenth Century* (New York, 1952, 1969).

NICHOLS, JOHN, *Literary Anecdotes of the Eighteenth Century*, 9 vols. (1812–15).

PARTRIDGE, ERIC (ed.), *The Three Wartons: A Choice of their Verse* (1927).

PERCY, THOMAS, *Reliques of Ancient English Poetry*, ed. Henry B. Wheatley, 3 vols. (1891).

PHILLIPS, EDWARD, *Theatrum Poetarum, or a compleat Collection of the Poets* (1675).

POPE, ALEXANDER, *Works*, ed. Joseph Warton, 9 vols. (1797).

——*Poems*, ed. J. Butt *et al.*, 11 vols. (1939–69).

——*Correspondence*, ed. George Sherburn, 5 vols. (Oxford, 1956).

——*Prose Works II*, ed. Rosemary Cowler (Oxford, 1986).

POTTER, ROBERT, *An Inquiry into some passages in Dr. Johnson's Lives of the Poets: Particularly his Observations on Lyric Poetry and the Odes of Gray* (1783).

PRIESTLEY, JOSEPH, *The Rudiments of English Grammar Adapted to the Use of Schools. With Observations of Style* (1761).

——*An Essay on a Course of Liberal Education for Civil and Active Life* (1765).

ROLLIN, CHARLES, *Method of Studying the Belles Lettres*, 4 vols. (5th edn., 1759).

RYMER, THOMAS, *Critical Works*, ed. Curt A. Zimansky (New Haven, 1956).

SAINTSBURY, GEORGE (ed.), *Minor Poets of the Caroline Period*, 3 vols. (Oxford, 1905).

SCOTT, JOHN, *Critical Essays on Some of the Poems of Several English Poets* (1785).

5555

55555

SCOTT, MARY, *The Female Advocate; A Poem. Occasioned by Reading Mr. Duncombe's Feminead* (1774), in Augustan Reprint Society 224, ed. Gae Holladay (Los Angeles, 1984).

SHADWELL, THOMAS, *Complete Works*, 5 vols. (1927).

SHERIDAN, RICHARD BRINSLEY, *Dramatic Works*, ed. Cecil Price, 2 vols. (Oxford, 1973).

SHERIDAN, THOMAS, *A Plan of Education for the Young Nobility and Gentry of Great Britain* (1769).

SHIELS, ROBERT, *The Lives of the Poets of Great Britain and Ireland*, 5 vols. (1753) [published under the name of Theophilus Cibber].

SIDNEY, SIR PHILIP, *An Apology for Poetry or The Defence of Poesy*, ed. Geoffrey Shepherd (Manchester, 1965).

SMITH, ADAM, *Lectures on Rhetoric and Belles Lettres*, ed. John M. Lothian (1963).

SMITH, G. GREGORY (ed.), *Elizabethan Critical Essays*, 2 vols. (Oxford, 1904).

SMOLLETT, TOBIAS, *The Adventures of Roderick Random*, ed. P. G. Boucé (Oxford, 1981).

The Spectator, ed. D. F. Bond, 5 vols. (Oxford, 1965).

SPENCE, JOSEPH, *Observations, Anecdotes, and Characters of Books and Men*, ed. J. M. Osborn, 2 vols. (Oxford, 1966).

SPENSER, EDMUND, *Works*, ed. John Hughes, 6 vols. (1715).

—— *Poetical Works*, ed. J. C. Smith and E. de Selincourt (1970).

SPINGARN, J. E. (ed.), *Critical Essays of the Seventeenth Century*, 3 vols. (Oxford, 1908).

SPURGEON, CAROLINE F. E. (ed.), *Five Hundred Years of Chaucer Criticism and Allusion (1357–1900)*, 3 vols. (Cambridge, 1925).

STOCKDALE, PERCIVAL, *Lectures on the Truly Eminent English Poets*, 2 vols. (1795).

STONES, GRAEME, and STRACHAN, JOHN (eds.), *Parodies of the Romantic Age*, 5 vols. (1999).

SUCKLING, SIR JOHN, *Works* (1709).

SWIFT, JONATHAN, *Prose Works*, ed. H. Davis *et al.*, 14 vols. (Oxford, 1939–69).

The Tatler, ed. D. F. Bond, 3 vols. (Oxford, 1987).

THOMSON, JAMES, *The Seasons and The Castle of Indolence*, ed. James Sambrook (Oxford, 1972, 1991).

TOLAND, JOHN, *A Collection of Several Pieces*, 2 vols. (1726).

WALLER, EDMUND, *Poetical Works*, ed. Robert Bell (1854).

WARTON, JOSEPH, *An Essay on the Genius and Writings of Pope*, 5th edn., 2 vols. (1806).

WARTON, THOMAS, *Observations on the Faerie Queene of Spenser* (1754).

—— *Observations on the Fairy Queen of Spenser... A New Edition*, 2 vols. (1807).

—— *The History of English Poetry*, 3 vols. (1774–81).

—— *History of English Poetry*, ed. David Fairer (1998).

—— *Correspondence*, ed. David Fairer (Athens, Ga., 1995).

WEEVER, JOHN, *Antient Funeral Monuments, of Great-Britain, Ireland, and the Islands adjacent* (1767).

—— *Epigrammes in the Oldest Cut and Newest Fashion* (1599), ed. R. B. McKerrow (Stratford, 1922).

WELSTED, LEONARD, *Of False Fame. An Epistle to the Right Honourable Earl of Pembroke* (1732).

WILLIAMS, LOAN (ed.), *Novel and Romance 1700–1800: A Documentary Record* (London, 1970).

WILMOT, JOHN, Earl of Rochester, *Poems*, ed. Keith Walker (Oxford, 1984).

WILSON, JOHN, 'On the Revival of a Taste for our Ancient Literature', in *Blackwood's Edinburgh Magazine*, 4 (1818), 264–6.

WINSTANLEY, WILLIAM, *The Lives of the most Famous English Poets, or the Honour of Parnassus* (1687).

WODHULL, MICHAEL, *Ode to the Muses* (1760).

WOMERSLEY, DAVID (ed.), *Augustan Critical Writing* (1997).

WOOD, ANTHONY À, *Athenae Oxonienses* (1691–92).

WOTTON, HENRY, *An Essay on the Education of Children in the First Rudiments of Learning* (1753).

WOTTON, WILLIAM, *Reflections upon Ancient and Modern Learning* (1694).

WORDSWORTH, WILLIAM, *Prose Works*, ed. W. J. B. Owen and Jane Worthington Smyser, 3 vols. (Oxford, 1974).

WORDSWORTH, WILLIAM, and COLERIDGE, SAMUEL TAYLOR, *Lyrical Ballads*, ed. R. L. Brett and A. R. Jones, rev. edn. (1984).

YOUNG, EDWARD, *Poetical Works*, 2 vols. (1896).

—— *Conjectures on Original Composition* (1759) (Scolar Press Facsimile, 1966).

Secondary

ADAMS, ELEANOR N., *Old English Scholarship in England from 1566–1800* (New Haven, 1917).

ALTICK, RICHARD, *The English Common Reader: A Social History of the Mass Reading Public* (Chicago, 1957).

BACKSCHEIDER, PAULA R., *Spectacular Politics: Theatrical Power and Mass Culture in Early Modern England* (Baltimore, 1993).

BALDICK, CHRIS, *The Social Mission of English Criticism: 1848–1932* (Oxford, 1983).

BARASH, CAROL, *English Women's Poetry, 1649–1714: Politics, Community and Linguistic Authority* (Oxford, 1996).

BARTHES, ROLAND, *Essais critiques* (Paris, 1964).

BASKER, JAMES G., 'Scotticisms and the Problem of Cultural Identity in Eighteenth-Century Britain', *Eighteenth-Century Life*, 15 (1991), 81–95.

BATE, W. JACKSON, *The Burden of the Past and the English Poet* (London, 1971).

BAUGH, ALBERT C., and CABLE, THOMAS, *A History of the English Language*, 3rd edn. (1978).

BELANGER, TERRY, 'Publishers and Writers in Eighteenth-Century England', in *Books and their Readers in Eighteenth-Century England*, ed. Isabel Rivers (Leicester, 1982), 5–25.

BENEDICT, BARBARA, *Making the Modern Reader: Cultural Mediation in Early Modern Literary Anthologies* (Princeton, 1996).

BLOOM, HAROLD, *The Anxiety of Influence: A Theory of Poetry* (London, 1973).

—— *The Western Canon: The Books and Schools of the Ages* (London, 1994).

BONNELL, THOMAS F., 'John Bell's *Poets of Great Britain*: The "Little Trifling Edition" Revisited', *Modern Philology*, 85 (1987), 128–52.

—— 'Speaking of Institutions and Canonicity, Don't Forget the Publishers', *Eighteenth-Century Life*, 21:3 (1997), 97–9.

BRAUDY, LEO, *The Frenzy of Renown: Fame & its History* (New York, 1986).

BRETT, R. L., 'The Aesthetic Sense and Taste in the Literary Criticism of the Early Eighteenth Century', *Review of English Studies*, 20 (1944), 199–213.

BREWER, JOHN, *The Pleasures of the Imagination: English Culture in the Eighteenth Century* (London, 1997).

BROWNLEY, MARTINE WATSON, 'Johnson's *Lives of the English Poets* and Earlier Traditions of the Character Sketch in England', in *Johnson and his Age*, ed. James Engell, Harvard English Studies 12 (Cambridge, Mass., 1984), 29–53.

CHANDLER, JAMES, 'The Pope Controversy: Romantic Poetics and the English Canon', *Critical Inquiry*, 10 (1984), 481–509.

COURT, FRANKLIN D., *Institutionalizing English Literature: The Culture and Politics of Literary Study, 1750–1900* (Stanford, Calif., 1992).

CRANE, RONALD S., 'An Early Eighteenth-Century Enthusiast for Primitive Poetry: John Husbands', *Modern Language Notes*, 37 (1922), 27–36.

CRAWFORD, ROBERT, *Devolving English Literature* (Oxford, 1992).

——(ed.), *The Scottish Invention of English Literature* (Cambridge, 1998).

CRESSY, DAVID, 'Literacy in Context: Meaning and Measurement in Early Modern England', in *Consumption and the World of Goods*, ed. John Brewer and Roy Porter (London, 1993), 305–19.

CURRAN, STUART, *Poetic Form and British Romanticism* (New York, 1986).

——'Romantic Poetry: The I Altered', in *Romanticism and Feminism*, ed. Anne K. Mellor (Bloomington, Ind., 1988), 185–207.

DAVIE, DONALD, *A Gathered Church: The Literature of the English Dissenting Interest, 1700–1930* (London, 1978).

DEMARIA, ROBERT, JR, *The Life of Samuel Johnson: A Critical Biography* (Oxford, 1993).

DIX, ROBIN, 'James Thomson and the Progress of the Progress Poem: From *Liberty* to *The Castle of Indolence*', in *James Thomson: Essays for the Tercentenary*, ed. Richard Terry (Liverpool, 2000), 117–39.

DOUGLAS, DAVID C., *English Scholars 1660–1730* (London, 1939).

DUFF, DAVID, *Romance and Revolution: Shelley and the Politics of a Genre* (Cambridge, 1994).

EAGLETON, TERRY, *Literary Theory: An Introduction* (Oxford, 1983).

——*The Function of Criticism: From The Spectator to Post-structuralism* (London, 1984).

——*The Ideology of the Aesthetic* (Oxford, 1990).

EGER, ELIZABETH, 'Fashioning a Female Canon: Eighteenth-Century Women Poets and the Politics of the Anthology', in *Women's Poetry in the Enlightenment: The Making of a Canon, 1730–1820*, ed. Isobel Armstrong and Virginia Blain (London, 1999), 201–15.

ENGELL, JAMES, *Forming the Critical Mind: Dryden to Coleridge* (Cambridge, Mass., 1989).

EZELL, MARGARET J. M., *Writing Women's Literary History* (Baltimore, 1993).

FAIRER, DAVID, 'The Origins of Warton's *History of English Poetry*', *Review of English Studies*, NS 32 (1981), 37–63.

——'Anglo-Saxon Studies', in *The History of the University of Oxford*, general editor T. H. Aston, vol. 5. *The Eighteenth Century*, ed. L. S. Sutherland and L. G. Mitchell (Oxford, 1986), 807–29.

FERGUSON, MOIRA (ed.), *First Feminists: British Women Writers 1578–1799* (Bloomington, Ind., 1985).

—— *Eighteenth-Century Women Poets: Nation, Class, and Gender* (New York, 1995).

FOLKENFLIK, ROBERT, *Samuel Johnson: Biographer* (Ithaca, NY, 1978).

FOXTON, ROSEMARY, 'Delariviere Manley and "Astrea's Vacant Throne"', *Notes and Queries*, NS 33 (1986), 41–2.

FRASER, DONALD, 'Pope and the Idea of Fame', in *Writers and their Background: Alexander Pope*, ed. Peter Dixon (London, 1972), 286–310.

FREEMAN, LISA A., '"A Dialogue": Elizabeth Carter's Passion for the Female Mind', in *Women's Poetry in the Enlightenment: The Making of a Canon*, ed. Isobel Armstrong and Virginia Blain (London, 1999), 50–63.

GORAK, JAN, *The Making of the Modern Canon: Genesis and Crisis of a Literary Idea* (London, 1991).

GORMAN, PETER, *Pythagoras: A Life* (London, 1979).

GREENE, RICHARD, *Mary Leapor: A Study in Eighteenth-Century Women's Poetry* (Oxford, 1993).

GRIFFIN, ROBERT, *Wordsworth's Pope: A Study in Literary Historiography* (Cambridge, 1995).

GRIFFITHS, ERIC, 'Dryden's Past', in *Proceedings of the British Academy* 84: 1993 *Lectures and Memoirs*, 113–49.

GROOM, NICK, 'Celts, Goths, and the Nature of the Literary Source', in *Tradition in Transition: Women Writers, Marginal Texts, and the Eighteenth-Century Canon*, ed. Alvaro Ribiero, SJ, and James G. Basker (Oxford, 1996), 275–96.

—— *The Making of Percy's Reliques* (Oxford, 1999).

GRUNDY, ISOBEL, *Lady Mary Wortley Montagu* (Oxford, 1999).

GUILLORY, JOHN, 'Canonical and Non-Canonical: A Critique of the Current Debate', *English Literary History*, 54 (1987), 494–503.

HABERMAS, JÜRGEN, *The Structural Transformation of the Public Sphere: An Inquiry into a Category of Bourgeois Culture*, trans. Thomas Burger (Oxford, 1989).

HALSBAND, ROBERT, '"The Female Pen": Women and Literature in C18 England', *History Today*, 24 (Oct. 1974), 702–9.

HANS, NICHOLAS, *New Trends in Education in the Eighteenth Century* (London, 1951).

HAVENS, RAYMOND D., 'Thomas Warton and the Eighteenth-Century Dilemma', *Studies in Philology*, 25 (1928), 36–50.

HELGERSON, RICHARD, *Self-Crowned Laureates: Spenser, Jonson, Milton and the Literary System* (Berkeley and Los Angeles, 1983).

HIDDEN, NORMAN, 'Thomas Hayward and "The British Muse"', *English*, 37 (1988), 217–22.

HOBBY, ELAINE, *Virtue of Necessity: English Women's Writing 1649–88* (London, 1988).

HONIGMAN, E. A. J., *Shakespeare: the 'lost years'* (Manchester, 1985).

——*John Weever* (Manchester, 1987).

HOWELL, W. S., *Eighteenth-Century British Logic and Rhetoric* (Princeton, 1971).

JOHNSTON, ARTHUR, *Enchanted Ground: The Study of Medieval Romance in the Eighteenth Century* (London, 1964).

JONES, RICHARD FOSTER, *The Triumph of the English Language: A Survey of Opinions Concerning the Vernacular from the Introduction of Printing to the Restoration* (Oxford, 1953).

——*Ancients and Moderns*, 2nd edn. (St Louis, 1961).

KEAST, WILLIAM R., 'Johnson and "Cibber's" *Lives of the Poets*, 1753', in *Restoration and Eighteenth-Century Literature: Essays in Honour of Alan Dugald McKillop*, ed. Carrol Camden (Chicago, 1963), 89–101.

KELLY, GARY, 'The Limits of Genre and the Institution of Literature: Romanticism between Fact and Fiction', in *Romantic Revelations: Criticism and Theory*, ed. Kenneth R. *Johnston, Gilbert Chaitin, Karen Hanson*, and Herbert Marks (Bloomington, Ind., and Indianapolis, 1990).

KINSLEY, JAMES, and KINSLEY, HELEN (eds.), *John Dryden: The Critical Heritage* (London, 1971).

KENDRICK, T., *The Druids: A Study in Keltic Prehistory* (London, 1927).

KENYON, JOHN, *The History Men: The Historical Profession in England since the Renaissance* (London, 1983).

KERNAN, ALVIN, 'The Idea of Literature', *New Literary History*, 5 (1973), 31–40.

——*Samuel Johnson & the Impact of Print* (Princeton, 1987).

KIELY, ROBERT, *The Romantic Novel in England* (Cambridge, Mass., 1972).

KLIGER, SAMUEL, 'The Neo-classical View of Old English Poetry', *Journal of English and Germanic Philology*, 49 (1950), 516–22.

KRAMNICK, JONATHAN BRODY, 'The Aesthetics of Revisionism, a Response', *Eighteenth Century Life*, 21 (1997), 82–5.

——*Making the English Canon: Print-Capitalism and the Cultural Past, 1700–1770* (Cambridge, 1998).

KUCICH, GREG, *Keats, Shelley, and Romantic Spenserianism* (University Park, Pa., 1991).

LASLETT, PETER, *The World We Have Lost* (London, 1965).

LEAVIS, F. R., *The Great Tradition* (London, 1948).

LEVINE, JOSEPH M., *Humanism and History: Origins of Modern English Historiography* (Ithaca, NY, 1987).

——*The Battle of the Books: History and Literature in the Augustan Age* (Ithaca, NY, 1991).

LOEWENSTEIN, DAVID A., 'Skelton's Triumph: The *Garland of Laurel* and Literary Fame', *Neophilologus*, 68 (1984), 611–22.

LOVEJOY, ARTHUR O., and BOAS, GEORGE, *Primitivism and Related Ideas in Antiquity* (Baltimore, 1935).

LIPKING, LAWRENCE, *The Ordering of the Arts in Eighteenth-Century England* (Princeton, 1970).

——*The Life of the Poet: Beginning and Ending Poetic Careers* (Chicago, 1981).

MCDERMOTT, ANNE, 'Johnson's *Dictionary* and the Canon: Authors and Authority', *Yearbook of English Studies*, 28 (1998), 44–65.

MACDOUGALL, HUGH A., *Racial Myth in English History: Trojans, Teutons, and Anglo-Saxons* (Montreal, 1982).

MCKILLOP, ALAN DUGALD, 'A Critic of 1741 on Early Poetry', *Studies in Philology*, 30 (1933), 504–21.

MCLACHLAN, H., *English Education under the Test Acts: Being the History of the Non-Conformist Academies 1662–1800* (Manchester, 1931).

MCLAVERTY, J., 'Pope and Giles Jacob's *Lives of the Poets: The Dunciad* as Alternative Literary History', *Modern Philology*, 83 (1985), 22–32.

MCMURTRY, JO, *English Language, English Literature: The Creation of an Academic Discipline* (Hamden, Conn., 1985).

MANER, MARTIN, *The Philosophical Biographer: Doubt and Dialectic in Johnson's 'Lives of the Poets'* (Athens, Ga., 1989).

MERMIN, DOROTHY, 'Women Becoming Poets: Katherine Philips, Aphra Behn, Anne Finch', *English Literary History*, 57 (1990), 335–55.

MICHAEL, IAN, *The Teaching of English: From the Sixteenth Century to 1870* (Cambridge, 1987).

MILLER, THOMAS P., *The Formation of College English: Rhetoric and Belles Lettres in the British Cultural Provinces* (Pittsburg, 1997).

MORRIS, DAVID B., *Alexander Pope: The Genius of Sense* (Cambridge, Mass., 1984).

MOSS, ANN, *Printed Commonplace-Books and the Structuring of Renaissance Thought* (Oxford, 1996).

MULVIHILL, MAUREEN E., 'A Feminist Link in the Old Boys' Network: The Cosseting of Katherine Philips', in *Curtain Calls: British and American Women and the Theatre 1660–1820*, ed. Mary Anne Schofield and Cecilia Macheski (Athens, Oh., 1991), 73–104.

MUMBY, F. A., *Publishing and Bookselling: A History from the Earliest Times to the Present Day* (London, 1930).

NEUBERG, VICTOR E., *Popular Education in Eighteenth Century England* (London, 1971).

NEWDIGATE, BERNARD H., *Michael Drayton and his Circle* (Oxford, 1941).

NEWTON, RICHARD C., 'Jonson and the (Re-)Invention of the Book', in *Classic and Cavalier: Essays on Jonson and the Sons of Ben*, ed. Claude J. Summers and Ted-Larry Pebworth (Pittsburgh, 1982), 31–55.

NUSSBAUM, FELICITY, *The Brink of All We Hate: English Satires on Women, 1660–1750* (Lexington, 1984).

O'BRIEN, P., *Warrington Academy 1757–86: Its Predecessors and Successors* (Wigan, 1989).

OSBORN, JAMES MARSHALL, 'Thomas Birch and the *General Dictionary* (1734–41)', *Modern Philology*, 36 (1938), 25–45.

—— 'The First History of English Poetry', in *Pope and his Contemporaries: Essays Presented to George Sherburn*, ed. James L. Clifford and Louis A. Landa (Oxford, 1949), 230–50.

—— 'Joseph Spence's "Collections Relating to The Lives of the Poets"', *Harvard Library Bulletin*, 16 (1968), 129–38.

OWEN, A. L., *The Famous Druids* (Oxford, 1962).

PAGE, EUGENE R., *George Colman the Elder: Essayist, Dramatist and Theatrical Manager 1732–1794* (New York, 1935).

PALMER, D. J., *The Rise of English Studies: An Account of the Study of English Language and Literature from its Origins to the Making of the Oxford English School* (Oxford, 1965).

PARKER, IRENE, *Dissenting Academies in England: Their Rise and Progress and their Place among the Education Systems of the Country* (New York, 1969).

PARKER, WILLIAM R., 'Winstanley's *Lives*: An Appraisal', *Modern Language Quarterly*, 6 (1945), 313–18.

PARRY, GRAHAM, *The Trophies of Time: English Antiquarians of the Seventeenth Century* (Oxford, 1995).

PATEY, DOUGLAS LANE, 'The Eighteenth Century Invents the Canon', *Modern Language Studies*, 18 (1988), 17–37.

—— 'The institution of criticism in the eighteenth century', in *The Cambridge History of Literary Criticism*, vol. 4. *The Eighteenth Century*, ed. H. B. Nisbet and Claude Rawson (Cambridge, 1997), 3–31.

PEARSON, JACQUELINE, *The Prostituted Muse: Images of Women Dramatists 1642–1737* (New York, 1988).

PERRY, RUTH, 'George Ballard's Biographies of Learned Ladies', in *Biography in the 18th Century*, ed. J. D. Browning (New York, 1980), 85–111.

PHILLIPSON, NICHOLAS, 'Politics, Politeness and the Anglicization of Early Eighteenth-Century Scottish Culture', in *Scotland and England 1286–1815*, ed. R. A. Mason (Edinburgh, 1987), 226–47.

PIGGOTT, STUART, *The Druids* (London, 1968).

—— *William Stukeley: An Eighteenth-Century Antiquary* (London, 1950, 1985).

PITTOCK, JOAN, *The Ascendancy of Taste: The Achievement of Joseph and Thomas Warton* (London, 1973).

PLANT, MARJORIE, *The English Book Trade: An Economic History of the Making and Sale of Books* (London, 1939).

POTTER, STEPHEN, *The Muse in Chains: A Study in Education* (London, 1937).

RICHETTI, JOHN, *Popular Fiction Before Richardson: Narrative Patterns 1700–1739* (Oxford, 1969).

RICKS, CHRISTOPHER, 'Allusion: The Poet as Heir', in *Studies in the Eighteenth Century III*, ed. R. F. Brissenden and J. C. Eade (Canberra, 1976), 209–40.

RIGG, A. G., *A History of Anglo-Latin Literature 1066–1422* (Cambridge, 1992).

RIGGS, DAVID, *Ben Jonson: A Life* (Cambridge, Mass., 1989).

RIVERS, ISABEL (ed.), *Books and Their Readers in Eighteenth-Century England* (Leicester, 1982).

ROGERS, PAT, 'Johnson's *Lives of the Poets* and the Biographic Dictionaries', *Review of English Studies*, NS 31 (1980), 149–71.

—— 'Classics and Chapbooks', in *Books and their Readers in Eighteenth-Century England*, ed. Isabel Rivers (Leicester, 1982), 27–45.

—— 'Thomas Warton and the Waxing of the Middle Ages', in *Medieval Literature and Antiquities: Studies in Honour of Basil Cottle*, ed. Myra Stokes and T. L. Burton (Cambridge, 1987), 175–86.

—— 'Boswell and the Scotticism', in *New Light on Boswell: Critical and Historical Essays on the Occasion of the Centenary of 'The Life of Johnson'*, ed. Greg Clingham (Cambridge, 1991), 56–71.

ROSS, MARLON B., *The Contours of Masculine Desire: Romanticism and Women's Poetry* (New York, 1989).

ROSS, TREVOR, 'Just When *Did* "British bards begin t'Immortalize"?', *Studies in Eighteenth-Century Culture*, 19 (1989), 383–98.

ROSS, TREVOR, 'Copyright and the Invention of Tradition', *Eighteenth-Century Studies*, 26 (1992), 1–27.

—— *The Making of the English Literary Canon: From the Middle Ages to the Late Eighteenth Century* (Montreal and Kingston, 1998).

RUNGE, LAURA L., *Gender and Language in British Literary Criticism 1660–1790* (Cambridge, 1997).

SANDERS, ANDREW, *The Short Oxford History of English Literature* (Oxford, 1994).

SAVILE, ANTHONY, *The Test of Time: An Essay in Philosophical Aesthetics* (Oxford, 1982).

SCHEFFER, JOHN D., 'The Idea of Decline in Literature and the Fine Arts in Eighteenth-Century England', *Modern Philology*, 34 (1936), 155–78.

SCHOFIELD, R. S., 'The Measurement of Literacy in Pre-Industrial England', in *Literacy in Traditional Societies*, ed. Jack Goody (Cambridge, 1968), 311–25.

SCHOFIELD, ROBERT E., *The Enlightenment of Joseph Priestley: A Study of his Life and Work from 1733 to 1773* (University Park, Pa., 1997).

SHATTOCK, JOANNE (ed.), *The Oxford Guide to British Women Writers* (Oxford, 1993).

SHILS, EDWARD, *Tradition* (Chicago, 1981).

SKINNER, QUENTIN, 'The Idea of a Cultural Lexicon', *Essays in Criticism*, 29 (1979), 205–24.

SPADAFORA, DAVID, *The Idea of Progress in Eighteenth-Century Britain* (New Haven, 1990).

SPUFFORD, MARGARET, *Small Books and Pleasant Histories: Popular Fiction and its Readership in Seventeenth-Century England* (London, 1981).

STALLYBRASS, PETER, and WHITE, ALLON, *The Politics and Poetics of Transgression* (London, 1986).

STAUFFER, DONALD A., *The Art of Biography in Eighteenth-Century England* (Princeton, 1941).

TERRY, RICHARD, '"Ill Effects from good": The Rhetoric of Augustan Mockery (with illustrations from Pope and Fielding)', *British Journal for Eighteenth-Century Studies*, 17 (1994), 125–37.

—— 'The Eighteenth-Century Invention of English Literature: A Truism Revisited', *British Journal for Eighteenth-Century Studies*, 19 (1996), 47–62.

—— 'Literature, Aesthetics and Canonicity in the Eighteenth Century', *Eighteenth-Century Life*, 21 (Feb. 1997), 80–101 [also 21 (Nov. 1997), 79–99].

TODD, JANET (ed.), *A Dictionary of British and American Women Writers 1660–1800* (London, 1984).

TOMPSON, RICHARD S., *Classics or Charity? The Dilemma of the Eighteenth Century Grammar School* (Manchester, 1971).

TREVOR-ROPER, HUGH, 'The Invention of Tradition: The Highland Tradition of Scotland', in *The Invention of Tradition*, ed. E. J. Hobsbawm and Terence Ranger (New York, 1983), 15–41.

TROWBRIDGE, HOYT, 'Joseph Warton's Classification of English Poets', *Modern Language Notes*, 51 (1936), 515–18.

VINCENT, DAVID, *Literacy and Popular Culture: England 1750–1914* (Cambridge, 1989).

WASSERMAN, EARL REEVES, 'The Scholarly Origin of the Elizabethan Revival', *English Literary History*, 4 (1937), 213–43.

—— *Elizabethan Poetry in the Eighteenth Century* (Urbana, Ill., 1947).

WATSON, RICHARD FOSTER, *The Beginnings of the Teaching of Modern Subjects in England* (1908; East Ardsley, 1971).

WEEDON, MARGARET, 'Jane Austen and William Enfield's *The Speaker*', *British Journal for Eighteenth-Century Studies*, 11 (1988), 159–62.

WEINBROT, HOWARD D., *Britannia's Issue: The Rise of British Literature from Dryden to Ossian* (Cambridge, 1993).

—— 'Samuel Johnson, Percival Stockdale, and Brick-bats from Grubstreet: Some Later Response to the *Lives of the Poets*', *Huntington Library Quarterly*, 56 (1993), 105–34.

WELLEK, RENÉ, *The Rise of English Literary History* (Chapel Hill, NC, 1941).

—— 'What is Literature?', in *What is Literature?*, ed. Paul Hernadi (Bloomington, Ind., 1978), 16–23.

—— 'Literature and its Cognates', in *Dictionary of the History of Ideas: Studies of Selected Pivotal Ideas*, ed. Philip P. Wiener, 4 vols. (New York, 1973), 3: 81–9.

WHEELER, DAVID, ' "So Easy to be Lost": Poet and Self in Pope's *The Temple of Fame*', *Papers on Language and Literature*, 29 (1993), 3–27.

WHITNEY, LOIS, 'English Primitivistic Theories of Epic Origins', *Modern Philology*, 21 (1924), 337–78.

—— *Primitivism and the Idea of Progress in English Popular Literature of the Eighteenth Century* (Baltimore, 1934).

WILES, R. M., 'Middle-Class Literacy in Eighteenth-Century England: Fresh Evidence', in *Studies in the Eighteenth Century I*, ed. R. F. Brissenden (Canberra, 1968), 49–65.

WILLIAMS, RAYMOND, *Marxism and Literature* (Oxford, 1977).

—— *Keywords: A Vocabulary of Culture and Society*, rev. edn. (London, 1983).

WILLIAMSON, MARILYN, *Raising their Voices: British Women Writers 1650–1750* (Detroit, 1990).

WINN, JAMES ANDERSON, *John Dryden and His World* (New Haven, 1987).

WOODMANSEE, MARTHA, 'On the Author Effect: Recovering Collectivity', in *The Construction of Authorship: Textual Appropriation in Law and Literature*, ed. Martha Woodmansee and Peter Jaszi (Durham, NC, 1994), 15–28.

WOOLF, VIRGINIA, *A Room of One's Own* (London, 1946).

ZIMANSKY, CURT A., 'Chaucer and the School of Provence: A Problem in Eighteenth Century Literary History', *Philological Quarterly*, 25 (1946), 321–42.

Index

Addison, Joseph 15, 44, 53, 163, 167, 185, 187, 193, 204–6, 226, 270, 284; 'Account of the Greatest English Poets' 50–1, 60–1, 71, 119–20, 123, 148, 288–92, 323; on Spenser 288–92; *Spectator* 13, 25, 61, 71–2, 175–6, 186, 197, 205, 242, 290–1
Ælfric 112
aesthetics 13, 22, 136, 171, 206, 211–15
Aeschylus 101, 165
ahistoricism 304–7
Aikin, John 191–2, 195
Akenside, Mark 102, 192, 230, 242, 292, 307; 'The Balance of the Poets' 304–5; *The Pleasures of Imagination* 57, 315
Alexander, Sir William 49
Alfrike, Bishop 112
allusion 302–3
Altick, Richard 172
ancients v. moderns 97–102, 136
Anderson, Robert: *Works of the British Poets* 241, 245–6, 252
Anglicization of Scottish culture 197–202
Anglo-Latin literary inheritance 108–11
Anglo-Saxon literary inheritance 94, 108–18, 297
anthologies 219–26; principles of selection in 223–6
Ariosto 309
Aristophanes 65
Arthur, King 140
Art of Knowing Women, The 270
Ashfield, Andrew 253
Astell, Mary 267
atavism 96
Athenaeus 125
Aubrey, John 233–4
Augustus, Emperor 55
Austen, Jane 142

Bacon, Francis 76, 192, 195
Bailey, Nathan 23
Bale, John 83, 111
ballads 174–5
Ballard, George: *Memoirs of Several Ladies* 265–7, 273, 276, 282
Barbauld, Anne 258
Barber, Mary 273–4
Barthes, Roland 11–12
Basse, William 87
Bate, W. J. 150
battle of the books 97–102, 136
Baumgarten, Alexander: *Aesthetica* 13, 206, 214
Bayle, Pierre 231; *Dictionnaire historique et critique* 232
Beattie, James 29, 199
Beaumont, Francis 18, 37, 38, 48–9, 51–2, 79, 227
Beaumont, Sir John 49, 88
Bede 110, 115–16
Behn, Aphra 78, 254, 258, 260–3, 269, 273–4, 277–8; canonization of 280–5
belles lettres 22–7, 191–2, 202–3
Bell, John: *Poets of Great Britain* 217–19, 252
Bentley, Richard 115, 308
Beowulf 114–15
Berners, Juliana 262, 266–7
Betterton, Thomas 48
Bible, the 176
Biographia Britannica (1747–66) 84, 226, 230–1, 261–4, 267, 276, 281
Biographia Britannica (1778–) 226, 230, 262, 265, 267
Birch, Thomas 230; *General Dictionary* 226, 228–32, 261–2, 292
Blackmore, Sir Richard 59, 151, 182, 216, 227–8, 244, 246
Blackwall, Anthony 181
Blackwell, Thomas 301
Blackwood's Edinburgh Magazine 286

Blair, Hugh 199; *Lectures on Rhetoric and Belles Lettres* 202–4, 208–9
Bloom, Harold 150, 167; *The Western Canon* 36; *see also* influence
Blount, Sir Thomas Pope: *Censura Celebriorum Authorum* 76; *De Re Poetica* 59, 76, 229, 279
Boccacio 103
Bodenham, John 221
Bonnell, Thomas 217
books, availability of 171–2
Boothby, Frances 260
Boswell, James 198–200, 216, 218, 234, 238, 249
Bouhours, Dominique 23, 206
Bowles, Thomas 176
Brewer, John 169
British Poets, The 220
Brome, Richard 145
Brooke, Frances 268
Brown, John: *History of the Rise and Progress of Poetry* 130–1, 135
Browne, William 49
Browning, Elizabeth Barrett 146
Buchanan, John 185
Bunyan, John 51
Burke, Edmund 200; 'Of Taste' 208–10
Burney, Frances 142
Burton, Robert 162
Butler, Samuel 42, 193, 227
Byron, George Gordon, Baron 91, 322
Bysshe, Edward: *Art of English Poesy* 180, 221–2

Caedmon 108, 110, 114–17, 141
Caesar, Augustus 154
Caesar, Julius 125; *Battle for Gaul* 126, 129–31, 133, 161
Camden, William: *Britannia* 108, 110, 124; *Remains Concerning Britain* 108–11, 118, 128–9
Campbell, John 230; *Polite Correspondence* 116–17, 139–41
'canon' 35–36
Carew, Richard 101–2; *The Excellency of the English Tongue* 96, 118, 122
Carew, Thomas 128, 245
Carter, Elizabeth 255–6, 258, 268, 273
Cary, Elizabeth 78, 257, 260
Catiline 235
Cato 161
Catullus 96, 101

Cavendish, Margaret, Duchess of Newcastle 78, 260, 262–5, 266, 273–4, 276
Celtic culture 125–6
Centlivre, Susanna 254, 258, 262, 269, 282, 284
Chalmers, Alexander 252
Chandler, Mary 259, 261, 265
chapbooks 174–7
Chapone, Hester 268
Charles II 154
Charlett, Arthur 115
Charlotte, Queen 249
Chatterton, Thomas 246, 312
Chaucer 12, 36–7, 42–3, 45–6, 48–53, 56, 60, 76, 78, 89, 96–8, 103–08, 123, 130, 143, 154–7, 162, 165–6, 205, 216, 218, 227, 247, 258, 312, 322–3; designer of the 'English tongue' 58–9, 119–20; difficulty of his language 62, 71, 94; first English poet or 'father' of English poetry 93, 108, 145, 147; in Poets' Corner 38, 153; unreadable because of linguistic change 71; *House of Fame* 68; *Knight's Tale* 321
chivalry 296–300
Chudleigh, Lady Mary 258–9, 262, 266, 273, 276
Churchill, Charles 148, 218
Churchyard, Thomas 48–9, 89
Cibber, Colley 101
Cibber, Theophilus 90, 228, 231, 261, 263, 265, 276, 284; *see also* Shiels, Robert
Cicero 181
circulating libraries 171–2
Clare, John 177
Clarendon, Edward Hyde, Earl of 16
'classic' 35–6
classical literary inheritance 95–102, 287
classicism 286–323
classics, role of in English education 100, 182–4
Cleveland, John 44, 76
Cobb, Samuel: *A Discourse on Criticism* 32; 'Of Poetry: Its Progress' 51–2, 93, 101
Collection of the English Poets, A 220

Collins, William 36; 'Epistle to Thomas Hanmer' 51, 53–4, 57, 94, 104, 138, 245
Colman, George, the elder 17
Colman, George, the younger, and Thornton, Bonnell: *Poems by Eminent Ladies* 272–4, 276
Comenius, Johann 184
Congreve, William 147–8, 163, 166, 222
Connoisseur, The 267, 273
Conrad, Joseph 142
Cooke, Thomas: *Pythagoras* 101, 165–6
Cooper, Elizabeth: *The Muses Library* 89, 228, 238, 256
Cooper, John Gilbert 207
Corneille, Pierre 283
Cornwall, Michael of 108
Cotgrave, John 221
Cotton, Sir Robert 114
Cowley, Abraham 39, 44, 48, 50–1, 53, 72–3, 123, 182, 222, 227, 257–8, 273, 277–8; death and burial 37–8, 153–4, 164–5; 'On the Praise of Poetry' 70–71
Cowper, William 193
Crashaw, Richard 44, 76
Crawford, Robert 204
Creech, Thomas 273
Critical Review 255
criticism 31–3, 92
Croxall, Samuel 145, 227–8

'dame' schools 178–9
Daniel, Samuel 49, 76, 96
Dante Alghieri 42, 69, 76
Darwin, Erasmus 193
Davenant, Sir William 43; 'Preface' to Gondibert 32, 71, 74
Davis, Norman 106–7
Davys, Mary 261
Day, John 112
Defoe, Daniel 15, 76, 100, 143, 151, 175
Denham, Sir John 40, 44, 50–1, 53, 58–61, 119, 123, 146, 229, 245, 257; 'Cooper's Hill' 117, 224; 'On Mr. Abraham Cowley' 37, 47, 93, 97, 153–4, 164–5
Dennis, John 24–5, 47; 'the celebrated English Poets Deceas'd' 41; *The Grounds of Criticism in Poetry* 32,

41; *The Impartial Critic* 73; *The Usefulness of the Stage* 93
De Piles, Roger 304
Dickens, Charles 142
Dilly, Edward 217–18
Diodorus Siculus 125–6
Diogenes Laertius 158
dissenting academies 183, 189–96
Doddridge, Philip 191, 195
Dodsley, Robert: *Collection* 255–6, 267; *The Museum* 304
Donne, John 42–4, 62, 218
Don Quixote 297
Dorset, Earl of 39, 244
Douglas, Gavin 88–9, 312
Drayton, Michael 38–9, 43, 76, 123; *Poly-Olbion* 127; 'To Henry Reynolds' 48–50, 58
'Dream of the Rood' 115
Druidical origins of English literature 124–33
Druids 45, 53, 94, 313–15; as verse-makers 126–33, 140
Drummond of Hawthornden 49
Dryden, Charles 147
Dryden, John 18, 32–3, 40, 42, 44, 46–8, 50, 52–4, 59–62, 78, 97, 101, 104, 181, 222, 238, 246, 257, 273, 290, 321–3; as improver of the language 58, 119–20, 123–4; in Poets' Corner 39; and tradition 142–68; and transmigration 159–64; *Absalom and Achitophel* 152; *Æneis* 159–60; *Don Sebastian* 28; *Fables Ancient and Modern* 60, 152, 154, 159, 163, 176; *Mac Flecknoe* 151–3, 160, 224; *Of Dramatic Poesy* 41, 79–80; *The State of Innocence* 31; 'To Godfrey Kneller' 57; 'To my Dear Friend Mr Congreve' 147–8; 'To the Pious Memory of Mrs Anne Killigrew' 154, 161–2, 277, 279; *Troilus and Cressida* 32; 'Upon the Death of Lord Hastings' 160–1
Dryden Jr, John 147
Duck, Stephen 176
Duff, William 136
Duke, Richard 245
Dunbar, William 312

Duncombe, John 267; 'The Feminiad' 267–72, 274–6, 278, 282, 284
Dyce, Alexander: *Specimens of British Poetesses* 252–3
Dyer, John 245

Eagleton, Terry: *Ideology of the Aesthetic* 22, 213–14; *Literary Theory* 12, 17, 20, 21
educational 'realism' 184–9
Eger, Elizabeth 253
elementary schools 170, 178–9, 188
Eliot, George 142
Eliot, T. S. 142
Elizabeth I 42, 95, 266
elocution 170, 192–4, 198–200, 211
Elstob, Elizabeth 266, 271; *English-Saxon Grammar* 116, 122–3, 257–8; *English-Saxon Homily* 258
Enfield, William 214; 'An Essay on the Cultivation of Taste' 212; *Exercises in Elocution* 191, 193–4, 213; *The Speaker* 18, 191, 193–4, 213
Engell, James 20
English Poets, The 220
Ennius 60, 97–8, 145, 160, 165, 315
Euphorbus 160, 162
Euripides 81
Eusden, Laurence 151, 246
Exeter, Joseph of 77–8, 108

Fairfax, Edward 43, 60, 147, 156
fame 65–75, 227, 230, 248, 251
fancy *see* wit
Fawkes, Francis see Woty, William
Felton, Henry: *Dissertation on Reading the Classics* 99
female canon, making of 252–85
Female Wits, The 254–5
Fenton, Elijah: 'An Epistle to Mr. Southerne' 36, 51–3, 56–7, 129, 227
Ferguson, Adam 197
Ferrar, Martha 268
feudalism 296–7, 300, 318
fiction 30–1
Field, Nathan 145
Fielding, Henry: *Covent-Garden Journal* 18; *Joseph Andrews* 28; *Tom Jones* 175
Fielding, Sarah 275; *Adventures of David Simple* 39–40

filiation, as a metaphor of tradition 145–56
Finch, Anne, Countess of Winchilsea 123, 257–9, 266, 268, 273, 281; 'The Circuit of Apollo' 281
Fitz-Geffry, Charles 157
Flecknoe, Richard 151
Fletcher, John 37, 48, 50–2, 62, 79, 128, 150, 153, 227
Flower-Piece, The 255
Flowers of Parnassus, The 255
Fontenelle, Bernard le Bovier 98, 100
Fowke , Martha 261
Foxe, John 69
Franklin, Benjamin: *Idea of a New School* 186–7
Freemantle, Bridget 176
Fuller, Thomas 249; *Abel Redevivus* 67, 82–3; *History of the Worthies* 75, 78–80, 82–5, 226

Garth, Samuel 47, 53, 182
Gascoigne, George 49
Gay, John 47, 167, 227–8
'Genesis' 115
Gentleman's Magazine, The 241, 243, 255
George III 249
Gerard, Alexander: *Essay on Taste* 137, 195, 208, 210
Gibbon, Edward: *An Essay on the Study of Literature* 16, 19; *Memoirs* 16, 19
Gibbons, Thomas: *Rhetoric* 181–82
Gibson, Edmund 112, 114–15
Gildas 140
Gildon, Charles; *The Complete Art of Poetry* 222; 'For the Modern Poets' 98; *Lives and Characters of the English Dramatick Poets* 81
Gloucester, Robert of 77, 108, 131
Goldsmith, Oliver 245; *The Beauties of English Poesy* 223–4, 257; *The Deserted Village* 178; *Poems for Young Ladies* 257
goths, gothic age, gothicism 55–7, 286–323
Gower, John 37, 44, 48–9, 76, 97, 105, 107–08, 123, 312
grammar schools 178–9, 182–3, 188, 189–90
Granger, James 262

Granville, George, Baron
    Lansdowne 53, 167, 247
Graves, Richard 266, 282
Gray, Lady Jane 260, 266
Gray, Thomas 42, 57, 91, 107, 124–5,
    133, 192–3, 193, 243, 245–6, 323;
    Common-Place Book 42–3, 105,
    131; draft-plan of English
    poetry 43–4, 47, 131; 'Elegy' 224;
    'Letter to Warton 15
    April 1770' 326–7; 'Progress of
    Poesy' 51, 54, 94, 139, 321
Greene, Edward Burnaby 102
Greene, Robert 35
Greenwood, James: The Virgin
    Muse 188, 257–58
Grierson, Constantia 261, 266, 273–4
Griffin, Robert 322
Griffiths, Eric 124
Griffiths, R. 228
Grub-Street Journal 174
Guardian, The 187
Guillory, John 204

Halifax, Marquess of 244–5
Hammond, James 102, 242
Hardwick's Marriage Act 172
Hardy, J. P. 226
Harrington, James 60
Hartlib, Samuel 184
Hauville, John of 108
Hawkins, Sir John 244
Haxby, Stephen 157
Hayley, William 276
Hayward, Thomas 249; The British
    Muse 220–3, 248, 257
Henly, J. 117
Henry I 107
Herrick, Robert 70
Hertford, Countess of 268
Hickes, George 112, 116, 124, 131;
    Thesaurus 113–15
Highmore, Susanna 268
Hill, Aaron 246
Hippocrates 162
historicism 303; see also ahistoricism
Hobbes, Thomas 32
Hobby, Elaine 283
Hoccleve, Thomas 44, 89, 103
Homer 28, 81, 95, 97, 101, 115, 117,
    141, 145–7, 160, 165–6, 175, 187,
    271, 299, 304–5, 312, 315
Horace 53, 60, 69, 97, 150, 165, 187

Huet, Pierre Daniel 134
Hughes, John: Works
    of . . . Spenser 291–2, 296,
    301, 309
Hume, David 185, 199
Hurd, Richard 42; Discourse on
    Poetical Imitation 248; Letters on
    Chivalry and Romance 57, 295–7,
    299–302, 310, 318
Husbands, John 138–41
Hutcheson, Francis 206; Inquiry
    into . . . Beauty and Virtue 13

Iamblichus 158
influence, anxiety of 150, 167–8
invention 30–1
Irwin, Countess 268

Jacob, Giles: Poetical Register 15, 73,
    227–8, 230, 238, 263
James I
James II 149
Jerningham, Edward 242
Jervais, John 316
Jervas, Charles 297
Job 135, 315
Johnson, Ralph 181
Johnson, Samuel 16–17, 173, 185, 199,
    267, 303; and anecdotes 234–7,
    243–4; Adventurer 255;
    Dictionary 15, 29, 30, 118–21,
    143; Idler 33, 40, 62, 137; 'Life of
    Addison' 234; 'Life of Butler' 232;
    'Life of Cowley' 239–40; 'Life of
    Dorset' 236; 'Life of Dryden' 60,
    81; 'Life of Gray' 238; 'Life of
    Milton' 15, 81; 'Life of Otway'
    236–7; 'Life of Pope' 29–30, 73,
    238–9, 248; 'Life of Roscommon'
    233; 'Life of Swift' 235; 'Life of
    Thomson' 235; 'Life of Waller'
    242; Lives 36, 77, 82, 90, 216–51;
    'London' 224; 'Preface to
    Shakespeare' 306–7; Rambler 33,
    75, 242; Rasselas 137; Works of
    the English Poets 248, 250, 252
Jones, Mary 258, 273
Jonson, Ben 18, 36, 39, 40, 48–9,
    51–2, 62, 76, 78–9, 80, 87,
    123, 150, 153, 157, 205, 227,
    238, 278, 303; as literary
    father-figure 145–6; in
    Poets' Corner 38–9; on

Jonson, Ben (*cont.*)
  Shakespeare 47, 70, 80; *The Golden Age Restor'd* 37; *Workes* 63–5
Joscelyn, John 111
Journal from Parnassus 48, 281
'Judith' 114
Junius, Francis 114
Juvenal 102, 163

Kames, Lord 195
Kant, Immanuel 209
Keepe, Henry 93
Kelly, Gary 20
Kennet, Basil 24
Kernan, Alvin 12, 17, 20, 21
Kibworth Academy 191, 195
Killigrew, Anne 154, 161–2, 258–9, 266, 273–4, 276–7, 282, 284
King, Edward 127
King, William 47, 236, 245
Kippis, Andrew 262, 265, 266
Knox, Vicesimus 249; *Elegant Extracts* 188, 225, 258–9; *Essays, Moral and Literary* 244–5, 247–8, 251, 287, 311–12, 323
Kyd, Thomas 37

Lady's Poetical Magazine, The 267
Langbaine, Gerard: *Account of the English Dramatick Poets* 77–8, 80–2, 87, 154, 228–30, 238, 240, 260, 263, 278–80; *New Catalogue of English Plays* 78
Langland, William: *Piers Plowman* 45, 103, 105
Laslett, Peter 172
Leapor, Mary 176, 258–9, 268
Leavis, F. R. 142
Lee, Nathaniel 51, 222
Leedes Intelligencer 172
Leland, John 83, 109, 111
Lennox, Charlotte 256, 275
Levine, Joseph 100
liberty, its effect on the progress of poetry 54–6
linguistic improvement 58–61, 118–22
Linus 96, 135
Lipking, Lawrence 36, 219
literacy level 171–4
literary history as a mortuary discourse 87, 89–91
literary 'school' 43

literary tradition 142–68
literature 11–34; as a word 14–22, 206
Livius Andronicus 96
Locke, John 187
Lockman, John 261
Longinus 206
Lonsdale, Roger 254
Lucretius 151–52
Lydgate, John 37, 42–4, 49, 89, 97, 103, 107, 123, 143, 312
Lyttelton, George, Baron 242

McKerrow, R. B. 88
McLaverty, James 227
Madan, Judith 268, 273; 'The Progress of Poesy' 51, 53, 55
Mallet (Malloch), David 200
Mandeville, Bernard de 174
Manley, Delarivier 254, 260, 269, 276, 280, 282, 284
Map, Walter 42, 103, 108
Marlowe, Christopher 37, 49, 96, 158
Mary Tudor 266
Marvell, Andrew 38, 47
masculinity as a criterion of good writing 277
Mason, William 42, 187
Masters, Mary 258, 273
May, Tom 38
medieval era 56–7, 315, 317
Meres, Francis 101–2, 288; *Palladis Tamia* 36, 88, 96, 162
Merlin 103, 132, 134
Mermin, Dorothy 253
metempsychosis see transmigration of souls
Michael, Ian 182, 188
Milton, John 17, 38, 42, 50–1, 53–4, 61–2, 70, 72, 99, 101, 147, 150, 156, 165–6, 176, 181–2, 187, 192, 218, 222, 227, 228, 245–6, 296, 299, 305, 312, 320–3; 'Comus' 321–2; 'Il Penseroso' 224, 322; 'L'Allegro' 224; 'Lycidas' 127; 'Of Education' 184, 190; *Paradise Lost* 224, 240, 259, 307; 'To Manso' 128
Minim, Dick 40
minor poets 247–9
Mirror for Magistrates 45, 105
Monboddo, Lord 29
Monck, Mary 259, 273, 276

Monmouth, Geoffrey of 108–9, 134
monosyllables 122–4, 257
Montagu, Elizabeth 275
Montagu, Lady Mary Wortley 258–9, 273, 279
Monthly Review 241
Moses 135, 315
Motteux, Peter 147
Mulvihill, Mary 283
Musaeus 135
Muses Mercury 119

Nashe, Thomas 49–50
Neckam, Alexander 108–9
Newbolt report 169
Newcastle, Duchess of *see* Cavendish, Margaret
Newcastle, Duke of 165, 263–4
Newcastle upon Tyne 211; Literary and Philosophical Society 211–13
New College, Oxford 316
Nichols, John 216
Numa Pompilius 161

Ogilby, John 151
Oldham, John 48, 51
Oldys, Alexander 47
Oldys, William 220–3, 230, 248–9, 256
Ormond, Duke of 152
Orpheus 96, 135
Orrery, Earl of 236, 278, 280, 283
Osborn, James 44–6, 229
Otway, Thomas 51–2, 222, 227, 236–7
Overbury, Sir Thomas 78
Ovid 96–97, 146, 154–5, 181; *Metamorphoses* 158–9, 163–4
Owl and the Nightingale 114

Parker, Matthew 111, 113
Parnell, Thomas 47
Patey, Douglas Lane 12, 17, 21–22, 36, 204, 206
Peachum, Henry 145
Pembroke, Countess of 79, 260, 261, 266
Pennington, Elizabeth 258, 268
Percy, Thomas: *Reliques of Ancient English Poetry* 297–9, 301–02
Perry, Ruth 266
Persius 160, 163
Petrarch 42, 76, 103, 105
Philips, Ambrose 166, 227–8, 245

Philips, Katherine 76, 79, 154, 162, 257, 260–2, 266, 268, 273–4, 278; canonization of 278–85
Philips, John 47, 187
Phillips, Edward 81; *Theatrum Poetarum* 75, 77–9, 81, 83, 85–6, 109–10, 226, 238, 240, 248, 251, 260, 262–3, 265, 280
Phillips, Teresia 269, 282, 284
Pilkington, Laetitia 258, 261, 269, 273–4, 282
Pindar 97, 101, 116, 141
Pindar, Peter *see* Wolcot, John
Pix, Mary 254, 280
Plato 165
Plautus 65, 81, 97, 166
Poetical Miscellany 257
poet laureateship 69, 149
'poetry', 'poesy' 27–30
Poets' Corner 37–9
politeness, polite learning 24–5
Pomfret, John 216, 246
Poole, Joshua: *The English Parnassus* 180, 221
Pope, Alexander 12, 18, 40, 44, 47, 53, 62, 69, 72–3, 91, 102–3, 107, 141, 148, 175–6, 182, 185, 187, 192–3, 227, 237, 242, 245–6, 273, 279, 290, 305, 312, 320–3; 'discourse on the rise and progress of English poetry' 41–3, 324–5; *Dunciad* 71–2, 151, 153, 155, 164, 228; 'Eloisa to Abelard' 322; *Epistle to Arbuthnot* 269–70; *Epistle to Augustus* 306; *Essay on Criticism* 32–3, 71, 207, 306; *Odyssey* 5; *Peri Bathous* 151; *Rape of the Lock* 224, 240, 271; *Temple of Fame* 104; *Windsor Forest* 117
Porphyry 158
Posidonius 125
Potter, Robert 241–3
Price, Sir John 140
Priestley, Joseph 27, 191; *A Course of Lectures on Oratory and Criticism* 195; *An Essay on...Liberal Education* 190; *Rudiments of English Grammar* 27, 185, 194, 203, 210
primitivism, ideas of 134–41
Prior, Matthew 44, 47, 53, 123, 166, 181–2, 192–3, 202, 227

progress-of-poesy poems 51–7, 130
Provençal origins of English
    literature 103–7
Provence 42–3, 45, 56
Puttenham, George 36, 288; *Arte of
    English Poesie* 28, 37, 95, 122,
    145
Pythagoras 158–60, 165; *see also*
    transmigration of souls

Quarles, Francis 78, 182

Rabelais 76
Radcliffe, Lord 150
Ralph, James 292
Ramsay, Allan 202
Randolph, Thomas 145–6
Rapin, René 22, 23, 24
Rawlins, Thomas 265
Reeve, Clara 193
relativism of critical judgements 292,
    294, 309–10, 318, 320
Revelations 69
Reynolds, Sir Joshua 316–19
rhetorical handbooks 180–2
Richard the Hermit 77
Richardson, Jonathan 309
Richardson, Samuel 142, 267
Richelieu, Cardinal 23
Ricks, Christopher 146, 149
Robertson, William 199
Rochester, Earl of 47–8, 76, 245,
    282
Rogers, Pat 226, 230–1
Rollin, Charles 23; *Method of Teaching
    and Studying the Belles
    Lettres* 208, 210
Roman de la Rose 324
romance, medieval 295–302; origins
    of 297–8
Romanticism 11, 288
Roscommon, Earl of 50–1, 181, 245,
    247, 273
Ross, Trevor: *The Making of the English
    Literary Canon* 214–15
Rowe, Elizabeth 258, 261–2, 268, 273,
    276; *Friendship in Death* 284
Rowe, Nicholas 53
Royal Society 184
Rymer, Thomas 33, 106–7, 134, 207; *A
    Short View of Tragedy* 23, 98,
    103–4, 124; *Tragedies of the Last
    Age* 31, 41

Sallust 235
Sappho 53, 162, 278–80
Saxon origins of English language
    118–24
Scott, John 245
Scott, Mary: *The Female
    Advocate* 275–6
Scotticisms 199–200, 204
Scottish invention of English
    literature 196, 204–6
Scottish universities 196–206
'Seafarer, The' 115
Sedley, Sir Charles 245
Seneca 161
Settle, Elkanah 151, 155
Seward, Anne 241, 257–8
Sewell, George 227
Shadwell, Thomas 74, 147, 149, 151
Shaftesbury, third Earl of 135, 205;
    'Advice to an Author' 207, 209
Shakespeare, William 17, 18, 37–40,
    46, 48–9, 51–2, 54–5, 58–9, 61–2,
    72, 76, 78–9, 80, 87, 96–9, 103,
    130, 146, 150, 153, 162, 165, 166,
    175, 177, 181–2, 185, 187, 192,
    202, 205, 222, 227, 238, 245–7,
    278, 290, 296, 304–6, 308, 320–2
Shenstone, William 242, 292; *The
    School-Mistress* 178, 224
Sheridan, Richard 172, 186
Sheridan, Thomas 186, 190, 193;
    British Education 198–9; *Plan of
    Education* 187–8
Shiels, Robert: *Lives of the Poets* 228,
    231, 238, 261, 263, 265, 276, 281,
    284
Sidney, Sir Philip 37, 40, 48–9, 76, 96,
    247; *Apology for Poetry* 28
Silvius Italicus 181
Skelton, John 37, 42, 49, 69, 88, 103,
    107
Smart, Christopher 58–9
Smith, Adam 205; *Lectures on Rhetoric
    and Belles Lettres* 25, 200–2;
    Wealth of Nations 197
Smollett, Tobias 26, 29, 135; *Roderick
    Random* 198
Somner, William 112
Sophocles 165
Southerne, Thomas 36, 52
Southey, Robert: *Specimens of the Later
    English Poets* 259
spelling books 182

Spence, Joseph 124; 'Collections Relating to the Lives of the Poets' 44–5; *Observations* 43, 45, 237, 290; 'Preface' to *Gorboduc* 45; 'Quelques Remarques' 44–7, 104–5, 117, 129, 134

Spenser, Edmund 37, 40, 42–3, 48–51, 53, 55, 58–60, 62, 76, 89, 96, 99, 123, 147, 153, 163, 205, 218, 222, 245–7, 296, 301–3, 305, 312, 316, 320, 322–3; in Poets' Corner 38–9; *Faerie Queene* 156–7, 239, 288–96, 299, 302, 309–10, 316; *Shepheardes Calendar* 63, 156

Sprat, Thomas 44, 86, 93, 245

Steele, Richard 166; *Spectator* 100, 184

Stepney, George 244–5, 247

Sterne, Laurence 91

Stockdale, Percival 242–3; *Enquiry into the Nature...of Poetry* 242; *Lectures on the...English Poets* 243, 310–11

Strabo 125–6, 131

Stukeley, William 133

Suckling, Sir John: 'A Session of the Poets' 47–8, 63

Surrey, Earl of 48–9, 53, 96

Swift, Jonathan 18, 24–5, 40, 47, 98, 185, 187, 192–3, 202, 204–5, 242, 273; *Battle of the Books* 148; *Gulliver's Travels* 173, 175; *A Proposal for Correcting...the English Tongue* 118–22, 205; *A Tale of a Tub* 32, 137

Tacitus 126

Taliessin 103, 132, 134, 139, 140–1

tartan kilts, wearing of 144–5

taste 136, 170, 186–7, 194–5, 206–15, 286–7; and reason 208; and the senses 207; teachability of 209–11, 212

Tate, Nahum 151

Tatler 15, 24–25

Taylor, John 151

Temple, Sir William 97–8, 100, 135, 186

Terence 166

test of time 306–7

textbooks 179

Theobald, Lewis 151, 155, 308

Theocritus 102

Thomas, Elizabeth 261, 277

Thomson, James 47, 102, 187, 192–3, 216, 245–6, 292; *Liberty* 55; *The Seasons* 314–15

Thornton, Bonnell *see* Colman, George, the younger

Thoyras, Paul de Rapin 129

Thwaites, Edward 112–14, 116

Tickell, Thomas 166, 226, 227

Tillotson, John 181, 187

Toland, John: *Specimen of...the Celtic Religion* 129, 132

Tollett, Elizabeth 275

'tradition' 142–45, 315

transcendent nature of literary value 305–7

transmigration of souls 145, 156–68

Trotter, Catharine 254, 258, 261–2, 268–9

Turner, Thomas 175

Turner, Revd William 211–12

Tyrwhitt, Thomas 94

Uniformity, Act of 189

Upton, John 292, 316

usefulness of English literature 171, 211–15

Vane, Lady Frances 269, 282

versification, improvement of 59–60

Verstegan, Richard: *A Restitution of Decayed Intelligence* 111–12, 119

Virgil 53, 60, 81, 95–7, 101, 115, 123, 146–8, 153, 164–7, 181, 187, 305

Wakefield, Gilbert 191

Wales, Gerald of 108–09

Waller, Edmund 39–40, 42, 44, 48, 50–1, 53, 58–61, 71–2, 119, 146–7, 157, 167, 182, 222, 224, 227, 257–8

Walsh, William 244, 248

'Wanderer, The' 115

Wanley, Humphrey 112–13, 115

Warburton, William 42, 271, 297

Warner, William 49

Warrington Academy 189, 191–6, 212–13

Warton, Joseph; 'The Enthusiast' 314; *An Essay on the Writings and Genius of Pope* 29, 234, 242, 320–1

Warton, Thomas 42–3, 107, 132–3, 220, 301, 312, 313–20, 326–7; edition of Milton's *Poems upon Several Occasions* 320, 322; *History of English Poetry* 41, 106, 125, 131, 294–5, 302, 316; *Observations on the Faerie Queene* (1754) 293–5, 303, 307–9, 311, 316, 319–20; *Observations* (1762) 294–5, 303, 310, 316; 'The Pleasures of Melancholy' 313–14; 'On Sir Joshua Reynold's Painted Window' 317–19

Watts, Isaac 216

Webbe, William 36, 124, 288; *Discourse of English Poetrie* 37, 95, 107

Weedon, Margaret 193

Weever, John 249; *Antient Funeral Monuments* 88–9; *Epigrammes* 48, 87–8

Wellek, René 17, 77, 219

Welsted, Leonard 92, 120–1, 207, 246

West, Richard: elegy on Ben Jonson 36, 65

Westminster Abbey 37–9, 87

Wharton, Anne 257–8, 261–2, 266

Whitehead, Paul 248

William of Orange 120

Williams, Raymond 13; *Keywords* 12, 20, 22; *Marxism and Literature* 14

Wilson, John 286

Wilson, Joseph 172

Winchester, Godfrey of 108

Winstanley, William: *England's Worthies* 75–6; *Lives of the most Famous English Poets* 65–9, 77–81, 83–90, 97, 109–10, 226, 228, 238, 240, 248, 250, 258

wit 32

Wither, George 151

Wodhull, Michael 55, 102

Wolcot, John 244

Wood, Anthony à: *Athenae Oxonienses* 76, 79, 229, 232

Woodmansee, Martha 219, 225

Woolf, Virginia 146

Wordsworth, William: 'Essay Supplementary to the Preface' 246–7, 251; 'Preface' to *Lyrical Ballads* 30

'works', semantics of 63

Works of the English Poets see Johnson, Samuel

'worthies' tradition of biography 82

Worts, William 101

Wotton, Henry 183

Wotton, William 113, 183; *Reflections upon Ancient and Modern Learning* 22, 98–9

Woty, William: *Poetical Calendar* 255, 267

Wright, Mehetabel 268

Wroth, Lady Mary 260

Wycherley, William 227, 282

Wyatt, Thomas 44, 49

Xenophanes 158

Yalden, Thomas 216, 227, 246

Young, Edward 18, 182, 227, 246; *Conjectures on Original Composition* 74, 248; *Love of Fame* 73–74